CONSULTATION

ROBERT R. BLAKE
JANE SRYGLEY MOUTON
Scientific Methods, Inc.

ADDISON-WESLEY PUBLISHING COMPANY
Reading, Massachusetts • Menlo Park, California
London • Amsterdam • Don Mills, Ontario • Sydney

ISBN 0-201-00594-8
EFGHIJ-HA-79

PREFACE

Consultation and education are probably the two most important influences behind the forward movement of society. In certain respects, consultation is even more important than education in giving society its forward thrust. The reason is that consultation alone deals with actual "here-and-now" problems—ones that, if solved, can make a real difference to real people in the way they live and work.

This book provides a systematic presentation of the scope of the consulting field. Only highly specialized kinds of consultation that are not of general interest have been excluded.

Emphasis throughout is on the dynamics of the interaction between consultant and client. Techniques employed by consultants have been described in each case to the degree necessary for learning something about the particular approach and its "how to do it" aspects. Numerous concrete examples illuminate these consultant-client interactions.

Each major approach to consultation has been examined from the standpoint of the assumptions underlying it, and in such a way as to demonstrate the relative richness or shallowness of the approach; as well as for comprehending under what conditions each of the many approaches is likely to be appropriate and consequential and where it would be inappropriate to employ a particular approach.

In Chapter 1 a cube of 100 cells is introduced which serves as the orienting framework for the book. The remainder of the text is concerned with illustrating how various consultation strategies are applied, as well as characterizing the client who is the recipient of the consultation. An individual consultant's intervention may be represented in only one cell of the cube. This does not imply that his or her work is limited to that intervention. It does mean that the consultant has supplied in the published literature an example which is useful for appreciating one kind of consultant intervention.

The fifth row of the Consulcube provides a basis for seeing how consultation

and education are interwoven in many modern applications, thus possibly providing for the first time a strategy of development and change that offers an
important and powerful way of breaking through barriers to effectiveness which
hitherto have resisted penetration.

Consultation will be of interest to a number of audiences. The undergraduate
and graduate student of the behavioral sciences who wishes to explore possibilities
of a career in consultation will find this book a useful orientation to the full range
of possibilities. The corporate executive and industrial manager will find the presentation useful for assessing what kinds of consultative assistance are likely to be
without merit. Consultants, whether internal-organization-development (OD) men
or external consultants retained by companies for specific purposes, will also find
it a useful basis for evaluating their own consultative approaches and for seeing
possibilities that are available to them but to which they may not have given the
degree of attention merited.

Reginald C. Tillam has provided invaluable support in the preparation of
Consultation. Tillam's experience as an ILO consultant in a major Iranian project
provided him a first-hand background of concrete knowledge about processes of
consultation. Along with our experiences as consultants over a period of twenty
years, this has led to the integrated presentation of consultation and education
which is depicted in the text. Also, our close personal acquaintance with consultants aided us in interpreting the various writings about consultation which are
reviewed here. Appreciation is expressed to the many authors included in the text
who have sought to reveal their approaches to consultation.

Austin, Texas   R.R.B.
January 1, 1976   J.S.M.

CONTENTS

**PART 3
CONFRONTATIONAL INTERVENTIONS**

1

CONSULTATION

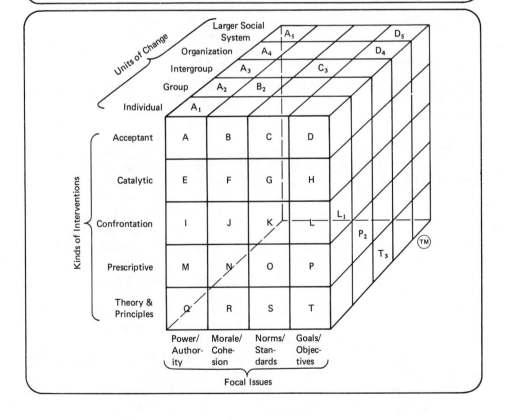

Consultation can be a useful tool in helping individuals deal with many of the complex difficulties they face today. Consultants offer assistance by *intervening*—that is, by taking some action to help a client solve his or her problem. These interventions involve much more than simply telling a client what to do or applying "common sense" remedies to a situation.

The range of situations encountered by today's consultant is as varied and distinctive as are the behavioral dilemmas people face in modern industrial life. In addition to classical management consulting areas, the field has expanded to include individual and group therapy and the rehabilitation of alcoholics and drug addicts. In business and government, consultation is no longer limited to aspects involving managerial competence: firms now recognize that alcoholism, drug addiction, and so on are as much organizational problems as they are personal problems. Thus numerous organizations are seeking assistance in understanding and coping with such varied dilemmas as helping an individual work through pent-up tensions; counseling someone who has lost patience with subordinates; dealing with teamwide frustrations; or launching a major effort to radically improve organizational effectiveness. In the latter sense, management development and organization development also are fields for intervention, as are vocational counseling, midcareer "retreading," and retirement planning and readjustment. Despite the seeming uniqueness of these situations, underlying principles link many of them into a common framework—principles that will become clear as our discussion progresses.

CYCLICAL NATURE OF BEHAVIOR

Behavior, whether that of an individual in solitude, of people within a group, or in a larger social setting, tends to be cyclical in character. In other words, a sequence of behavior repeats its main features, within specific time periods or within specifiable settings. For example, an alcoholic might start each day with a drink. His first is not necessarily at exactly the same time every day and he may depart from his pattern occasionally by skipping a day or two. But such deviations are variations on a regular theme. The same holds true with smoking: the smoker consumes, say, one or two packs per day on the average, even though there may be temporary intermissions. Likewise, the heroin addict may shoot up daily, except for forgoing a fix when temporarily out of funds. Ghetto residents as well as the inhabitants of malfunctioning communities around the world find themselves entrapped in the day-to-day routines of the "poverty cycle." A business or government executive arrives at work each day at about the same time, attends about the same meetings with about the same people, week after week. Often, too, he or she finds the same kinds of problems repeatedly occurring. The boss gets angry in a similar way and to more or less the same degree whenever problems of one or another particular category crop up. A corporate management group might perennially be unable to finish its meetings' agendas even though the session time is increased. In the broader corporate setting, one fiscal quarter follows another and this year's annual report is often very similar to last year's publication. A few old problems were solved, a few new ones cropped up, but the major themes recycle from period to period.

Cyclical behavior can become so habitual as to be beyond the conscious or "self" control of the person, group, organization, or community whose performance it characterizes. As long as this repetition stays within certain situational bounds, it can be advantageous. For example, many such cycles help to free intellectual and emotional resources for concentration on less programmable aspects of behavior. Outside these bounds, however, an unreviewed behavior cycle can be harmful, even dangerous. Take a simple example. An American in London who looks to the left before crossing the street may be in for a rude shock. In most cases, fortunately, he or she gets immediate feedback—via squealing brakes and tooting horns—which enables him or her to snap out of a stateside behavior cycle and construct a different one for getting across streets intact. But many of life's situations give no such immediate warning of inappropriateness. Indeed, a person, a group, or an organization may perform behavior cycles in ignorance, or in reckless disregard of possibly harmful and self-defeating consequences. The consultant's function, therefore, is to help a person, a group, an organization, or a larger social system identify and break out of these damaging kinds of cycles.

CYCLE-BREAKING INTERVENTIONS

An intervention occurs whenever someone does something to someone in the context of a cycle-breaking endeavor. Who does what to whom for what purpose, of course, involves a whole spectrum of interactions. A teacher criticizes a student's essay in the hope the pupil will stop repeating the same grammatical, stylistic, or spelling mistakes. A therapist interprets a patient's "transference," hoping to enable the patient to identify the background of certain feelings entering into his relationship with the therapist and possibly with his boss and colleagues as well.

In other interventions, an encounter-group leader suggests arm wrestling to two participants antagonistic toward one another. A management consultant tells a corporate president that the repetitive pattern of low profit margins should be broken by carrying out a 15-percent manpower reduction. A team-building practitioner suggests that a boss and his subordinate examine problems existing within their patterns of decision making, difficulties caused to some extent by the lack of openness and candor in their discussions. An organization development consultant confronts members of a large company with evidence of how their reliance on precedent and past practice hampers problem solving and suggests that directions for improvement might be seen if they move outside of their corporate "selves" to take a "fresh look" at problem areas. The social worker shows an unsupported wife how to fill in application blanks and accompanies her to the government agency when she applies for assistance.

Lippitt sums up the consultant-client relationship in the following way:

> Consultation, like supervision, or love, is a general label for many variations of relationship. The general definition of consultation... assumes that
>
> 1. The consultation relationship is a voluntary relationship between

2. a professional helper (consultant) and help-needing system (client)
3. in which the consultant is attempting to give help to the client in the solving of some current or potential problem,
4. and the relationship is perceived as temporary by both parties.
5. Also, the consultant is an "outsider," *i.e.*, is not a part of any hierarchical power system in which the client is located.

Some additional clarification of this condensed definition is needed. The client is conceived to be any functioning social unit, such as a family, industrial organization, individual, committee, staff, membership association, governmental department, delinquent gang, or hospital staff. The consultant is usually a professional helper, such as a marriage counselor, management consultant, community organizer, minister, social worker, human relation trainer, psychiatrist, applied anthropologist, group therapist, or social psychologist. The role of psychological "outsider" may sometimes be taken by a consultant located within the client system, such as a member of the personnel department. (R. Lippitt, 1959, p. 5)

Recent trends toward employing internal consultants and using paraprofessional consultants in community projects make it difficult to be more precise in specifying "who" a consultant is. Fortunately, however, it is of greater import to identify what he or she does—to whom and for what purpose.

KINDS OF INTERVENTIONS

The character, context, and focal issue of an intervention are all-important aspects of its prospective success. With this in mind, five main kinds of interventions can be identified.

Acceptant.   The intention is to give the client a sense of personal security so that when working with the consultant he or she will feel free to express personal thoughts without fear of adverse judgments or rejection. The client may thus be helped to "sort out" emotions in a self-reliant manner and thereby get a more objective view of the situation.

Catalytic.   Catalytic intervention assists the client in collecting data and information to reinterpret his or her perceptions as to how things are. In this way, the client may arrive at a better awareness of the problem and how to handle it.

Confrontation.   This challenges a client to examine how the present foundations of thinking—usually value-laden assumptions—may be coloring and distorting the way situations are viewed; that is, the client may screen off one or more alternative options which, if he or she were aware of them, could lead to the selection of more effective actions.

Prescription.   The consultant tells the client what to do to rectify a given situation or does it for him. This consultant takes responsibility for developing the evidence for the diagnosis and formulates the solution as a recommendation to be followed.

Theories and *principles.* By offering theories pertinent to the client's situation, the consultant helps the client internalize systematic and empirically tested ways of understanding. When learned so well as to be personally useful, these principles permit the client to view his or her situation in a more analytic, cause-and-effect fashion than had hitherto been possible. Thus the client becomes able to diagnose and plan how to deal with present and future situations in more valid ways. From the outset, he or she can specify how to rectify the immediate situation and further improve matters by choosing from discerned alternatives.

Consultant interventions may be "pure" acceptant or "pure" catalytic, "pure" confrontation, and so on. Some consultants employ "mixtures," taking an acceptant stance at one point, shifting to catalytic at another and confrontational at still another, often in ways that are more impulsive than planned. However, the majority appear to develop one intervention style and to rely on it, sometimes to an excessive degree. The intervention approach employed should, of course, be based not on the consultant's favorite techniques but rather on the client's diagnosed need.

FOCAL ISSUES FOR INTERVENTION

Yet another dimension must be added: the focal issue an intervention is addressing. Of the four focal-issue categories, the first involves the exercise of *power/authority,* a second relates to *morale/cohesion,* the third is centered in problems that arise from *standards or norms* of conduct, and the fourth comprises any issue in the *goals/objectives* area.

Power/authority, morale/cohesion, norms/standards, and goals/objectives are interdependent. When change is initiated in any one of them, changes may be observed in one or more of the other three, whether at that moment or later. For example, reduction of a boss's excessive use of authority may increase morale/cohesion. Other similar interactions will suggest themselves.

For consultant purposes, the *focal issue* is that aspect of a situation presently causing the client's difficulty. It may be any one of the four focal issues or any combination of them. The consultant centers attention on what he or she thinks the focal issue to be, even though other issues may in some way be linked to it.

The kind of intervention employed—acceptant, catalytic, etc.—may also be dictated by what the focal issue is or is thought to be. Focal issues involving morale/cohesion seem to be most responsive to acceptant interventions, though there are many exceptions; power/authority issues may require confrontation; norms/standards issues might be resolved following catalytic interventions. Theory-and-principles interventions can be appropriate to the entire range of focal issues; however, it is impractical to intervene with theory when an issue's intensity is at too low or too high a level. An apathetic and uninvolved person, or, at the other extreme, a fanatic believer, is not going to be open to the possibilities suggested by a theory intervention. A severely depressed person is unable to sit back thoughtfully and study theory that might help identify the origin and potential resolution of his or her own situation. Thus, theory-and-principles interventions seem most suitable when the problem is of middle-range intensity. In general, consultant effectiveness depends on the consultant's ability to identify correctly the focal issue, introduce the kind of intervention the situation objectively requires, and deal with the real client.

UNITS OF CHANGE

The social context of an intervention is determined by the individuals or group toward whom the consultation is directed. An *individual* may be the client of an intervention. Another context may be a *group or team*—whether a husband-wife couple, a small working group, or some larger assemblage—whose members share some basis for continued association. A still larger unit of change is the context of *intergroup* relationships between, for example, two divisions or departments. A fourth possibility would be an entire *organization,* such as a corporate body, a government agency, a school, a church. The fifth category comprises *larger social systems,* such as a community, a city, or a group of states or even nations.

It is very important for a consultant to determine "who" the real client is. Trying to focus change on an individual group member as a *separate* entity is only likely to generate resistance, for such change would make him or her a deviant, rejected by other group members who would have no understanding and even less sympathy for the client's behavior shift. The real client, in that case, is the group —in other words, the members need to change simultaneously and together if any one of them is to change. An effective consultant continually asks, "Is *this* the real client, or is the *real* client—the one needing to solve this problem—a larger or smaller social unit?"

THE CONSULCUBE ™

The three dimensions—kinds of interventions, focal issues, and units of change— form the Consulcube depicted in Fig. 1.1. Within it are a hundred cells, each of which represents the characteristics of a particular kind of intervention being applied to a particular client who is facing a particular problem of breaking out of an unproductive or self-defeating cycle. Using the Consulcube, then, any given intervention can be described in three ways: what the consultant *does, what issue* it is intended to help resolve, and *to whom* he does it.

The coding system of the Consulcube, illustrated in Fig. 1.1, will be utilized throughout our discussion. On the front of the cube an alphabetical letter designates each intervention/focal issue combination: for example, *A* denotes an acceptant intervention with power/authority as the focal issue, *B* an acceptant intervention with morale/cohesion as the focal issue, and so on. The numbers along the third dimension represent the five units of change. As affixed to letters, they reference each of the hundred cells. Thus J_3, for example, means "a confrontational intervention to help resolve a morale/cohesion problem within an intergroup situation"; S_5 "a theory/principles intervention to help resolve a problem of norms/standards in a larger social system"; and so on.

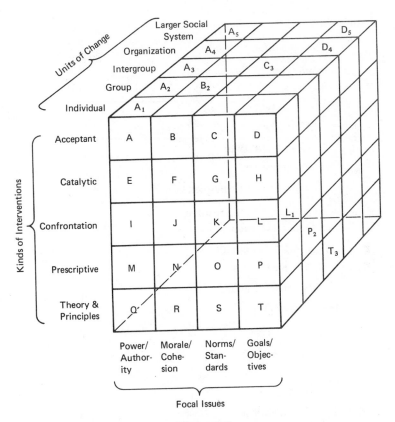

Figure 1.1
The Consulcube TM

Now the first part of the question, *Who* does what to whom for what purpose? may be reexamined. Often, evocative words are used to describe those who engage in consulting activities—psychiatrist, priest, counselor, trainer, helper, social worker, teacher, nun, pastor, expert, confidant, colleague, and so on. Some of these terms imply health; others imply pathology. Some suggest strength; others connote weakness.

Any language for identifying the "who" has some emotional coloring, but a sound working rule is to use language that does not get in the way of understanding. For the purposes of our discussion, the person who is intervening is called *consultant*. The person, group, or other "whom" receiving the intervention is spoken of as the *client*. The problem to be solved is referred to as the *focal issue*.

Of course, the consultant is usually an individual. However, the consultant-team concept is also well accepted and generally takes either of two forms: two or more consultants simultaneously working together, or two or more consultants working in tandem, one after the other.

Thus, to summarize,

WHO	– the *consultant* does
WHAT	– some kind of *intervention* such as
	– Acceptant
	– Catalytic
	– Confrontational
	– Prescriptive
	– Theory and Principles
WHY	– to address and/or resolve a *focal issue* such as
	– Power/Authority
	– Morale/Cohesion
	– Norms/Standards
	– Goals/Objectives
TO WHOM	– the *client* as
	– Individual
	– Group
	– Intergroup
	– Organization
	– Larger Social System

The Consulcube schema enables comprehensive definition and pertinent focusing on the dynamics of consultation, and represents an integration and extension of earlier work (Blake and Mouton, 1961, 1974). Alternative ways of characterizing consultant interventions include those of Ronald Lippitt, Watson, and Westley (1958), Gordon Lippitt (1969), Nadler (1970), Miles and Schmuck (1971), Golden (1972), Lieberman, Yalom, and Miles (1973), Morrill, Oetting, and Hurst (1974), and Geis (1969). Recent studies, not of interventions but of traditional management consulting, by Hollander (1972) and Fuchs (1975), might also be mentioned. They are not referenced further in *Consultation*.

ORGANIZATION OF THE BOOK

The field of consulting is rich in case studies, clinical reports, and field research, in addition to having produced some basic research investigations. The Consulcube serves to organize many disparate reports into a systematic and coherent whole in such a way that the respective consultants' assumptions can be identified and the particular interventions evaluated. Those reports that fit together in a specific cell have been summarized to provide the gist of what took place and a basis for seeing the strengths and limitations of each. Not all cells are represented by examples, because certain focal issues coupled with certain units of change result in circumstances where interventions are unlikely to be sought by the client system. Interventions reported throughout the wide-ranging consultation field have been viewed as representative of one or another kind of strategy of intervention.

A word about empirical evaluation. The field of consultation is still in the process of taking shape in many of the hundred Consulcube "spaces." First the field needs organization in systematic terms; then, basic similarities and differences among approaches can be recognized. Thereafter, meaningful evaluative research and skill development for impactful consultation become a realistic possibility. Occasionally the original authors may not have been sufficiently explicit to ensure that interpretations of their work are complete in all significant aspects. Nonetheless, with each report selected we have endeavored to identify as accurately as possible its general thrust.

REFERENCES

Blake, R. R., and J. S. Mouton. *Group Dynamics—Key to Decision Making.* Houston: Gulf Publishing Company, 1961.

Blake, R. R., and J. S. Mouton. "The D/D Matrix." In J. D. Adams, ed., *Theory and Method in Organization Development: An Evolutionary Process.* Washington, D.C.: NTL Institute for Applied Behavioral Science, 1974, pp. 3–36. (Originally published Austin, Texas: Scientific Methods, Inc., 1972.)

Fuchs, J. H. *Making the Most of Management Consulting Services.* New York: AMACOM, 1975.

Geis, H. J. "Toward a Comprehensive Framework Unifying All Systems of Counseling." *Educational Technology*, March 1969, pp. 19–28.

Golden, W. P. "On Becoming a Trainer." In W. G. Dyer, ed., *Modern Theory and Method in Group Training.* New York: Van Nostrand Reinhold, 1972, pp. 3–29.

Hollander, S. C. *Management Consultants and Clients.* East Lansing, Michigan: Michigan State University Studies, 1972.

Lieberman, M. A., I. D. Yalom, and M. B. Miles. *Encounter Groups: First Facts.* New York: Basic Books, 1973.

Lippitt, G. L. *Organization Renewal: Achieving Viability in a Changing World.* New York: Appleton-Century-Crofts, 1969.

Lippitt, R., J. Watson, and B. Westley. *Planned Change: A Comparative Study of Principles and Techniques.* New York: Harcourt, Brace, 1958.

Lippitt, R. "Dimensions of the Consultant's Job." *Journal of Social Issues* 15, no. 2 (1959): 5–12. Reprinted by permission.

Miles, M. B., and R. A. Schmuck. "Improving Schools through Organization Development: An Overview." In R. A. Schmuck and M. B. Miles, eds., *Organization Development in Schools.* Palo Alto, Calif.: National Press Books, 1971, pp. 1–27.

Morrill, W. H., E. R. Oetting, and J. C. Hurst. "Dimensions of Counselor Functioning." *Personnel and Guidance Journal* 52, no. 6 (1974): 355–59.

Nadler, L. *Developing Human Resources.* Houston: Gulf Publishing Company, 1970.

1

ACCEPTANT INTERVENTIONS

2

ACCEPTANT INTERVENTIONS: AN INTRODUCTION

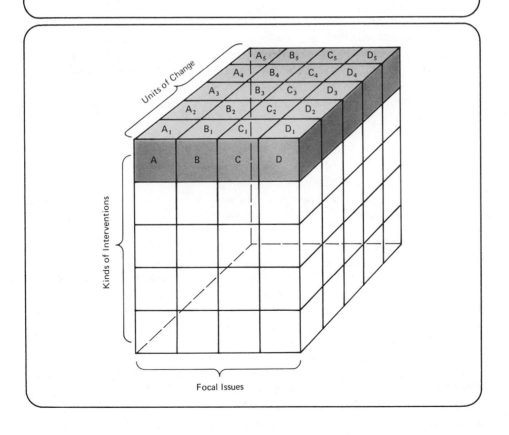

Invariably, human existence is punctuated by emotionally charged experiences. Many are uninvited and unwanted, upsetting and disturbing. Sometimes emotions produced by these experiences fade with no apparent aftermath. If they persist, the person might be able to turn his or her thoughts inward and identify the emotions blocking normal functioning. Introspection is a means of bringing negative emotions under control by viewing the disturbing influence from a calmer perspective—hopefully, one is then able to resume activities feeling "as good as new." Sometimes, however, clusters of negative feelings continue to burden the individual, making it difficult or impossible to carry on normal activities. Indeed, a person may exclude intense emotional reactions from conscious awareness, although these forces are still in operation. The technical term is *repression.*

For most practical purposes, one who is able to be objective is not under the influence of disabling emotions. Being *completely* objective would imply being emotionless and much else that is not within the scope of any human being. Yet the ability to take an objective view of the situation, or of oneself, or of both, is an essential first step toward tackling many self-defeating cycles. Emotionally charged attitudes about one's boss, for example, may so hinder a person that he or she loses effectiveness. This is a power/authority issue. By comparison, a morale/cohesion problem may exist when a person's feelings of self-worth are so low that feelings of helplessness impede corrective actions.

Or norms and standards may be the focal problem. This issue arises, for example, whenever a person is rejected by his or her colleagues for being a "rate-buster" or a "goldbrick." In either case the individual is violating group norms by working too much or too little in their estimation. Goals/objectives may be the focal issue when, for example, a person continuously "fails" because he or she sets out to achieve unrealistic goals.

Any of these four focal issues can be made even more difficult than the situation warrants because emotions are contributing to faulty thinking in the interpretation of what is going on. Frustrations, anger, anxiety, even vague feelings that something is wrong can block constructive problem solving. When a person—or several in a group, or numbers of them in larger social units—is emotionally off balance, a consultant may help relieve the situation by indicating ways to deal with emotional disturbances.

This involves *catharsis* of the sort that can be induced by acceptant intervention. Catharsis, a technical term, refers to a process of "cleansing" that brings about a release from tensions. When a client can express and work through the emotions hampering performance or disturbing behavior in unwelcome ways, it becomes more likely that the situation can be approached in an objective, problem-solving fashion. In other words, cathartic release permits the client to free his or her thinking from disabling emotions.

Acceptant consultation attempts to aid a client through sympathetic listening and empathic support. It might seem that any good friend of the client can do this just as well—but some clients have no good friends and, in any case, the consultant avoids certain actions that friends might take. For example, the consultant does not adopt a partisan point of view and help the person justify the reasonableness of his or her own positions and feelings—the client's behavior cycle must be broken not perpetuated. The kind of acceptance and support offered by the consultant, who is neutral in regard to interpersonal aspects of the focal issue, helps the client relax his or her defenses, confront disabling emotional reactions, and study better ways of dealing with the situation.

Sometimes a person does not talk about how he or she feels but simply opens up in the presence of another person. The sense of being accepted gives a client a feeling of "safety" not experienced with nonconsultants or when alone. The letting down reduces emotional pressure and opens avenues to thought.

The following example illustrates acceptance per se. As reported by Calia and Corsini (1973), the consultant never spoke except to greet the client at the beginning of the session and ask her at the session's end if she wanted to come again. Thus there was neither spoken communication of the sort where the consultant would listen to what the client had to say and then acknowledge understanding, nor any other overt effort to "help." Rather, acceptance and support, implicit in the consultant's silent presence, constituted the only intervention over four sessions, at the end of which the client's feelings of depression had lifted and she was able to resume her normal activities.

In a manner of speaking the incident was nothing, for the girl said nothing when she came in. I mean this literally. She knocked on the door, and I went to open it, and greeted her pleasantly. At my invitation she sat down, and we looked at each other. I waited for her to say something, to explain, complain, or ask questions. I looked at her trying to be as pleasant and as accepting as I could. Her eyes filled with tears and the tears rolled down her face, but she said nothing. I wondered what I should do. The simplest and most natural thing might have been to say, "What is bothering you?" But it must be remembered that I had been trained precisely not to ask questions or to give advice, and so, feeling quite foolish, I just kept looking at the girl. For half an hour, nothing happened. I then said to her, "It is time to end our session. Would you like to see me again?" Somewhat to my surprise and relief, she nodded, and when I suggested another appointment at the same time next week, she nodded again, and went out without having said a single word.

The following session was a repeat of the first one. We looked at each other, she cried silently, I waited, and then she once again accepted my invitation for another session without a word being said. Not to weary the reader, we had two more sessions and they were all exact duplicates of the first two, though several times I thought that the student was about to talk. At the end of the fourth session, when I again asked if she wanted to have another session, she shook her head, and walked out.

The client, a high school student, returned at a later time and reported the following:

"I want to thank you very much for what you did for me, Mrs. ————."

"But I did nothing!" I impulsively cried out. "I wanted to so much help you, but I just did nothing but look at you."

"You did a great deal. You changed my whole personality. That you had the kindness and love to wait for me to talk, to just be there, and not to ask me questions, or try to make me talk, that you were willing to just be there, and not be critical, and not complain that I was wasting your time was the best and most wonderful thing. While we were looking at each other I was thinking how wonderful the silence was, how good it was for you to understand me, and make me feel good and important. I felt you were loving and comforting. I just couldn't talk, and if I had it would have been banalities. Because you valued me so much, that you just were willing to be with me, I realized that my crazy thoughts that no one loved me or cared for me, were wrong. You loved me and you cared for me and you were patient and kind and understanding and warm, and you didn't put any pressure on me or try to get me to talk or to manipulate me. I felt so comfortable with you, and the relationship was so real. No, you did a great deal for me, and as a result I decided I was worthwhile and I was a good person and I was one to be respected, and I was able to solve my problems which I had sorely exaggerated." (Calia and Corsini, 1973, pp. 7–8, 8–9)

This is the acceptant method working in an almost "pure" form. The client reveals that the consultant was giving her complete acceptance without reservations or qualifications. Within this relationship, she was able to "let go" and to benefit, perhaps permanently, from the release of tensions associated with her feelings of unworthiness. The consultant's acceptance provides a basis for the client to reestablish her own self-confidence and to become more objective and problem solving.

The following are some ground rules a consultant might establish when working with a client as an acceptant interventionist. He or she:

1. tries to understand the client's situation from the client's own point of view, without necessarily accepting it as valid for problem solving. This may mean vicarious sharing in the sense that the client becomes aware the consultant "feels" the problem. Or, as an essential minimum, the consultant offers the response, "This is what I hear you saying. . . . "
2. practices active listening. Encourages the client to talk more, that is, looks him or her in the eye, smiles, nods acceptance of what is being said, says, "Uh-huh."
3. helps the client talk about how he or she sees the situation. Encourages with "tell me more" expressions.
4. helps the client *clarify* his or her feelings and *accept* their existence. Says, for example, "You've described the situation. How do you *feel* about it?"
5. might restate this last remark, if the client falls silent, in a way that lets him or her know the consultant fully understands and accepts—without judgment—what has been said.
6. stays *out* of participation in the *content* of the client's problem. Neither agrees nor disagrees with what the client says, and takes no sides.

7. might say, "What do you think the problem is? What ways are open for dealing with it?" *All* diagnosis comes from the client.

8. expects the client will make progress by this acceptant approach in defining his or her *real* problem and successfully solving it. The entry problem is unlikely to be the real problem, which will unfold as the client builds skill and confidence in dealing with his or her own frustration, anger, or low self-esteem.

Another client—also an adolescent girl—gives her evaluation of longer-term interaction with an acceptant consultant.

> I've been thinking about what you are to me. It's as though you were myself—a part of me. You're a balance wheel; you're not a person. It's almost as if I were talking to myself, but with someone listening and trying to think on it. I'm not getting rid of anything but a lot of stored up feeling. I don't come for advice. No, sometimes I do. But then I'm conscious that I want advice. It really bothers me when you become a person. What you do is let a person talk and put in comments that keep it going instead of stewing in a circle. That's why I say that you're a balance wheel. It's different now. When I first met you, you were a person. I disliked you because you were touching sore spots. Now I know you'll be a person when I need you to be. Other times you're someone to blow off steam to and to talk to so I can make up my mind. (Lewis, 1940, p. 184)

This reaction adds another facet to understanding how the acceptant consultant works. The clue comes from the client's indication that the consultant's active and sympathetic listening and supportive ways of intervening do make a positive contribution beyond simply creating a secure climate where the client feels free to explore personal quandaries. Climate is of undoubted importance, but the point here is that the consultant introduces specific comments to aid the client in moving forward in her thinking rather than moving in circles.

By general attitude, nods of agreement, positive comments, and by empathic sharing through nonevaluative acceptance of whatever is expressed, the consultant supports the client so that the latter can unload tensions, anxieties, frustrations, and hostilities in a one-to-one situation; or share such feelings with others in the client membership if several are involved. The consultant gives no advice, no suggestions. It is the consultant's basic assumption that, if these things are done well, the client will be helped to diagnose his or her own situation in a more objective manner, see what is causing it to be as it is, and see how to improve matters.

REFERENCES

Calia, V. F., and R. J. Corsini, eds. *Critical Incidents in School Counseling.* Englewood Cliffs, N.J.: Prentice-Hall, 1973. Reprinted by permission.

Lewis, V. W. "Intensive Treatment with Adolescent Girls." *Journal of Consulting Psychology* 4, no. 5 (1940): 181–84.

ACCEPTANT INTERVENTIONS

3

POWER / AUTHORITY

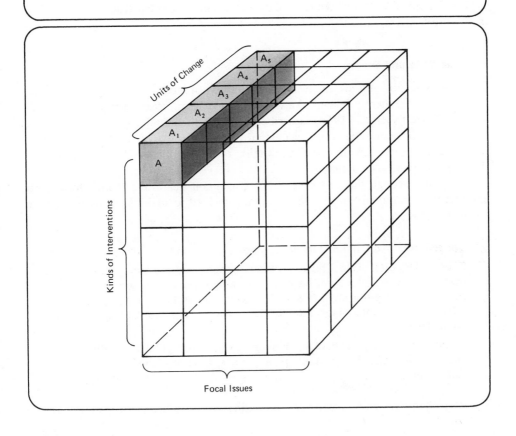

Power/authority is a particularly critical source of difficulties in modern society. The general problem is of a two-way nature: some persons who possess power/authority exercise it ineffectively; others who know they are subject to power/authority have trouble accepting that fact, whether or not the power/authority is presently being exercised upon them and in whatever manner. How people react to power/authority can be a factor in increasing or decreasing their effectiveness and personal satisfaction. When attitudes toward authority in general or toward a specific person in authority arouse antagonisms or the sense of being threatened, the client becomes less objectively competent to deal with his or her situation. Thinking may become distorted and recurring and self-defeating cycles of behavior may result. This is so whether the authority is an abstract concept such as "The Establishment," or specific individuals, such as a boss, a parent, a teacher, the police, and so on. When these kinds of distortions occur the consultant's task is to intervene in such a way as to release the client from these unproductive reaction cycles.

INDIVIDUAL (A₁)

Under certain conditions, acceptant interventions can be useful in helping individuals break out of cycles where the focal issue is emotion-laden reactions to persons in authority.

Anger at Boss and Others

The first of several studies involves consultation with factory workers. Inside a factory tensions, frequently related to a worker's supervisor, arise spontaneously. Dickson and Roethlisberger (1966) describe acceptant interventions with an employee on the shop floor, interventions calculated to help the worker deal with his emotional tensions more effectively. The situation took place in the Hawthorne Plant of the Western Electric Company.

Walking through the department, the consultant heard Joe talking to another employee in emotional tones. The consultant decided to make himself available to Joe then and there.

> *Consultant:* Well, hello, Joe. What's been going on?
>
> *Client:* Oh, hell, Bill. These goddam bosses around here, they aren't worth a dam. They . . . you have a raise coming and they won't give it to you. They give other guys raises all around you and they won't give you a raise. This goddam place stinks. The sooner I can get out of here the better I'll feel.
>
> *Consultant:* Well, gosh, Joe, this apparently has got you pretty upset. What do you say we go upstairs and have a smoke and talk it over till quitting time.

The consultant avoided "polarizing" by siding with the boss and getting a rebuff from Joe. Instead, he expressed sympathetic interest and invited Joe to talk. But he didn't take Joe's side either.

> *Client:* Well, I'll tell you, Bill. I heard that some of the boys around here got a merit increase in their pay so I simply went up asking for a raise and he tells me that getting a raise around here is a matter of luck. Boy, that burns me up. I am working for the Western Electric Company, I'm working, not gambling. If this goddam thing is a gamble, I don't want any of it—I don't want to gamble. I can go across the street here in these dives and gamble my money. I came here to work, I didn't come here to gamble. If it is all a matter of luck, I don't want any of it. I want to get a job where I can work and get ahead on my merit.

A sympathetic attitude coupled with readiness to listen and to "accept" his feelings are all it takes. Joe easily gets started toward breaking out of his repetitive cycle by "unloading." Very evidently he's mad, "burned up." He wants recognition for his merit, nothing more, nothing less.

Joe continues to ventilate his feelings.

> *Client:* ...Yeah, it seemed to me as if I had a reasonable squawk why I should get a raise. I simply asked the department chief for a raise and boy, he just flew all over me. A guy that talks like that to me...why I haven't any use for him...I won't work for him at all. I told him too that he wasn't the Western Electric Company, that he was only a representative of the Western Electric Company, and that I wasn't working for him, but by God, if I can't convince a man like that that I deserve a merit increase, why how in the hell am I ever going to get ahead? He tells me that I am at the top of Grade 34 and I can't get any higher, that's as far as I can go....

The conversation continues in this general tenor for some time. Joe rambles from one complaint to another. Later he gets to talking about learning as a way of advancement. Then he takes off on the "machine setters."

> *Client:* ...Why hell, Bill, we don't learn anything—they won't explain anything, they shove you out of the way, they do everything they can to keep you from learning anything, and it is a hell of a hard racket. You know how those machine setters are, especially screw machine men, they won't tell you anything.

All the time, the consultant has been listening. Often he does little more than reflect his sympathetic understanding of what is being said by repeating it in a way that shows he accepts what he's being told without putting a "good" or "bad" on it. Now he makes a comment, and Joe's reaction comes through loud and clear.

> *Consultant:* I see. They seem to be pretty selfish about their knowledge of screw machines.

Client: Selfish isn't the right word. They are absolutely tight. They won't tell you anything. As a matter of fact, if you try to learn anything, they try to hide it from you. Take for example, when I got in there, I wanted to get some books on this subject. Now, there is another case too, if the department chief had been on the up and up he could have gotten me some books on that stuff, so I could learn, but no, he sits you down there and leaves you cold. He never would make any attempt to get you to study. The only way I got my books was that another department chief that I used to work for came through our place one day, and he stopped me and he said, "Oh, so you are working on screw machines now." I said, "Yes," and I said, "I would like to have some books so I could read. . . ." (Dickson and Roethlisberger, 1966, pp. 280–81, 282)

Joe rambles on, almost without interruption. His emotional tensions lead him to gripe about one thing after another. From the consultant's view, this is all necessary. Joe can't think straight until these pressures have been relieved. Slowly the conversation gets away from gripes. It begins to move toward problem solving. The consultant still does not offer suggestions. He prefers to help Joe by supportive listening, clarifying, and empathic sharing.

With these tensions off his chest Joe's mind turns to what constructive action he might take and he reaches the conclusion that it would be worth his while to have a talk with his department chief. Now he is able to do so more calmly and probably more effectively than if he had tackled this supervisor while under the influence of emotions that now have been discharged. Afterwards Joe decided to stay on his present job. The consultant contacted Joe several times subsequently and Joe seemed to be satisfied with the decision he had reached (Dickson and Roethlisberger, 1966, p. 287).

This consultant's interactions with Joe were acceptant in nature. He encouraged Joe to talk about his problems, while at the same time avoided participating directly in these matters. He neither recommended solutions nor prescribed actions, but his approach encouraged Joe to think through his situation and to reach his own conclusions. Thus Joe retained "ownership" over the problem at all times.

Anger at a Teacher

H. G. Ginott (1965), a consultant especially concerned with the parent-child relationship, emphasizes the importance of parent interventions of the supportive and accepting kind. By encouraging catharsis, the parent can help to reduce the child's frustration and promote a problem-solving attitude.

In this example, a mother is following a recommended intervention, interacting as a professional consultant with her son. Ten-year-old Harold came home cranky and complaining.

Harold: What a miserable life! The teacher called me a liar, just because I told her that I forgot the homework. And she yelled. My goodness, did she yell! She said she'll write you a note.

Mother: You had a very rough day.

Harold: You can say that again.

Mother: It must have been terribly embarrassing to be called a liar in front of the whole class.

Harold: It sure was.

Mother: I bet inside yourself you wished a few things!

Harold: Oh, yes! But how did you know?

Mother: That's what we usually do when someone hurts us.

Harold: That's a relief. (Ginott, 1965, pp. 27–28)

Once the child experiences the security inherent in the parent's nonjudgmental *acceptance,* he then opens up. This permits the parent to understand the child's true feelings and provides an initial basis for helping him understand his frustrations. The acceptant intervention helped free Harold and increased the possibility of his moving toward a constructive solution.

Frustrations towards Parents

Emotional tensions can be so severe as to disorient the child who is too young to cope. Moustakas (1970, 1973) seeks to intervene in an acceptant way in these circumstances by being passive and supportive while providing a play therapy situation for the young client, an approach that appears to encourage the client to talk. A key to this intervention is in creating a situation where the child can express himself in actions as well as words.

A variety of playroom materials such as sand, water paint, and clay, and items such as toy guns, knives, and swords, are available in the consultation area. Dolls, puppets, and other representations of human figures often are provided for the child to use in whatever way he or she wishes. These props function in much the same way as do auxiliary doubles, alter egos, and so on, in psychodrama (see Chapter 21). Both the Axline and Moustakas approach described below and psychodrama help the client to act out in words or motions the emotions and feelings causing his or her subjective difficulties. When representations rather than real people are interacted with, the client usually feels very free to respond to them as his or her emotions direct. There are no "others," apart from the consultant, who might get hurt, or would seem to have some capacity for retaliation. A child can stomp on a doll that, for him, is his "real" bossy brother, or plead for affection from "mother" or express fear toward "father," with or without words. The consultant helps the child to release tense, pent-up feelings most likely produced by antagonisms toward authority figures and to experience his or her own insecurities in ways that can restore a capacity for problem solving.

At the beginning of the third session Richard's hostility reached a climax as he screamed out at the therapist: "I'll drill the whole place full of lead!

Do you hear me? I'm gonna dirty this place up so far that I don't think you'll be able to clean this stuff up with all the water in the world. I'm gonna really fix this stuff, I'm telling you. I'm gonna mess this room up like a coyote. And then I'll take this jackknife and cut everything up. Then I'll try it on you next!" (Moustakas, 1970, pp. 35–36)

The consultant abstains from evaluation. His contribution is in "reflecting" phrases that enable the child to express aggressive feelings. As this progresses, differentiation is often noticeable from the child's initially diffused or indirect expressions to a more focused, direct expression of negative and positive feelings (see Moustakas, 1970, pp. 37–44).

Dibs is a five-year-old boy who, for two years, has rarely spoken to other children in his nursery school and acts in such a way as to be classified as mentally defective. The focal nature of the power/authority issue is revealed in Dibs' acting out frustration and fears engendered by punitive parental chastisements at an earlier time. Axline describes how emotions were blocking Dibs' capacity to relate not only to adults but to children as well. The acceptant character of her work with Dibs is shown in the following play-therapy incident which occurred after several months of once-a-week sessions.

Dibs had arranged a tea party on a small table by filling nine plastic cups with water. In one sense Dibs is talking to himself. In another he is talking to his consultant.

"We will use our good tea set, today." His tone of voice changed. It became restrained, a little on edge. He imitated perfectly the precise inflection and expression of his mother's voice. "If there is to be a tea party we will do it properly," he said. "Yes. There will be tea, a little tea in each cup, then fill it up with milk. That is too much tea. I said a *little* tea in each cup, then fill it up with milk. If you want more water, that will be all right. But no more tea. And no arguments." He spooned water into each cup. "Cup six has too much tea," he said, with a note of severity in his voice. "Please remove some of the tea from cup six and follow my instructions more accurately. And that is enough sugar for children. *Enough sugar.* It should not be necessary to repeat everything I say. If you want to have a tea party you will sit down quietly at this table and you will wait until everyone is served. You may have a piece of cinnamon toast with your tea. You do not speak with food in your mouth."

Dibs set the table. He drew a chair up to the table. His manner became meek, subdued, quiet as he drank his tea in the little cup.

He continued in this way until

he reached across for the toast and upset one of the cups. He sprang up from the table, a frightened expression on his face.

"No more party," he cried. "The party is over. I spilled the tea!" Quickly he emptied the cups and returned them to the shelf.

"The party ended because you spilled the tea?" I asked.

"Stupid! Stupid! Stupid!" he cried.

"It was an accident," I said.

"Stupid people make accidents!" he shouted. There were tears in his eyes. "The party is over. The children are all gone! There is no more party." His voice choked on the tears. This had been a very real experience to him. "It *was* an accident," he told me. "But the party is over."

"It frightened you and made you unhappy," I said. "The accident of spilling the tea ended the party. Did the boy who upset the tea get sent to his room?"

Dibs paced around the playroom, wringing his hands. "He did. Yes. Yes. He should have been careful. It was very stupid of him to be so clumsy." He kicked over a chair. He swept the cups from the shelf. "I didn't want a party," he shouted. "I didn't want any other children around!"

"It makes you angry and unhappy when something like that happens," I said.

Then Dibs wanted to get out of the playroom and they went out together. Later, after a long time spent in silence, he began to talk again.

"I'm sorry."

"Sorry? Why are you sorry?" I asked.

"Because I spilled the tea," he said. "I was careless. I shouldn't have been."

"You think you should have been more careful?" I asked.

"Yes," Dibs said. "I should have been more careful, but I am not stupid."

"You were careless, perhaps, but not stupid?"

"That's right," said Dibs. There was a smile on his face.

Dibs had successfully weathered this storm. He had discovered a strength within himself to cope with his hurt feelings. (Axline, 1964, pp. 132–34)

By not acting as authority the consultant was able to release emotions and attitudes that probably would have remained hidden and unresolved. In summarizing her work, she describes the strategy used for this and other acceptant interventions.

I attempted to keep my comments in line with his activity, trying not to say anything that would indicate any desire on my part that he do any particular thing, but rather to communicate, understandingly and simply, recognition in line with his frame of reference. I wanted him to lead the way. I would follow. I wanted to let him know from the beginning that he would set the pace in that room and that I would recognize his efforts at two-way communication with some concrete reality basis of a shared experience between the two of us. (Axline, 1964, p. 44)

Social Withdrawal

Acceptant interventions may produce beneficial effects even with young children who are so seriously disturbed that they are treated in a live-in school devoted to their rehabilitation. Bettelheim (1950) describes a treatment strategy that promotes cathartic release through acceptance, yet has significant catalytic elements. Children are attended by counselors who react to their behaviors in a nonjudgmental and supportive way. For example, they are given full opportunity to vent their hostilities on the counselor even though these feelings originated prior to entering school. While such feelings might have arisen first with parents, they often have come to apply to all adults in general.

Bettelheim draws an implicit distinction between criteria for using acceptant and catalytic consulting approaches. His view is that when an expression of hostility can be diagnosed as having some specific cause, it should be answered. When hostility seems to be of the indiscriminate type, the counselor should be accepting so as to let it flow out.

> If the child's hostility is due to some discomfort that the counselor can relieve either through talking or realistic assurance . . . the counselor should make an effort to work through the child's hostility and help him with the underlying problem that gave rise to it. But if the child's aggression toward the counselor is more the outward expression of an internal battle between the child's efforts at control and his asocial drives, then it is best if the counselor suffers the child's aggression quietly and submits— as far as he can realistically do—to the child's hostile whims. (Bettelheim, 1971, p. 105)

Not only hostile, but also fear-related behavior can be helped through counselor acceptance. These emotions may be most prominent with children as they are waking up. Bettelheim remarks (1971, p. 107) that "All therapeutic functions of the counselor are greatly in focus during the awakening period; it is perhaps the time of day when the child needs his counselor most." An example of this is Walter, aged 10, who is being helped to start a new day.

> Walter seemed to withdraw during the night even more deeply than the others. When he fell asleep at night only his body was covered, but every morning he was all covered up, even his head. His counselor would pat lightly on his blanket and talk softly to him until somewhere from beneath the covers a hand would appear. If the counselor took it and held it quietly for a few minutes, Walter would finally poke his head out. But even after such contact he was still too removed from reality to meet it, and pretended he had gone back to sleep. Repeatedly she would come back to his bed and talk to him for a minute; each time he would again pretend to have fallen asleep, but each time he was in better contact than before. The conversation would increase from a soft "hello," to comments about

how he felt and what he might like to wear. Then he would slowly let her help him get dressed, though he was still not quite in this world. She had to help him in orienting himself by letting him find out certain things for himself. He was usually pleased when he had figured out for himself which day of the week it was, and what activities would be going on that day. By then he was ready to get up and start to play, but this process took an average of forty-five minutes. (Bettelheim, 1971, p. 111)

The approach in this orthogenic school, then, is for the consultant to help the child perceive the nonthreatening reality aspects of his current surroundings more clearly. The child is in control. He can "test" the adult-consultant in his own way at his own speed, thereby reaching his own conclusions for what is "safe" for him to do. This confidence-building support assists him in reestablishing his own right and induces self-control rather than feelings of powerlessness.

Summary

Rejection by someone who is personally significant to oneself and who possesses power or authority—like a parent, boss, teacher, or older brother or sister—is certainly a cause of much difficulty. Why do *they* do it? From the standpoint of the person having authority or power, a refusal or put-down, given without explanation, can quickly eliminate disagreement, reestablish control, and permit "progress" on the authority person's terms. From the angle of the person rejected, elimination of disagreement in this way amounts to suppression, pure and simple. When taken seriously by the rejected person, the meaning comes through that one has been weighed in the balance and found wanting—that to the power figure, one is unworthy. People find rejection and suppression of this sort difficult to take. An immediate reaction is to become antagonistic toward the authority person—often the rejected individual will start fighting back or griping with a bitter sense of personal "rightness." Others may simply walk out, removing themselves from the authority person's field of power and influence, although in situations of childhood and adult dependency this might be a practical impossibility. Still others, accepting the authority of the rejection, seem to conclude that yes, they *are* unworthy. They may buckle under and follow commands, but somehow they are not the same from then on.

Whatever the reaction to being rejected through suppression, strong emotions are involved. Feelings such as resentment, hostility, frustration, or self-rejection in the belief that "I am a worthless person," can lead to unhealthy, unproductive, and even self-destructive behavior.

Intervention by a consultant who is acceptant, particularly when this consultant is viewed as an expert authority also, communicates the very opposite. The intervention says, "Accept yourself and value yourself as a worthy person," a theme that helps the client express and come to terms with feelings provoked by rejection and suppression by authority.

GROUP (A₂)

Interventions relating in one way or another to the feelings of a group of subordinates toward boss-based power/authority are investigated here. Inherent in the boss-subordinate relationship are blocks to the open and free exchange of feelings; consequently, counterproductive tensions and strains may build up.

Alienation

Kuriloff and Atkins (1966) report examples of acceptant interventions that helped to release emotional tensions within a management group. Kuriloff had recently become vice-president and general manager of this manufacturing organization, so this was "his" group. All who participated, and who reported to him, held responsible posts. Atkins was the consultant brought in to help. This episode took place during one of the group-building sessions.

Helen, the office manager, is talking with Bob, the distribution manager. He had once been her boss, and at that time they had had a good relationship. But they don't have it now and she doesn't know why. The unknown trouble between them disturbs her.

> "Bob, I give up," Helen said, painfully and with deep puzzlement. "What do you want from me?" she begged. Bob did not respond. Perhaps the group had shut him up. Perhaps he could not answer. He listened. Her voice shaking, Helen explained that they had gotten along well when they both started with the company a year ago, when she worked for him. What had happened?

Describing his work situation as a never-ending cycle of burdensome responsibilities, Bob responded to Helen, "Every time I get someone trained to help me, they're taken away."

On hearing this, Helen, who was on the verge of tears, was addressed by the consultant, "I have the feeling that you've been wanting to cry."

> "I wish I could," she mumbled. "I'm afraid I'll look foolish."
> "We won't laugh," the consultant promised.
> She began to weep. The group was quiet, apprehensive.
> We waited.
> She stopped.
> Then softly, as she wiped her eyes, she said, "I feel much better. Thank you for being so patient." (Kuriloff and Atkins, 1966, pp. 77–78)

The Helen-Bob story doesn't end here, of course, yet progress had been made because a recurring cycle of repeated misunderstandings had been brought into the open. It was the beginning of a fuller breakthrough to mutual understanding, reached only after additional interventions. But without Helen having expressed the feelings she had been holding back or Bob revealing the frustration he felt, it is unlikely that much constructive progress could have occurred.

Resentment

When the boss of a work team is too "strong," i.e., exercises a high degree of direction and control, frustration and resentment are likely to be generated among subordinates who are afraid to "talk back." Sometimes tight control is on a one-to-one basis rather than on a one-to-all basis, creating suspicion and distrust among team members. An intervention discussed by Margulies and Raia (1968) illustrates such a situation.

They describe an intervention in a utility firm with a group of clerical personnel and their supervisors which cleared the air and paved the way for increasing effectiveness of the work group. The initial "felt need," a turnover problem, that led to the consultants being invited in by a member of management was *not* the problem they eventually helped with. As they interviewed employees, the consultants found that people in the employment office preferred to talk about their *immediate* problems. The intense reactions provoked by the interviews served as the beginning of the acceptant-intervention process.

Having conducted the interviews, Margulies and Raia summarized them and fed back their findings. In this way they were able to focus attention on the stresses arising from a climate of low trust. The interview data produced a sense of despair among participants for it portrayed a situation worse than they had perceived. As often happens, it also generated motivation to do something about this lack of trust and produced a plan for four meetings over a period of several weeks. Here is what happened in the first session:

> There appeared to be a good deal of anxiety and nervousness in the group. The participants, seated in a circle, clustered in small sub-groups. Barbara, Joann, and Judy, all of whom had come to the employment office less than six months ago, sat next to each other. A second sub-group included Louise, Lorraine, and Pauline. These were "old-timers" who had worked in the office for a number of years. Jerry and Sandy, who had come to the employment office from another department, seemed to be uncommitted to any sub-group and resisted overtures from the other participants. Mary, the selection supervisor, sat tapping a pencil on the notebook on her lap and seemed generally unconcerned. Nick, her boss, the Employment Manager, was also present.

> Most of the session was spent struggling with ways to express feelings toward the supervisor.

> "Mary," Judy said at one point, "I wish I could tell you how difficult you make it for me around here. And I know that some of the others feel the way I do, but just won't say it."

"O.K.," Mary replied, "Go ahead and say what you want to, all of you. It's your meeting."

"Well, it's *that* kind of comment and the way you look right now that makes it awfully hard for me to say how I feel," said a somewhat flushed Judy. Suddenly she cried to the rest of the group, "Where are the rest of you in this! Doesn't anyone else care about what goes on around here?"

Barbara offered some support. Hesitantly, she said, "Yes, Judy, I do feel the way you do about Mary's behavior. I just wonder if it's worth exposing myself. But I'm willing to try if it will do any good." Several others, in a very detached way, shared some of their impressions of the supervisor's behavior.

Judy's catharsis started a process among the women of expressing and sharing their tensions and emotions.

With some help from the trainers, a few of the participants were able to explore their relationships with the supervisor. Much of the discussion centered around the feelings of frustration and dependency, aroused in the newer girls by what appeared to them to be Mary's persistent need to know everything and to control everyone. Barbara told of how she had cried at home the night before after being "scolded" by the supervisor earlier in the day.

"I only stopped in to ask Judy a question about the interview form," she said to her supervisor, "I was only in there a couple of minutes when you came in and chewed me out."

"Our job is to process those applicants," Mary replied. "If you have any questions, if you want to know something, you should come to me. That's what I'm here for."

Throughout the meeting Nick remained silent. At times, particularly during some of the emotional exchanges between Mary and the younger girls, he seemed uncomfortable. Although Mary appeared to be composed during most of these exchanges, she was visibly shaken at the end of the session. (Margulies and Raia, 1968, pp. 5–6)

The authority-obedience assumptions characteristic of Mary's supervision had long prevented the women from giving her any meaningful feedback. Once it started, Mary "heard" attitudes that either she previously had been deaf to, or that perhaps had been hidden from her by the women for fear of consequences. For Mary, such emotional expressions from her subordinates had an "insight" effect. They provided her with information that altered her self-perception.

"I didn't know they felt this way," she said to one of the trainers, "I didn't know I was such a terrible supervisor." (Margulies and Raia, 1968, p. 6)

Significant changes in Mary's supervision resulted. Morale perked up after the clearing-the-air sessions, and, with the subordinates less fearful of punitive consequences, it eventually became possible to focus on and successfully solve significant work problems that, once relieved, increased productivity and work satisfaction.

Weakness on the Part of the Boss

Fordyce and Weil (1971, pp. 29–35) describe a situation in which subordinates were frustrated not because the boss was too strong and controlling, but because his subordinates found him too weak and vacillating. Rather than attempting to correct unprofitable business practices, he allowed them to continue.

A consultant-initiated group activity involved unblocking through cathartic release of emotions. The consultants interviewed members individually, in an acceptant way, about the changes each wanted and how the various team members presently interacted with the top man. These interviews provided an X-ray of feelings and tensions existing within the section, and indicated that team members needed to open up and share their anxieties and misunderstandings directly with one another and with the boss. When the top man invited subordinates to air their complaints, three major concerns surfaced. First, subordinates felt weak because the top man didn't give them the backing they wanted. Second, they felt blocked because he wouldn't take decisive action to stop what they identified as unprofitable activities. Third, they felt impotent because he didn't follow through on their recommendations to fire incompetent managers. Fordyce and Weil call this airing of feelings a "garbage out" process that helps clear the air.

The consultants contributed (1) by encouraging participants to express their feelings in an unfiltered, authentic way, and (2) by ensuring that participants listened to one another understandingly and appreciatively to hear what was really being said. As participants did this, they began supporting one another in expressing their various feelings and emotions. For example, had the top man in the example above "answered" complaints or justified them by "explaining" them, his subordinates' frustrations would probably have been increased rather than reduced. The consultants reinforced the free expression of feelings by the nondefensiveness in their own behavior.

Loss of Control

Many times a need for action is recognized, yet group members are hampered by vague fears as to the possible consequences of their actions. Frequently they believe they will lose their present positions, prestige, or control, unless they can clearly see how their power will be maintained or enhanced. Fear of the unknown has a "better not risk it" effect, and so releasing participants from ill-defined fear may be a first step toward progress.

Gibb (1972) describes a situation pertinent to this point. Group building was about to get started in an organization, but there was resistance to participation. This was diagnosed as "fear" by the consultant. He explained the advantage of dealing with fear rather than brushing it aside, for failure to resolve such feelings can result in "foot-dragging," absenteeism from team-building sessions, or taking part with minimal interest and involvement.

Several top men who were to participate in the team-building sessions came together in a preview session, and the consultant provided them the opportunity to explore as many of their fears about team building as they were able to ventilate. In an acceptant way, the consultant helped participants to freely share their doubts and reservations. For example, managers initially feared that team building could reduce their power to deal with subordinates. They felt that if they began to permit subordinates to have more involvement and participation, poorer decisions might result than with boss-determined decisions and one-to-one implementation. After exploration of such feelings, participants began to discover that some of their fears were imaginary. A number of constraints and barriers that might have doomed the team-building program were thus removed, and other more realistic fears were identified and faced as potential risks.

Summary

Disruptive emotions can occur whenever one person imposes his or her will on others in a manner that pushes them to do things differently than in the past, and/or in ways they do not fully understand, and/or without perceived opportunities to voice reservations and doubts. In adult life this kind of imposition of will usually comes from one's boss, though we know that if children could seek out help, they would report similar feelings.

Three kinds of group situations where the focal issue is one of power/authority —or even its remnants—seem to be helped by acceptant interventions. The first involves tensions in here-and-now relations based on present or former subordinate-boss relationships, as was the case between Helen and Bob. The next two examples illustrated situations in which a common group tension shared by every team member is focused upon the boss. In the utility-firm report by Fordyce and Weil the boss was considered too weak. In the third type situation, tensions are shared among equal-rank colleagues engaged in a designated activity. The Gibb example described the use of acceptant interventions to bring out the feelings of managers *prior* to a training activity that they perceived as potentially threatening to their authority.

All three kinds of situations share a common element: the individuals involved have "bottled up" their emotions and have been "blocked" from sharing. Such feelings prevent members from finding immediate solutions, and must be worked through before real progress can occur.

INTERGROUP (A₃)

Power/authority dynamics can function between two or more groups just as they may operate between two or more individuals. Awareness of the differentiated degrees of power/authority possessed by each can produce antagonism on the part of the weaker of the two groups, which in turn can result in polarized disagreements or a readiness to defer rather than confront. Given this kind of situation, some or most of the associated emotions stay bottled up. Hurt feelings can fester and produce a chronic demoralization. When these feelings are prevalent among members of either group, it becomes necessary to treat the problem in group-dynamic terms. Why? Even though it might be possible under one-to-one acceptant consultation to relieve someone's feelings, when the individual returns to the group he or she is likely either to feel alienated from other members who are as yet unrelieved; or his or her former emotions may be reactivated through interaction with these others. The two examples to be presented involve emotions arising between groups of unequal power/authority. In the first example, a union is the weaker party; in the second, a headquarters is clearly the stronger group.

Union-Management Antagonisms

Union-management relationships are susceptible to the kinds of emotional disturbances that provocative win-lose position taking can produce. Frequently, in order for each group to gain something—to win—the other must "give"—and giving is often equated with losing. Each new contract-bargaining round begins in the shadow of past embittered contests. Bickering, mutual suspiciousness, exaggerated demands, accusations and counteraccusations have become standard reactions. The true reasons for such emotions and frustrations are rarely even approached in ongoing bargaining.

In the following example, contract bargaining is under way. It is more or less hopeless, getting nowhere. The management and union representative groups voice their frustrations by griping about one another, yet these expressions give little relief —they are mere wisps of steam escaping from two overpressured vessels. A consultant suggests that both groups take a fresh look by getting away from the bargaining table and sitting down in a special no-bargaining conference. The underlying purpose is to explore, express, and, hopefully, heal the negative feelings obstructing collective action. Union and management agree to give it a try.

Two acceptant-oriented consultants help a cathartic process to take place. One works with the union throughout, joining in both private meetings and face-to-face interactions with management. The other works with management under similar circumstances. Realizing the importance of airing emotions before trying to grapple with operational problems, one consultant focuses the union members' attention on their feelings toward management. He suggests that, "If the relationship with management is as tight and rigid as you report it to be, it is important to start out by examining your own feelings, whatever they may happen to be right now." His openended query is, "What are your complaints?" He goes on, "As you identify your feelings, they can be written on this flip chart. After examining them later you may decide some are repetitious, or that, while true, they are not really pertinent."

As remarks are made, the consultant helps participants enlarge upon their statements by reflecting or restating in different words what he hears being said. In this way they become accurate descriptions of feelings and reactions. This help is often necessary as members try to express themselves on topics about which they feel tense and blocked. The other consultant follows similar procedures with management.

Having completed this study on an each-group-by-itself basis, they convene in a joint session. To increase acceptance of what is being said, each group "speaks" to the other via its respective selected spokesman. This arrangement reduces confusion and increases the responsibility for being accurate and for avoiding tension-increasing accusations. Because consultants are not *partisan,* and because they do accept each group as sincere, they create a climate of openness and trust even while pointing up emotionally generated aspects of the intergroup tensions. They help reduce the defensiveness that has routinely made it difficult for either group to listen objectively to the other.

Here is a "fantasy" unveiled during three intense days of union-management catharsis. The actual events had occurred thirty years earlier.

> "In 1933," the union said to management, "you S.O.B.'s had us down and out because of the depression. And what did you do? You cut everybody's pay in half, and, having done so, then you turned us out into the yard to dig up all the pipe and repack it. How do you expect us to bargain with a bunch of cutthroats that would do that to human beings who are down?"

The managers did a retake. They said, "Oh, but that wasn't us; that was five dynasties ago!" But this disclaimer did nothing to mollify the union. It was a "logical" answer to emotion-based attitudes that had resulted from the story being told and retold and kept alive for thirty years.

Later, the 1963 management walked the 1963 union back through time in an attempt to reconstitute the thinking that had characterized 1933 management.

> "We shouldn't let people go home with no job; we have a responsibility to keep them going somehow, despite hard times. We can't employ them full time because we don't have that much production scheduled—market demand is way down. Rather than laying off people wholesale, the human thing to do is keep people productively occupied somehow. With operational activities currently at such low levels, the only thing we can do that has long-term usefulness is to dig up the yard pipe and repack it for maintenance purposes."

The 1933 management's intentions were probably well-meant, even though clouded by overtones of paternalism. The union's legend regarding those intentions, endlessly repeated, portrayed them as malicious and exploitative. Eventually the 1963 union, after reconsidering the management's dilemma in that past era, agreed that the prior management had taken a responsible attitude toward employees. Slowly the old legend dissolved.

The emotions and feelings discharged in those three days were intense, deep-rooted, and both potentially and actually destructive. But fantasies of misdeeds from the past finally were unloaded. This cathartic freeing up permitted the bargainers to break their cycle of mutually antagonistic interactions and get back to their deliberations in a more problem-solving way than had characterized negotiations in recent years. But only by getting those kinds of emotionally colored misunderstandings into the open, and worked through, was it possible for union and management to restore a businesslike basis of working toward a contract (Blake and Mouton, 1974, pp. 8–9).

Plant Management Embarrassment with Headquarters

Ill feelings and tensions are sometimes characteristic of groups in a hierarchical relationship, one having power over the other. The subordinate group is likely to keep negative feelings hidden for fear of the consequences that might result. The stronger group, of course, is likely to be impatient with and reject what it interprets as criticism of itself.

A hierarchical situation that benefited from acceptant interventions involved a headquarters and a plant. In accordance with a long-term practice that had become tradition, the president and three vice-presidents journeyed to each of the plants on a more or less regularly scheduled basis. The key managers there convened to work with them. Occasionally these sessions were productive but over time they had become more a matter of protocol. Agendas were made up on the spot and limited to topics that were *not* likely to touch on tender problems. However, this particular year, rather than starting the discussion in the customary way, a consultant (one of the authors) suggested that each group meet separately to review their feelings about the other. The consultant's reason for making this suggestion was to enable participants to clear the air so that when the session moved to an examination of operational problems, these might be discussed in a more open and straightforward manner than in recent years.

Headquarters representatives concluded that although the plant's problems were real and quite serious, their own feelings toward the plant's leadership were on the positive side. They found little to communicate to them on a "feelings" plane. But they said they were prepared to listen.

Not so with the plant's managers, however. Their dominant feelings were ventilated in the following way.

"When you four visit, you embarrass us because you don't act in a businesslike manner. You [the President] show up in a sports coat, open shirt, wearing a cap. You other three are comparably informal. This embarrasses us with our own people, for although they work hard, they don't see you taking us seriously. We notice that you don't dress this way in your own office. Many comments are heard about the Acapulco playboys from headquarters. Not only do others in our own organization feel as we indicate, but we do too. It gives us the feeling that you don't come to visit us for serious business but, rather, as an interlude when you can relax. Our real concern is not with the way you dress as much as with our feelings that the way you dress indicates how you feel." (Blake and Mouton, 1972)

This catharsis resulted in headquarters management seeing the effect their behavior had upon the plant managers' attitudes toward them. They shifted to a problem-solving basis and developed agreement with the plant's leadership on the importance of increasing the purposefulness of their visits and of dealing with significant matters.

Summary

The existence of undisclosed feelings often can be accounted for by one of the two interacting groups being and feeling weaker than the other, and/or dependent on the other for its security. The weaker group then avoids open criticism or other overt rejections of the stronger group, and hides feelings that might provoke negative reactions. In a similar manner, since the stronger group does not receive emotional feedback, it is likely to come on stronger, sometimes to the point of arrogance. These two basic features of a relationship can result in increased misunderstandings and reduced capacity for problem solving as time goes on.

Acceptant interventions that create a degree of security sufficient for the weaker group to unveil its emotions for the stronger to understand and appreciate can be a sufficient basis for reestablishing mutuality and a problem-solving approach.

ORGANIZATION (A₄)

Many consultant interventions are concerned with power/authority as a focal issue. This is especially understandable in the context of organization activities, since operations are usually carried out through the exercise of direction and control within boss-subordinate relationships.

When the use of power/authority blocks effectiveness it may become essential to deal with the problem; otherwise, organizational integration and the potentials for synergistic efforts toward successful overall results remain impaired. However, the acceptant mode of intervention is rarely utilized by consultants within an organization.

Nonetheless, there have been occasions when this mode has proved useful. Paternalistic organization leadership can stir organization-wide emotions and yet prevent expression of them. By relieving these tensions, energy for constructive action can be released, particularly when a new management takes over after a departing paternalistic management. This often occurs when a family-owned company is taken over by a publicly owned corporation.

Bartlett (1967) describes such a catharsis-inducing experience, implemented through a dramatic acceptant intervention in a company where there had been an influx of "new men." The men were being assigned by a paternalistic president to take over a number of responsibilities that had been handled poorly in the past.

As Epsilon grew, the Vice President (VP), a fine line supervisor, had gradually been drawn in on managerial problems and policies so far over his head that he began to avoid decisions. As a result, the formal process of decision making had broken down except on a "management-by-crisis" basis. This left each department head to operate like a feudal baron: equal in power, independent, and in direct competition with all others. (Bartlett, 1967, p. 383)

In response to the ensuing difficulties, the president had begun hiving off, sector by sector, various of the vice-president's responsibilities and importing new men to undertake them. Lower down in the organization, supervisors and foremen had chosen up sides as supporters of the vice-president or the general manager. The last-mentioned person had been methods/personnel director before being promoted to his recently created position. Currently the vice-president was reporting to him.

Throughout the organization both open and hidden resentments, as well as procedural confusions made worse by sabotage, were rife. A series of interventions were utilized to reach many levels of the organization membership.

1. Lower-level members expressed their true feelings of frustration to one another on a mutual sharing basis;

2. with anonymity preserved through voice-disguised tape recordings, these expressions of frustration by lower-level members were fed back to the executive level;

3. an acceptant consultant helped the executive level to "believe" the existence of such feelings and to express their own emotional and other reactions to the expressed lower-level frustrations;

4. the executives were encouraged to ask the lower-level members to continue this process of openness, but on a face-to-face basis;

5. intermediate hierarchy levels were included to help executive levels become more responsive, and to explore and express their own feelings.

This organization-wide catharsis led to a search for reasons why these pent-up emotions had developed in the first place. Solution-seeking proposals to improve operations and relationships followed.

This illustrates in principle that the pent-up and often hostile emotions felt toward people at higher levels who exercise their power/authority in a paternalistic manner can be successfully reduced. Through acceptant interventions, a more constructive basis of relationship can be established, and those who have felt frustrations are given an unprecedented opportunity to ventilate their feelings in a nonthreatening environment.

LARGER SOCIAL SYSTEM (A₅)

There are two ways of viewing interventions that deal with larger social systems. The first views a given larger social system as a set of arrangements established to provide members with food, clothing, shelter, and safety. By this concept of larger social system, a community has such properties, as does a nation. A hospital is a special case of a larger social system in that, in addition to providing these basic requirements, it is organized to aid clients solve mental or physical problems. A residential college or university also qualifies as a larger social system.

Alternatively, larger social systems may be regarded in terms of the numerous individual problems created and perpetuated by the system's existing conditions. This being the case, fundamental resolutions per medium of system-wide changes are called for. Examples are such current and critical social problems as alcoholism and other forms of drug addiction, delinquency, or underachievement that is apparently not related to an individual's social adjustment.

Several of the approaches to solving individual problems such as these, which in aggregate are symptoms of difficulties in the larger social system, involve creating special simulated or truncated social systems within which individual members are provided special opportunities of support for breaking out of self-defeating cycles.

Educational Underachievement

Underachievement in high school is a chronic problem facing American education. Academic failure by students who had demonstrated at least the potential to succeed blocks their possibilities of going to college and later beginning professional careers. With rare exceptions it means that the underachiever will be less effective later in life than if the causes of his or her present underachievement could be identified and removed, or significantly reduced.

One focal issue that may be a widespread source of underachievement is negative attitudes held by youth toward authority. An example illustrating this point begins with about a hundred ninth- and tenth-grade students being selected for participation in a summer campus residential program, Upward Bound.

> The students came from poor socioeconomic backgrounds (their parents' incomes all met the Office of Economic Opportunity's poverty criteria), had low educational aspirations, and in spite of their good scholastic potential, most experienced failure in school. A high percentage (22 percent) of the students came from fatherless homes and 45 percent of the families were welfare recipients. Thus, these students suffered not only monetary but also psychological deprivation. (Bakal, Madaus, and Winder, 1968, p. 17)

Their attitudes toward authority were either withdrawing or hostile in nature.

> It became apparent from contact with some students that their distrust and fear of authority brought about either total compliance or overt and aggressive acting out. Consequently, the students were either timid, submissive, and withdrawn or hostile, defiant, and aggressive. The feelings toward authority manifest in these two types of behavior do not permit the students to function effectively in the public schools, which they re-

ject. The public school system is a middle-class institution. Its classroom
size and inflexible curriculum tend to make it highly structured and authoritarian. Therefore, it increases the students' feelings of alienation so
that they remain on the periphery, almost completely cut off from the
school culture. (Bakal, Madaus, and Winder, 1968, p. 18)

In this live-in setting, several features of the social system were utilized as part of
the intervention process. One, acceptant in character, involved student government,
organized in such a way that the staff could only convey understanding and acceptance of its actions.

The idea of self-government was presented to the students early in the
program but it was adopted only after positive student reaction became
evident. There were no preconceived plans or rigid guidelines. The students were allowed to assume the responsibility for their own student
council and the staff merely responded to their initiative. The responsibility, powers, and duties of the student council were established through
the students' frank discussion with the administration. In general, they
were given the authority to exercise broad power in almost every area
of the program, except the strictly academic. Mutual involvement was encouraged by which both the administration and student body could raise
issues of mutual concern. However, the students after evaluating the staff's
opinions were free to make the final decision themselves. . . .

But the students' acceptance of the student council's authority did not
evolve easily. Initially, they were resentful of accepting discipline from
peers. As one student said, "I resent the fact that I have to be judged by
my friends." However, when the student body observed that the staff was
supporting the council's opinions and backing its decisions, they began
to accept the idea of student authority. The staff's expression of full confidence in the council's decisions greatly increased the council's prestige.
(Bakal, Madaus, and Winder, 1968, pp. 19–20)

Within this framework of acceptance, group counseling occurred four times a week.
It was led by staff members who aided students in expressing feelings about their
educational experiences. They could discuss any problems of current personal concern to them.

Another purpose of group counseling was to provide a setting in which
the students could express their feelings of alienation from school and
their attitudes toward authority and so work through their problems. The
group's permissive atmosphere encouraged this. The group counselor as
an authority figure was perceived by the students to be representative of
society—the teacher, school system, or parent. The group served as an
arena in which transference relationships with the group counselor, resident counselor, or other group members were formed. Furthermore, the
group counselor could deal with a hostile group without becoming angry,

could handle strong feelings without being threatened, and could control the group without punishment. For all the students this was probably a unique experience.... The students seemed to be asking the counselors: "Are we backward?" "Are we really hopeless?" The counselors' acceptance of their feelings gave the students reassurance that they were not backward and that staff attached much worth and importance to them and their feelings. (Bakal, Madaus, and Winder, 1968, pp. 21–22)

One objective of the summer program was to help participants prepare for entering college. Its emphasis was future-oriented rather than being in any sense an attempt to build positive attitudes toward the home environments and public schools experienced to date. Nonetheless, it was recognized that "looking back in anger," however justifiably, at unfortunate situations of the past can significantly affect one's approach in the present and future. When attitudes color perception so as to make learning experiences in general seem unattractive, acceptant interventions can aid the client to see his or her past in a more purposeful way and the now-and-future situation in a more positive light. This appears to be particularly true when the causes of negativism are traceable to disturbed relations between the client and those previously in authority over him or her. The opportunity to experience nonjudgmental, supportive adults in a nonthreatening atmosphere can enable the client to review and reject past-influenced antagonistic attitudes and to replace them with a more constructive orientation toward those authority figures encountered in future situations.

Sometimes a larger social system, such as a new community, is created to receive a large number of citizens who have been uprooted as a result, for example, of urban renewal. Such a new town creates many problems of community development. One such dilemma is how best to cope with and reduce or eliminate delinquency.

One view of delinquency, applied particularly to youngsters who have never known a self-respecting relationship with grown-ups, is that they are acting out resentments against authority, looking for others who likewise resent what they see as the hypocrisy of grown-ups. Externally imposed authority is accepted by them only in the presence of those able to exert it. As soon as the authority is absent the youngsters are ready to vent their hostilities in antisocial and sometimes violent ways.

Given this concept of delinquency, what kind of interventions might be expected to decrease readiness to engage in delinquent behavior? Wilson (1963) discusses delinquency in a new community in Great Britain and suggests how social workers might approach a resolution through acceptant interventions.

The only possible approach is "permissiveness," out of which may come a measure of self-understanding. But the first effect may appear to be worse, as the youngsters test out the professed goodwill of the worker. This means that the worker must be prepared to bear the most tremendous tensions—from the youngsters testing the worker out, and from the neigh-

bourhood wondering why the worker does not apply "discipline" and re-
senting more fiercely than ever the appalling behaviour of the gang.
(Wilson, 1963, pp. 33–34)

By the consultant giving warm, empathic, and acceptant understanding, youngsters
are provided the opportunity, through catharsis, to ventilate and work through their
hostilities. During the initial period, when they are testing the adult's credibility
prior to ventilation, the delinquent behavior may appear to worsen. Yet they are
simultaneously learning to trust adults who can help them. Wilson points out, however, that citizens of the community, particularly those in positions of authority,
are likely to repudiate the "testing" behavior and believe the community organizer's
acceptant interventions are making the situation worse. For this concept of coping
with delinquency to have any chance of success, the consultant must be prepared
to accept this kind of testing and members of the community must also be aware
of the fact that increased antisocial and destructive behavior may be a prerequisite
for establishing the kind of contact that can eventually reduce the severity of delinquent behavior.

The kinds of behavior that appear in individuals, but which have their origins
in malfunctionings of the larger social system, are not likely to be resolved in an
effective way solely through acceptant intervention. When such problems become
chronic, different kinds of interventions are needed than the sort that releases tensions through modes of emotional expressiveness, talking out, and acting out.

IMPLICATIONS

Power/authority can evoke strong emotions in persons on whom it is exercised.
Reactions include experiencing feelings of self-doubt, fear, alienation, hurt, and
even more severe responses that lean in the direction of autistic behavior.

Acceptant interventions may be useful when such emotions are bottled up or
otherwise hidden. As we have seen, it is possible for the person experiencing such
emotions not to be consciously aware of them; he or she may even deny their existence. Though the acceptant intervention process is often slow and tedious, the
client's experience of the consultant and intervention circumstances as acceptant,
nonjudgmental, supportive, and not "deadlining," offers the security that permits
the client to formulate and express his or her feelings. Next the client may begin to
differentiate fantasy-induced emotions from those that might better correspond to
"arousal factors" in his or her objective circumstances. When fears and anxieties
are not rejected and when the client can express them in a non–self-rejecting way,
he or she has taken the first major step toward dealing with power/authority in an
objective manner.

REFERENCES

Axline, V. M. *Dibs in Search of Self*. New York: Ballantine Books, 1964. Reprinted by
permission.

Bakal, Y., W. Madaus, and A. C. Winder. "A Motivational Approach to Compensatory Education." *Social Work* 13, no. 2 (1968): 17–22. Reprinted with permission of the National Association of Social Workers.

Bartlett, A. C. "Changing Behavior as a Means to Increased Efficiency." Reproduced by special permission from *Journal of Applied Behavioral Science* 3, no. 3 (1967): 381–403.

Bettelheim, B. *Love Is Not Enough.* New York: Avon Books, 1971. (Originally published by The Free Press, 1950.) Reprinted by permission.

Blake, R. R., and J. S. Mouton. "The D/D Matrix®." In John D. Adams, ed., *Theory and Method in Organization Development: An Evolutionary Process.* Washington, D.C.: NTL Institute for Applied Behavioral Science, 1974, pp. 3–36. (Originally published Austin, Texas: Scientific Methods, Inc., 1972.)

Dickson, W. J., and F. J. Roethlisberger. *Counseling in an Organization: A Sequel to the Hawthorne Researches.* Boston: Division of Research, Graduate School of Business Administration, Harvard University, 1966, pp. 280–82. Reprinted by permission.

Fordyce, J. K., and R. Weil. *Managing with People: A Manager's Handbook of Organization Development Methods.* Reading, Mass.: Addison-Wesley, 1971.

Gibb, J. R. "TORI Theory: Consultantless Team-Building." *Journal of Contemporary Business* 1, no. 3 (1972): 33–41.

Ginott, H. G. *Between Parent and Child.* New York: Macmillan, 1965. Reprinted by permission.

Kuriloff, A. H., and S. Atkins. "T-Group for a Work Team." Reproduced by special permission from *Journal of Applied Behavioral Science* 2, no. 1 (1966): 63–93.

Margulies, N. P., and A. P. Raia. "People in Organizations: A Case for Team Building." *Training and Development Journal* 22, no. 8 (1968): 2–11. Reprinted by permission.

Moustakas, C. E. *Psychotherapy with Children.* New York: Ballantine Books, 1970. (Originally published by Harper & Row, 1959.) Reprinted by permission.

Moustakas, C. E. "Psychotherapy with Children." In G. and B. Stanford, eds., *Strangers to Themselves.* New York: Bantam Pathfinder Editions, 1973, pp. 218–31.

Wilson, R. "Difficult Housing Estates." *Human Relations* 16, no. 1 (1963): 3–43. Reprinted by permission.

ACCEPTANT INTERVENTIONS

4

MORALE/COHESION

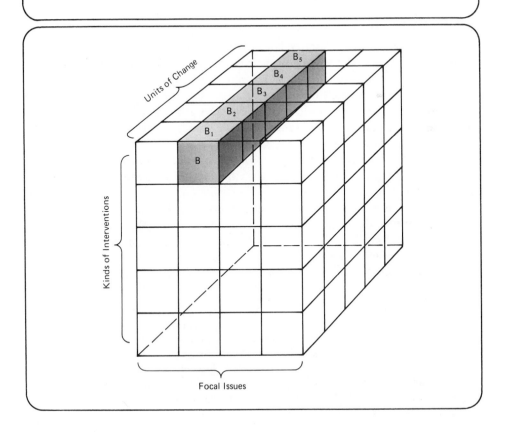

Focal Issues

When uncorrelated with objective circumstances, feelings and emotions associated with a sense of well-being or with attitudes of despair can lead to less than rational behavior. One end point on the scale—the euphoria of "cloud nine" well-being—can lead to mania. The opposite end point—the despair of depression—can result in loss of identity, self-rejection, and personal disintegration. These extremes and much in between are characteristics of morale/cohesion whether or not the subjective emotions are within a single individual, typify an organization, or are spread throughout a larger social system.

INDIVIDUAL (B₁)

Certain dilemmas people face are associated with low morale. Discouragement on the job, indecisiveness in career choice, demotion, fear of failure, loneliness, and despair are just a few examples. Lowered morale can diminish the capacity to cope with the ordinary stresses and strains of everyday life. It is not surprising, therefore, to find that acceptant interventions are useful in aiding clients to overcome the listlessness or uncertainty produced by emotions they themselves are unable to resolve.

Work Discouragement

Schwartz and Will (1961) describe how a nurse was helped to correct a low-morale problem. After a period of being away from the job, Miss Jones returned to her duties eager to get back to work and discovered that the regular charge nurse was away. Therefore, the so-called disturbed ward of the hospital was being supervised by a substitute. The ward was overcrowded. There was a shortage of personnel. Preestablished treatment plans were not being fulfilled. The patients themselves were uneasy about the disorganized conditions. Miss Jones thought they had become much more "difficult" than before. The other ward staff members had become tired and discouraged so were less effective than usual in coordinating procedures and in dealing with patient needs.

Miss Jones thought things would settle down in a few days and she and the staff could improve the functioning and climate of the ward. But conditions did not get any better. Instead, Miss Jones herself gradually became discouraged. By the end of the week she was having the same feelings and attitudes as other staff members. Her functioning was similarly ineffective. She reports,

> ... I began to be more and more unsuccessful in my relationship with patients. My hostility toward them was most disturbing. I actually began to visualize them as irritating, demanding people. This was sensed by them as they seemed to withdraw from me. Aggressive patients began to snarl at me. Miss F's remarks about my being ineffectual were more frequent and my anger was personal and intense. Disparaging remarks from other patients would upset me and I would keep away from them. . . .
> (Schwartz and Will, 1961, p. 568)

During the second week, she started talking with one of the consultants. During these discussions the consultant's general approach to Miss Jones was, "If you're able to find out something about the *content* of your low morale, how it developed and what it's related to, you might be able to help yourself and other nurses prevent it in the future." At first Miss Jones found it difficult to express herself. After the first few discussions she was talking more frankly and in detail about her work experiences and the feelings that had accompanied them.

The following provides an example of the consultant's method of intervention during this period. Previously he had observed an incident between this nurse and a patient.

> Breakfast trays were served. Miss Jones brought in Miss Q's tray: "Ready to eat breakfast?" Miss Q did not reply. The tray was placed beside her. Miss Jones started fixing the egg, but did not sit down.
>
> She soon left and went to the office, returning about five minutes later. "You haven't started to eat. Don't you want your breakfast?" No reply. Miss Jones picked up a spoonful of egg and started to feed the patient. Miss Q scooped the egg off the spoon and smeared it on her bathrobe. "Really, Miss Q, you can do better than that." Miss Q started muttering and holding on to her dish of eggs. "Damn it, damn it." The next several spoonfuls she refused. Miss Jones walked away, saying, "I'll check back in thirty minutes for your tray." However, in about five minutes she returned with some hot coffee. "I brought you some more coffee." Miss Q was still sputtering and as Miss Jones approached her, Miss Q threw the tray of food on the floor.

Later, in terms of the approach he had suggested, he asked the nurse how she had experienced the incident. She replied,

> It had a lot to do with how I was feeling, I think. I certainly didn't approach her as I had before. I got sort of tired of her messing around, I guess. As I cleaned up the food, I was not really angry. I felt I didn't care if she ate her food or threw it at me, and I didn't speak to her or offer to get her more breakfast.
>
> I didn't report this incident or put it in the patients' record, partly because I felt I had failed and partly because I felt no one else would care, or read the notes. Also I felt rather isolated from the rest of the personnel and didn't want to discuss the problem with them or seek their advice. (Schwartz and Will, 1961, p. 573)

The opportunity to ventilate her feelings was a source of relief in itself, for up to this point she had concealed her anger and resentment. In the course of her "talking out" experience she noticed that the consultant voiced no criticism; consequently she had no need to feel defensive, or to justify her situation, or to "explain it away." She felt increasingly freer to explore her own feelings, and found they did not seem as "terrible" as she had previously thought. This in turn made it easier for her to share with another person her sense of personal failure.

After several discussions, both consultant and client noticed some positive changes in how she participated with other staff members and patients. As the discussions continued, she gave increasingly full expressions to her feelings and continued to modify her behavior from what had characterized it previously. After a couple of weeks, she was performing as effectively as before her absence. By intervening in a nonjudgmental supportive way, the consultant was able to help Miss Jones free pent-up emotions and regain a positive outlook on her work situation.

Indecisiveness

Indecisiveness, such as in regard to a career choice, may cause low morale and indicate deeper uncertainties about one's own competence. It is associated with feelings of failure "before the event," and may result in a person continuing to drift through life rather than attempting to shape his or her future. Vocational counseling can sometimes aid a client in making a career choice, but this is not always so. The following example occurs during an interview in which the particular topic being discussed by the student is the grades he is making in his college work. The conversation's wider context, however, regards study habits, attitudes toward school, and choice of a career. It illustrates another acceptant-intervention approach to a focal issue of low morale.

Consultant: Sometimes you feel that way about your courses, and sometimes you don't.

Client: Yeah, that's right. Sometimes it looks like everything is against you and other times everything is pulling for you, but I like all of my studies this quarter, so that should be in my behalf or something.

Consultant: Perhaps that makes it a little easier to put off the problems you'll meet at the end of the quarter.

Client: Yeah. I believe it would. *(Pause and laugh.)* At the end of the quarter I'm going to have the problem of what to take next quarter and all that.

Consultant: You don't like to think about that, though, do you?

Client: No, boy! *(Laugh.)* I don't like to think about that until I come to it. Oh, I've been thinking, when I had some free time, trying to figure out what to take next quarter and all that, but oh, I don't know, it's a kind of material you want to put off.

Consultant: You want to put it off if you can?

Client: That's right.

Consultant: That's one of the things that—

Client: You shouldn't do, I know.

Consultant: No; well, you feel that people would disapprove of it. That's one of the reasons why you feel two ways about coming in for an appointment like this, because here there's always a risk you might get to thinking about some of those problems that you'd rather put off.

Client: Well, that might be, I doubt it.

Consultant: It is a lot more comfortable to put them off, isn't it?

Client: Yeah, that's right. But people—*(pause)* and it would be better for you if you wouldn't put them off, that's one sure thing.

Consultant: But it takes a lot of courage sometimes, to really think them through ahead of time. *(Very long pause).*

Client: About this question of studying, do you think—ah, what do you think is the best way to study for a midterm? Do you think you ought to make an outline of the material you've had and then go through that outline and the parts you don't know, or . . . *(He continues in this vein.)* (Rogers, 1942, pp. 56–57)

This episode exemplifies the use of an acceptant mode to help solve a decision problem that has been reducing morale. The "lead" in defining the content to be discussed remains with the student. The consultant's contribution is active listening, and restating and reaffirming what the student has said. Carried out sympathetically, this approach is sufficient to give the client a lift in morale and permit him to face the real issues in his situation.

Demotion

Promotion often produces a sense of elation and joy because it signals to a person that he or she is well regarded by those in supervisory positions. Demotion, unanticipated early retirement, or firing can arouse feelings of self-doubt as to one's competence or value to others, even though the basic reasons for the reduction or separation may not be the person's accomplishments.

Golembiewski, Carrigan, Mead, Munzenrider, and Blumberg (1972) describe a situation in which people were offered a demotion as an option to early retirement or separation and discuss what they as consultants did when the reality of the situation brought individuals face-to-face with doubts about their personal adequacy, worth, and value to the organization. The intervention proved useful in fostering the readjustments that demotion required.

The first step toward helping those demoted to adopt a more realistic attitude toward their new jobs was to assist them in expressing and working through the tensions, frustrations, and hostilities aroused by the implication of rejection. That step was followed by further cohesion-building contacts with their new supervisors conducted in such a way that harmonious, even warm, feelings arose. Those affected came to appreciate that they could expect helpful support from their new bosses, who were compassionate and sympathetic rather than criticizing and pressuring during the transitional period. The general method, rather than a sink-or-swim approach, was to help employees deal with emotions engendered by self-doubt and actively plan with their supervisors ways to remove potential barriers to future success. This action planning was catalytic in character, as will be described in a later chapter.

Fear of Failure

College students, living in a relatively free environment, enjoy a substantial degree of autonomy. But problems of low morale can prevent a student from using the college situation for his or her own learning and growth. In academic settings, acceptant interventions have long been relied upon to help such students "find" themselves after emotions have blocked learning.

> Paul, a college student, comes to the counselor without appointment and says that he is feeling desperate. He feels he is under much tension, he cannot face social groups, his hands sweat, and so on. An appointment is given for the following day and the student comes in for his first interview. This initial interview commences as follows (phonographic recording):
>
> *Consultant:*   Well, now, yesterday I sent you off before we really got started talking. This will be a good time when we can talk things over. Do you want to tell me what's on your mind?
>
> *Client:*   Yes. I told you that I experienced—uh—excessive tension whenever—uh—my personality to any degree is concerned, that is, whenever I—uh—when any issue was at stake, even if small, it's—uh—exceedingly gotten worse, and as I told you it's become quite unbearable, and I really have to do something about it, because I'll make a perfect flop of my college career. I can't waste my father's money.
>
> *Consultant:*   You really feel it's interfering a lot with your college career?
>
> *Client:*   Tremendously, oh, tremendously. I'm—uh—in some subjects I'm failing which I wouldn't fail, I'm sure of, if I wasn't feeling this way, and I'm so despondent and I haven't got any morale at all. (Pause.) As examples, I can't get up, I told you I couldn't get up to a blackboard and illustrate problems which I knew very well, and when I was called I was so tense that I couldn't think straightly and—uh—it seems all out of proportion—this tension.
>
> *Consultant:*   In what way?
>
> *Client:*   I said I couldn't even go into a restaurant without feeling tense, which seems very queer, but I—uh—that's the problem I'm confronted with nevertheless. (Pause.)
>
> *Consultant:*   You feel you've gotten to a point where you've just got to do something.
>
> *Client:*   Yes, I have to, definitely. It's been going on, I should say—I can recall I was twelve years old, the first time, when I was asked to read a—

a composition that I did. I was rather proud of it, and when I got in front of the class, why—uh—my hands started shaking like anything, and I had to sit down. I was extremely humiliated, too.

Consultant: You felt very much humiliated.

Client: Very much so.

Consultant: In what way?

Client: In the fact that I felt abnormal, because everybody else could do it and I couldn't. (Rogers, 1942, pp. 66–67)

Paul is sufficiently distressed about the situation as to be eager to talk about it. With the supportive listening of the consultant Paul is able to move toward a more focused definition of his problem: that the character of his tensions, related to feelings of low self-worth, is out of line with the actual demands of the situations he faces. He is making implicit comparisons between unlike episodes. Perhaps the key one is where he tells *himself*—as well as the consultant—that he has an *unusual* problem of feeling tense when entering a restaurant, and traces this feeling to earlier times when he experienced the more common problem of stage fright during a classroom presentation.

Lack of Confidence

Low morale and reduced self-worth can stem from relations with parents and friends if the client feels duty bound to fulfill their expectations, yet is unable to do so. Although power/authority dynamics may have caused the problem, the intervention that helps resolve it may focus on morale/cohesion aspects. Once self-confidence has been increased, the client may be able to grapple with the basic problem.

Ginger, a sixteen-year-old above-average student, exemplifies this. In a group consultation session,

the leader mentioned she looked depressed, and while she denied it, she seemed willing to talk if the leader was interested.

After a little coaxing Ginger described herself as feeling that "I don't really exist." Everything she did was for other people—although, she quickly added, what they wanted was the right thing, so she did not mind. She said, "I would probably do them anyway, but they won't let me decide." She described her parents as genuinely concerned but very covertly making demands on her, at the same time denying that they were making demands.

She talked about her Sunday-school group, how kids in it were wasting time, not doing anything in particular, and how she felt that she could not make them change. Essentially, Ginger felt powerless with both her friends and her parents, fulfilling their demands, living a life over which she had no control, unable to be angry because she was only being asked to do things that were for her own good.

Ginger's twisting a piece of paper, her expression of sadness which her face assumed when she did not know she was being watched, her helplessness, all disappeared when she began to express her anger, resentment, and frustration—feelings she had never felt comfortable in expressing because they seemed "wrong" and "I feel guilty because they only try and do what is right for me." As they talked about the ways her parents gain (in pride, satisfaction) from her successes, she began to see that their statements of selflessness were not entirely true, and she began to feel that she could now express more of her resentment at their pressures upon her. (Clark and Jaffe, 1973, p. 190)

Two weeks later Ginger told the consultant she had talked with her Sunday school class about her criticism and they had responded to her suggestions. She also had been able to talk with her parents about their expectations regarding her school and social life. The consultant concludes,

The issue of resentment and demands continually occurs with young people, who often bury their anger because they feel guilty about it, as Ginger did. Demands are often covert, understood, or they are covered over with disclaimers of any gain for the person making the "legitimate expectation" demands. However, with Ginger and many others, the inability to comment directly on demands made on them creates a general state of confusion and helplessness, and often a vague feeling of emptiness, of being a form existing for, and conforming to, outside pressures, with no existence within itself. (Clark and Jaffe, 1973, p. 191)

Loneliness

When the client is facing an immediate crisis, telephone counseling permits the person to contact a professional quickly for help in getting through the crisis episode.

Whenever a caller presents a specific difficulty, the staff member's interest increases. Results are tangible, some sort of resolution is possible within the period of one call. Common experiences leading to the typical crisis call are loneliness, confusion, anxiety, and depression, while the typical problems fall under four categories: self, others (sexuality), parents, school. The following example comes from Number Nine's phone log.

10:00 p.m. Girl, Jane called. 16 years old. She was very lonely and afraid to talk, but wanted to. She says she can't relate to people, and feels withdrawn. She said she feels like she's falling off a cliff backwards and can't feel anything. She talks about animals and really digs them, but all of a sudden, after talking for 45 minutes she just withdrew, and wouldn't talk anymore. (Clark and Jaffe, 1973, p. 156)

In time, the crisis counseling led to the consultant assisting through extensive acceptant interventions.

Despair

Numerous people have resorted to drugs as an avenue of escape from life. However, handled in an accepting way, the drug experience may provide insights that restore a sense of self-worth. An example is fifteen-year-old Sara, who tried LSD out of a sense of despair, and began what evidently was a "bad trip." Her friends took her to a crisis center, where several consultants assisted by encouraging her to express the thoughts and feelings she was experiencing. Many of these thoughts and feelings had been "buried." They concerned matters of sex, both in aspects of her childhood upbringing and most recently with a boyfriend who had rejected her, wishes for greater intimacy with her parents, guilt about physical exposure, and so on.

Sara's account of what she felt during her trip (taped when she returned two weeks later) shows the importance of setting in transforming an initial negative set.

"I was feeling very depressed, and I had tried to kill myself, so I thought I'd just become an acid head or speed freak or something. I expected it to be like going crazy and I was surprised it turned out so differently, because of the state of mind I was in. Maybe it was the surroundings. I'll never forget what happened in that room, because it's been so important to me . . . "

At first Sara huddled in the corner and cried out in Spanish, her native language which she had not used regularly for years. "Mike Samuels I love you. I need you. I want to die." Yvonne was called in because she is Spanish also, and Jerry and Billy, two other staff helpers, also came. Sara repeated those phrases in a common trip sign of a wish (in this case for love, closeness, and sexual pleasure) and fears and guilt associated with satisfying it (punishment by dying), which indicates that the conflict is not being resolved. Yvonne encouraged Sara to express the feelings she blocked and work through a fantasy solution, which will then be vividly remembered as the experience which resolved the conflict.

Sara was afraid and in need of support and security. She was on such a regressed level that the most meaningful support would be physical contact with a surrogate mother (of either sex). Yvonne took this role, telling her not to be afraid and bathing her hands and feet with a wet handkerchief. Yvonne saw her withdraw slightly, and took this as a sign that she was working on negative feelings about touching her body. It is easy to build rapport with someone who is tripping, even when the guide and tripper have never met before, because the tripper relates to people mainly as fantasy versions of parents and other important figures in his life.

Mothering is best when it is physical and direct. Words are confusing and often not understood, because the tripper may regress to a period before language. The integrity and self-awareness of the guide in this role is critical. He or she must move with the tripper, not seeking power or advantage over him because people on psychedelics are usually sensitive to such maneuvers. . . . A mother surrogate, whose love is more unconditional than the original, can undo some of the damage in people who are much more fearful than Sara. The trip out of psychosis, while much longer, can be similar and demands the same kind of patience from the guide-mother.

Once contact is made, the guide can tune into the conflict the tripper is experiencing. There are only a small number of themes which make up the human condition, though they exhibit infinite variations. Since they involve sexuality, guilt, union with parents, or desire for closeness and intimacy, the guide can test for the relevant theme by suggesting phrases which relate the tripper's words or actions to possible sources of the conflict; he can then judge from the reaction whether the supposition is correct. If the theme suggested by the guide is not relevant the tripper will simply ignore it, since LSD frees one almost totally from social games and polite conversations. Under acid all relationships relate directly to central needs. (Clark and Jaffe, 1973, pp. 92–93)

Sara's report of her experience in retrospect includes the following.

When she came back two weeks later, she was beaming and smiling, wearing colorful clothes and a bright rainbow shawl. As she thanked us for the experience, her face was as radiant as it had been during the trip, in sharp contrast to the subdued demeanor before and immediately after it. Her account validated our impression of the significance of the trip, and of the amount she had uncovered and learned to accept about herself.

She ends her narrative with her conclusions:

"Right after the trip I didn't really know what I had done, but I felt guilty anyway. When I woke up it was so different. Then I started reconstructing things, and I realized it was true, that's your subconscious and that's how you feel. I started feeling that we really have to live to satisfy ourselves. Not be selfish you know, but you can't satisfy anyone if you're not satisfied yourself. That's my main goal now. Before, I was so afraid of being hurt that I built this wall and made myself a prisoner in it. I've changed now. Like before I'd just nod. My feelings have been blocked and sterile. I couldn't communicate with people. Like I wanted to shout 'I love you' or 'I just want to hold your hand' or something like that, but I couldn't because I was so restrained. We have only one of those things we call lives, and we breathe and walk around and things like that, and poof, it's gone. As far as I'm concerned there's nothing else, as far as positive proof is concerned, so I'd better make sure I make something of it, enjoy myself."

The trip intervention turned what was intended as an act of self-destruction into an opening-up peak experience. Because of her tremendous insight and capacity to integrate learning, Sara has since been freed to trust people more and to express herself without drugs, and she has no desire to trip again. Through counseling and group experience at Number

Nine, she continues to relate her insights to her everyday life. She contacted her parents and told them about what she is doing and about some of the feelings she was holding back. She visited home, and her family agreed that she could continue to live in New Haven in a residential job-corps program. (Clark and Jaffe, 1973, pp. 96–97)

This process of nonjudgmental, understanding-based acceptance permitted Sara to rediscover buried thoughts and feelings. By talking and acting them out she was able to reassess and to replace them with functional ways of thinking and feelings that are basic to a sound adult adjustment.

Gordon offers an acceptant-consultation strategy useful to teachers dealing with classroom relationship problems. The teacher first decides, Whose problem is it? It belongs to the child if it impedes that child's learning but has no deleterious impact on other students or the teacher. It is the teacher's problem if the student's behavior reduces the leader's ability to teach or reduces the classroom learning opportunities of others. In the first case the child-as-client is dealt with through acceptant interventions; confrontation is the intervention approach in the latter case.

An example of acceptant intervention concerns a student having difficulty finishing a school project. The consultant, a classroom teacher, is talking with a girl about producing the school paper.

Client: I'll never get the paper out. I think I'll quit.

Consultant: (*Silence, nods*)

Client: I've been here since three this afternoon. Everybody else split. They seem to think because I'm the editor that I have to do all the work. That's a bummer.

Consultant: Uh-huh.

Client: Ellen didn't get the typing done and Maryanne still has to do those layouts—and look at that mess over there that Steve calls the sports page.

Consultant: (*Nods*)

Client: (*Pause*) The problem is that everybody is waiting for somebody else to do something. We need a list of things that have to be done and the order they must be done in. That way everybody will be able to see what the next job is and who has to do it.

Consultant: I see.

Client: I can make the list at home tonight. See you tomorrow.

Consultant: Right. (Gordon, 1974, pp. 62–63)

Encouraged by this nonjudgmental attitude of acceptance, the client discovers a personal solution and is freed from the tensions that were tearing down morale a moment before.

Walling Off Emotions

For years, an author had been unable to establish a realistic basis of adjustment even though her psychiatric treatment had been extensive. Depression led to drinking, drinking led to further withdrawal in a series of ever-deepening cycles. While past efforts had involved a conversational approach, the new effort described below was calculated to assist her to experience her emotions more directly by beginning acceptant interventions on a nonverbal basis.

In expressive therapy interventions, the client expresses himself or herself by using media with which he or she has little or no prior experience—clay modeling, water colors for painting, or dancing either by oneself or with others. Whatever the medium, the client must deal with it in an expressive way, and as a "primitive" artist because it is an unfamiliar form. He or she does not have a programmed way of response, stereotyped or stylized over the years. Such neutral media for artistic expression can be used in conjunction with a consultant who aids the expression of buried emotions by helping the client feel it is "safe" to reveal his or her feelings. In the following example, a client learned to get in touch with her emotions through a variety of methods.

Her first experience was with dance therapy. She went through a practice session believing that she was doing well. However, the instructor's evaluation was, "Professorial, knows it all." Apparently, expressiveness was lacking.

> The next hour J. had me lie down on the floor and close my eyes. I was to feel my body touching the floor, the back of my head, my shoulders, my arms, my back, my buttocks, my thighs, my legs, my heels. Then I was to open my body to the air, to let it touch me all over, let it caress me. As I was lying spread-eagle fashion, J. said all the parts of my body where the air was touching my skin. She then put on a record, and asked me to imagine that the music was flowing over me. Music soon turned into waves; I saw myself at the edge of the ocean; waves were lapping over me, washing me back and forth. I felt like crying.

> It seems to me now that it took me a long time to cry, to be angry, to be sad, to be sensuous. I had always *felt like* crying, being angry, or being joyful. I had screened myself from perceiving motion and emotion and regarded the former as merely useful or necessary, the latter as an uncomfortable hindrance at best, a weakness at worst. At first, after an hour of beating in anger on a beat-up bed, of shouting, of moving sensuously, of dancing with exhilaration, I felt rather guilty, even though I thought I had repudiated prudishness. (Mahlendorf, 1973, pp. 318–19)

Later, the consultant provided acceptant support while the client enacted her recollections of anger and rage.

> Anger caused us more trouble in acting out than anything else; perhaps, I should rather say rage. What is so frightening is not only the realization of one's destructiveness and one's fear of retaliation, but also the terror

of losing control and of never regaining it. Let me illustrate. I dislike my-self worse when I felt in myself reactions, motions, belief patterns, which, consciously, I rejected years ago. They are residues of my mother's in-fluence upon me that I experience as alien. I should add that some of my mother's *traits* in me do not provoke such self-dislike. I demonstrated to J. a childhood day when I was ill and my mother's reaction to my illness. I was the child in pain; I was the mother calming down the child. I stopped the acting-out, too petrified to go on. I felt I was entering a terrible dark-ness that I could not tolerate. J. told me that she would go into the dark-ness with me. Her words felt like the hand of my brother to whom I had clung when small and frightened.

I reenacted the scene and this time *played* it through. When the mother admonished the child to be quiet and not to make a fuss, the child stopped crying and went rigid. The mother continued saying: "See, there is not much the matter with you, you are quiet now." I felt the child get up and hit out at the mother, hitting to kill. Beating and trampling about, I saw a bloody body; as this image came, I felt sick with fear and col-lapsed sobbing. J. held me in a manner that conveyed to me that she believed the reality of my feelings, the pain, the rage, the fear and the grief. She was not afraid of these feelings in me, hence not afraid of losing control. Since this was so, I could let her take care of me.

It does not really matter whether or not this incident constitutes a memory of an event that happened—namely the child pleads for help, the adult denies the plea and hence the child's feelings, the child believes that in her rage over the denial she has killed her mother. What does matter is that this scene showed the essence of the child's relationship to her mother; a denial of emotion and its reality on the part of the mother; a cutting off of emotions and an underlying rage that is perceived as omni-potent by the child. It does matter that J. believed the emotions, accepted them as real and was not afraid of losing control. She provided me with the consolation and courage that my brother had given me, a help I could accept in the initial stages of the scene. (Mahlendorf, 1973, pp. 320–321)

The focal morale/cohesion issue has now become a power/authority issue, showing the close linkages between these two focal concerns.

She also worked with both clay and wood carving to express in art form what she had been unable to put into words.

Let me summarize: In the last few years I have learned to express my emotions in a way that is meaningful to me and to my friends. As the art work gave clearer expression to my emotions, I became more comfortable with myself. My life is taking on a new shape, I am beginning to know what I need and I feel surer of the ways to satisfy my needs. The need to dull emotions by alcohol disappeared. Expression of emotions is not re-stricted to working through a medium: clay, wood, or words; it is not a substitute for relationships to others. I can equally well express emotions through touch or words, for I have gained the assurance that whatever expresses me honestly is acceptable. Sculpture or a piece of writing are merely more durable and they may reach more people. (Mahlendorf, 1973, p. 326)

Finally, the significance of the consultant's or the paraprofessional consultant's acceptant mode of relating, and of group support as well, is pointed out.

The art therapist need not be a person trained in artistic skills. It is best if she is a patient with artistic inclinations who is a little further along in her therapy—she has been there, she knows what mental illness feels like, she can encourage expression, she is not afraid of emotion. It is wise not to ask the patient to pursue a skill he had before therapy. If I had tried writing as a medium of expression, I could not have done anything with it, it had ceased to help me express myself; know-how and long habit had removed feeling expression from it.

Finally, it is important that several patients share an art activity, explore the possibility of new media, and share the enjoyment of their new discovery. An analogy with a supportive family describes the situation best; the therapists as parents encourage emotional expression and provide means for such expression; fellow patients like siblings participate in and enjoy together a common task. All members of the family support the achievements of each individual. (Mahlendorf, 1973, p. 327)

Various nonverbal expressive modes for intervention seem to be quite useful in working through emotional difficulties when the client is blocked in some way from discussing his or her feelings directly with the consultant. In one respect, it is similar to play therapy as described earlier (Chapter 3) by Axline and Moustakas in connection with focal issues in the power/authority area, in that the consultant's role of nonjudgmental support makes it possible for the client to "be himself" and thereby gain release from tensions. But the difference lies in the client's attempts, as expressiveness increases, to transmute this into some unique creative "product" of feelings which represents integrated-whole *outcomes* of therapy rather than fragmentary episodes within it.

Summary

Acceptant interventions appear to be particularly applicable to problems on the low-morale/cohesion end of the scale. This suggests that the acceptant mode of intervention helps a person unload burdensome thoughts and reactions and enables the client to reorient his or her thinking toward a more objective appraisal of the surrounding situation. The commonsense aspects of this dynamic are suggested by such phrases as "getting it off your chest," "getting it out of your system," or "having a good cry."

GROUP (B₂)

Inappropriate use of power/authority, whether it be between persons of equal rank or between a boss and a subordinate, can result in problems involving issues of morale/cohesion. In the first example given, involving a team-building session, group members were building up antagonisms toward one another which the consultant tried to ease. In the next, an organizational situation was fraught with negative aspects of morale—i.e., frustration, antagonisms, internal conflict, suspiciousness, and hostility among work-team members—so intense as to be disruptive of work.

Interpersonal Tensions

As illustrated below, team building is one approach for investigating how feelings among team members influence their effectiveness, as well as for acquiring interpersonal skills for dealing in a more constructive way with interpersonal tensions (Oshry, 1966).

> B is a drawling Texan who had the habit of accentuating points in the group by telling rather long and very funny stories ranging in dialect from Texan to Irish to Cajun to Jewish. Each story was followed by widely shared group laughter, although some group members, A in particular, appeared to be getting annoyed at the amount of group time being taken up by B. The group had discussed some of their reactions to B's story-telling behavior for about twenty minutes when the following interchange took place.
>
> A (to B): It just seems to me that you might be more effective if sometimes you came right to the point. Some people might not enjoy your stories and might not understand what you were getting at.
>
> B: Didn't you enjoy them?
>
> A: Oh yes! I think they're great, I wasn't talking about me; I was thinking of other people who might not appreciate . . .
>
> C: Well how did you feel when B was telling his story?
>
> A: I felt he might be more effective if he came to the point more directly.
>
> C: That's what you thought, but how did you feel? Were you angry?
>
> A: Oh no!
>
> C: That's funny, you looked angry. Maybe irritated then?
>
> A: No.
>
> C: Even a little irritated?
>
> A: No.
>
> D: (In exasperation.) For crying out loud! Then if it didn't bother you, why have you been kicking it to death for the last hour?
>
> A: I just felt that B would be more effective if . . .

Postscript: Two sessions later, *A* admitted how much *B*'s behavior had bothered him, and then added, "But now that I've come to know you, it doesn't bother me any more." (Oshry, 1966, p. 40)

Although the consultant had tried to intervene early and get the feeling into the open, his initial attempts were unsuccessful. Oshry has summarized how feelings can influence problem solving in a team situation such as exemplified above.

Effects of Feelings on Ideas

Feeling	*Effects on Openness, Expression, and Experimentation with Ideas*
A feels competitive toward *B*. In any group interaction, he is motivated to increase his own status and decrease *B*'s.	1. *A* takes premature potshots at *B*'s ideas, thus decreasing the opportunity for others to evaluate or build on *B*'s ideas.
	2. *A* saves his best ideas for those times when *B* is not present.
	3. *A* tends not to express incompletely conceived ideas, which in open discussion might have been productively developed, for fear that critical judgment might lower his status relative to *B*.
A is *irritated* by a persistent pattern of *B*'s behavior. (For example, he is annoyed by *B*'s domination of group discussion.)	4. *A* tends to tune out *B* or to distort what *B* says.
A feels unsure of his own ability, which may in fact be equal to or greater than the ability of others in the group.	5. *A* prefers not to build on others' ideas for fear that his contributions will not be significant.
A feels dependent on his superiors' good will.	See 3 and 5 above.
	6. *A* tends not to critically evaluate or alter in any way his superiors' ideas for fear this will threaten the relationship between them.
A likes B personally and wants him as friend.	See above. (Oshry, 1966, p. 41)

Because people tend to shy away from hostile and antagonistic emotions, the natural inclination is to leave a "hot" situation alone in the hope that it will cool off. This is not likely to happen as people reenact in memory what caused the problem. In the next example it is likely the situation would have deteriorated further had not management arranged channels for working through the destructive emotions.

Frustrations, Antagonisms, and Suspicions

At the Weldon Manufacturing Company, prescriptive interventions concerned with work study, incentive rates, and so on (described in Chapter 21) were having negative rather than their intended constructive effects on production. Suspicions, hostilities, and fears for the future were rampant among managers and supervisors. Morale was at a low ebb. In an effort to get at these problems, an acceptant kind of consultant intervention was "superimposed" on the first, or prescriptive, step.

This second intervention focused on "family groups." It started with the top team of the Weldon organization, but the consultants interviewed members individually in advance, partly to provide themselves with background but more significantly to explore and moderate or allay apprehensions—an acceptant intervention in itself—as well as to encourage hope for the future among prospective participants.

Here is how the situation appeared:

> It was believed at that time that progress potentially available through the various technical improvements was being blocked by the hostilities, suspicions, and fears of the Weldon managers and supervisors in their work relations with one another. Not that these had become worse, but just that they had not become better. It was felt, further, that these conditions among the higher-level people had their effects among the lower-level supervisors and operators as well. Coordination between the merchandising and manufacturing divisions remained poor and a constant source of difficulty. The plant managers and supervisors clearly were performing at a level well below their capacities. (David, 1967, pp. 95–96)

Then group sessions of two to four days were scheduled. Each session commenced with a *problem census,* which is usually a catalytic-intervention technique (see Chapter 10). Soon, strongly felt emotions both in regard to operations and toward one another were expressed.

> The training period ran from the evening of the first day through noon of the fourth day, and the work was continuous and intensive, with breaks only for meals, brief recreation, and sleep.
>
> The "program" was unstructured at the beginning, as is conventional in this type of training. The first evening discussion began with a problem census, often a rather neutral opening process but in this case one that very soon led to strongly emotional expression of concern. (David, 1967, pp. 95–96)

Acceptant interventions permitted long-suppressed hostilities and anxieties to be shared, and slowly it became possible to deal with human and mechanical barriers to organization effectiveness.

> By the following day the participants had begun to express their feelings toward each other quite directly and frankly, something they had rarely done in their daily work. As the discussion progressed it became easier

for them to accept criticism without becoming angry or wanting to strike back. As they began to express long-suppressed hostilities and anxieties the "unfreezing" of old attitudes, old values, and old approaches began. From the second day onward the discussion was spontaneous and uninhibited. From early morning to long past midnight the process of self-examination and confrontation continued. They raised questions they had never felt free to ask before. Politeness and superficiality yielded to openness and emotional expression and then to more objective analysis of themselves and their relationships at work. They faced up to many conflicts and spoke of their differences. There were tense moments, as suspicion, distrust, and personal antagonisms were aired, but more issues were worked out without acrimony. (David, 1967, pp. 99–100)

Thereafter, more constructive response became possible, replacing the resistance that had been shown to the prescriptions of the first interventions.

INTERGROUP (B₃)

By their nature, the conditions under which low morale/cohesion is the focal issue between two groups make it highly unlikely that intervention will be sought. The rationale is this: when two groups despair of coordinating effort, they tend to become more separately encapsulated and to withdraw even further from one another. Each may develop its own resources rather than rely on outside help. When this occurs, a condition of autonomy becomes "natural," and thus neither group is likely to seek consultant assistance to deal with the morale/cohesion issues, even if an effective intervention could restore a circumstance of interdependence.

ORGANIZATION (B₄)

Lowered morale/cohesion can become a problem for the membership of an entire organization. At least two factors are involved in creating such conditions. One is organization trauma whereby some critical event causes members who previously had a strong group commitment to feel a sense of loss and thereafter withdraw their identification from the organization. Consequences of this include apathy, indifference, or feelings of rejection.

The other cause of reduced morale/cohesion is more difficult to observe but no less important. It occurs when organization members experience a succession of small disappointments over a more extended period of time, with each disappointment causing participants to withdraw emotional commitments to some small degree. Nonetheless, the cumulative effect over time of a succession of disappointments can have the same consequences for organization morale/cohesion as a single traumatic event.

Few documented examples of successive disappointments leading to morale/cohesion problems are available, but an acceptant approach for bringing about organization-wide relief from tensions associated with change is described by Levinson

(1973). One year previously, a consulting firm had prescribed a reorganization that resulted in the stripping of authority from many who had previously held significant positions. As a consequence, widespread depression and anger was generated.

> Following the devastating effect of the reorganization of a company . . . and a subsequent year of turmoil, a consultant was asked to undo the situation. Initial interviews with the executives indicated the severity of the depression each was experiencing and provided information on the turmoil in the rest of the organization. Building upon a clinical understanding of depression following the experience of loss, an appreciation of the sense of responsibility the managers in the organization felt, the sensitivity of the new leadership, and important changes in external forces which the organization now confronted, the consultant recommended that the 100 top management people be brought together for a meeting to last several days. During this meeting, on the consultant's recommendation, the chief executive officer presented the history of the organization, its achievements, its present state, and its future potential, and indicated clearly what was happening in the outside environment and what drastic changes had to be made. This was followed by an opportunity for the 100 men, in small groups, to discuss and analyze what they had heard and to mourn the loss as well as to confront reality. While regretting the past, they could begin to see clearly what the future held and what kinds of adaptive efforts might have to be made.

The consultant's acceptant intervention permitted these managers to "mourn"—that is, to discharge the feelings associated with their giving up an attachment to extinct realities. The president's presentation in historical perspective of their situation provided organization members an opportunity to identify the emotion-provoking problem and thereafter to express their feelings of frustration, anger, loss, and so on. The consultant's second-step recommendation (a catalytic phase) permitted study and shared perception of their new reality. Later still, freed from their counter-productive emotions, managers began to deal with the current organization situation in problem-solving terms.

> They were then reconvened to hear presentations about future trends in their field, as well as in society at large, and to set in context what they were up against. They then had the opportunity to discuss and digest their impressions and to see how such forces related to them. On the basis of those small-group discussions, they established priorities for action, coalesced them in large plenary sessions, and evolved a charter for their functional operations. Thus, they began to turn their aggressions outward on real problems, which they faced together, while working through their sense of loss and depression. (Levinson, 1973, pp. 166–67)

Without the prior cathartic release from tensions, this new attitude of constructive desire to meet and master organization realities would probably not have been possible. Furthermore, had this catharsis been experienced on a one-by-one basis or by only a few individuals, the absence of sharing would probably have minimized the change brought about.

Congruent with Levinson, Davis (1967) emphasizes that organization development efforts that concentrate on but limit themselves to promoting cathartic release among organization members are counterproductive.

> There is no real growth—there is no real development—in the organization or in the individuals within it if they do not confront and deal directly with their problems. They can get together and share feelings, but if that is all they do, it is merely a catharsis. While this is useful, it has relatively minimal usefulness compared with what can happen if they start to relate differently within the organizational setting around task issues. (Davis, 1967, p. 4)

His solution is to provide work teams with on-the-job support for problem-solving efforts *after* they have attended emotionally freeing sensitivity training sessions. In a certain sense, and allowing for the significant differences between Davis' and Levinson's respective acceptant methodologies, the sequences they describe illustrate constructive follow-up intervention possibilities.

LARGER SOCIAL SYSTEM (B₅)

Acceptant interventions can contribute to the restoration or maintenance of the mental health of members of the larger social system.

Trauma

Sometimes survivors or relatives of victims of a catastrophe, such as an explosion, or bus accident, or tornado, experience great difficulty in regaining mental balance. Aroused emotions can be so intense that participants are unable to cope with them, so unbearable that they can "disappear" from consciousness. Calm returns. But the traumatic experience has not gone away: it has been "buried." While the individual feels no immediate pain, the buried emotions may exert effects on later behavior. Acceptant interventions in such trauma situations can be used to reduce the likelihood of future adverse mental-health consequences by enabling participants to talk about their feelings as soon as possible after the episode. If the several who have suffered the disaster can share their emotions with one another, then the distortions that might otherwise result may be reduced or entirely avoided.

The following incident exemplifies the beneficial results that can flow from emotion-releasing interventions. Tuckman was involved with a situation where forty-three school children had been in a bus accident. Five had been killed; only one person escaped hospitalization (Safran, 1973). Tuckman's crisis team quickly intervened, but even then found that some children had blocked the accident from conscious thought, denying everything that had happened. Others had reactions involving guilt and uncontrolled anxiety. The Tuckman team provided the children the opportunity to face their losses and injuries by sharing with one another their feelings toward what had happened. The consultants also worked with the victims' parents, teachers, and classmates in a similar manner. Cohesion returned and personal morale was restored with a minimum of emotional damage.

Other examples of emotional release in larger social systems involve customary, long-established acceptant intervention "mechanisms." Examples include traditional mourning procedures where close friends comfort the person who has suffered the loss of a loved one. A minister may also contribute, or friends of the deceased may come together and hold a wake where they have the opportunity to mourn together. In larger social systems as wholes, cathartic experiences of this kind occur at the time of the death or funeral of a respected and beloved leader.

From Problem-Laden "Cells" to Feelings-Sharing "Hive"

The majority of adults have not been hospitalized for mental-health difficulties; yet for many their ways of adjusting to the larger social system or the constraints of their present situations are characterized by various mental ill-health symptoms. Such aspects include loneliness, isolation, and withdrawal in daily contacts. Given this degree of isolation, such persons go unnoticed even though suffering many of the same problems of adjustment that characterize those who are hospitalized.

Within a larger social system, small families may be living in relative isolation from one another even though the living units are side by side. Moreover, where one or more of a family's members are away at work or school for a significant part of the day, the sole occupants of its living unit may be a mother burdened down with young children or keeping house in total solitude. Mothers who find coping difficult and who do not maintain social contact with others may need to ventilate dissatisfactions in order to reestablish perspective. Depressed mothers, who may benefit from active and acceptant support with accompanying opportunities for catharsis, often remain unidentified unless the community consultant takes active steps to find them.

> The choice of ten mothers for membership of the new group was made partly on their own relationships with one another and partly on the caseworker's assessment of their emotional needs and the stresses which seemed to be troubling them.
>
> Through her diagnosis of the mothers' needs she quickly recognized that what was necessary above all else was a group from which they could gain "support" for the strains and stresses of family life. These stresses were particularly heavy, and they were unable to derive from the neighbourhood the support which most mothers get from friends and relatives. "We are all in the same boat together and got to cope," as one member said.

Her (i.e. the worker's) method was not to make plans for talks from visitors, nor arrange outings, nor, during the last nine months of the group when the members met in each other's homes, to fix up accommodation in the Meeting Rooms. The planning and organization she left to the members themselves. But it was certainly to encourage and facilitate activity and to make it easier for them to do the kinds of things which secretly they hoped for, but had not the energy or initiative to do without encouragement, such as the planning of a party or an outing with their families. Above all, it was to help them to make relationships which would be a source of support. When invited—and this happened on several occasions —the group worker joined the mothers and their families on special occasion such as a visit to the approved school to see one of the children, or a grammar school commemoration service in the Cathedral. (Wilson, 1963, pp. 36–37)

Wilson summarizes the acceptant basis of intervention for these most impoverished mothers.

The worker's method was not dependent on the programme. She welcomed and accepted the mothers as they were, encouraging them to feel comfortable and to feel free to talk about some of the things that they felt troubled about in themselves and their families. In the early days she dropped in for a chat in their own homes as well as meeting them in the group. Within the group, the worker regarded it as her job to ease the relations between the members themselves, so that they came more and more to a sense of mutual support. For the first six months the group met in the Meeting Rooms, but for the rest of the two years over which the work lasted it met in one or another of the members' homes. There was never a programme. The aim was that they should enjoy one another's company enough to be able to give each other a sense of support and so to establish confidence in human relationships. (Wilson, 1963, p. 38)

The general outcome of the community worker's numerous interventions with individual "cell inhabitants," then, was the creation of an informal therapeutic community.

Building Self-Confidence

When mental-health problems concerned with self-rejecting behavior become unmanageable, hospitalization is one recourse. Psychiatric hospitalization has been described as producing an unusual degree of dependency in that the patient is called upon to exercise minimal responsibility for himself or herself. When or if a patient eventually is released from hospital confinement, whatever degree of morale/cohesion he or she possesses by that time may easily be shattered, for the patient is now called upon to operate in an unprotected environment. A number of acceptant interventions are available within a halfway house, where the discharged patient is encouraged to build up realistic self-esteem as he or she seeks to cope with the everyday external world.

Clark and Jaffe (1973) describe conditions under which a therapeutic living community may be organized around strengthening the dynamics of morale/cohesion. The intervention is correlated to the fact that the members of this live-in community are former mental patients. During hospitalization they had accepted being dependent upon prescriptive consultation and had either lost or failed to gain such social skills as are essential for self-confident living in the wider society.

The needed support was available in New Haven in the form of a transitional community, referred to as the New Haven Halfway House. Participants could interrelate with one another in a trusting, accepting, loving, and helpful way, in order to build the confidence and skill essential for coping in real-world terms. The atmosphere of the house is described as follows:

> The pressures and problems a resident faces at the House are not so much authority problems, problems of dealing with a structure of rules and demands, than they are those of getting close to people, living together, and making personal decisions about the future and about methods. The burden of handling himself and getting along with others is placed on the resident, and he can neither blame his past, his illness, restrictive rules or external circumstances for his own failings in the House. (Clark and Jaffe, 1973, p. 231)

Interviews with residents demonstrate how they reacted to the environment and its benefits.

> —People are supposed to unravel some of their problems. This is supposed to be a community, so you're not supposed to be evasive. Maybe people can help you if you come out of your shell. Most people try to work on their problems alone, but they find they need an understanding person to listen. The House gives people a responsive attitude to themselves, to know there's another life when they leave here. They're learning to accept other people, so they can go out and accept others. The House is a lantern to show the way out.

> —You go to the hospital because you feel nobody needs you and say to hell with life. I couldn't develop a relationship and didn't feel wanted. Here I find I can contribute, so relating is a two-way street. People listen to me and sometimes they accept it. It makes me somebody because they need me.

> —You act like yourself here. You don't have to be phoney. I don't feel I have to put on shows or acts. Like if I get mad, I won't be threatened with being put back into the hospital. I feel no pressure, strain, or anything. (Clark and Jaffe, 1973, p. 231)

The residents-as-clients recognize from their own direct experience the morale/ cohesion building aspects of learning to accept and support one another, and the importance of this for coping with outside life.

The backup consultation mode provided by the house director was primarily catalytic. Her routine administrative responsibilities included such things as the assignments of chores, collecting rent, and so on. When conflict arose she frequently mediated the differences as well as reinforced the rules or norms of the House. University students who also lived in the House as part of their learning of clinical dynamics provided the former hospital patients a basis of comparison and reality-checking data. This also is in the catalytic mode.

The Santa Barbara Psychiatric Foundation is a similar community created to provide its members, themselves also recently released from a mental health institution and still "patients," with cohesion-building opportunities necessary for the growth and development of self-confidence (Carleton, 1973). The New Haven House and Santa Barbara Foundation together verify the importance of acceptant interventions for reestablishing self-esteem.

"Deep Dive" Therapeutic Environments for Disturbed Persons

Communities have been created to help more severely disturbed persons by providing a milieu within which these clients can "work themselves through" their subjective experiences. The character of this "milieu as an acceptant intervention" can be contrasted with the help-giving values characteristic of the New Haven Halfway House, which mostly accepts residents after their release from mental hospitals.

In London's East End, the Philadelphia Association (P.A.) leases Kingsley Hall, an old settlement house.

> Madness, especially the form known as schizophrenia, is seen by members of the P.A. as a response to a family or other interpersonal situation where contradictory demands make the person feel that no response he makes is right. The schizophrenic child has lived in fear of irrational, punitive behavior by his parents and feels prohibited from pointing it out. Such a person never is able to feel at home in a world which is perpetually fearsome and inconsistent. At best the child learns to face the world with a false self of either rigid conformity or bizarre eccentricity which shields him from destruction by the hostile world. But when life gets too stressful, the fears and desires that he has been holding back burst out; he breaks down and goes mad. Support for this theory has come from several quarters of the United States.

> Laing and his group see madness as a natural coping mechanism in an intolerable living situation, much as a fever is a sign that the body is combatting disease. The mental hospital, by simultaneously treating the patient as if he is sick, by not allowing him to experience the integrative possibilities of his madness, and by trying to stop the process with drugs and social reinforcement techniques to reduce the "symptoms," further cuts

off the patient from experiencing things which are his own, not the expectations and demands of those around him. The patient thus is once again in a situation like that of his family. His madness is usually an attempt to assert his autonomy by fleeing a family which has never allowed him any experience that is his own, by always telling him what to do.

At Kingsley Hall the individual's rebellion is supported, and he is allowed to experience his autonomy. There are no rules, and nothing is prescribed as conventional. There are people available to help one go through the experience, but only if asked. The hope is that undergoing a period of madness, in a place where one is helped not to fear oneself and where others understand and sanction the process, can often lead to a natural resolution. . . . (Clark and Jaffe, 1973, p. 241; cf. Barnes and Berke, 1971)

While both the halfway house and Kingsley Hall milieux constitute acceptant interventions through community organizations, Kingsley Hall is intended for people in more severe predicaments. While a halfway house can offer positive and active support, the Kingsley Hall situation can respond best to an individual's unique needs once help has been sought.

Summary

Miniature social systems that provide a supportive environment and nurture the self-esteem of members can sometimes deter certain of the more severe mental-health problems typical of those found in psychiatric hospitals and strengthen the individual as he or she seeks to cope with the realities of the larger social system. Other-than-residential acceptant interventions can be made available to individuals immediately after they suffer traumatic experiences. Such timely interventions help to reduce the likelihood that more serious emotional problems, such as loss of self-worth, will occur.

REFERENCES

Barnes, M., and J. Berke. *Mary Barnes: Two Accounts of a Journey into Madness.* New York: Ballantine Books, 1971.

Carleton, L. "The Therapeutic Community and the Workshop." In J. L. Carleton and U. Mahlendorf, eds., *Man for Man: A Multidisciplinary Workshop on Affecting Man's Social Nature through Community Action.* Springfield, Ill.: Charles C Thomas, 1973, pp. 329–33.

Clark, T., and D. T. Jaffe. *Toward a Radical Therapy: Alternative Services for Personal and Social Change.* New York: Gordon and Breach, Science Publishers, 1973. Reprinted by permission.

David, G. "Building Cooperation and Trust." In A. J. Marrow, D. G. Bowers, and S. E. Seashore, *Management by Participation.* New York: Harper & Row, 1967, pp. 95–109.

Davis, S. A. "An Organic Problem-Solving Method of Organizational Change." Reproduced by special permission from *Journal of Applied Behavioral Science* 3, no. 1 (1967): 3–21.

Golembiewski, R. T., S. B. Carrigan, W. R. Mead, R. Munzenrider, and A. Blumberg. "Toward Building New Work Relationships: An Action Design for a Critical Intervention." *Journal of Applied Behavioral Science* 6, no. 2 (1972): 135–48. Reprinted by permission.

Gordon, T. *T.E.T. Teacher Effectiveness Training.* New York: Peter H. Wyden, 1974.

Levinson, H. *The Great Jackass Fallacy.* Boston: Harvard University, 1973.

Mahlendorf, U. "Experiential therapy." In J. L. Carleton and U. Mahlendorf, eds., *Man for Man: A Multidisciplinary Workshop on Affecting Man's Social and Psychological Nature through Community Action.* Springfield, Ill.: Charles C Thomas, 1973, pp. 311–33. Reprinted by permission.

Oshry, B. I. "Clearing the Air in Human Relations." *Business Horizons* 9, no. 1 (1966): 35–46.

Rogers, C. R. *Counseling and Psychotherapy.* Boston: Houghton Mifflin, 1942. Reprinted by permission.

Safran, C. "How Mental First Aid Can Pull You through a Crisis." *Today's Health* 51, no. 9 (1973): 67–68.

Schwartz, M. S., and G. T. Will. "Intervention and Change in a Mental Hospital Ward." In W. G. Bennis, K. D. Benne, and R. Chin, eds., *The Planning of Change.* New York: Holt, Rinehart and Winston, 1961, pp. 564–83. Reprinted by permission.

Wilson, R. "Difficult Housing Estates." *Human Relations* 16, no. 1 (1963): 3–43. Reprinted by permission.

ACCEPTANT INTERVENTIONS

5

NORMS / STANDARDS

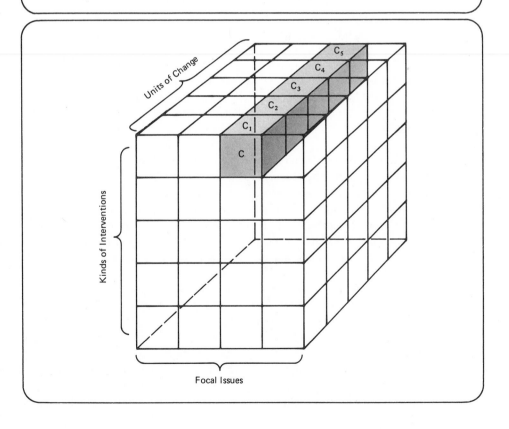

Norms and standards sometimes resist change because they are reinforced by feelings and emotions rather than by logical justification, and any effort to change norms/standards which disregards these emotional underpinnings is likely to prove unsuccessful. Therefore, such an intervention should identify and focus on the critical issue that is provoking the emotions aroused in relation to a particular norm or standard.

The two examples below demonstrate the acceptant-intervention strategy as used to aid people work through their emotions and feelings prior to the change of norms/standards at the level of organization-wide membership.

ORGANIZATION (C₄)

Norm-based emotions may be corporate-wide. For example, even though a management may claim, on a public-relations level, that it desires to deal with its plant's union representatives in a solution-seeking way, more deeply rooted and widely diffused antiunion attitudes may repeatedly surface to stifle the effort. Under these circumstances the problem cannot be solved simply by working with the management bargaining committee (the organization's representative in negotiations with the union), for committee members can move in a problem-solving direction *only* when they are confident of management's wholehearted support at all levels.

Norm Formation

An example of an organization-wide acceptant intervention for setting new norms and standards of conduct is reported by Blake and Mouton (1974, pp. 9–10). The entire management engaged in a cathartic experience prior to union-management bargaining. A series of one-day conferences was held with approximately 100 members of management. The purpose of these meetings was to identify feelings about the union through answering a key question, *Can* better relations between union and management be created?

Participants discussed the question in three *diagonal slice* groups of ten or so people during each conference. The only repeaters from one session to the next were the plant manager who sat in one group during each conference, the operations superintendent who sat in another group, and the personnel chief in a third. These three "led" the discussions. Their goal was to promote a true exploration of feelings rather than guide the discussion toward predetermined conclusions. Consultants met with each group to help people identify and express their feelings.

Consultant interventions focused discussions in each group on a basic question: What are your attitudes toward the union? These interventions occurred repeatedly as the discussions unfolded, particularly at points where participants were voicing fears and anxieties and needed reassurance that these feelings were acceptable. To promote either clarification of thinking or differentiation of ideas, other interventions restated, rephrased, or reflected comments made. When the consultant, who had no vested interests in management attitudes toward the union, voiced in pithy summaries the attitudes aired, the echo effect permitted management to hear themselves talk.

Group after group came to recognize the one-sidedness of their viewpoints as well as the dead-end quality of hopelessness they connoted. How did this come about? Time and time again some member would become impatient eventually with the bitter feelings the others expressed and would say so. At that point, the consultant would ask other members to examine *why* their feelings were as they were. This phase of cathartic release seemed an essential prelude to the next step.

As deep-lying attitudes and feelings were identified, expressed, shared, and looked at from many points of view, constructive concepts began to surface. The groups realized that one can look forward to an improvement in union-management relations only when subjective attitudes that block problem solving are eradicated or at least given an experimental adjournment in the minds of management.

Though no single generalization was reached at all conferences, the following newsprint summary of the consensus reached at one conference gives the gist of what transpired. It was concluded that, "Regardless of what the union officers are, personality-wise, and what their history has been, the only way for bringing about a resolution of conflict is through treating them as *officers,* according them the dignity and respect that people who have been duly elected should receive. Our role is to meet with these people and to search for whatever conditions of cooperation and collaboration are possible."

Cathartic release had permitted an organization-wide norm regarding warfare relations with a union to be replaced by a new one that guided management in building a more problem-solving relationship. Thereafter it was possible for the management's bargaining committee to take a more collaborative stance toward the union. This eventually led to the solution of many problems that had become chronic standoffs.

Shifting a Norm

Another approach to organization norm setting also starts from the premise that organization life in modern times is fear provoking, characterized by high levels of member distrust. If change is to occur it is necessary to help organization members shift their trust levels upward so they may interact not according to implicit role requirements and norms of defensiveness, but rather out of spontaneous feelings or problem-solving requirements. The intervention may rely heavily on emotional release—i.e., helping participants "let down their guard." Described by Gibb (1972) under the acronym of the TORI (Trust, Openness, Realization, Interdependence) Community, one such approach aids participants to experience and share with one another their community relatedness.

The consultant works with participants congregated in an open place or a large but sparsely furnished room, so that each can directly experience all the others simultaneously. Nonverbal activities are organized or undertaken spontaneously in order to engage participants in uncustomary modes of relating, intended to create communication clearer than words sometimes can convey. As old norms begin to break down, a contagion effect is produced. Aroused feelings can be expressed, talked about, worked through. Acceptant interventions stimulate activities that range from several people collaborating in lifting and rocking another person, to touching and feeling one another while blindfolded, to Indian wrestling, and so on. One person might lead another who is blindfolded on a walk, helping the other experience his or her surroundings by smell and feel rather than through words or sight. Engaging in such activities automatically violates old norms of "keeping your distance," being formal, and staying in role. A new sense of closeness and mutual dependence between people which is not necessarily experienced in conversational interaction is communicated.

Gibb describes the new norms and standards of conduct he believes this emotion-freeing intervention produces. One aspect is deep interpersonal acceptance as indicated in such words as being personal, people-oriented, intimate, and close. Individuals become more authentic, transparent, honest, available, assertive, and direct. Rather than controlling others, individuals become more allowing, less intrusive, and less manipulative, more collaborative and more sharing. He points out that following these organization-building experiences it is possible to use the climate of high trust and acceptance for initiating problem-solving activities that continue to be carried out in the "each to all" community setting.

Different interpretations regarding the impact of TORI nonverbal activities are possible. One is that physical contact serves to reduce participants' inhibitions, Another is that under a no-words convention, and within the overall TORI environment, it becomes easier for a participant to communicate acceptance of others. In any case, whether within the TORI experience or in other situations involving close contact, there are risks that can hardly be anticipated and obviated unless the particular consultant has previously gained deep understandings of individual participants.

> As part of a development effort in a company, thought to be a wise course to "open people up," a trainer undertook encounter experiences that involved having the executives touch each other and engage in activities that brought them physically closer to each other. Two executives, whose latent homosexual impulses (unconscious and well controlled) could not tolerate such closeness, had psychotic breaks, and had to be hospitalized. (Levinson, 1973, p. 164)

Summary

Generalizations about changing norms and standards through organization-wide catharsis include the following. First, an organization is a reference group for its individual members—no one member really can change his or her attitudes until other members are ready to change theirs. The impracticability, for example, of using acceptant interventions to solve *organizational* problems on a *one-to-one* basis is apparent. In the management-ideology case discussed earlier, for example, each individual, in working through his own feelings with a consultant, might have come to the same end point in terms of altered feelings toward the union. But without a basis for *sharing* these feelings with others in order to reach a new consensus, each person would probably have felt compelled to get his emotions and feelings back into line with the perceived norms of his reference group rather than shifting to a new and more constructive basis.

A second generalization concerns the source of the intervention when norm changing is involved. Usually, it is more feasible for the intervention to be introduced by an outsider-insider consultant combination. An outsider can be emotionally neutral, whereas an insider is expected to share a common membership norm. The insider is more likely to be treated as "one of us," and may be putting his or her career on the line if he or she gets *out* of line. Organization members—initially, at least—usually presume that the outsider consultant has no personal axe to grind. Accordingly, the insider can be a consultant to the outsider, who in turn is in a better-informed position to be a consultant to the organization.

A third generalization relates to norms that traditionally have been regarded as representing the "rational man" concept of management. Behavioral science has shown us that feelings and emotions can sometimes overwhelm logical analysis of facts and data, and cause people to hold irrational positions. When feelings and emotions can be identified and worked through *prior* to attempting to deal logically with a problem, it becomes possible to bring about the kind of development needed for more effective functioning of the organization.

LARGER SOCIAL SYSTEM (C₅)

Trade associations and other professional meetings have certain characteristics that make them temporary as contrasted with permanent or enduring communities. Even so, they exemplify models of a larger social system (actual or potential), because people are associated in an exchange of information as well as in resolving matters regarding food, clothing, and shelter.

Such a temporary social system has characteristic properties, often involving sociometric networks of friends who cohere versus strangers who are isolates with either no real membership status or only a minimal one. As a result, those who have already established friendships maintain their interaction, but do not expand it, and those who are strangers have little or no contact and, therefore, can only profit from the meeting's formal presentations, exhibits, and so on.

Acceptant interventions are useful in preparing people to be more emotionally expressive and responsive to one another when attending such meetings, for individuals characteristically interact according to norms of formality and distance rather than informally and with intimacy. Part of the warm-up for breaking away from conventional norms and embracing new ones engages people in positive emotional experiences with one another. Similar procedures are used in organization-growth situations. Gibb (1972) describes typical procedures used in a large space, often without furniture to impede the interaction. An acceptant consultant may start things off by engaging participants in a mingling experience. People move along in two circles, traveling in opposite directions. As one person passes the next, introductions are exchanged, with each person telling something about himself or herself that ordinarily would not be discussed with a stranger. This kind of sharing creates "instant" warmth and mutual friendliness. A second activity might involve participants sitting on the floor in pairs, or in small five- or six-man clusters, with participants looking intently at one another in silence. After a few minutes, participants talk about what each "saw" in looking at the other, and how each felt being able to look but not talk. Participants usually make remarks that are pleasant and intimacy-producing. A basis for liking the other person is established, and new functional norms replace conventional norm-based formality to permit free and easy exchange in the temporary community.

IMPLICATIONS

This review of acceptant interventions in the context of norms/standards suggests several significant conclusions. First, because norms and standards are aspects of behavior difficult to define in operational terms, they are rarely regarded in consultant activity as being maintained and perpetuated by existing emotions and feelings. Therefore, other modes of intervention than the acceptant approach are generally relied upon to bring about changes in norms/standards. Prescription (Chapter 23), for example, rather than being an effective intervention, may unwittingly block norm changing although the norms/standards focal issue has been accurately identified.

Second, when an individual deviates from group norms, he or she is likely to experience feelings of rejection. When the problem is experienced in this way it becomes a morale/cohesion issue for him or her rather than a consequence of deviation from norms. Therefore, the one-to-one intervention is likely to be made in the morale/cohesion area, rather than in terms of the person's feelings toward group norms and standards.

REFERENCES

Blake, R. R., and J. S. Mouton. "The D/D Matrix®." In J. D. Adams, ed., *Theory and Method in Organization Development: An Evolutionary Process*. Washington, D.C.: NTL Institute for Applied Behavioral Science, 1974, pp. 3–36. (Originally published Austin, Texas: Scientific Methods, Inc., 1972.)

Gibb, J. R. "The TORI Experience as an Organizational Change Intervention." In W. W. Burke, ed., *Contemporary Organization Development: Conceptual Orientations and Interventions*. Washington, D.C.: NTL Institute for Applied Behavioral Science, 1972, pp. 109–26.

Levinson, H. *The Great Jackass Fallacy*. Cambridge, Mass.: Harvard University Press, 1973.

ACCEPTANT INTERVENTIONS

6

GOALS / OBJECTIVES

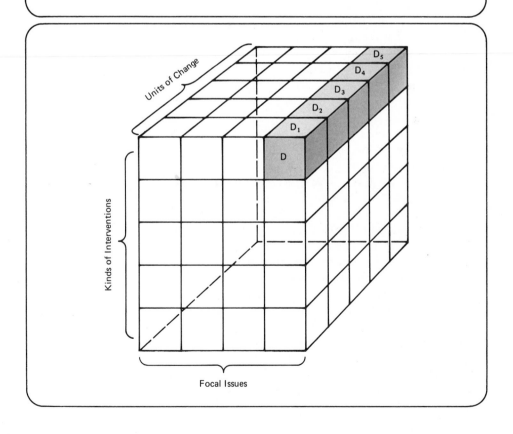

There is little if any evidence that acceptant interventions are ever relied upon when the focal issue involves establishing or changing goals/objectives. One reason is that when individuals fail to reach already-established goals, the issue in question is not their commitment to the goal—an issue that might be worked through in an acceptant-intervention way. Rather, the issue involved is the individual's lowered morale/cohesion. As a result, the intervention is more likely to deal with the emotions of loss, failure, or lowered self-regard than to aid a person in exploring emotions more intimately associated with unfulfilled goals/objectives (D_1).

Although the same may be true at the group level, the goal is likely to have been boss-set. Therefore, when failure to realize the objective occurs, or when frustrations with attempting to achieve it are experienced, the resultant focal issue is more likely to be the power/authority rather than goals/objectives (D_2) aspect of the situation.

In the intergroup context it is rare to find any kind of intervention, whether acceptant (D_3) or otherwise, because the concept of *superordinate* goals/objectives —that is, goals that could be pursued with high commitment by otherwise separate groups—is not a concept sufficiently developed to enter into the thinking of participants, even though they may in fact share a formal goal with another group which could be achieved by intergroup collaboration. Instead, focus is likely to be on the distinctive properties or goals of the two groups—and when these become incompatible, power/authority rather than goals/objectives is the focal issue.

Focal issues that invite acceptant intervention at the organization level (D_4) do not involve goals and objectives either—if this can be inferred from the absence of acceptant interventions. The setting of objectives for organizations is likely to be seen "naturally" as a top-team versus organization-wide activity. Therefore, the membership of an organization is unlikely to feel a sense of loss or depression associated with the failure to realize goals. Accordingly, consultant interventions to deal with feelings of loss or failure are improbable.

Acceptant interventions with a goals/objectives focal issue are absent at the larger-social-system level as well. Rarely does the membership of a larger social system participate in the setting of system-wide goals, and no sense of emotional loss can be experienced for failing to meet goals that do not exist. Although in some larger social systems there is a concept of national planning, this planning is normally of a strategic economic character. Thus the achievement is dependent on technology rather than on the behavior of the people as a whole, precluding the need for acceptant interventions in the event of failure.

Again, in larger social systems that within living memory have been created on ideological as well as socioeconomic grounds, the "crisis" (Spiro, 1956, ch. 7) may come many years later as the group's pioneers, themselves the creators of the ideology-referenced goals/objectives, recognize that the newer generations are drifting away from commitment to such goals. Problems such as these tend not to be approached in the goals/objectives focal-issue area of acceptant intervention. Rather, if addressed at all by that mode, they are viewed as individual or senior-citizen-group problems linked with tendencies to idealize the past and mourn its—and their—passing from relevance.

REFERENCE

Spiro, M. E. *Kibbutz: Venture in Utopia.* Cambridge, Mass.: Harvard University Press, 1956.

ACCEPTANT INTERVENTIONS

7

SUMMARY
AND
IMPLICATIONS

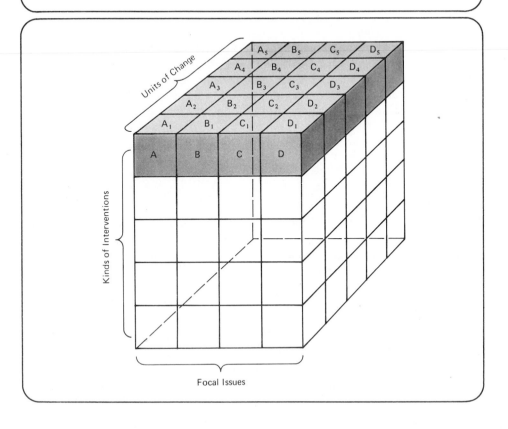

The ability to express feelings and emotions freely and appropriately is basic to psychological health and to behavioral effectiveness. Blocked emotions can cause many difficulties in thinking, decision making, and problem solving; resulting tensions and anxieties may lead to physical illnesses.

An important aspect of consultation involves interventions in which the client is assisted in clearing up emotional blockages in order to engage in more objective problem solving. Acceptant interventions bring about the unblocking step through a process of catharsis, intended to trigger a free flow of emotions.

The use of acceptant interventions to activate a cathartic process is most valuable when the client feels weak in the sense of being unable to deal in a constructive manner with whatever obstacles are preventing him or her from taking appropriate actions. This does not necessarily mean that the client is *weak* on some absolute scale of strength, but only relative to the obstacles impeding progress in focusing on and dealing with problem issues.

WHAT AN ACCEPTANT CONSULTANT DOES

An acceptant consultant helps the client to think through his or her situation in a manner that relieves the blocking aspects and ensures that the client retains a sense of personal "ownership" in resolving problems. This is accomplished in two ways. (1) The consultant gives passive support by attentive listening and nonevaluative responses. He or she avoids a partisan stance and suspends all judgments regarding what the client is saying or doing. (2) The consultant may intervene more actively by creating conditions under which the client experiences emotional release, but he or she does so in a nonprescriptive way. Again, this kind of intervention avoids a partisan orientation and provides the client a sense of support by implying that any action is acceptable regardless of its content.

LIMITATIONS

Two possible limitations are of sufficient importance to be emphasized. One is that the client, after working through and relieving his or her emotions via a cathartic process, may come to *accept* the circumstances that caused the problem rather than taking the initiative to correct them.

A second pitfall is possible when disturbed emotions involve, not one's personal and subjective experience, but interpersonal or intergroup relationships. The person who "in public" goes into catharsis some time after having become accustomed to doing so within private acceptant-intervention situations may arouse hostile reactions of the "You're being a baby" kind, particularly among those whose tensions make them want to "fight it out." In a hostile social climate, cathartic release may be so contrary to a tradition of resolution via aggression as to be impractical.

WHY IS THE CATHARTIC PROCESS HELPFUL?

The answer to this question has many facets:

1. By seeking to define his or her problem to an acceptantly listening and commenting consultant, the client many times is enabled to gain a fuller perspective on the problem, which lessens the earlier sense of uneasiness.

2. By exploring the content of subjective experiences, the emotional tensions associated with insufficiently examined situations may be reduced.

3. An acceptant intervention permits the client to explore variables in his or her own experience—concepts to which words may previously never have been attached. By finding words to characterize these dimensions of experience, the client may be assisted to see in more precise terms the extent to which his or her emotions are appropriate to the situation and the extent to which these responses are untenable in the light of operating circumstances.

4. By working backwards to identify presumed causes for present problems, the client is able to pinpoint what is really causing what and therefore is in a better problem-solving position.

5. When a client is able to connect things that previously had seemed separate or disparate, the insights thereby gained can reduce tensions associated with the earlier contradictions.

6. By sorting out his or her various feelings, the client may be assisted to see in more specific and concrete terms exactly what aspects of his or her circumstances are producing anxiety.

7. By testing in words the consequences of an anticipated action, tensions and fears associated with the real-life action may be reduced.

POSSIBLE CLIENT BENEFITS FROM ACCEPTANT INTERVENTIONS

Successful acceptant interventions may result in the client:

1. experiencing improved self-acceptance,

2. enjoying greater spontaneity,

3. developing the capacity, through learning how to talk with himself or herself, to deal in more objective terms with emotional problems that may arise in the future,

4. reactivating and experiencing in a more healthy way dimensions of emotions that may previously have been repressed or denied,

5. developing an increased ability to experience reality-based emotions appropriate to the given circumstances,

6. formulating more objective definitions of the problem or situation faced, thereby increasing his or her problem-solving capacity.

PART

2

CATALYTIC INTERVENTIONS

8

CATALYTIC INTERVENTIONS: AN INTRODUCTION

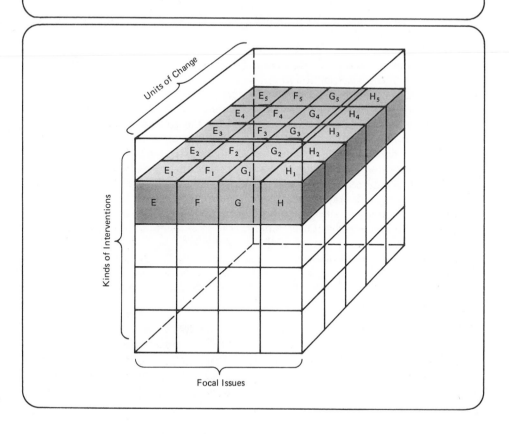

A client is often hampered either by not being able to see a situation or not seeing it clearly enough to take needed actions. Though emotions may be involved, the actual cause is lack of data—either unavailable or uncommunicated—or faulty discussion methods. Such problems indicate a need for perception building, and catalytic interventions are often relied on in these circumstances. They help the client to widen his or her view of the situation by gaining additional information or by verifying existing data.

Catalysis is a concept most often employed in chemistry to describe a certain kind of reaction. A catalytic agent, when added to certain other substances, brings about a change in speed of reaction. The change would not have occurred had this agent not been introduced.

In intervention, a catalytic consultant is the agent. He or she enters a situation with the intention of increasing the rate at which a process is occurring. The status quo is accepted as a given. His or her goal is to assist those within the status quo to do what they are doing in an improved way.

The consultant may employ a number of approaches to gain cooperation from the client in order to help with the problem. He or she tries to get inside the client's frame of reference, see the situation from the client's point of view. In this way, the consultant can collaborate with the client in a catalytic way.

Caplan (1970) offers a consultant's point of view of a catalytic intervention used in a mental-health setting.

> First, he has accepted no coercive authority from the director, and so collaboration of the staff, although authorized, must be freely volunteered by them and is more likely in regard to certain issues than others. Second, the consultant is continually aware that while he is collecting information he is also building relationships that will form the vehicle for eventual consultation intervention. In fact, his intervention usually starts at the moment of his first contact with his potential consultees, who may from the beginning be watching such things as his way of asking questions and the areas of his major interest, as part of the process of identification with him that is one of the major ways in which they are influenced. Third, although the area of his inquiry has not been predetermined by a request to deal with a particular administrative predicament, and so is apparently wide open to include any or every aspect of the organization, the consultant realizes that the resources at his disposal are necessarily limited. He must therefore narrow his focus to those issues that the consultees feel to be currently most pressing, and which they are thus likely to want to discuss. (Caplan, 1970, p. 276)

"Deal[ing] with . . . those issues that the consultees feel to be currently most pressing . . ."—this is the meaning of "getting inside the client's frame of reference. . . ." The advantage is that the client's interest in being helped is aroused. However, it could be that the problem definition formulated by the client, based on his or her feelings, is wide of the mark. If so, consultant and client would be collaborating on solving the wrong problem.

Rather than relying on pedestrian step-by-step diagnosis as the basis for planning strategy, intuition is the consultant's tool for finding out about the client's problem. How the consultant goes about this is revealed below.

> The special skill which consultants develop with increasing experience, and which is similar to the "intuition" of a clinician in following productive leads in psychotherapy, is that of superficially scanning the entire field of the life of the organization and then making quick judgments of the "hottest" areas for deepening his inquiries—that is, choosing those topics that provide leverage points in regard to salience and feasibility for the consultees. An ongoing systematic examination of such statistics as staff turnover in different departments, patient, client, or product movement, or staff absenteeism or sickness rates should form the background of his data collection and may suggest leads for further exploration. But the consultant's main method of scanning will probably be that of moving about as a participant observer within the life space of the organization and chatting with as many people as possible at different administrative levels, so as to find evidence of unusual behavior or preoccupation that may indicate administrative difficulty. (Caplan, 1970, pp. 276–77)

The way this works in practice is suggested in the following passage, depicting how the consultant proceeds to test for "felt needs."

> If the consultee appeared interested, the discussion would progress. If not, some other topic would be discussed. The plan, if any, that emerged would be that of the staff member or group involved, and not that of the consultant, who would guide the unfolding of the process only by his choice of contacts, which would determine the area of the social system and the levels of the administrative hierarchy involved. In addition, the consultant would catalyze and facilitate a rational investigation of the issue and the development of an effective remedial plan by supporting his consultees in confronting the problems and by helping them overcome emotional or cognitive obstacles in their reactions. (Caplan, 1970, p. 280)

When issues have been identified that the consultant and client agree need attention, the consultant may intervene based on several related but additional assumptions characteristic of the catalytic approach. One is that more information about the problem will have a significant impact on changing the perception of the situation. This means that whatever is preventing improvement of the situation can be dealt with by utilizing available information that is not presently being brought to bear on the dilemma at hand. Secondly, a catalytic intervention can focus on the ways and means of gathering more information through alternative data-gathering methods. These may involve assisting a given individual through the use of revelatory tests and measurements to see himself or herself more accurately. Or, perhaps several people may be encouraged to talk about their work as a group, or intergroup contacts, or organization activities, or even activities within larger social systems in a free and open style. *Procedural* suggestions by the consultant can help the client system to gather information that sheds a new light on the situation. Although these procedures usually are immediately understandable to participants, they either have not been considered before or have not been given the consideration they are recognized to merit once the consultant draws attention to them.

The consultant either assists clients as they gather impressions to illuminate their situation or does this work himself. Indeed, often the client is not skilled in the gathering and analysis of pertinent information, and through observation, interviews, or research the consultant is able to fill this gap. Information, often called "data" in a loose sense, need *not* be physical-reality facts or mathematical relations —often it consists of social "facts," or a summary of the existing state of the client's attitudes and emotions. These are not considered "live" emotions of the type an acceptant consultant might induce in a cathartic interaction. The presumption here is that feelings are information. Once recognized, allowances for them can be made in searching for solutions. Thus emotional matters can be presented informationally, without the need to deal with them in any direct way. The communication is most likely to be "cool" information, not feelings as subjective realities.

An example of this approach is provided by Crockett (1970), who at the time was Deputy Secretary of State for Administration. He describes a State Department project in group development. The consultants, Ferguson and Seashore, initiated the approach by interviewing all twelve members to probe subsurface reactions. Anonymity was promised to each respondent.

With participants seated in a large circle, the first session was started by Ferguson. He reviewed the agenda and procedures to be employed during the next two days, indicating that he would present summarized interview-based information regarding each respective member. Then each of the pictured persons could react to these summaries, with others joining the discussion to whatever degree they wished.

The interview-gathered information on each man was displayed on a large board. In order to reduce hostility or embarrassment, the summaries were presented in anonymous fashion and categorized so that the frequency of each distinctive description of an individual was indicated. As an example, these are the reactions posted to describe Crockett.

> ... For example: "He doesn't delegate properly." "He gives contradictory instructions to different people so that there are binds within the group." "He makes unilateral decisions relating to our responsibilities without first talking them over with us." "He takes action in our areas without telling us." "We are not generally informed about what's happening in the whole group." "We are kept ignorant about one another's activities." "He doesn't like confrontation and conflict." "He can't make tough (people) decisions." "We can't get in to see him." "He sees the wrong people." "He doesn't give us his attention when we do see him." "He has too many irons in the fire at one time." "He confuses us about priorities." "He is manipulative." (Crockett, 1970, p. 297)

Then participants discussed with one another the meanings which came through from the posted information.

> ...But here again the consultants tried to give us an understanding of the deep difference between a cold, hard, objective, critical "appraisal" by the boss on the one hand and a legitimate (even if critical) "feedback" that is given in a climate of trust and warmth and caring, on the other. We discussed the obligations which were imposed upon all who opted into such a group; specifically, we were reminded of the obligation of "caring" for other group members. Members who "cared" had obligations both individually and collectively to help the others to understand how they "came through" and "were seen," how they were "felt" and "perceived," how they were helpful or were hurtful in their communications. Each had an obligation to give and to receive feedback, and to give coaching to the others. (Crockett, 1970, p. 299)

How it worked out in practice is seen in the following session with Crockett.

> For example, where one had said I did not delegate, I denied it by saying, "I am the best delegator in the Department. You all have authority. You have responsibilities in your area. And it is up to you to get them done." And then the anonymity would disappear because the person who had put this item on the list would come in hard to justify his stand. And so with illustration of time and place and circumstance he would prove when I had not delegated properly or how I would fall back after I had given them authority, or how I had made a decision unknown to them or how, before evidence had come in, I had changed their decision, and so on. This kind of confrontation only started the conversation. Chuck would not let any of us off so easily. He probed deeply. How did my action make them feel? How did they see me? What were my motives? How did this affect the group's work together? This and many more questions that he asked would give me the opportunity to reply, "Yes, but you don't realize the pressure I am under from the White House... or from the Congress... or from the Secretary...." And the whole complexity of relationships, the pressures upon me, and explanations for my seemingly erratic behavior would come out. From such explanations and probings came understanding and a sense of sharing that had never before existed in the group. (Crockett, 1970, p. 300)

This kind of "feelings about relationships-as-facts" approach not only reduced pluralistic ignorance within the group regarding how each reacted to the others, it also aided some members to reduce individual blind spots.

Many group leaders are plagued by doubts concerning the real state of affairs existing between themselves and those who report to them. Should they ask these people point-blank, "How are things going between us?" The answer may be little more relevant than are many diplomatic remarks. If they don't ask, the real situation remains obscured. They can listen to rumor and scuttlebutt, but the validity of such sources cannot be taken at face value either.

With this initial background, further technical understanding of catalytic interventions can be gained by studying examples of the various types of methodologies employed in different situations. Some may be used solely with an individual or a group; others, although the format will vary, occur in situations where the unit of change may range from an individual to a larger social system. Thus a general description of the more widely used methodologies is presented first in order to avoid duplication of material throughout the various applications.

PROCESS CONSULTATION

Knowing something about aspects of behavioral dynamics, a catalytic consultant recognizes that interaction skills are difficult to acquire on a teacher-tell basis. An alternative is to intervene in a group, intergroup, or organization setting and use their problems as case material. He or she may even act as a "mirror" to individuals, although this is rare. By the consultant asking pertinent questions, information can be produced to be studied and insights derived as to what is going on. The goal is to focus members' attention on studying their own situation so they are in a better position to consolidate aspects that are desirable and to change what is unwanted. The consultant may limit his or her participation to inviting group members to "look at" their interactions in order to stimulate information gathering and informational feedback. He or she may exercise more initiative by suggesting alternative approaches or possibilities that permit the gathering—whether through interview, survey methods, questionnaires, or other means—of information that is not readily available from here-and-now behavior, but is needed. In using the client's "felt needs" to govern his or her own interventions, the catalytic consultant is likely to offer suggestions that are little more than a step away from what people are prepared to do on their own initiative. In other words, the consultant avoids introducing suggestions that people might be prepared to accept purely out of confidence in the consultant's expertise. If the consultant's suggestion is so far from current realities as to be accepted on blind faith, it is too far removed to release a process in a catalytic manner. By formulating tentative possibilities that participants can accept more or less as a restatement of their own ideas, the consultant ensures that responsibility for the consequences remains with the client.

Another consideration that makes this possible is the consultant's special role vis-à-vis the client. First of all, he or she is *invited* in because help is wanted. Yet because the consultant is not a member he or she does not share the everyday pressures members may feel, and thus can more easily focus their attention on procedures, processes, and relationships. Since he or she is not a "carrier" of group history, the consultant probably will not have the same unknowing commitment to consistency with the past, nor the same blindness to new possibilities. Although the past may no longer be pertinent to the here and now, the group may unwittingly be acting out of habits of response. A catalytic consultant can comprehend the group situation more fully than members do and work indirectly to fill vacuums in their awareness. By contrast, a confrontational consultant would forthrightly state perceived discrepancies between consultant and client comprehensions.

This catalytic reticence in turn tends to preserve another consultant advantage: he or she is not likely to be party to participant-centered frictions, antagonisms, and cliques. Beyond that, he or she is relatively free from the pressure and discipline that members often feel when they are part of a power structure created by formal authority relationships, if the situation is a more formal one than obtained in a friendship group. In other words, as consultant, his or her interventions are "membership free." They can be accepted for the help they offer, without regard for hidden purposes or vested interests that might otherwise be present. The same holds true for an internal consultant who is not a member of the unit with whom he or she is consulting.

An example of catalytic process consultation within a group setting is provided by Culbert (1970). By proposing two kinds of interventions, Culbert sums up several of the issues trainers must deal with in conducting a T Group. The first intervention involves *phase-shifting*—assisting a group to shift from the initial and often shallow search for commonalities to a more here-and-now perception-exchanging basis of interaction. While the examples offered are from a T-Group setting, the same approach can be employed in organizational "family-group" development. Progress can be stimulated by exploration of one another's immediate thoughts and feelings. This brings about a new phase of summary, recapitulation, and closure. The following exemplifies a phase-shifting intervention calculated to move the group into the last-mentioned phase.

> I'd like to state my understanding of what we have been doing so far as a group. We began by agreeing that important personal learning could be had by exploring interpersonal differences. When we began our small-group discussion, however, we were confronted with trust issues. It was as if we really couldn't expose our differences until we found out more about one another; and we proceeded to talk at a low-risk level about things we have in common. At least, this is my understanding of why we have been so much in agreement. It's as though the implicit task in what we have been working on is to find out that we are enough alike to risk revealing some of the ways in which we might be different. Soon I expect that some of you will begin risking more by making personal statements which will express your differences from the others in the group. (Culbert, 1970, p. 26)

A second example, also seeking to bring about a shift from one phase to another follows.

> We began the group by acknowledging the learning value to be gained from exploring personal differences. However, when the group began, we were confronted with the work that needed to be accomplished in cre-

ating a climate of trust. As a group, we tried to get to know one another without risking disagreement. We now seem to have come to a point where sufficient trust has been developed to allow some of you to take risks through making personal statements which expose your "differences." The trust question still appears to be with us, for most of the self statements being made sound fairly encapsulated to me. It seems that we are still more involved in finding out how others will react to our differences than we are in possibly learning from their reactions. My last statement is based on the "yes, but" character I hear in reactions to attempts by others to give feedback. It seems to me that as the trust level increases we shall begin to be more open to the comments of others and begin to interact more. In this way I think we'll become more effective resources for one another's learning. (Culbert, 1970, p. 27)

The other kind of intervention, termed *phase-relevant*, is intended to enable whatever is presently going on to continue in a better or deeper way. Both appear to be catalytic in intention. Though Culbert utilizes his own personal map of progression to guide clients from one development phase to another, this map is not taught to participants or in other ways internalized by them. The opposite happens. When the consultant determines they are ready, his interventions crystallize what he anticipates will become a felt need and gives public expression to what members are privately sensing. The intervention tips the scales and a new activity gets under way.

In addition to here-and-now, direct process consultations, so many different strategies and tactics are involved in catalytic interventions that on the surface each may appear distinctive and unique. When examined from the standpoint of what the consultant's assumptions are and what he or she does, however, it turns out that they really are adaptations of a basic methodology engineered to fit local circumstances. Since the catalytic consultant relies on information that can be fed back in a summarized but nonevaluative way, various additional interventions for information gathering and feedback can be categorized according to how the information is gathered and used.

MODELING

Another belief widely shared among catalytic consultants relates to modeling—i.e., the consultant envisages his or her own behavior as setting an example of how others ought also to behave. By identifying with the consultant, the client may change by imitation, following the consultant's example in such matters as personal openness, giving feedback, and caring. This aspect of change may never be explicitly pointed out, as the mechanism may work best when it is not deliberate and calculated. Consultants emphasizing the importance of modeling include Ferguson (1968, p. 190), Bennis (1965, p. 353), and Golden (1972, p. 21), among others.

A combination of process consultation with an individual, which invites modeling, is summarized by Caplan in the following selection.

In addition to such personally idiosyncratic distortions, mental health consultants often identify misperceptions and stereotyped expectations among administrators based upon cultural prejudices, and such as those that relate to rejected ethnic, religious, or racial groups or to members of other professions or occupations which are believed to be inferior. One way of handling this, in addition to acting as a mediator to bring the parties together so that they can meet each other as people rather than as stereotypes, is for the consultant to ask his consultee for a factual account of the professional behavior of the person who is being stereotyped and then to discuss this in such a way that the realities of the situation begin to shine through. In this conversation, the consultant temporarily lends his perceptual apparatus, as it were, to his consultee. He gives him specific ego support by using the leverage of the consultation relationship to enable the consultee to identify with him and to stand back for the moment from his preconceptions and, along with the consultant, take a fresh look at the other person. The consultant will usually have to begin by pointing out some specific details of his own perceptions or inferences about the case, and then he can start to involve the consultee in the joint task of adding items to the list.

Another method, which can be used on its own or to supplement the above, is for the consultant to recount an anecdote from his memory or his imagination about his own experience with a person of the category under discussion. He indicates his respect for this person by his tone of voice and by the admiration with which he talks about him, and perhaps drives the message home by telling of the surprise he felt when he discovered how effectively the hero of his parable operated, and how much he himself had learned from that encounter. (Caplan, 1970, p. 289)

Confrontational consultants, particularly those in the psychoanalytic tradition, would see this kind of identification with the consultant as positive transference, and frown upon its use in inducing change. They would view the tendency to model through imitation as something the client should be assisted to understand, and only to engage in as a deliberate, conscious decision, based on rational considerations.

GATHERING INFORMATION THROUGH INTERVIEWING

A catalytic consultant usually prefers *not* to enter a situation cold. He or she may rely on any one of several ways to gain some understanding of the problem before actually meeting with the client. When the client is a larger unit than an individual, one approach is to interview each member separately with regard to a number of more or less standard topics. For example, he or she may ask about openness, trust, frictions, operational procedures, and so on, as well as use broader or more open-ended questions. Possibilities include:

"How are things going around here?"
"What changes would you like to see?"

"How do you think this organization could be more effective? What do you feel it does best? Does poorly?"

The interviewer may also ask about managerial behavior.

"How would you describe the management style of Mr. X? How do you think he could be more effective?"

The consultant may introduce a question or two calculated to stimulate the person being interviewed, but thereafter keep the discussions open-ended. He or she can follow the client's lead as to what topics are pertinent, and thereby keep closely in touch with the felt needs of the system. At the same time the consultant avoids introducing private, personal thoughts about what he or she considers the more important or more trivial topics.

Questions may also be asked about relationships with other parts of the organization.

"Whom do you like to work with most? Least?"
"Who is most influential in your organization?"

And about relationships with other organizations and units:

"When there are problems with other organizations, what can you do about them?"
"Can you give examples of unresolved issues with other organizations?"
"Do you think you could give them advice that would help them do a better job?" (Fordyce and Weil, 1971, pp. 140–41)

As indicated by these lines of inquiry, interviewing is an approach for gaining access to the private views and feelings of each individual on a wide range of topics. The consultant then studies the replies and attempts to summarize them into a number of functional categories. These often furnish the principal basis for a consultant intervention.

In meetings that take place after the individual interviews, the discussion is likely to be initiated by the consultant. He or she feeds back the summarized findings, being careful not to reveal the identity of particular interviewees. Anonymity offers the consultant a detour around the candor problem because participants are usually prepared to be frank when their identities are concealed. In addition, personal exposure of thoughts, feelings, and convictions that could result in face-to-face acrimony among members is avoided. Anonymity is maintained by grouping reactions from different members into categories so that in most cases more than one person will have made the same or similar point. A view held by one person only is not likely to be reported.

When feeding back information about members' behavior the consultant usually avoids specifically reporting to the group verbatim reactions to such questions as, "How would you describe the management style of Mr. X? How do you think he could be more effective?" This would expose Mr. X to data he would be compelled to react to without knowing its source.

Interview-based information gathering with feedback, and with the consultant helping in processing the information, is the most common catalytic version of group development. Members' participation in planning development sessions and in determining how to handle meetings is sought in order to get support for carrying this activity to its conclusion. This may involve such matters as, Who gets his feedback first?, Should the summary be put on newsprint? or, Should we have night sessions?

Development meetings for a group can be as brief as two days or last up to five days or even more. An extensive use of interview-based information gathering with group-development feedback is described by Davis.

> We have also conducted more than 85 team development efforts. These vary in format, but a typical one involves interviews with each of the members of the team (a job family consisting of a supervisor and his immediate subordinates) and then perhaps a three-day off-site meeting where the interview data are fed back for the groups to work with. The team ends the meeting with explicit action items. Follow-up to the off-site meeting involves implementing the many action items. (Davis, 1967, p. 292)

Through interviewing, the consultant becomes the information-gathering instrument as well as a resource for helping the group respond to the data revealed. His or her direct group-development contributions include offering procedural suggestions, inviting alternative explanations, asking pertinent questions, and so on.

SCALES AND INSTRUMENTS

An approach different from direct interviewing but calculated to serve the same purpose involves the use of tests, questionnaires, and scales. The gathered reactions can then be utilized to formulate the agenda for development discussions.

One advantage to using a set of scales is that the consultant, by selection of the items included in it, can ask participants to deal with issues they might not have recognized as important prior to the consultant-initiated discussions. For example, questions concerned with mutual trust and mutual support, communications, listening, objectives, conflict, use of member resources, how control is exercised, and group climate can be included. While these are known professionally to be significant barriers to effectiveness, most of them are not issues that managers spontaneously raise in day-to-day work meetings, even though they are in fact latent needs that become felt needs as soon as the scales are introduced. These particular questions are not the only ones that might be asked—indeed, group members could be invited to "invent" the scales to be used by their group.

In an intergroup setting, Mangham (1972, p. 71) provides an example of a questionnaire that, according to him, is based on Blake and Mouton instruments.

The instructions invite groups to evaluate their own teamwork. Categories such as "objectives" and "conflict" are provided, as are multiple-choice options from which participants can select the answer most descriptive of their situation.

In a company where the questionnaire approach was employed, one department of eight employees ranged in background from Ph.D. with long experience to a recently hired process trainee. The development meetings were held at the work place. Prior to the first meeting, each member filled out the questionnaire and added whatever comments seemed pertinent. This information was collected so that it could be summarized and fed back anonymously, all in accordance with the supportive, nonconfrontational nature of Mangham's intended catalytic intervention. However, members felt little would be gained through anonymity and, therefore, they identified their own scores. This he agreed with, given the ground rule that people who did not want to do so would not be pressured to conform.

When participants began to see the collated data, they noticed many discrepancies between their individual answers to identical questions. This came as a surprise. Presumably, they had taken for granted that every other person would see the group's mode of operation in the same way. The consultant noted that the most penetrating item—in the sense of the intensity of reactions it produced—was "conflict." The scores indicated that participants preferred to "let sleeping dogs lie" in their work situations.

A catalytic intervention ensued when the consultant tried to help the group use these data. First, he asked members to throw out ideas of what conflict meant to them by speaking the first words that came to mind in connection with it. The list of associations included "violence," "destruction," "vicious," "cruel," "hurt," "smash," "batter," "war," "fight," "bitter struggle," "immature squabble," and so on. The significance of these associations was discussed and a brief paper on conflict was distributed. The consultant then pointed out that conflict (1) can be positive, and (2) can be worked through and resolved. Other catalytic interventions took place later. For example, Mangham asked, "What does this discussion mean for the [group] here and now? What conflicts do we envisage in talking about the problems we have in working together?" Open-ended questions such as these focus attention on an issue, but permit the consultant to avoid showing his hand.

SURVEY RESEARCH

The term survey research refers to the technique of having a large number of people complete the same questionnaire. Mann (1951) has provided a summary of its use as an organization intervention and reviews those strategies that seem likely to produce successful outcomes. Central to each of these seven statements is a reliance on client participation.

1. *Concern for superiors*—and particularly those at the top of the organization. Where superiors took a genuine interest in the findings, studied them and tried to apply them, the data were discussed more adequately

and used more constructively in working out action steps than in those units where superiors showed no such interest.

2. *A high degree of participation and personnel involvement.* Where superiors and subordinates were involved to a high degree in the research planning and particularly in the analysis and interpretation of the findings the results were better understood, emotionally accepted, and utilized in making changes than where a high degree of participation was not achieved.

3. *Participation in the form of self-analysis.* Analyses and interpretations of data and their relevance for change were more likely to be followed by change if the relevant individuals or members of a group made these analyses rather than an outsider.

4. *Objective survey data about one's own organization.* Quantitative summaries about the attitudes and perceptions of subordinates and associates facilitate critical self-evaluations.

5. *Timing and pacing.* It was preferable to let those who were to change set the pace at which the change process went. Too fast a rate for intellectual and emotional acceptance resulted in little or no change; too slow a rate resulted in dissipation of motivation.

6. *Group forces.* Group discussions leading to group decisions about action steps were found to facilitate attitude and behavioral changes in human relations under most circumstances. Decisions concerning changes were carried through when made by all members of the group because of the reciprocally binding nature of such decisions. In a few instances it appeared that objective information identifying the strengths and weaknesses of particular sub-units should not be presented simultaneously to all of the members of an organizational family unless the group had already had some experience in working together as a team towards the solution of human relations problems.

7. *Membership character of the change agent.* Line superiors were able to exert more force toward change than members of either the company personnel staff or of the university research team. (Mann, 1951, pp. 58–59)

These points were drawn from early work, yet they continue to reflect pivotal issues in effective survey research.

A refinement of the survey-research model calculated to avoid weaknesses of earlier approaches is reported by Bowers and Taylor (1973). They point out that survey results, as fed back in conventional approaches, are likely to be received in any of three ways, none of which are likely to have positive organizational effect. Instead, the data will be:

1. set aside for consideration at some undesignated future date,

2. handed to subordinates with a general recommendation to "do something with them,"

3. used to serve partisan ends, e.g., to bolster or justify performance of certain managers.

Bowers' and Taylor's interventions have attempted to reduce these weaknesses by strengthening both the participatory basis of information gathering and feedback steps. Rather than tailoring interviews or questionnaires to the individual client, a standardized questionnaire assessing four basic areas of organization has been developed. These are "leadership," "organizational climate," "group process," and "satisfaction." This is not a morale survey, but rather a descriptive survey of organizational conditions and practices. Two-thirds of the questions are perception based; the remainder deal with reactions, feelings, desires, and satisfactions. The answers are read electronically and can be stored on magnetic tape for future reference or used in longitudinal analyses of progress.

Bowers and Taylor indicate that while the instrument can spot strengths and weaknesses, organization executives and others often "prefer not to hear bad news." This suggests that data feedback is insufficient to bring about desired results. When "cold" information produced by statistical summaries is involved and fed back to an "untreated" authority system, catalytic consultants must also intervene in the power/authority system. Unless feedback takes this into account, the information is unlikely to have the impact of which it is potentially capable. The devised catalytic solution to this defensiveness or resistance is to use a resource person trained to provide each supervisor and his or her immediate work group with a set of findings, an explanation of the information, and suggestions concerning its interpretation and use. Private counseling of supervisors on how to use findings with their own subordinate groups is also provided. Since the approach, which advocates participative management, does not rely on training the managers themselves in skills of effective participation and does not formally teach a theory of participation, its impact rests on the catalyzing effects of the information, reinforced by consultation regarding this information's interpretation.

While Bowers and Taylor in the above description emphasize the consultant's role, one of the first examples of action research by J. R. P. French, Jr., emphasizes the importance of client participation.

About three years after opening its new Virginia plant, Harwood experienced problems in developing an expanded work force. World War II had created a manpower shortage, and Harwood was confronted with changing the traditional aversion of its supervisors toward employing "older" workers. Growing labor shortages made it necessary to employ older people; yet such hiring was resisted. At the time this was a critical issue to the company, and it is a problem that illustrates how Harwood has learned some things about management.

Dr. John R. P. French, Jr. was then director of personnel research for the company. He cited scientific proof that older people did have the kinds of skills and aptitudes required for the jobs in this plant, but the staff attitude remained unchanged. Dr. French realized that merely telling the staff that their attitude was contrary to the facts would not persuade them. It would have been easy to impose a new hiring policy, but it was felt that this approach would be self-defeating. He concluded that it was necessary for the staff to unlearn their mistaken beliefs and that this would occur only if they would seek out the facts for themselves. Only then could they recognize the discrepancy between facts and belief.

Accordingly, Dr. French sought to involve the staff members in research of their own. A modest project was suggested to them. If older workers were inefficient, it would be advisable to determine how much money the company was losing by continuing the employment of those older women who were already in the plant. There were a number of such women, those who had several years of service, or who had been taken on more recently as a favor to the community—a widow, possibly, or a hardship case.

Full responsibility for designing the project was placed, not with the research director, but with the members of the management staff. They were to determine the best methods of collecting data. The project was theirs, not his, and so would be the credit. They could come up with something which was of their own devising.

The findings were in sharp contrast to the staff's expectations. Not age, but other factors, determined success or failure on the job. But the analysis being their own, the staff trusted it. Thus being enabled to re-examine their beliefs through first-hand exploration, they were helped to new understanding. In the process, they "unlearned" some of the beliefs they had been convinced were true and were now ready to affirm quite different ones. They also learned something about the value of research applied to organizational problems.*

This experiment is a good example of the kind of action research that Lewin advocated and that Harwood used when feasible. It points up that when members of a group take part in a fact-finding inquiry of this sort, the very circumstance that the findings are their own inspires them to change their attitude and subsequent behavior. As Lewin put it, "This result occurs because the facts become really their facts (as against other people's facts). An individual will believe facts he himself has discovered in the same way that he believes in himself." When the findings are their own, people cannot challenge them as inadequate, or impute any bias to the fact-finders. They then recognize they must have been mistaken before. (Marrow, Bowers, and Seashore, 1967, pp. 24–26)

In contrast to action research (examined in the next section of this chapter), then, survey-research techniques are information-gathering and feedback devices that have evolved from an academic tradition of research. Survey research often deals with such issues as employee satisfaction, the concerns of individuals and groups about

---

* Marrow, A. J., and J. R. P. French, Jr. "Changing a Stereotype in Industry." *Journal of Social Issues* 12 (1945): 33–37.

particular problems such as morale and productivity, the character of leadership and supervision, or how grievances are handled. These data are not of the here-and-now variety, which depict what group members see as going on within and between themselves momentarily. According to Bowers and Franklin (1972, p. 46), survey-research instruments usually describe *end conditions*—satisfaction, morale, and productivity—rather than identifying process variables, such as openness or trust, or interpersonal variables, such as win-lose competitiveness, which may be causing them.

Typically, an outside survey-research consultant and organization participants collaborate from the beginning, first in perfecting the instrument by identifying specific or unique, as well as basic, features that should be engineered into it. Analyzing and interpreting collected information also are joint activities. However, the survey-research instrument may be taken without much change from any of the classical versions. One of the most inclusive is presented by Likert (1967). When standardized versions are used and instruments are completed by participants in more than one segment of the organization, it is often convenient to summarize the information through computer analysis. Decisions as to who is to receive information, and when, are collaboratively arrived at by survey-research consultants and organization representatives. In reaching such decisions the survey-research consultant may offer procedural suggestions as to desirable courses of action and introduce alternatives that participants may not previously have considered. Then summaries, correlations between various questions, and cross-department comparisons on a group-by-group basis can be made available to each participating group for its own study, interpretation, and evaluation. Information usually is fed back to the respondents and possibly to others at higher levels. Though usually not pointed out by the consultant, anonymity, which bypasses the openness issue, is a characteristic feature.

A closer glimpse at survey research is afforded by examining a sample survey-research instrument prepared by Likert. Data regarding group meetings were generated by posing the following kinds of questions to managerial personnel:

Are there any *group meetings* in which the non-supervisory people in your department can discuss things with the supervisors? (Check one.)

_____Yes, and they are always worthwhile.

_____Yes, and they are usually worthwhile.

_____Yes, but usually nothing much is accomplished.

_____Yes, but they are just a waste of time.

_____No, we never have such group meetings. (Likert, 1961, p. 123)

Miles, Calder, Hornstein, Callahan, and Schiavo (1970) explain how survey-research information used for group development may be handled. The example is a useful one for showing how traditional status-quo values set the boundary limits for consultant interventions in the catalytic mode.

Often, though not always, the data are shown first to the "head" of the family group, at which point his presentation of the data to the rest of the group may be discussed or rehearsed. Then the data are presented to the rest of the group, who are, in fact, "heads" of other family groups. Subsequently, they will examine the data with their groups. Thus, the survey feedback takes place through an interlocking set of conferences. Typically, outside staff members are present at each of the conferences.

Ordinarily, examination of the data leads to action planning in response to problems made salient by the data. Consequently, these feedback conferences provide activities in the presence of outside staff members who attempt to use their training skills to help members of the group improve their work relationships. (Miles, Calder, Hornstein, Callahan, and Schiavo, 1970, p. 357)

It is now possible to summarize standardized features of survey research as a catalytic intervention. A three-step sequence of activities usually is involved. First, information-gathering instruments are created or prefabricated instruments are utilized and information is gathered. Second, various groups—actual groups one level above where the information was gathered or the head of the family group itself—have meetings with the consultant to discuss this information and plan how to use it. Finally, if the procedure is carried to its natural conclusion, the survey-research consultant may work with the client groups on problems the survey information identified. The client groups themselves are supported as they analyze and interpret their own interactions in live information sharing. The consultant facilitates the group's interpersonal interactions, identification of norms, and evaluation of their problem-solving procedures. His or her comments make it legitimate to focus group study on such here-and-now phenomena.

The consultant may then recommend that participants attempt to relate this personal feedback to their own actual behavior, by trying to act according to the feedback given them rather than according to habit. This, in turn, can become a stimulus, producing further information about personal reactions. The hoped-for effect is that client effectiveness will be enhanced.

ACTION RESEARCH

Lewin (1946) introduced the concept of action research. Ideally, in terms of the Bradford-Gibb-Benne definition (1964, p. 33), it "is an application of scientific methodology in the clarification and solution of practical problems . . . also a process of planned personal and social change." In essence it is a method of empirical data gathering for action planning. Extensive collaboration between a consultant and client is involved regarding concrete uses to be made of data, including how to gather it, discussion of its meanings and implications, and explicit planning of action as a consequence of data-based findings. Evaluation of an action taken in one cycle becomes the data for a second cycle, and so on. While descriptions of the steps and the sequence vary in detail, the actual steps are essentially the same. As described by W. French (1972), the main ones are:

1. *Diagnosis.* As an initial step, usually the most senior-ranking member of the client system and the consultant reach a joint assessment. As an additional sub-step, subordinates may be interviewed to procure supplemental data. Questionnaires and survey feedback may be used to round out the diagnosis. French points to the importance of working with the client's "expressed needs" by indicating the importance of postponing or going slow, rather than confronting consultant-client differences in problem perception. The client is never "caused" to recognize his or her problem as different from what he or she previously felt it to be.

2. *Information Gathering.* After initial problem-definition is agreed upon by consultant and client, interviews are relied on to get at the facts in more specific and concrete terms, but questionnaires or survey-research procedures may also be developed.

3. *Feedback.* Feedback sessions to report the findings from the data-gathering procedures are arranged, most typically in the form of group-development sessions. The consultant summarizes common problems and participates by process observations that commonly result in a T-Group–type experience.

4. *Action Planning.* This step culminates the cycle of action research, involving further data gathering and team-building sessions with lower-level teams. French is not specific in commenting on how this takes place or what the intervention of the consultant might be.

The action-research approach constitutes a catalytic intervention in much the same way as does the approach initiated by interviews, or by questionnaires and scales, or by survey research. All share the basic proposition that information collection and feedback are the necessary and sufficient conditions for bringing about change. The major difference in action research is that the sequence might be thought of as the consultant's *planned* approach.

The key assumption behind action research is that the only thing participants require is access to information. Since its diagnoses are always kept within the client's framework of expressed needs, the consultant automatically accepts the status quo as given, not subject to challenge or confrontation. An accompanying assumption is that change will not be resisted when the facts of a situation are brought to the attention of participants in the manner indicated. However, it is known that traditions, precedents, and past practices are forces that may operate on participants in silent and therefore unrecognized ways. The readiness of participants to reject information through rationalization, or to distort its meaning through defensiveness, projection, and so on, is another blind spot in the action-research approach. Further learning of theory, techniques, or skill as a basis for comprehending dynamics underlying behavior is not made a focus of intervention either.

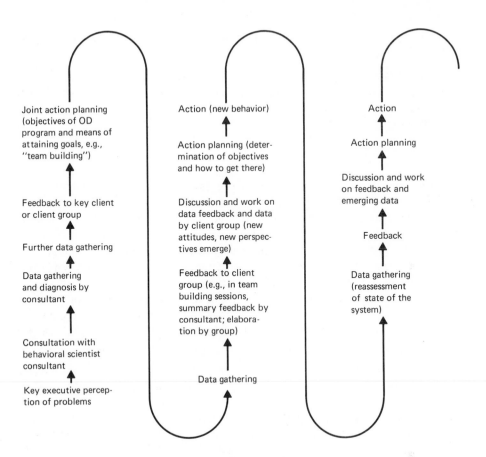

Joint action planning
(objectives of OD
program and means of
attaining goals, e.g.,
"team building")

↑

Feedback to key client
or client group

↑

Further data gathering

↑

Data gathering
and diagnosis by
consultant

↑

Consultation with
behavioral scientist
consultant

↑

Key executive percep-
tion of problems

Action (new behavior)

↑

Action planning (deter-
mination of objectives
and how to get there)

↑

Discussion and work on
data feedback and data
by client group (new
attitudes, new perspec-
tives emerge)

↑

Feedback to client
group (e.g., in team
building sessions,
summary feedback by
consultant; elabora-
tion by group)

↑

Data gathering

Action

↑

Action planning

↑

Discussion and work
on feedback and
emerging data

↑

Feedback

↑

Data gathering
(reassessment
of state of the
system)

Source: W. French, "Organization Development: Objectives, Assumptions and Strategies," *California Management Review* 12, no. 2 (1969), p. 26. © 1969 by The Regents of the University of California. Reprinted by permission.

Figure 8.1
An action research model for organization development.

SUMMARY

The ground rules for the way a catalytic consultant operates include the following. He or she:

1. Starts an intervention with informal conversation to create an easy-going non-authoritarian atmosphere, an informal give-and-take situation. "How are things?"

2. Invites the client to describe his or her situation, and accepts the needs described by the client as the only legitimate frame of reference to work within. As the consultant listens, he or she tries to formulate suggestions for gathering

new information that may illuminate some aspect of what the client seems interested in pursuing.

3. Suggests procedures that might be followed to gather more information. These may range from, "Why not just freewheel about your situation. No need to outline, just tell it as it comes out," to using action-research or survey-research methodologies.

4. Gives encouragement whenever possible by supporting the client's efforts at defining or redefining the problem at hand.

5. Avoids giving specific suggestions. Even procedures for data gathering are offered in a *very* tentative way. The consultant seeks to stay within the limits he or she thinks the client would *readily accept,* taking clues about client needs from what the client reveals about his or her thinking. The consultant may know what the client "should" do, or may know the client is not "facing up," but to impose his or her will on the situation or to challenge the client's self-deception would possibly promote resistance, which in turn might shift responsibility for solving the problem from client to consultant. To ensure that the client feels and knows that he or she retains control over the situation the consultant does not overstep these bounds. "How about this possibility?", "Do you think this would work?" are as far as the consultant is willing to go.

6. Encourages the client to make his or her own decisions. The consultant is graceful about it, but will *not* make them for the client, tip the balance one way or another, or confront the client whose definition of the situation is what is blocking progress. Consequently, the client feels that whatever action comes about was of his or her own choosing.

While catalytic interventions are calculated to alter the rate of change occurring within the status-quo system, there is no assurance that reactions of clients will provide added impetus to this rate. The catalytic approach, probably more than any other, can stimulate reactions, the characteristics of which are difficult to predict. The most common miscalculations result in either (1) the client rejecting the entire approach, or (2) confrontations between participants which become win-lose struggles.

REFERENCES

Bennis, W. G. "Theory and Method in Applying Behavioral Science to Planned Organization Change." *Journal of Applied Behavioral Science* 1, no. 4 (1965): 337–60.

Bowers, D. G., and J. L. Franklin. "Survey-Guided Development: Using Human Resources Measurement in Organizational Change." *Journal of Contemporary Business* 1, no. 33 (1972): 24–26.

Bowers, D. G., and J. Taylor. "Survey of Organizations." As reported in University of Michigan Institute for Social Research *Newsletter* 3, no. 6 (1973).

Bradford, L. P., J. R. Gibb, and K. D. Benne, eds. *T-Group Theory and Laboratory Methods: Innovation in Re-Education.* New York: Wiley, 1964.

Caplan, G. *The Theory and Practice of Mental Health Consultation.* New York: Basic Books, 1970. Reprinted by permission.

Crockett, W. J. "Team Building—One Approach to Organizational Development." Reproduced by special permission from *Journal of Applied Behavioral Science* 6, no. 3 (1970): 291–306.

Culbert, S. A. "Accelerating Laboratory Learning through a Phase Progression Model for Trainer Intervention." Reproduced by special permission from *Journal of Applied Behavioral Science* 6, no. 1 (1970): 21–38.

Davis, S. A. "An Organic Problem-Solving Method of Organizational Change." Reproduced by special permission from *Journal of Applied Behavioral Science* 3, no. 1 (1967): 3–21.

Ferguson, C. K. "Concerning the Nature of Human Systems and the Consultant's Role." *Journal of Applied Behavioral Science* 4, no. 2 (1968): 179–93.

Fordyce, J. K., and R. Weil. *Managing with People.* Reading, Mass.: Addison-Wesley, 1971. Reprinted by permission.

French, W. "Organization Development: Objectives, Assumptions and Strategies." © 1969 by The Regents of the University of California. Reprinted from *California Management Review* 12, no. 2: 26, by permission of The Regents.

Golden, W. P., Jr. "On Becoming a Trainer." In W. G. Dyer, ed., *Modern Theory and Method in Group Training.* New York: Van Nostrand Reinhold, 1972, pp. 3–29.

Lewin, K. "Action Research and Minority Problems." *Journal of Social Issues* 2 (1946): 34–46.

Likert, R. *New Patterns of Management.* New York: McGraw-Hill, 1961. Reprinted by permission.

Mangham, I. "Building an Effective Work Team." In M. and P. Berger, eds., *Group Training Techniques.* Epping: Gower Press, 1972, pp. 69–82.

Mann, F. C. "Changing Superior-Subordinate Relationships." *Journal of Social Issues* 7, no. 3 (1951): 56–63. Reprinted by permission.

Marrow, A. J., D. G. Bowers, and S. E. Seashore. *Management by Participation.* New York: Harper & Row, 1967. Reprinted by permission.

Miles, M. B., P. H. Calder, H. A. Hornstein, D. M. Callahan, and R. S. Schiavo. "Data Feedback and Organizational Change." In R. T. Golembiewski and A. Blumberg, eds., *Sensitivity Training and the Laboratory Approach.* Itasca, Ill.: F. B. Peacock, 1970, pp. 352–61. Reprinted by permission.

CATALYTIC INTERVENTIONS

9

POWER / AUTHORITY

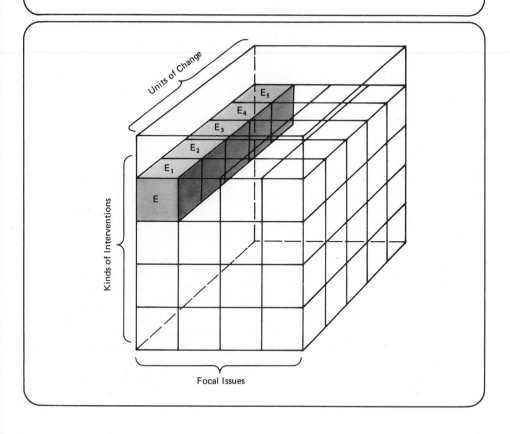

When power/authority is identified as the focal problem issue, the catalytic consultant works to bring this issue more into the client's field of awareness. Usually he or she employs some methodology that does not involve direct consultant participation in diagnosing the problem and recommending solutions. Instead, the client is helped to collect pertinent information which he or she can then interpret and act on.

INDIVIDUAL (E$_i$)

A catalytic intervention intended to aid a person to be more effective on the job is described by Bavelas and Strauss (1955). Their client was a foreman responsible for an assembly-line operation. He was in trouble. Women were complaining about pay, speed, heat, and so on. The consultant worked with the foreman to assist him in altering his style of supervision—use of power/authority—when dealing with the complaints.

> The consultant who was brought into this picture worked entirely with and through the foreman. After many conversations with him, the foreman felt that the first step should be to get the girls together for a general discussion of the working conditions—something, incidentally, which was far from his mind originally and which in his own words would only have been "begging for trouble." He took this step with some hesitation, but he took it on his own volition.

> The first meeting held ... was attended by eight girls. They voiced the same complaints again ... [emphasizing physical] ventilation. ... The foreman promised to discuss the problem of ventilation and temperature with the engineers, and he scheduled a second meeting to report back to the girls. ... (He did so, but could get no cooperation from the engineers or his boss.)

This first meeting probably had cathartic components, but it is also likely that the facts of poor ventilation and high temperatures, which had previously been interpreted as gripes, were now seen as real problems to be resolved. The character of the intervention strategy is revealed in the following.

> The foreman came to the second meeting with some apprehensions. The girls ... had a proposal of their own to make. They felt that if several large fans were set up so as to circulate the air around their feet, they would be much more comfortable. After some discussion the foreman agreed that the idea might be tried out. (Immediately after the meeting, he confided to the consultant that he probably shouldn't have committed himself to this expense on his own initiative; also he felt that the fans wouldn't help much anyway.) The foreman and the consultant discussed the question of the fans with the superintendent, and three large propeller type fans were purchased.

One after another, the complaints were handled by a similar procedure. Information gathering through discussions as to what the real problems were and what possible alternatives were available brought many solutions to the fore. The foreman secured agreement from his boss, the engineer, and the superintendent.

Against this background of success the final problem identified related to the women's dislike of the constant speed of the endless chain of hooks that carried objects in and out of their spray-painting booths.

> ... The group's leader frankly explained that the point wasn't that they couldn't work fast enough to keep up with the hooks, but that they couldn't work at that pace all day long. The foreman explored the point. The girls were unanimous in their opinion that they could keep up with the belt for short periods if they wanted to. But they didn't want to because if they showed that they could do this for short periods they would be expected to do it all day long. The meeting ended with an unprecedented request: "Let us adjust the speed of the belt faster or slower depending on how we feel." The foreman, understandably startled, agreed to discuss this with the superintendent and the engineers.

The consultant's catalytic influence had by now helped focus the power/authority issue as an interesting contrast between the operator's viewpoint and that of industrial engineering.

> The engineers' reaction naturally was that the girls' suggestion was heresy. Only after several meetings was it granted grudgingly that there was in reality some latitude within which variations in the speed of the hooks would not affect the finished product. After considerable argument and many dire prophesies by the engineers, it was agreed to try out the girls' idea.
>
> With great misgivings, the foreman had a control with a dial marked, "low, medium, fast" installed at the booth of the group leader; she could now adjust the speed of the belt anywhere between the lower and upper limits that the engineers had set. The girls were delighted, and spent many lunch hours deciding how the speed of the belt should be varied from hour to hour throughout the day.
>
> Production increased, and within three weeks (some two months before the scheduled ending of the learning bonus) the girls were operating at 30 to 50 percent above the level that had been expected under the original arrangement. Naturally the girls' earnings were correspondingly higher than anticipated.

But the solution of one set of problems created another set of problems that had not been anticipated.

... The girls were earning more now than many skilled workers in other parts of the plant. Management was besieged by demands that this inequity be taken care of. With growing irritation between superintendent and foreman, engineers and foreman, superintendent and engineers, the situation came to a head when the superintendent without consultation arbitrarily revoked the learning bonus and returned the painting operation to its original status. The hooks moved again at their constant, time-studied designated speed, production dropped again, and within a month all but two of the eight girls had quit. The foreman himself stayed on for several months, but, feeling aggrieved, then left for another job. (Bavelas and Strauss, 1955, abridged from pp. 91–94)

Relying on a catalytic approach, the consultant had aided the foreman to view the group-dynamic issues facing him and to get more worker involvement as he sought to deal with difficulties existing among these paint-room operators. By shifting the supervisor's use of power/authority to one that promoted information gathering through discussion, the supervisor was able to see not only how to solve gripes but how to improve productivity as well.

His efforts failed, however, because the status quo itself came under scrutiny. Eventually the assembly-line situation was brought back to where it had been in the beginning. The failure seems to have been caused by the consultant working with the supervisor *as an individual* when he should have been working as an organization consultant, involving all those who must support change: the foreman, the foreman's boss, the superintendent, the engineers, and the women as well. Because this was not done, new resistances related to challenged authority arose, which neither the foreman nor the consultant could resolve.

The consultant's objective in this example was to help the client gather and interpret data regarding his situation, and to offer procedural suggestions (for example, "Why not ask the girls?"), yet to avoid taking part in the client's final decisions. This remained the complete responsibility of the client. The failure should not be taken as a limitation of the character of the intervention; it simply reflects the kind of problem that can arise when the consultant intervenes with the "wrong" client.

GROUP (E₂)

Misperceptions regarding the use of power/authority are particularly pertinent as focal issues in group functioning. The boss views his behavior one way, many times in terms of his "good intentions." Each subordinate, however, is likely to have a different perspective of the boss's behavior, especially as this impinges on the subordinate's own job responsibilities and status in the group.

Catalytic interventions within groups can aid members to share their perceptions, pool information, clear up misunderstandings, and thereby increase the likelihood that more valid problem solving can take place unfettered by misuse and abuse of power/authority.

The New Boss

A description of a catalytic consultant specializing in process consultation depicts what took place in a small manufacturing organization. The intervention involved a "family" group composed of heads of different departments with their new general manager. Kuriloff, introduced earlier in Chapter 3, is the boss. These meetings were being held to identify and to resolve interpersonal difficulties (as revealed in the example earlier) and interactions (now to be described) that had been slowing the solution of economic problems. Power/authority was frequently the central issue. The following dialogues took place during the first session.

Participants understood they had convened to study how they work with one another and how they might work together more effectively. The general manager called the meeting to order. Finally someone asked Jack, one of the consultants: "What are we supposed to do?" The consultant started things off with procedural suggestions of the catalytic kind: suggestive but tentative, direction-giving but not demanding, approving but not indulgent, instructive but not didactic.

> Jack . . . explained that the purpose of our getting together was to explore our feelings and relationships . . . . "It's important to express feelings about one another, including us trainers. No holds are barred. . . . However, everyone should also feel free *not* to respond if it becomes too difficult or too uncomfortable. Openness is valued, but so is the right of privacy."
>
> After a slow beginning, something happened.
>
> Jim . . . voiced concern about his relationship with Rod. . . . "What's happened to us? Lately we can't seem to get anywhere on design problems."
>
> "Strange," Rod replied, "I've noticed it, too." (Kuriloff and Atkins, 1966, pp. 70–71)

Rod went on to say that once Jim was no longer subordinate to him, Jim's whole philosophy of management seemed to change from what it previously had been; and that this came through to Rod as "dishonest." Jim and Rod tried to clarify this misunderstanding. Other participants stepped in from time to time to assist this process.

The consultant had been successful in getting these two members of the group involved in critique and feedback.

> "If you had only let me know how you felt," Jim implored, "we could have straightened this out long ago."
>
> "Well, I got the message that you didn't much care what I thought," Rod countered. "When you invited the engineering people to come to your house for that barbecue, you didn't invite me. I assumed you wanted the opportunity to solidify your position with your new people." (Kuriloff and Atkins, 1966, p. 72)

Jim explained that no slight was involved—Rod hadn't been invited because Jim understood Rod would be out of town. Soon afterward a cathartic by-product of the mutual feedback emerged.

> The first session ended, and during the coffee break Rod and Jim stood in the hall, drinking coffee and talking busily. Excited, Rod said, "I'm sure glad we could clear the air! I feel a lot better now that I got it out in the open. I think I can sit down and work with you now. My feelings won't be standing between us." Rod extended his hand. He did not smile. (Kuriloff and Atkins, 1966, p. 73)

This kind of communication about "feelings-as-data" gives each person the additional information essential for interpersonal problem solving. In this instance, feelings associated with changes in status were in the forefront. By sharing emotions and respective interpretations of events, perceptual clarification was increased.

The consultant in the Kuriloff and Atkins situation is primarily facilitative in the sense of hastening the process. However, as an outsider, he can see and point out for particular attention what insiders have accepted without second thought.

> Finally, the trainers employ their skill in pointing out the group's processes, that is, when they are evading important issues or avoiding expression of feelings. They also lend support and protection to those who find it difficult to function in a group. (Kuriloff and Atkins, 1966, pp. 89–90)

This latter function is particularly relevant where there are real or different perceptions of the use of power/authority.

Levinson describes the consultant-as-intermediary intervention as an appropriate strategy when members of a team are so stirred up that direct or face-to-face consultant interventions would lead, not to constructive outcomes, but to destructive results. Feelings and emotions are too deep lying to be channeled constructively. Under these conditions an intervention approach that moderates tensions and provides a way for nonconfrontational awareness building can offer the possibility of useful though not necessarily dramatic progress. Levinson reports such an explosive situation and how it was dealt with.

> A president with a good managerial history was brought in to head a scientific company whose key men neither understood nor wanted to be subject to professional management. When they threatened to resign, and some did, urgent consultation was requested. Diagnosis of this situation took into account organization history and scientific values, desertion by the company's founders, exploitation by a previous president, cohesion of the in-group, and the need to retain adaptive profitability. On the basis of a comprehensive assessment, it was decided to hear the men out in individual interviews, then summarize those interviews and present them simultaneously to the interviewees and the president. This procedure

produced problems and issues to be dealt with, without subjecting the group to the possible exploitation of the president, whom they feared, and without running the risk of their destroying him under confrontation attack. The consultant became, in effect, an intermediary. On the one hand, his job was to help the president understand the nature of the complaints and the kinds of people he was dealing with as well as certain basic psychological principles. On the other hand, his task was to help the group recognize its need for a professional manager and to offer these men more constructive ways of giving the president support and guidance. After the initial contact of three, three-day sessions, the consultant maintained a distance from the group so that he would not be seen as "running the company." Many of the key managers individually took part in executive seminars to learn more about the psychology of management, and the consultant was available to all of them as individuals by phone or personal contact. This enabled the president and his key figures to develop a working relationship in which all could count on the distant but supportive influence of the consultant and the new and consistent pattern of leadership the president established.

This case example is one where power/authority is at the core of the problem, yet significant issues of morale/cohesion need attention also.

Once general comfort was attained in these relationships and the men could come to trust the president (in part because the consultant drew off some of their hostility toward him), they decided that it would be wise to get together as a group at monthly intervals in order to open up avenues of communication, which they knew needed opening but which would have been destructively explosive had they been opened before. The group continues to function effectively together, now more closely than ever. However, this process of carefully differentiated steps extended over a three-year period. (Levinson, 1973, pp. 165–66)

This intermediary kind of role—almost one of keeping protagonists separated—is a way of preventing a status quo explosion. By offering suggestions as to ways to proceed and through preserving the anonymity of interviewees, the consultant aided the president on the one hand, and his subordinates on the other, to enlarge and objectify their mutual perceptions, yet without really teaching them to be open and candid in face-to-face interactions. Eventually they did improve their communications, but how they did so is not indicated.

Boss Inaccessibility

Frequently bosses think they have open-door policies; that is, subordinates are free to come in whenever they need to. Often subordinates hear the *words* but, for whatever reason, still see the boss as inaccessible. This can create a power vacuum, which is unrecognized by either boss or subordinates. In effect, there are "invisible seals" within the system, keeping two or more individuals' perceptions and information separate and preventing shared insights into power/authority problems and their resolution.

Harvey and Boettger (1971) identified and intervened in this kind of situation. The consultation involved a Corporate Services group, including a vice-president and fifteen division directors. Referred to as COSCOM (Corporate Services Committee on Operations Management), it met periodically to exchange information, to discuss problems, and to find and evaluate solutions to them. Most COSCOM members had already engaged in an "unfreezing" experience involving T-Group participation. Because of this they expressed interest in applying laboratory method to improving COSCOM functioning. The consultants then interviewed the boss and division directors concerning their view of problems, including problems facing the total company, those in their own divisions, those involved in how they worked with other divisions, and the concerns each had as to his own work in the company. Each interview lasted approximately an hour.

Interview findings were summarized and a variety of problems identified. One set of issues concerned difficulties division directors had in communicating with their boss, the COSCOM vice-president: "The vice president is inaccessible"; "The vice president has too many people reporting to him for me to have the time that I need to talk with him"; "The vice president does not seem to want to know what I think." All of these point to a power/authority focal issue. A particular facet of the problem was that interviewees identified some personal frustrations from being required to reply to memoranda from their boss.

> "It seems as if every morning when I show up for work my desk is loaded with a bunch of memos."
>
> "I spend half of my time around here trying to answer those _____ memos the vice president sends me, and my staff spends half of their time getting me enough information to answer them."
>
> "I have a hard time getting my work done. I am always busy fielding his 'rockets'."

Such reactions to memoranda suggested an important communication problem. Complaints about the frequency of memos might be objective. To check this possibility, the consultants extended their data gathering by finding out how many memos actually were transmitted over a six-month period. Three hundred sixty-seven memos had been sent to fifteen subordinates. Interview information was then fed back to the COSCOM members as a team.

In the joint-action planning phase, the following information-gathering strategy was designed.

1. Each participant would provide the consultant with the most inappropriate (confusing, irrelevant or unessential) memo the vice-president had sent him.

2. The vice-president would do something similar, except he would be providing the consultants with replies he had received.

3. After memos had been projected on the screen, for all to see, each person wrote

   a. What he thought the memo said to do.
   b. What action he would take in response to the memo.
   c. What priority he would give work on the memo—high, medium, or low.

4. Each participant, other than the actual instigator and recipient, read aloud the conclusions reached under (3) to the total COSCOM group.

5. The recipient of this missive reported how he had understood it and what action he had to take, and the priority given it.

6. The vice-president did the same in regard to his intention when he had composed the memo.

7. The next day entailed diagnosis of "communication" problems between the vice-president and memo recipients. Recommendations for action were also developed. (Harvey and Boettger, 1971, p. 164)

After some discussion of the information, participants developed a cooperative spirit and set higher goals of achievement. Savings resulted as well, but this was not quantified. The project was reported to have had a successful outcome.

Viewed from the perspective of an action-research strategy, the key executives of this organization perceived the possibility that problems existed. Consultants were invited to apply the "laboratory method" with which these executives already had some familiarity. Initial exploratory information gathering and diagnosis by the consultants took place and then a second round to test a second hypothesis was followed by feedback to the client group. In turn this led to joint-action planning as a means of obtaining desirable goals. This action-research strategy provides a sequence of interventions that can have a catalyzing effect, quickening the readiness to solve problems sensed on a felt-needs basis but not previously recognized with enough clarity for their negative impact to be fully appreciated.

Simultaneous Hierarchy and Equality

Because of widespread recognition of the problems that can result from unilaterally exercised power/authority, particularly within an hierarchical structure, various *structural* solutions have been formulated regarding how to gain the benefits of equality while preserving the official hierarchy that itself connotes inequality of power/authority.

Collateral system is an intervention that preserves the power/authority status-quo, while creating an alternative to it. Several authors have actively intervened in an organization to bring about power/authority "splits," while others have commented on possibilities that might prove feasible.

One example is provided by Zand (1974). The rationale of this collateral-system intervention rests on the following. The functioning of a work group is strengthened to the degree it can flexibly shift its operating style to accommodate changing and diverse problems. This may mean, for example, that one particular problem situation calls for authority to be highly focused in a single individual with several others implementing solutions he or she alone has devised. Another type of problem may profit from more widely shared solution-seeking participation, with contributions based on personal capabilities rather than on rank. These two contrasting styles of exercising authority by no means exhaust the possibilities, but they are the two systems concentrated on in collateral-system interventions.

The idea that problems are of two types—well-structured and ill-structured— is the second premise of this approach. Well-structured problems according to Zand (1974, p. 89) are suited to resolution through organized routines under close supervisory management. In contrast, ill-structured problems are complex—hard to define and to solve under established procedures and tight or close supervision. Work supervised under tight control is more effective when dealing with well-structured problems than with those in the ill-structured category. However, a more general supervision, with free give-and-take, is more suited to the solution of complex, difficult-to-define problems.

Given the premise that work-group inflexibility is not subject to change, the alternative is to form a *collateral organization*. Although this group might include the same individuals who man the small work group, when operating in the collateral mode, they are expected to see themselves in a different light and act accordingly.

This intervention encourages the work group to use the collateral organization whenever a manager becomes aware that he or she is faced with an ill-structured problem or opportunity. In the collateral organization, hierarchy-based relationships and attitudes are set aside to facilitate creative problem solving.

An example involves the vice-president of a bank. Mr. Brady wanted to increase his department's competence to meet competition in the worldwide market. While the goal itself was clear, many ill-structured issues needed to be identified and resolved in a coordinated way if these goals were to be successfully met.

In daily work, this vice-president interacted routinely in an authority-production mode. Mr. Brady was in the habit of masterminding solutions to daily operations problems, and his subordinates were largely implementers of these solutions. Thus, as the vice-president began discussing strategy issues with several key subordinates, he found them unable to delve into these problems in an effective manner. Each subordinate seemed to view the "whole" from a position close to his own sphere of responsibility.

Zand's intervention approached the situation in a catalytic manner. First he interviewed Mr. Brady and his subordinates, in addition to observing their daily work and the many decisions they made. He apparently concurred that they would have great difficulty dealing productively with these strategy matters even though, as individuals, they were competent and had the international-banking knowledge essential for identifying valid solutions to ill-structured problems. He concluded that somehow they would have to depart from the usual pattern of power/authority production-centered work.

> The OD specialist explained the need for a collateral organization to Mr. Brady and his group. He proposed an initial three-day meeting, at which strategy and operating issues would be discussed, analyzed, and if possible, resolved. (The men were so busy they insisted it be from Friday afternoon to Sunday evening.) Aware that collateral organizations frequently fail because managers may have unrealistic expectations and cannot foresee the difficulties of a collateral mode, the specialist stressed setting limited, attainable goals. He suggested that the group try to identify key issues but discuss only two or three priority issues in detail. Since there would be many unanswered questions after the meeting, they would also have to approve some structure which could be used to work on finding answers after they returned to work. Finally they should discuss how they could organize to solve ill-structured problems more effectively in the future.

> Ten days before the meeting, the OD specialist interviewed each manager, gathering information for the meeting and answering questions about format. Each manager described the issues he most wanted discussed, the outcomes that would make him feel the meeting was worthwhile, and the difficulties that might interfere with managers being reasonably open about important issues. The interview process itself stimulated managers to think about norms that departed from those of the primary mode. (Zand, 1974, p. 73)

The consultant introduced the following considerations in a general session presentation that served as a preamble to this outside meeting.

> The power difference in the formal organization would still exist when the managers returned to work. Mr. Brady, the vice president, was the group's superior, and this was his meeting, not the consultant's. The group or its members could make recommendations, but Mr. Brady would have to approve any proposal before it could be implemented. Regardless of formal position, managers usually have valuable insights and proposals that cut across many different areas. It would be the responsibility of the high managers to facilitate expression and use of these views. The OD specialist would suggest procedures and ask questions to help the group's problem solving. (Zand, 1974, pp. 73–74)

This summary illustrates the consultant's two-headed theme of "preserve the formal structure for well-structured problems, but switch out of it for solving nonroutine problems." Operating in a catalytic mode,

> the specialist then reported a summary of the issues managers wanted to discuss. At first, the group operated in an authority/production mode. Man-

agers frequently proposed solutions before a problem had been clearly defined. The specialist made process observations to alter these norms. Discussion was brought back to managers whose views had not been heard adequately. There was regular testing to ensure that any problem was understood by all before solutions were discussed in depth. Regardless of status, managers began contributing important information and insights. This helped the senior managers see how the open channels of the collateral mode improved problem solving.

On the second day, the managers agreed to experiment with a collateral mode after they returned to work. They would set aside "unstructured" time (multichannels, free questioning, and so on) to study several ill-structured problems. Based on their new experience, they also adopted a special norm for their collateral mode: incomplete ideas, although not thoroughly reasoned and defendable, were welcomed. This was a deliberate and significant departure from behavior in their primary organization. It was intended to stimulate search and creativity. They reiterated, however, that in the hierarchical (primary) organization, a recommendation would still have to be supported by thorough reasoning and documentation. They had grasped the distinction between primary and collateral modes without falling into the trap of insisting that one had to displace the other. (Zand, 1974, p. 74)

Upon completing this intervention on how to operate as a collateral organization, members returned to their everyday assignments. While continuing to operate the business in a formal mode, they dealt with several sticky problems on a one-morning-per-week basis over the next six weeks in the collateral mode. This helped to stabilize their skills in this mode, yet preserved the sharp demarcation between power/authority and catalytic modes of problem solving.

A number of comparisons of the formal-collateral modes are possible. One involves a *temporary system* as discussed by Miles (1964) and elaborated on by Bennis and Slater (1968). A temporary system is an association of two or more people for some specific purpose, with shared understanding that it is temporary, i.e., has a limited duration and will dissolve when the objective for organizing it has been met or when individual members' current interests are no longer meaningfully served.

By comparison, a collateral organization is likely to dissolve for at least two reasons. One is when the kind of unique problems the collateral organization is capable of solving cease to exist. Another is that the formal organization may "internalize" the particular power/authority mode of the collateral organization, making formal distinctions between these and traditional modes unnecessary. In other words, needs for switching back and forth from formal to collateral organization no longer exist. In a team-building sense, the needed flexibility to deal with both well-structured and ill-structured problems has been achieved.

A parallel use of the collateral-organization basis for intervention is described by Weisbord, Lamb, and Drexler (1974). The client in this case is the police department of Urban City, where authority-obedience was suspended to permit problem diagnosis and solution recommending.

First, data about the bureau was gathered by interviewing and observing the police officers in their daily activities. From this data emerged a strategy to be used to build a more effective middle management. All supervisors would be given an opportunity to name the most pressing problems, trained in group problem-solving techniques and then immediately given a chance to use their new skills in special task forces which would be organized to solve the problems they had named. (Weisbord, Lamb, and Drexler, 1974, pp. 4–5)

One aspect of the collateral organization rests on the use of diagonal slices of the organization to define problems.

These task forces would cut across the lines of rank and divisions to include those with authority over the problem, those with the skill to solve it, and those most affected by it. The task forces would be "collateral" or parallel to the formal organization. That is, they would include the same men as the formal organization, but in new relationships, working under special ground rules, whose task would be to solve problems not easily handled in a formal way. The task forces would supplement the usual decision-making process, not replace it; they would have the power only to recommend solutions to the commissioner and chief. Underlying the use of task forces are the assumptions that several people of varying backgrounds together can solve joint problems more creatively than by working alone, and that people are more committed to carrying out decisions they have had a part in making.

Sessions were scheduled at various times so that all men could attend, regardless of shifts worked. The program involved half a dozen formal meetings, varying in length from two hours to one and a half days, plus several informal meetings arranged by the men themselves.

In the first session, each of the four groups, which were mixed by rank, made a list of the problems they saw in the bureau. The lists were then combined and the problems sorted into long- and short-range designations and assigned priorities by the officers working in peer groups by rank. Then the resulting lists were merged according to the priorities assigned. (Weisbord, Lamb, and Drexler, 1974, p. 5)

Task force assignments of the same personnel were then made.

From this came a task force assignment list, with each task force centered around a specific problem the officers had named, such as vehicle maintenance, discipline, the reporting system, and the promotional system. The men were then given training in group problem solving, including theory, a personal style questionnaire, observation of groups at work, and a training problem (interference at crime scenes) for all the men to work through together. (Weisbord, Lamb, and Drexler, 1974, p. 5)

The close resemblance of collateral organization to the confrontation meeting described in Chapter 9 is revealed in the following.

The men were asked to select the task force they preferred. Each task force thoroughly investigated its assigned problem and made recommendations in an oral presentation and written report to the chief and the commissioner. Some answers were given by the chief and commissioner on the spot, and some further assignments were made; then the recommendations, responses, and actions taken were summarized in a memo from the commissioner and the chief to all the men. In addition, some new task forces were created as a result of questions raised by the first groups. This necessitated a second round of task force work and the same kind of reporting sessions and memo back to the officers as in the first round.

Most of the men found the training sessions useful, particularly the aspect of being able to discuss mutual problems in groups. Many also said that the training seemed to improve their communication and problem-solving skills (on all levels) in their daily work. (Weisbord, Lamb, and Drexler, 1974, p. 5)

Even though based on subjective data, an evaluation of impact was attempted and the following conclusions drawn.

As for changes made to correct the problems facing the bureau, in a survey comparing the bureau before and after the sessions, the officers felt that 15 out of 18 items in the questionnaire had improved after the training and task forces. As further proof, the survey was also given to patrolmen, who were not directly involved in the training, but certainly would be able to see its effects. They, too, reported improvement in most of the critical problems facing the Bureau of Police. In addition, interviews with senior officers a year later indicated that task force problem solving had become standard operating procedure for difficult, non-routine problems. In short, the "collateral organization" had become a new administrative tool as intended. (Weisbord, Lamb, and Drexler, 1974, p. 5)

All of these examples are interesting commentaries on the ability of people in groups to shift with the rules of the game. In a way, though, the focal issue is how to distribute power/authority. It is the acceptance of norms/standards that vary from situation to situation which makes the shift possible. Again, this points to the close interrelatedness of the focal issues and the simplification of focus that is necessary to emphasize the broader generalities.

Challenging the Teacher's Authority

Teachers' classroom problems are legion. A developing conviction is that if teachers understood themselves more fully—particularly in their use of power/authority and their reactions if challenged by students—they could replace actions that provoke difficulties with others that preclude difficulties. The consultant focus, then, shifts from child behavior *per se* to helping teacher-as-client. Sometimes this process is facilitated by working with teachers in groups instead of in one-to-one consultations.

An example of such an approach is offered by Dinkmeyer and Carlson (1973). In the following excerpt, the consultant is with a group of classroom teachers and, through his interventions, focuses issues and assists teachers to share their experiences with one another.

Teacher 3: "I think he is fighting her. Whatever she says, he is going to do the opposite."

Consultant: "You believe it is his need to be in control?"

Teacher 3: "Yes, some think they are in charge."

Consultant: "You feel challenged by these students?"

Teacher 3: "Right. I can't let them get by with anything."

Consultant: "What do some of you think about that?"

Teacher 4: "I recognize I have the same problem about wanting to be in control."

Consultant: "If it's important for you to have the power, what do you think the child experiences?"

Teacher 1: "I imagine our real problem is getting involved in fighting with them."

Teacher 2: "I've found things go better when I refuse to become involved in power contests."

Consultant: "Let's look at this in another way. What if you're busy writing and somebody comes by and says, 'That's really good work. Now I hope you keep that up.'"

Teacher 4: "No, I don't think I would like that..."

Teacher 5: "You're not satisfied with it." (*laughter*)

Consultant: "Yes, what is the implication?"

Teacher 4: "Well, I don't expect you to really finish."

Teacher 1: "...that he won't cooperate."

Teacher 4: "It's like a backhand slap."

Teacher 1: "That's really true, because I don't expect him to finish and I gave him the clue."

Teacher 2: "I can do that with the brighter children and say, 'Oh, that sounds like a good story,' or 'Oh, that sounds like it's going to be exciting; go on and finish it.' That excites them to want to go on. With the slower children, or the child who needs discipline, why should it work in a reverse order?"

By this open-ended inquiring the consultant successfully keeps teachers focused on their own behavior, which comes to be seen as involving a communications problem. An alternative interpretation, though, could be that the basic issue is, How we as teachers use our classroom authority to control students. The discussion continues:

Teacher 4: "We have to learn to be more aware of our communication and the messages we send."

Consultant: "It seems difficult to understand, but our communication does affect the child's motivation."

Teacher 2: "It really has to be a habit, where you have to be able to do it unconsciously, always positive."

Consultant: "And I think that you are right about a habit. It takes a long time to get to that because you're so used to doing it the other way."

Teacher 4: "One thing, I don't know whether I mentioned it here, but I have found it is a tremendous help if I really take some time out when the children come in and call five or six of them out in the hall and say to each, 'Robert, I'm so thrilled that you are here because you were such a good boy this morning and it was so nice to have you in my room.' I suppose it would be like the boss coming along and saying to you he's proud of your work. I reflect on that and my afternoons go ten times better!"

Teacher 2: "I have got to try that. That sounds good."

Teacher 4: "But a lot of times I come in and begin spelling and say, 'Sit down, be quiet.' This is like throwing the monkey wrench into the machinery."

Consultant: "Or, when you come in you could say something like, 'I noticed that you were really working at that math this morning.' . . . just some little encouragement." (Dinkmeyer and Carlson, 1973, pp. 229–30)

Beyond functioning as a discussion rallying point, the consultant's contribution is mainly in asking "What if . . . ?" kinds of questions that aid participants in expressing their thoughts and feelings. Through this sharing, common-sense wisdom can be marshalled and made available to the teacher. The limitation is that the issue may, as seems to be true in this case, be defined as a communication and reward problem, when the underlying dynamics actually concern misuses of authority and obedience as a means of control.

Changing the Principal

A catalyzing strategy often employed in consultation is to create an explicit discrepancy between what is actual and what is wanted, rather than letting the gap remain on an implicit level. An intervention-based experiment involving several hundred elementary-school principals and their teachers, intended to hasten change, is reported by Daw and Gage. The teachers described their *actual* principal and their *ideal* principal in regard to the following twelve criteria (Daw and Gage, 1967, p. 184).

1. Encourages teachers with a friendly remark or smile.
2. Gives enough credit to teachers for their contributions.

3. Does not force opinions on teachers.
4. Enforces rules consistently.
5. Criticizes without disparaging the efforts of teachers.
6. Informs teachers of decisions or actions which affect their work.
7. Gives concrete suggestions for improving classroom instruction.
8. Enlists sufficient participation by teachers in making decisions.
9. Demonstrates interest in pupil progress.
10. Interrupts the classroom infrequently.
11. Displays much interest in teachers' ideas.
12. Acts promptly in fulfilling teacher requests.

Some of the principals were told how their teachers had rated them in comparison with an ideal principal; others, who had also been rated, were not given this information feedback. Thus it was possible to evaluate the effect of "pure" information feedback on reducing the size of the real/ideal gap. The feedback did effect positive changes in the principals' behavior. This appears to be a situation where both principals' and teachers' values were in alignment. What was needed was to reduce pluralistic ignorance; that is, aid both groups in recognizing their shared perceptions. This then stimulated the desire and action to change.

Academic Warfare

A small academic department was split into factions or camps on major activities. The usual interpersonal tension problems, such as mutual distrust, accusations of boss-manipulation for personal benefit, and so on, were evident. This department became the client for two different catalytic change strategies: an unsuccessful intervention by an external consultant followed by a more successful internal-consultant intervention. The report is by Varney and Lasher (1973).

Within the department, indications of increasing ineffectiveness were becoming evident. In response, a one-day team-building session was arranged. It was led by an outside process consultant and initially appeared to have been successful in identifying the causes of manifest problems which could thereafter be dealt with more openly. However, two or three faculty members were outspoken in questioning the need for ". . . some outsider to come in and help us solve department problems." These attitudes had a veto effect and the consultation fell victim to the cleavage it was intended to heal. Furthermore, efforts by colleagues to reduce divisiveness were not accepted either.

The next step was initiated by an insider, an administrative officer of the university who also held a faculty appointment. Along with the two authors, he joined a group of interested students and requested permission of the department faculty to conduct a survey. The data from this, organized on an "as is" versus "ought to be" basis, would be summarized and fed back to them as clients for reflection and diagnosis. Agreement to do this was reached.

Data were fed back at two departmental meetings attended by all faculty. Real issues were identified and articulated. Action plans included the preparation of working papers as a means of thinking through and sharing points of view. Sharing of feelings also became more apparent, cooperation improved, and pride in organization was indicated by the department wanting to bring about ". . . changes geared toward making the department the most effective in the college."

Summary

In each of the examples above, power/authority was initially more or less centralized, whereas the end state was one of more equal distribution. An egalitarian value system seems to underlie many catalytic consultant's actions. This is to be contrasted later with the direction solutions take under prescriptive formulations.

INTERGROUP (E₃)

Catalytic interventions have been used to help solve intergroup problems. As already seen in individual and group applications, these share a common emphasis. Gathering empirical information and feeding it back to both groups is the fundamental strategy.

One of the difficulties that interdependent groups who need to cooperate encounter in their interactions is inappropriate or unclear power relations. When each group suffers from pluralistic ignorance as to what the power relationship is or should be, needed coordination can hardly follow.

This line of reasoning led Alderfer (1973) to view the classroom relationship between faculty and students in the following manner. The consultant observed that students often talk to one another about courses, but that similarly pertinent discussions between students and teachers, where the data generated could have potent change effects for all participants, are rare. Since it is even more rare for faculty members to discuss their teaching practices on a colleague-to-colleague basis, they do not influence one another to any significant degree either.

The intervention design did not entail communication between already intact groups. Instead, a faculty committee concerned with teaching and learning convened a sample group of faculty members—three each from humanities, social sciences, and natural sciences—for an evening of discussion with a representative group of their students. One student was randomly chosen from courses taught by each attending faculty member. After introductions, two separate groups, one of faculty and one of students, were formed for an hour-long discussion of, "How the student-teacher relationship affects teaching and learning." Consultants sat with each group. Faculty members are reported to have had greater difficulty in discussing the topic than did the students.

Points on which two or more participants agreed were recorded. Then two new groups were formed, this time with a crisscross composition, each group half faculty, half student. The agenda for this one-hour discussion was to identify similarities and differences between the faculty and student lists produced during the previous hour.

The four hours of discussion were video recorded and then edited to a one-hour summation that was shown to the original discussion participants. A summary of findings follows.

Students' View of Faculty	Faculty View of Itself
Faculty should be more available for discussion and clarification	Feedback from discussion sections useful in assessing progress
Initiative in evaluating course progress rests with teacher	
Teachers' enthusiasm for subjects and students very important	
Faculty should be prepared and well organized in their presentations	Scanning audience useful to see if the lecture is making sense
Professor should establish his right to teach and should earn the respect of his students	
Primary responsibility for lecture course rests with teachers	Lecture format creates an enormous distance between faculty and students (Alderfer, 1973, pp. 6–8)

Perceptions of how students see faculty in comparison with how faculty see themselves have little in common. This kind of intergroup design can be useful to those who participate in it, but since the individuals in this situation were not participating as members of an intact group, nor even as chosen representatives of their respective membership groups, the intervention is not likely to have any significant effect in terms of shifting such power/authority aspects as one-way communication, responsibility, and initiative taking.

ORGANIZATION (E₄)

The solution to organization problems may be through *supplementing* the exercise of power/authority rather than through strengthening its use. The basic strategy is for the consultant to *act in behalf* of those in authority to stimulate organization problem solving. The consultant convenes various lower-level groups for problem diagnosis. Anonymity is promised. A quantity of information is generated at these sessions and the consultant groups this information into categories and feeds it to senior authorities for their reactions, recommendations, or decisions. The facts made available by this approach may be quite different from the "facts" available to authority levels through reliance on the line organization's report. But neither the recipients of the information nor the members themselves have been subject to change intervention. When new problems that cannot be solved by conventional line procedures arise, it can be predicted that a repetition of this same procedure will be called for.

Suspending the Conventional Power/Authority Systems to Solve Problems

Creating openness and candor in identifying problems existing within an organization is a first step toward change in Jaques' approach to organization intervention. Its distinctive feature is that, after initial discussions, Jaques synthesizes conclusions reached in a written report that is then widely circulated.

Jaques (1948) describes approaching the diagnosis and solution of problems through a number of diagonal-slice groups, composed so that major contemporary tensions from the larger organization are represented within each subgroup. A group is free to discuss any matter. Gripes tend to dominate early discussions.

> There is very rapid fire discussion, which gradually takes on the character of a grouse session. There seems to be nothing good in the company. The executive feels the workers are lazy and junior management inadequate; the supervisors feel they can get no cooperation from above and are a target for nothing but abuse from below; the workers feel that they are getting a raw deal generally and that they cannot trust anybody. The picture grows worse and worse, until suddenly someone suggests they have been over-elaborating difficulties caused by other people, and should perhaps have a look at their own behaviour. There is a silence. Then others begin to agree, and from that point the discussion veers round to a more constructive tone.

In a nonthreatening way the consultant encourages members to proceed.

> There seems more to the initial grousing than just the group "getting things off its chest." We suggest to the group that it has been seeing whether we were prepared to face any difficulties, reasonable or not, without taking sides or passing moral judgments. There is a bit of rather tense laughter, followed by relaxation and agreement that perhaps this may have been the case.
>
> This interpretation seems to have produced considerable reassurance about us. The group begins to get down to considering its own differences. We suggest that these reflect here-and-now some of the differences between various sections of the community, and suggest it might be useful to examine them together. The group then begins to make a discovery for itself. It finds that while it is easy to criticise and scapegoat members of other sub-groups in their absence, some of the criticisms seem less reasonable in their presence. There is not time to pursue this further, however, because the next group is waiting and we find that we have already carried over our time. Previous experience, however, leaves us assured that the discussion will be continued outside, both during and after working hours. (Jaques, 1948, p. 544)

The common themes expressed in such discussions suggest a diagnosis of tensions within the organization, and a written report based on this diagnosis receives the widest possible circulation. Thereafter, additional diagonal-slice groups convene to follow up on the report's conclusions. In such discussions

> it is commented that the problem has been more thoroughly aired, with a different orientation, than has previously been the case. Issues which have been lying around unexpressed have come out openly for the first time. It is agreed to stop at this point, and to meet again after there has been a chance to think matters over further.
>
> This discussion is followed by others with the same and with other groups. There is a general pattern of talking round problems in such a way that a broader perspective about intergroup difficulties is obtained, on the basis of which executive action is eventually taken.

This catalytic approach generates an initial unloading which is at least quasi cathartic and is interspersed with encouragements calculated to make participants aware of their own attempts to escape from painful frankness. Tentatively and in a manner inviting friendliness, the consultant draws attention to various defensive strategies and unwitting collusions. In the following example the consultant brings a contradiction into focus.

> Our suggestion seems to be overlooked, however, since the discussion turns to complaints about wasting time talking, and the desire is expressed that the executive should decide what should be done and take action without consulting anyone. We point out that there is some inconsistency between such desires and previously expressed resentment about being dominated by those above, and ask whether this can be related to the wish to get away from a painful situation. If this is so, it appears easier to recommend more democracy and opportunity for participation for other people in the firm, than to cope with the difficulties and complex issues which arise when given the opportunity to participate yourself. (Jaques, 1948, p. 547)

This kind of intervention keeps consultant suggestions on a clue level—he is not forced to reveal his actual opinion and thereby induce a confrontation. Though it permits escape, it also provides organization members the opportunity to deal with problems that previously had been beyond their reach.

One of the earliest interventions relying on survey research as the basis for feedback is by Baumgartel (1959). Survey instruments were answered by members of six accounting departments in various operating components of a large insurance company. These instruments focused on three aspects: the work itself, human relations, and the organization. Sixty supervisors and 640 nonsupervisory employees in six departments took part. All six departments completed evaluation instruments both before and after the survey-research instruments were administered, regardless of whether or not they received feedback. Then four of the six departments received data feedback—which they discussed over a twelve-month period. Two control departments did not get the feedback. This strategy provided an answer to the question, Did the feedback of survey-research data provide any change in regard to the power/authority focal issue? Responding to a second survey two years after the first one, relatively more members of departments that received feedback and discussed it felt their supervisors were: (1) better at "handling" people, (2) better "leaders," and (3) more "likeable."

The consultant concluded,

> The results of this study suggest that the creative use of new information for conferences and meetings at all levels of departmental organization may be one of the best and most dynamic avenues to management development and organizational growth. (Baumgartel, 1959, p. 6)

The confrontation meeting is a catalytic way of gathering data about an organization in order to feed it back to the key executives in the authority system. It also is a procedure that temporarily suspends the traditional power/authority structure of the organization. Its title word, "confrontation," is a misnomer. This intervention is led by an outsider or by a staff member, and relies on the participatory activity of those in attendance, several echelons of a department that have a common boss. Often, though not always, the boss and the key people who report to him or her are not involved in the study of the problems. But once the problems have been identified by lower echelons, an arrangement is created whereby the information is fed to the top person and his or her group, under circumstances where they are expected to listen and, to the degree that they interact with lower levels, to limit their participation to queries for clarification.

A typical confrontation meeting schedule follows:

  9:30 to 10:00 Introduction
 10:00 to 11:00 Data collection–problem generation
 11:00 to 12:00 Information sharing and categorization
  1:30 to 2:45 Priority setting and action planning
  2:45 to 4:30 Confrontation and implementation

Providing an indication of the character of information that is gathered, one group listed the following (Bennis, 1969, p. 8):

- Meetings like this should start on time. "Minor irritants," like postponed meetings, are rarely communicated to people.
- The authority structure is unclear. Who's my boss: Who judges my work?
- Until recently, there has been little cross-fertilization.
- The Director is inaccessible. Members of the power structure are very accessible to some, but Dr. X (Associate Director) doesn't return my calls. As a result, the number of memos has increased.

- There is no system of setting priorities on distribution of materials. Does a policy exist? Is it possible to have one?
- It is a problem for newcomers to discover who does what in the organization.
- There are too many people employed and then not permitted to exercise the skills they were hired for.
- Too many meetings are held without a specific agenda.
- How do information and decisions that come out of these meetings get communicated?
- Taking over responsibility as acting project director has taken me away from my primary interest—this is irritating and annoying.
- Difficult to get a sure assessment of people's strengths and weaknesses.
- Who makes decisions around here?
- Funding is chaotic. Whom do we go to for funds?

This kind of information, generated by strategies that bypass ordinary reporting channels, is calculated to have a catalyzing effect on the upper-level group to whom it is addressed. Corrective actions on many of the issues identified are not difficult to set in motion, for most lower-level suggestions tend to accept the status quo and seek to bring about improvements in how it operates. The catalytic interventionist's contribution is primarily in helping introduce the participatory norm. Though Beckhard calls this approach a confrontation meeting, it is an identifiable kit of catalytic strategies. First, it involves a one-day activity, designed to suspend established lines of communication and decision making and make it possible to bring together widely diverse segments of the organization for diagnosis, priority setting, and action recommendations. As depicted in his description, a confrontation meeting does not involve confrontation. Rather, anonymous, more or less off-the-cuff feedback, itself not based on deep study or analysis, is forwarded to a higher-level group from lower-level personnel. The meeting, in other words, is designed according to catalytic assumptions and focuses on exploiting participation.

Two criteria are particularly indicative of a need for this kind of meeting. One is when the organization is under an unusual stress: new top management, loss of a customer, a launch of a new product. The second is when top management is a cohesive unit but a culture/communication barrier exists between it and lower echelons. The purpose is to bridge the gap in a quick mobilization of the entire organization toward change and improvement.

Following is a description of how the confrontation intervention works, reconstructed from Beckhard's experience in one organization. From the top man to front-line supervision, the management comprises about eighty people. All take part. The time allocated is two sessions, perhaps three hours one afternoon or night session, followed by three hours the next morning. The intervention begins with the management head or the consultant giving an introduction that spells out the meeting's purpose and encourages participants to express themselves fully and freely. Assurances that anonymity will be respected and no one punished are included.

The eighty then subdivide into five- or six-person subgroups on a diagonal-slice basis, so that no boss is in a group with his or her subordinates. Same-level colleagues also are split up. Top management meets together, except for the highest-level executive.

> The groups are assigned the following task: "Thinking of yourself as a person with needs and goals in this organization, and also thinking of the total organization, what are the behaviors, procedures, ways of work, attitudes, etc., that should be different so that life would be better around here?" Each group is asked to make a list of its items. They have about an hour for this task. (Beckhard, 1969, p. 39)

The eighty participants then reconvene in a general session. Subgroups' lists are posted and categories of common problems identified.

The second session starts with a total meeting and individual items are placed in the categories developed during the first session. New group alignments are formed on a functional basis, each guided by one of those who report to the top boss. For example, Manufacturing gets together under the leadership of its own boss, Marketing with its boss, and so on.

Instructions for each functional group are:

> 1. Go through the entire list and select three or four items which most affect you or your group. Determine what action your group will take on those and the timetable for beginning work on the problems. Be prepared to report this out to the total group.
> 2. Go through the list again and select those items to which you think top management should be giving highest priority. (Criteria for inclusion on this list is that your group can't deal with it.)
> 3. Since this is a large meeting, and all of us are off the job, develop a tactical plan for communicating what happened at this meeting to those who are not here. (Beckhard, 1969, p. 39)

Later, another general session is held in which each functional group indicates its three or four top-priority items and its plans for dealing with them. Beyond this, each functional group puts forward, for top management to consider, action problems that require higher-level handling. The top boss is expected to offer some commitment to action in response to these suggestions.

A follow-up program is built in before the session begins. Beckhard recommends a two-hour general meeting five or six weeks hence, in which each manager reports progress on the items on his or her list.

A third example also provided by Beckhard (1966) indicates that his strategy relied on participatory gathering, feedback, and action planning as the basic steps of change. One- to two-hour interviews, nondirective in character and ranging over a wide variety of topics, were conducted by the consultant with all general managers and central-staff department heads, and with a sample of lower-ranking personnel. Interviewees were informed as to why they were being interviewed, and what uses would be made of the information. They were assured that their anonymity would be preserved in findings or conclusions reached.

Findings from interviews were arranged under a series of headings.

1. Communications between president and line (or staff)
2. Line-staff communications
3. Location of decision making
4. Role clarification or confusion
5. Communications procedures

The interview results were then listed under these categories and color-coded to identify the category of respondent (i.e., general manager, staff head, staff assistant, and so on). (Beckhard, 1966, p. 9)

An off-site, three-day meeting attended by the president, general managers, and central-staff heads was begun by the consultant reviewing these interview findings. Some ninety items that needed attention had been identified. The group as a whole then spent most of the first day arranging items into a priority listing. Solutions for most problems, it was felt, must come from the group itself. As a change in pace and to provide alternate perspectives on some of their problems, the consultant introduced some ideas about organization communication the first night.

During the next two days, problem causes were diagnosed by tracing their origins to history, structure, personality, or the nature of the business. Practices, procedures, and attitudes that constituted barriers to progress were identified. Beyond the procedural steps the consultants had introduced, they also offered the group *process consultation.*

During the discussions, the consultants' contributions pinpointed how the group was functioning, guidelines for working on a problem, bringing conflict to the surface where it could be worked on, and systematic diagnosis of the causes of some of the problems that were identified. (Beckhard, 1969, p. 10)

Since only a start had been made, a second session was scheduled for a month later. During the intervening period the group lost ground in terms of being able to work effectively together, and it was necessary to spend a few hours reestablishing the earlier climate of trust. The manner in which this was accomplished is not indicated.

A major outcome was top management's increased awareness of the concerns of subordinate levels of management, and greater readiness to pay attention to these. A series of meetings similarly designed—information gathering, feedback and discussion, and action planning—was set up for two different sets of subordinate managers. An additional feature, however, was to bypass several layers of management and arrange for the president to receive feedback from the subordinate managers during the last half-day of the conference. The ground rule was that the president should indicate his thinking or decision regarding each issue presented.

Building such meetings into the organization's regular practices is one way to avoid the regressions that occur when people refocus on operating problems of the day-to-day sort. It also is a way of increasing the likelihood that further progress will be made.

> These meetings have proved to be continually effective and are held today on a semiannual or annual basis in all of the hotels. They have become a "way of life" for identifying current concerns, organizing work to deal with them, and planning action. The consultants' role has become that of "sponge" (collecting their data), "water faucet" (giving the information back to them), and "catalyst" (bringing all elements of management together). (Beckhard, 1966, p. 14)

Such a participatory basis momentarily takes problems out of the power/authority hierarchy, and then puts them back in at the point where authorization and approval for needed change is available.

Fordyce and Weil (1971) describe a catalytic mode of organization intervention for information gathering which also bypasses power/authority systems in a manner similar to the confrontation meeting. The arrangements are suitable for forty to a hundred representatives from large organizations and require a two-day meeting period. As in many such approaches, the consultant begins the sessions with a plea for candor. Then:

1. Participants are divided into subgroups of five or six individuals from different parts of the organization. The top group, however, remains intact, except for the absence of its top man.

2. An hour is provided each group to list changes in any area of functioning—objectives, procedures, policies, and so on—that would be organizationally and personally beneficial if they were to be brought about.

3. Using chart pads, each subgroup reports its list to the total group. Commentary for clarification is permitted but debate is discouraged.

4. The consultant studies the lists and identifies general categories that information fits into.

5. Each participant receives a copy of all item lists and of the categories. Then, in general session, all take part in classifying proposed changes into categories.

6. New subgroups, each led by a key manager and attended by those participants who are from his organization compartment, meet for three purposes:

   ■ To select the three or four items most important to them, and determine what action they will take and when they will start.

- To select the items to which they believe top management should assign highest priority.
- To plan for communicating the meeting results to others in the organization who are not in attendance.

7. Each subgroup reports its conclusions in general session with time for discussion provided. The top man now enters the situation and makes decisions, though possibly only in a preliminary or tentative way, regarding each item referred to him. Follow-up planning ends the meeting. (Fordyce and Weil, 1971, pp. 93–97)

This kind of development activity runs the risk of superficiality because (1) time is insufficient for deep analysis; (2) if participants have process problems in reaching agreement they are unable to get issues into the open for broader examination; and (3) the compulsion to compromise is high and can diffuse accountability so broadly that no one feels responsible for seeing to it that results are achieved. Accordingly, people become excited in the group sessions but later on feel let down because changes they expected to happen have not occurred.

A somewhat more formal intervention for organization diagnosis, referred to by Fordyce and Weil as a "manager's diagnostic team meeting series," provides for continuing efforts toward assessing effectiveness as contrasted with focusing on a particular problem needing change. The composition of the team includes:

- The top manager or a principal assistant.
- A consultant from outside the organization.
- A staff assistant or assistants with organization-wide responsibility, such as the personnel manager and the administrative or business manager.

This group may be enlarged from time to time, and it may bring in a needed specialist for particular purposes. Basically, however, it meets to pool information on organizational health and to recommend changes. Information gathering is by sensing, interviewing, questionnaires, and instruments. Findings from these sources lead to recommendations for action. The team may become the steering committee for a more extended development effort and thus become a more formal piece of apparatus in the power/authority system (Fordyce and Weil, 1971, pp. 91–92).

Culbert (1974) describes a "pocket of interest" approach to OD which is intended not so much to help the organization be more productive as to help employees be more mature, complete, and fulfilled as individuals. It seeks to redress the imbalance of power/authority between the unresponsive organization that has power and employees who have needs for greater self-realization but who lack the strength to bring it about. This catalytic intervention is consciousness raising for organization liberation in a manner comparable with consciousness raising for women's liberation.

The strategy is directed toward middle and lower layers of management and proceeds through a succession of five stages geared to help participants learn to express their personal needs more fully. Initial stages assist participants, who inter-act in support groups with other employees of like-minded interests, to convert vague feelings of uneasiness into a recognition of the discrepancies causing them— generally a divergence between what would best serve their self-interests and what the organization expects of them.

Later stages involve formulating operational recommendations for how individuals might redress perceived injustices created by the power/authority imbalance. This step may move in a confrontational direction. While power/authority is the focal issue, the formation of individuals into a support system, particularly to analytically explore causes, effects, and possible alternatives for change, is effective in increasing morale/cohesion for participants.

While acceptant and confrontational interventions are a part of the multistage approach, the underlying assumptions are mostly catalytic in character. As Culbert (1974) noted, "The basic problem in catalyzing self-management within the middle and lower levels lies in getting people the information they need to build a more comprehensive picture of reality and the support they need to act on it." While emotional aspects may be and are present, particularly in stage one, here again we see emphasis on empirical-rational data gathering as the essential condition for bringing about change.

Corporate Reorganization

Argyris (1967) describes the application of a catalytic model in the context of corporate reorganization. He initially questioned how executive management might reduce resistance to structural changes. Could this be done by involving management employees directly in the design and execution of the reorganization? A reorganization intervention was begun by involving managers from all levels in a diagnosis of the organization's existing problems. Groups composed of representatives from various functions but of about equal rank were assembled, with each group meeting twice for several hours. Brainstorming was used to identify problems, although solutions were not requested.

Information from these meetings was fed to a steering committee composed of all managerial ranks. Blind spots or inconsistencies in the findings were pinpointed and major questions that needed to be answered before the overall diagnosis could be considered valid were identified. Smaller task forces composed of personnel with relevant functional knowledge dealt with these questions. Based on task-force answers, the steering committee attempted to formulate a new organizational structure. Since vested-interest resistances to the reallocation of power/authority began to be encountered within the steering committee itself, an educational course was designed that helped members deal with intergroup rivalries, emotionality in groups, and hidden agendas.

Thereafter it was possible to prepare a final reorganization plan which was discussed fully with top executives and then with key representatives of all departments. Alternative suggestions were invited and given serious consideration. Further data gathering followed, using a questionnaire to critique the plan. New suggestions resulted. A final plan received top-management approval along with an implementation time schedule extending over the next seventeen months. Success is reported (Argyris, 1967, pp. 52–55).

This approach is based on felt needs and therefore does not consider possibilities outside participants' vision or experience at a given point in time. It accepts the organization's present products, people, and processes existing within already established traditions, precedents, and past practices. Catalyzing change within the boundaries of the here-and-now status quo apparently was an acceptable definition of the problem. Its major difference from the past was that it introduced a new *participatory* norm that reduced resistance to change.

Another organization restructuring intervention is described by Bourn (1973). It took place in a welfare organization in Great Britain.

> As with other Health Departments, the range and scope of the services provided by this Department had grown away from the historical conception of preventive medicine as concerned mainly with improving environmental hygiene, through inspection and regulation. It had moved toward a broader conception of preventive medicine which included the fostering of community health by the provision of a wide range of personal and social services, in such fields as school and child health, subnormality, mental health, nursing, midwifery, health visiting, speech therapy and child guidance. (Bourn, 1973, p. 114)

Allaway and Bourn were asked to lead problem-solving discussions using "Exploration Groups."

> The purpose of these Exploration Groups was to provide an opportunity for the staff of the Health Department to participate in an unstructured review of its aims, functions and organisation. The Exploration Groups were not expected to produce actual blueprints for change, but rather to consider whether change was needed and, if so, the broad outlines for a new system. (Bourn, 1973, p. 113)

A series of steps premised upon catalytic assumptions followed. Two Exploration Groups, composed exclusively of senior professional and administrative staff members, examined how best to restructure the organization to meet its present requirements. They were not asked to come up with detailed plans for organization.

The consultants accepted the status quo premise that emerging solutions could not threaten the historical status and position of either the professional or the administrative groups, and worked to prevent any intergroup or interpersonal confrontation of these vested interests.

> . . . The opening sessions of the Groups were slow and hesitant, the members feeling rather apprehensive about the whole idea of open and un-

structured discussion of such potentially sensitive issues. However, this anxiety did lead participants to question some of the hitherto accepted attitudes common in the Department.

... At first, when no-one could foresee the outcome of the review, the discussion was more concerned with protecting the established positions than with trying to envisage fresh approaches to the work of the Department.

... The majority difficulty was that, for any alternative form of organisation to be accepted, not only did it have to promise increased Departmental efficiency, but it also had to preserve the essential interests of all the major sections and groupings represented in the Exploration Groups. This explains why, as the ideas behind the Divisional Structure emerged from the discussion, the atmosphere changed from being negative and defensive to being positive and even enthusiastic.

... This change of heart seemed to be due to the changing balance of anticipated advantages accruing to the various sections of the staff. As their initial fears were allayed about the way in which the reorganisation was likely to affect their own interests, so the climate of the discussions changed from resisting to supporting change. (Bourn, 1973, pp. 120–21)

Eventually a reorganization was brought about which improved functioning without threatening rupture of existing relationships.

Of all groups in the Department, the Senior Medical Officers and the Deputy Medical Officer of Health gained the most from the reorganisation. The increased emphasis in the Department's work, on the provision of an integrated range of professional, social and medical services for the community, strengthened the professional basis of the authority of the senior medical staff, whilst their co-ordinating role in the new divisional structure increased the importance of their administrative work. Because they had previously felt unsure of their role as medical administrators, the senior medical staff were at first anxious about the idea of unstructured discussion. As they saw a new and enlarged role emerging for themselves, however, they began to favour the proposals for reorganisation. (Bourn, 1973, p. 122)

Significant limitations arising from this approach to organizational change involved hidden personal maneuverings beneath the cloak of "What's good for the Department had better be good for us."

In the case being reported here, each section and level of the staff contributed to the pool of information on which the ultimate decisions were based and almost all the staff who participated in the change programme were strongly committed in the proposed re-organisation. At the same time, the form of the re-organisation was influenced by sectional and group pressure. However, as staff co-operation was the key to making the Department more flexible in its response to community needs, the anxieties of the staff could not simply have been overriden or ignored. They had to be taken seriously, and carefully worked through in the Exploration Groups. However, because the Exploration Groups contained senior staff in a service organisation, the process of inter-group adjustment was not conducted explicitly. The only legitimate subject on the agenda was the effectiveness of the Department and its services; to have openly avowed sectional interests would have been unacceptable to the proclaimed sentiments of the members of the Groups, especially the members of the Professional Staff Group. At this senior level it was only considered legitimate to argue a case on whether or not it would advance the Department's interests. This meant that, because the true reasons for opposing change often could not be revealed, many of the arguments put forward were of a rather tangential and asked kind. Therefore, the process of adjustment and accommodation to sectional interests in the Department was disguised, a latent function hidden behind a discussion which, on the surface, appeared to be solely concerned with ways of improving the effectiveness of the Department. (Bourn, 1973, p. 123)

The rationale for using this kind of catalytic intervention, where the methodology of unstructured discussions is employed, is explained by the consultants in the following passage.

I would conclude that such unstructured discussion can ease the process of organisational change provided that (a) there is a minimum level of commitment to organisation goals, (b) the divisions of interests within the organisation are not so sharp that they cannot be resolved without recourse to sanctions, and (c) the discussion is not used merely to rubber-stamp decisions already taken at the top. If these conditions are satisfied, methods of this kind can make a genuine contribution to unfreezing bureaucratic structures and engendering a new spirit of commitment and cooperation. (Bourn, 1973, p. 125)

Beyond the elitist aspects of this approach, which limited the planning of change to the organization's top echelons and resulted in a strengthening of their power/authority, no efforts were made to

1. work through and resolve vested interests on the basis of insight;
2. involve those lower in the hierarchy so they could contribute their insights as well as derive increased convictions for implementing the change;
3. design an ideal model unencumbered by tradition, precedent, or past practice for what the organization could become as an effective health-delivery system.

A third example relates to resolving problems created by a "classical" merger of several school boards into a single school system. The so-called organization that resulted had all the classic behaviors and attitudes of any large-scale merger: mutual suspicion, cries for autonomy, generalized hostility to the head office, competition for resources, and a collection of principals who were clustered in groups that were somewhat isolated from each other and from the total system.

In this situation, the basic problem was, "How can we create an organic entity out of this collection of discrepancies?" (Duffin, Falusi, Lawrence, and Morton, 1973, p. 37)

The intervention was begun with interview-based problem perception. Once the problem had been identified, functional work groups of eight to ten participants were convened to study it and to design various possible solutions. Each of these was tried out in a role-playing session so that consequences could be dramatically versus literally experienced and evaluated. As participants did so, consultants focused participant awareness on their strategies of decision making, approaches to conflict resolution, communication barriers, trust levels, and so on. Sometimes the solutions that had been pretested during the learning phase were such that goals could be set for future "culture building." Suggested administrative and operational decisions were arrived at, or at the least, policies for follow-up or specific action proposals for problem solving were agreed upon.

The intervention is reported to have been successful. Since the problem involved a merger situation characterized by mutual suspicions, hostile feelings toward the head office, competition for resources, and so on, such an approach can help participants develop patterns of collaboration where none had previously existed. Reduction of a mutual ignorance produced by lack of a shared history can bring about cooperation of the kind needed to strengthen organization effectiveness. The new processes of information gathering and decision making may become embedded in the emerging system and increase its future efficacy.

Another set of interventions which also resulted in power/authority reorganization was premised on introducing wider participation to supplement the conventional exercise of power/authority. The intention was to quicken the rate of change. It took place in the State Department and is described by Levinson (1973, pp. 148–58). He recommended that a number of task forces be formed to look into various aspects of State Department functioning. The assumptions guiding this recommendation were:

1. Organization members want to manage themselves in a better manner.
2. Top management can promote internal progress but cannot create it.
3. Task forces, formed mostly on a diagonal-slice basis, can identify needed changes.
4. Once authorized by top management, these changes can be implemented.

These task forces are reported to have worked well. As seems necessary in most catalytic approaches, they had to be assured from time to time that openness was okay, they would not be punished, their findings would be paid attention to, and so on. Eventually the reports of thirteen task forces were integrated and a final report prepared for the top decision maker. Nearly all the findings were given approval. Then specific recommendations were grouped according to handling: (1) those to be implemented immediately; (2) and (3), those to be implemented within 90–180 days respectively; and (4) those needing further study. Results were unavailable when this approach was reported but progress was encouraging.

Levinson's description indicates that it is not necessary to (1) intervene in an educational way, i.e., help people see things differently or more clearly; or (2) aid managers in developing skills of teamwork, of conflict management, or of reducing communications deficiencies that prevent problem solving. Culture, as evidenced in traditions, precedents, and long-established practices, is deemed to be relatively insignificant in impeding change; and so, under that assumption, can be ignored. By contrast, the needed element provided by the intervention is widespread support through introduction of a participatory basis, making it legitimate for many members to offer suggestions for change.

Collateral Organization

Collateral organization as developed by Zand or Weisbord involves the same organization members engaging in two distinct problem-solving systems. A different kind of collateral organization, intended to produce organization change results, is employed by the Institute of Social Research at the University of Michigan.

The strategy is to identify a work unit from among many, or to create a synthetic group from representatives of others, and then set its operation up in a way that permits it to function independently of the "old" culture. Thereafter, it is helped to develop more effective problem-solving techniques, unhampered by the traditions, precedents, and practices of the past. It is collateral since it operates "alongside" other similar groups who remain free to continue their conventional practices. These similar groups may themselves incorporate changes they observe in the collateral group, or be "broken out" of conventional practices for similar change purposes at a later time.

One of these experiments has already shown promising results in the area of employee performance. Late in 1973, the Rushton Mining Company in Rushton, Pennsylvania, established a joint steering committee composed of representatives from both labor (United Mine Workers) and management. With the help of a consultant, Professor Eric Trist of the University of Pennsylvania, the members of this committee formulated a plan for an experimental work group with 27 volunteers from among the regular work force, 9 on each shift. All of the workers were put on top pay, and all were trained so that they could rotate to any job in the team. Each shift foreman has sole responsibility for the safety of his crew, and all responsibility for the production of coal rests with the crew itself. Grievances were also agreed to be the responsibility of the crew, and during the experiment workers have no recourse to either a foreman or the mine's grievance committee.

Although it is too early to draw definitive conclusions, the researchers report, there are hints that exciting changes are taking place in this experiment. As the men in the experimental work crews describe it, the incentives for working hard are very low in the rest of the mine. Most employees cannot wait to leave at the end of the day, and they are glad when the machinery breaks down so that they can get free time.

"We Mattered"

But in the experimental group: "Suddenly we felt that we mattered to somebody. Somebody trusted us. . . . When a machine busts down nowadays, most of the time we don't bother to call a maintenance man. We fix it ourselves, because, like I said, we feel it's as much ours as our car at home." Often the men linger around the locker room past quitting time to resolve any problems that have come up during the day and to discuss the next day's work.

In short, the mine is saving money in this area, even though the pay is higher. The experimental group of mine workers boasts lower supply costs, higher production rates, lower absenteeism, lower turnover, a record low accident rate, and the lowest number of safety violations in the mine's history. The ISR researchers caution that as yet they have no proof either that the system can be implemented in the rest of the mine or that these improvements will become stabilized over time. The staff will continue to monitor the experiment and collect and analyze data on all aspects of it in order to determine the full implications of these preliminary findings. (Lawler and Seashore, 1975, pp. 2, 6)

How the "Hawthorne" effect dilemma is handled once the project is over is not indicated, nor is the anticipated spread effect resulting from the creation of these demonstration models described.

School System Renovation

Derr (1972) provides a case study of an organization intervention premised on consultant information-gathering interviews followed by feedback and process consultation. Though the project was unsuccessful, the report is instructive, for the project's failure is related to the same survey-research weakness reported by Bowers and Taylor (1973). In both cases, the data tended to be dispersed by being (1) tabled or filed, (2) handed to subordinates with instructions to "Do something," or (3) used in a partisan manner.

The client organization consisted of fourteen special-service departments in a big-city school system. Consultants were to suggest ways to reorganize them so as to increase their effectiveness. Getting started was a problem. The school system was defensive about outsiders coming in at all, as evidenced by a two-month delay before an exploratory meeting between consultants and school officials took place. Finally information gathering, through twenty-four interviews, each from thirty to ninety minutes in length, got under way with interviewees representing a diagonal slice of the organization. Senior school officials had no active participation in or understanding of the consultants' intervention methods, and consultants were committed to confidentiality of interview sources.

This approach identified four perceived problem areas: (1) poor coordination, (2) inadequate communication, (3) poor adaptation, and (4) destructive power struggles. Information feedback sessions with department heads to verify the diagnosis and to achieve consensus about ways of improving the system took place, but certain key members declined to attend these feedback sessions. Instead, they requested that the consultant team prepare a written report. This was submitted and administrative action on restructuring took place, but it was outside the intent or recommendations of the consultants.

Original interviewees were reinterviewed a year later. Findings were that feedback sessions were a useless exercise, since no change in capacity to exert upward influence had occurred during the interim. The same problems remained unsolved.

Another intervention combining survey research and feedback, along with a catalytic version of process consultation, is reported by McElvaney and Miles (1971) in a change project also within a school setting. The interventions focused on two issues:

1. the ease and accuracy with which information flows throughout the organization
2. the character of problem solving within boss-subordinate relations, whether based on authority-obedience or collaboration, or to what degree it is based on each.

Information gathered from participants was expected to serve as a perception mirror in which they might see themselves more objectively. With improved perception they should be better able to determine what self-correcting actions needed to be taken.

The school involved first became interested when asked to provide survey information as a control unit in an experiment where other schools were the experimental units. The administration inquired as to the possibility of getting its own information back in summarized but uninterpreted form, so that school personnel could evaluate the information's meanings.

In the first session, when selected materials were fed back, with anonymity of interviewees protected, the information available was of too great a quantity to be worked over. The first feedback session was attended by eleven participants from the district, including the supervisory principal, his associate, three secondary and four elementary principals, and the district's business manager. It involved the following activities.

1. Examination and review of their information: analyzed initially item by item, then for themes, then broken down so that building-by-building comparisons could be made.

2. Problem identification by subgroups, leading to a number of agenda categories, such as district philosophy, communication issues, role confusion, quality of staff meetings, and so on.

3. Short lectures on pertinent concepts such as trust, decision making, and group operations.

4. Process critique—i.e., examination of problem-solving effectiveness among participants and their reactions to the session.

5. Assignment of particular problems to specific task forces for recommendations of improvement steps.

6. Next-step planning for future meetings, additional feedback of information to teachers on a building-by-building basis.

The catalytic character of the interventions related to process consultation can clearly be seen in the following participant description of one of the two consultants. His procedural contributions are emphasized:

> ... he's observant; he steps in and quizzes us on what we mean. He gets things straight. He's a catalyst between the administrators and the principals ... he's made his presence necessary for progress' sake. He's done a fine job of directing and redirecting the group's thinking toward specific goals. (McElvaney and Miles, 1971, p. 132)

As reported by the consultants, top administrators made progress in operating more effectively together: facing negative feelings promoted greater openness among them; intergroup suspicions were reduced; some improvement in communication was noted; policy clarification resulted. The authors' final conclusion provides a basis for assessing impact.

> ... although constructive change has often seemed to be painfully slow, the authors feel it highly probable that basic methods of functioning have changed for the better and that the health of the district will continue to improve. (McElvaney and Miles, 1971, p. 137)

LARGER SOCIAL SYSTEM (E₅)

Many larger-social-system interventions involve citizen-clients near or beneath the poverty line, and much of the assistance provided entails the consultant serving as a rallying point for group formation. He or she works at the level of felt needs, aiding participants to make progress within their status quo expectations. In addition to the more routine methods of catalytic consulting, he or she frequently introduces social mechanisms that provide participants with new competency-building experiences.

Problems cropping up within larger social systems often are associated with lack of opportunity or lack of skills for exercising power/authority over matters most citizens expect to be able to control. Several examples of catalytic interventions in the focal-issue area of power/authority reveal different aspects of the problem, and indicate how community structures can be designed to provide people, who themselves are unskilled or inexperienced in exercising authority, with access to the skills essential for doing so.

Community Action

Zurcher's (1970) description of an intervention permits evaluation of the catalytic assumptions underlying certain activities of the Topeka Office of Economic Opportunity. A city-wide committee, formed to design a community-action program, eventually incorporated as "The Economic Opportunity Board of Shawnee County, Kansas, Inc." Its charter provided that at least one-third of the board's membership would be composed of elected representatives of the poor, themselves selected from chairmen and vice-chairmen of a larger number of local Target Neighborhood Committees. While on the one hand this particular structure was used to implement the Economic Opportunity Act, it was also designed to provide an "experience in social process" for poverty-neighborhood participants. Zurcher points out that the design required the board and its other components to engage in "equal status" pursuit of mutual goals. It was intended to break down stereotypes, encourage communication and broader understanding, and engender social change (Zurcher, 1970, pp. 17–19). By participating as board members the neighborhood people might learn to expand their social roles and skills, and thereby acquire more capacity for influencing community decisions affecting their lives.

Therapeutic Community

Mental hospitals constitute a living and treatment social structure that differs from many public institutions, particularly in terms of the diagnosed sicknesses of the inmates. Jones (1952, 1973) conceived the idea that a mental hospital could nonetheless be transformed from a doctor-oriented social system into a community of "members." The hospital-as-community would thereby be made more therapeutic because the basic shift in power/authority between staff and patients would call for more mature and reality-oriented behavior on the part of the latter. Certain responsibilities for the hospital's well-functioning were to be placed on patients' shoulders —not completely, but to a significantly larger degree than in mental hospitals of the past.

Jones reviews the underlying strategy of this kind of intervention:

> The social structure of a therapeutic community is characteristically different from the more traditional hospital ward or decentralized unit. The whole extended community of staff, patients, and their relatives is involved, in varying degrees, in treatment and administration. The extent to which this is practicable or desirable of course depends on many

things, for example, the attitude of the leader and the other staff, the type
of patients being treated, and the sanctions afforded by higher authority.
The emphasis on free communication both within and between staff and
patient groups and on permissive attitudes which encourage free expression of feeling implies a democratic, egalitarian rather than a traditional
hierarchical social organization.

In a therapeutic community, staff and patient roles and role-relationships
are the subject of a frequent examination and discussion. The aim of this
is to increase the effectiveness of roles and sharpen the community's
perception of them. For example, it may be felt that a nurse's role is more
effective if it is made less formal, and if she therefore ceases to wear
uniform. It may take many hours of discussion to decide that, say, a nurse
only feels secure enough to discard uniform when she has been on the
ward for an average of four months. To share this discussion with the
patients is to increase their awareness of the difficulties of the nurse's
role and may in time modify their relationship to her. The aim is to achieve
sufficient flexibility of role behaviour so that at any one time it can reflect
the expectations and needs of both staff and patients collectively.

An essential feature of the organization of a therapeutic community is the
daily community meeting. By a community meeting, we mean a meeting
of the entire patient and staff population of a particular unit or section.
We have found it practicable to hold meetings of this kind with as many
as 80 patients and up to 30 staff; we think that the upper limit for the establishment of a therapeutic community in the sense that the term is used
here is around 100 patients. . . . (Jones, 1973, pp. 263–64)

The above comments depict a catalytic strategy for increasing perceptual objectivity
through improved information gathering and interpretation, based primarily on
critique and feedback to the entire community of ongoing happenings.

The next selection, also from Jones, describes an increase in the extent of patient participation through an even more basic shift in power/authority relationships.
Though the approach remains catalytic, albeit with a readiness to shift to a prescriptive mode when required, it places patients in potential "confronting" kinds of relationships with one another and with staff as well.

Another approach which has been widely tried is that of patient government or patient councils. The function of these ward councils varies con-
siderably from hospital to hospital, but in the main they are limited to the
handling of practical ward details, such as privileges, arrangements for
ward cleaning, rosters, and so on. Nevertheless, through time they tend
to take on increasing responsibilities. In our opinion, they should not assume too much responsibility unaided and should be supervised by staff
and the content of their discussions fed back to the community meetings.
Much good can come from the development of patient responsibility skill-

fully supervised, but it would be foolish to assume that this kind of development can occur without considerable conflict. . . .

This principle of expanding the role of patient to include that of therapist is, I think, a fundamental one in community treatment procedure. It can of course be mistakenly seen as the handing over of ultimate responsibility to the patients, which, in my opinion, is neither practicable nor desirable. What one wishes to do is to give patients that degree of responsibility which is compatible with their capacity at any one time. In no sense do the staff or the doctor in charge relinquish their ultimate authority, which merely remains latent and can be invoked when necessary. The application of this more flexible principle calls for considerable experience and skill. As an example, a community may be functioning fairly smoothly and effectively and the patients may be carrying a considerable amount of responsibility. Then, on a particular day, four or five of the most responsible and successfully treated members leave to be replaced by four or five new patients who may be in a state of considerable disorganization. The loss of patient leadership within the ward and the effect of the disturbed newcomers may be such that the ward functioning is materially altered for the worse, and at this point, the staff have to step in and play a more active and controlling role than they were previously doing. This is fundamentally similar to what happens in individual or group treatment sessions when ego strength fails or anxiety level rises and the therapist feels it necessary to be largely supportive for a time.

The sort of patient responsibility I am considering here is of a higher order than one usually understands by the term "patient government." Patient government is usually restricted to decisions on relatively minor matters of ward organization and activities. What I have in mind is the sharing of fairly major decisions with the staff, involving such matters as interpersonal problems, difficulties in staff-patient relationships, the handling of acting-out behaviour, the discharge of patients, or their transfer to other wards, and the choice of disciplinary action when deviant behaviour occurs. This sharing of serious responsibility with the staff is one of the most effective ways of overcoming the lack of confidence, the low self-estimate and the over-dependency which all too frequently characterizes the patient in the psychiatric hospital. The fostering of responsibility can also be extended to the patients' work roles, and if the hospital can undertake productive work for the community the range and scope of such roles is greatly enhanced: one can have patient foremen, timekeepers, etc. (Jones, 1973, pp. 267–69)

The possibility of effecting such a shift in the power/authority balance is limited by the readiness of hospital staff to share responsibility for the care of the patient population, and so on. This is analogous in some respects to the situation described by Zurcher (1970) in which a "poverty warrior" consultant intervened to promote information and power-sharing among city, business, and neighborhood leaders during the process of community development.

Dilemmas of Industrial Philosophy

The creation of social awareness through drama is not limited to psychodrama or other improvisation techniques. Formal drama also has been used for catalytic intervention purposes.

An example of this is provided by Dvoretsky, a Russian playwright whose *Calling in an Outsider* focused widespread attention on a basic dilemma of modern Soviet society. The play explores the assumption that concern for production and concern for people necessarily conflict in modern technological society.

The central character of the play, Cheshkov, is a manager called in to improve the productivity of a factory department. Its present unsatisfactory state is largely due to "people who are living in the traditions of their former reputation, which has imperceptibly developed into complacency and indulgency in their working relations" (Lvova, 1973, p. 171). Cheshkov uses an authority-obedience (9,1) managerial style in his attempt to turn the pleasant, easygoing (1,9) factory culture around. He enforces rigid discipline, demands fulfillment of production plans, and produces deep conflicts and tensions by trying to shift tradition in this arbitrary manner. Although Cheshkov "wins" in the end, his victory follows a climax in which most of his engineer and foreman subordinates resign.

The play, a smash hit in several of the Soviet Union's main cities, by its nature invites members of the audience to identify either with Cheshkov or with the engineers and foremen—that is, to respond either to efficiency values or to cherished traditions. Lvova (1973, p. 172) reports that *Calling in an Outsider* has been the subject of numerous conferences of theatergoers, with factory workers, engineers and students actively participating. Thus it is having a catalyzing effect on Soviet society by facilitating a widespread dialogue regarding alternative ways of achieving production through people.

Inter-Nation Problem Solving

While he has not described his intervention strategies in any detail, evidence at hand suggests that Kissinger's Middle East efforts, seeking to resolve differences between Egypt and other Arabian states on the one hand, and Israel on the other, at least up to the breakdown in the discussions that occurred in March 1975, were almost entirely *catalytic* in character.

His basic strategy involved assisting each side in clarifying its positions and options and then serving as a personal go-between, helping the other side digest the data reported and then recycling. Seeking to resolve problems in this step-by-step way, he tried to find areas of agreement on the easiest items first, hoping the nations would be able to grapple with the more difficult issues thereafter.

That prescriptions were not involved is demonstrated in the postbreakdown fears of Israel's Foreign Minister, Yigal Allon, who cautioned the United States against offering its own peace plan. "Such a prescription," he said on June 19, 1975, "would create a pressure-cooker atmosphere that could destroy progress." *

---

* "Allon Warns U.S. Not to Offer a Peace Plan for Negotiations," *The International Herald Tribune,* 19 June 1975.

The absence of confrontational interventions is demonstrated by the fact that the parties to the disagreements were never in direct face-to-face contact, and, beyond that, the parties themselves have indicated that Kissinger served each side as a reliable reporter when meeting with the other. There are no indications that his approach involved theory-based interventions. While there may have been acceptant kinds of active listening, these certainly were of a secondary character.

Many believe that these catalytic interventions have proven too weak to dislodge either side from fixed positions. The result is a step-up of pressure on both sides to face one another in a Geneva type of confrontation peace conference. Stepped up progress premised on third party prescriptions and other power pressure tactics also is in the wind.

IMPLICATIONS

In each of the larger-social-system examples, the intervention's success depended on shifting perceptions toward *who* held power/authority as well as toward how it could be used. Catalytic interventions assist people in becoming aware of and coping with power/authority problems.

In a laboratory or industrial chemical process the effect of some particular catalytic agent is predetermined by laws that without exception govern the interaction between catalyst and units of change. In human affairs, however, simple cause-effect deterministic processes, if they operate at all, are not readily discernible to the catalytic consultant as he or she interacts with a client—hence the almost infinitely greater possibility of unpredicted and/or unknown effects of consultant interventions. Given this situation, it is understandable that the catalytic consultant does not employ power/authority as a mode of operating, but instead tries to work within the client's power/authority system so as to aid it to change itself.

A typically low-key way of achieving this is to create conditions in which previously unrecognized aspects of the power/authority focal issue are brought to light. Most often this is accomplished by assembling and presenting pertinent information —as when subordinates who have been unwilling to confront their boss directly regarding his use of power/authority are enabled to deliver this information by means of an anonymous-response survey tabulation, no longer restrained by fear of reprisals.

REFERENCES

Alderfer, C. P. "A Video Assist to Student-Faculty Dialogue on Teaching and Learning." *Social Change* 3, no. 2 (1973): 6–8.

Argyris, C. "Today's Problems with Tomorrow's Organizations." *Journal of Management Studies* 4, no. 1 (1967): 31–55.

Baumgartel, H. "Using Employee Questionnaire Results for Improving Organizations." *Kansas Business Review* 12, no. 12 (1959): 2–6.

Bavelas, A., and A. Strauss. "Group Dynamics and Intergroup Relations." Abridged from W. F. Whyte *et al., Money and motivation,* pp. 91–94. Copyright © 1955 by Harper & Row, Publishers, Inc. By permission of the publishers.

Beckhard, R. "An Organization Improvement Program in a Decentralized Organization." Reproduced by special permission from *Journal of Applied Behavioral Science* 2, no. 1 (1966): 3–25.

Beckhard, R. *Organization Development: Strategies and Models.* Reading, Mass.: Addison-Wesley, 1969. Reprinted by permission.

Bennis, W. G. *Organization Development: Its Nature, Origins, and Prospects.* Reading, Mass.: Addison-Wesley, 1969. Reprinted by permission.

Bennis, W. G., and P. E. Slater. *The Temporary Society.* New York: Harper & Row, 1968.

Bourn, C. J. "Planned Change in Welfare Organisation." *Human Relations* 26, no. 1 (1973): 113–26. Reprinted by permission of Plenum Publishing Company, London, England.

Bowers, G., and J. Taylor. "Survey of Organizations." As reported in University of Michigan Institute for Social Research *Newsletter,* Spring-Summer 1973, pp. 3, 6.

Culbert, S. A. *The Organization Trap and How to Get Out of It.* New York: Basic Books, 1974.

Daw, R. W., and N. L. Gage. "Effect of Feedback from Teachers to Principals." *Journal of Educational Psychology* 58, no. 3 (1967): 181–88.

Derr, C. B. "Organization Development in One Large Urban School System." *Education and Urban Society* 4 (1972): 403–19.

Dinkmeyer, D., and J. Carlson. *Consulting: Facilitating Human Potential and Change Process.* Columbus, Ohio: Merrill, 1973. Reprinted by permission.

Duffin, R., A. Falusi, P. Lawrence, and R. Morton. "Increasing Organizational Effectiveness." Reproduced by special permission from *Training and Development Journal* 27, no. 4 (1973): 37–46. Copyright 1973 by the American Society for Training and Development, Inc.

Fordyce, J. K., and R. Weil. *Managing with People.* Reading, Mass.: Addison-Wesley, 1971. Reprinted by permission.

Harvey, J. B., and C. R. Boettger. "Improving Communication within a Managerial Workgroup." *Journal of Applied Behavioral Science* 7, no. 2 (1971): 164–79. Reprinted by permission.

Jaques, E. "Interpretive Group Discussion as a Method of Facilitating Social Change: A Progress Report on the Use of Group Methods in the Investigation and Resolution of Social Problems." *Human Relations* 1, no. 4 (1948): 533–49.

Jones, M. *Social Psychiatry: A Study of Therapeutic Communities.* London: Tavistock, 1952.

Jones, M. "The Therapeutic Community." In G. and B. Stanford, eds., *Strangers to Themselves.* New York: Bantam Pathfinder Editions, 1973, pp. 263–69. Reprinted by permission.

Kuriloff, A. H., and S. Atkins. "T-Group for a Work Team." Reproduced by special permission from *Journal of Applied Behavioral Science* 2, no. 1 (1966): 63–93.

Lawler, E., and S. Seashore. "Joint Planning Teams Improve Management." As reported in *ISR Newsletter* 3, no. 3 (1975): 2, 6.

Levinson, H. *The Great Jackass Fallacy*. Cambridge, Mass.: Harvard University Press, 1973.

Lvova, G. "The Human Element in the Scientific and Technical Revolution." *Social Sciences* 42, no. 12 (1973): 171–83.

McElvaney, C. T., and M. B. Miles. "Using Survey Feedback and Consultation." In R. A. Schmuck and M. B. Miles, eds., *Organization Development in Schools*. Palo Alto, Cal.: National Press Books, 1971, pp. 113–38.

Miles, M. B. "On Temporary Systems." In M. B. Miles, ed., *Innovation in Education*. New York: Columbia University, 1964, pp. 437–92.

Varney, G. H., and J. Lasher. "Surveys and Feedback as a Means of Organization Diagnosis and Change." In Thomas H. Patten, Jr., ed., *OD—Emerging Dimensions and Concepts*. Washington, D.C.: American Society for Training and Development, 1973, pp. 75–82.

Weisbord, M. R., H. Lamb, and A. Drexler. *Improving Police Department Management through Problem-Solving Task Forces: A Case Study in Organization Development*. Reading, Mass.: Addison-Wesley, 1974. Reprinted by permission.

Zand, D. E. "Collateral Organization: A New Change Strategy." Reproduced by special permission from *Journal of Applied Behavioral Science* 10, no. 1 (1974): 63–89.

Zurcher, L. A. *Poverty Warriors: A Human Experience of Planned Social Intervention*. Austin, Texas: The University of Texas Press, 1970.

CATALYTIC INTERVENTIONS

10

MORALE / COHESION

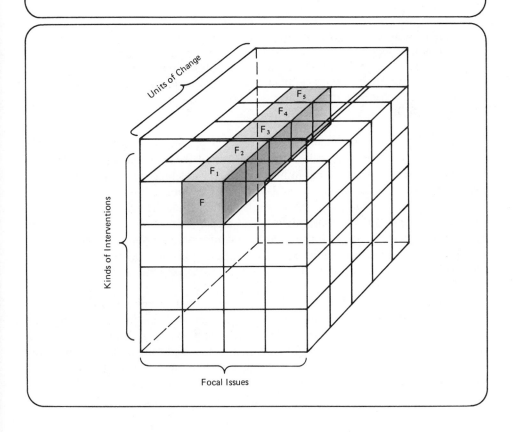

In contrast to the acceptant consultant, the catalytic consultant is more likely to take an active role in suggesting and recommending various approaches the client can try in order to alleviate his or her distress.

INDIVIDUAL (F_1)

The catalytic mode of intervening with an individual client is described in the next example, in which the consultant helps the client gather her own information and teaches the client to observe herself as she goes about her work. Consultant and client then discuss the client's self-observations, with the consultant aiding the client to crystallize her perceptions and to generalize from them as to how she might alter her behavior.

This facet of the catalytic approach is illustrated in a case study introduced earlier, in Chapter 4. The intervention involved Miss Jones, the ward nurse who was frustrated and demoralized. Discussions of a cathartic character helped bolster Miss Jones' morale and she gained relief from her tensions and frustrations by talking out her feelings. The consultant then seemed to shift to a catalytic mode: he proposed that she step up her information gathering by being more observant of what was going on as she participated in ward activities.

> Instead of focusing only on your failures, your difficulty in functioning, your poor relations with patients and staff, and your discomfort on the ward, you might be able to take a little different approach. In addition to participating on the ward with low morale, you might also become an observer of this low morale and see how it works. (Schwartz and Will, 1961, p. 578)

Miss Jones at first had difficulty in becoming a participant observer of her own activities. As the consultant raised questions about the experiences she related to him, though, she gradually came to have less intense feelings about her low morale. She started to see, reflect upon, and examine the connections between her low morale, the ward situation, and her relations with patients. The catalytic tone of the intervention suggested that she might adopt an *attitude of inquiry* toward herself and her relations with others through gathering information about what actually was taking place in a given situation. By seeing things in this new perspective she might be enabled to reduce her subjective reactions and to respond more objectively to events.

Additional aspects of the discussions were devoted to helping Miss Jones develop a new outlook on the dynamics of her interpersonal relationships. Consultant and client-nurse explored in depth the nurse's interactions with patients and colleagues, and sought to identify alternative action possibilities that might prove more constructive. In line with the earlier cathartic interventions, she was also encouraged to express freely her feelings about ward situations.

This example demonstrates the use of more than one type of intervention in the same consultation. Cathartic interventions paved the way for catalytic interventions by first dealing with emotional blockages—cathartic intervention *alone* might have been insufficient to bring about the changes that were actually achieved. The authors sum up their conclusions as to the effect of these catalytic interventions on Miss Jones.

> She had been preoccupied, on the one hand, with escaping from the situation of low morale and, on the other hand, with altering it by pulling herself up by her bootstraps. Failing to do either, she continued to feel she was a failure. In the discussion, she changed her goals to that of learning about the ways in which her low morale developed and of understanding the interpersonal processes constituting it. With this new perspective she focused less of her attention on her failure in the ward situation and more on the possibility of deriving something positive from a situation which up to this point had appeared to her as exclusively negative. (Schwartz and Will, 1961, pp. 578–79)

A strength of the participant-observer approach to information gathering is that it helps the client concentrate on situational "facts" and on ways to examine and evaluate behavior that previously may have gone unnoticed. The consultant remains detached from the client's problem but the catalytic intervention sets up a basis for here-and-now self-consultation. Responsibility for diagnosis is retained by the client.

On-the-job perceptions of one's own behavior are inescapably limited by biases and distortions, but these are more likely to go unchecked by a catalytic intervention than by, for example, a confrontational approach. Therefore, gains that could be made if such distortions were eliminated probably will not be fully realized under catalytic intervention unless increased self-knowledge is "fully" available from self-observation and persistent blind spots cleared up.

GROUP (F₂)

When a group loses its sense of esprit de corps, frequently its members begin dispersing until the group collapses. An exception is when the group is part of a larger entity and is held together by virtue of common organization membership, with replacement members being recruited as others leave. Examples of such groups are found in the intergroup or organization sections that follow.

INTERGROUP (F₃)

When groups that must interact feel positively toward one another, needed cooperation is often forthcoming; but when feelings are antagonistic, each group is likely to feel threatened by the other and withhold the kind of support needed to get the job done.

Headquarters versus Field

One example provided by Golembiewski and Blumberg (1967) involved a divisional management's efforts to bring about operational improvements—in particular, to reduce or even eliminate "we-they" anticohesion feelings between the headquarters organization and the field sales force. Forty-six participants from a large drug company took part in three days of intervention meetings.

A "cafeteria" selection procedure was used for identifying the two sides in any existing intergroup problem relationship, and exchanges were arranged on a "taxi dance" basis. For example, if Group A wanted to have an exchange with Group B, Group A was to get Group B's agreement to do so. Then their exchange was "booked." The meeting took place if a ninety-minute time slot was available.

Table 10.1

A Sample 3-D Image by One Regional Aggregate* with *Promotion* as the Relevant Other

---

A. How members of regional aggregate I see themselves in relation to promotion department

1. Circumvented	7. Production
2. Manipulated	8. Instrument of their success
3. Receiving benefits of their efforts	9. Have never taken us into their
4. Nonparticipating	confidence in admitting that a
(relatively)	promotion "bombed"
5. Defensive	10. The field would like to help, but must be
6. Used	a two-way street

B. How members of regional aggregate I feel promotion department sees them

1. Insensitive to corporate needs	6. As lacking understanding about their
2. Noncommunicative upwards, as	sales objectives
holding back ideas and suggestions	7. Belligerent
3. Productive in field saleswork	8. Overly independent operators
4. Naive about the promotion side of	9. Not qualified to evaluate the promotions
business	sent to us
5. Unappreciative of promotion efforts	10. Honest in opinions

C. How members of regional aggregate I characterize promotion department

1. Autocratic	8. Naive
2. Productive	9. Progressive in promotion philosophy and
3. Unappreciative of field efforts	programs
4. Competent with "things" but not	10. Overly competitive within own
"people"	department
5. Industrious	11. Plagiarists who take field ideas but do
6. Inflexible	not always give credit
7. Unrealistic	

Source: Golembiewski and Blumberg, 1967, p. 534.

* One of three field-division-manager groups formed for learning purposes during the three-day experience.

Among the forty-six participants many intergroup conflict combinations that could be approached in this manner were possible. The consultants attempted to provide periods for intergroup representatives of any two groups who shared some degree of interdependence in their relationship to come together for discussions. Before meeting the other side, each group in private created the images it wanted to exchange. Although an exchange period of up to ninety minutes may not be sufficient for exploring the historical background or feelings associated with a problem in any significant depth, or for planning developmental steps, it may be enough time to communicate a certain amount of data and give participants a sense of the issues.

The strategy used to deal with the core issues identified during the previous two days of intergroup exchanges was to design implementing steps for solving these recurrent problems. Using a self-selecting or cafeteria basis for organizing the effort, participants signed up to be members of whichever core group they felt themselves most interested in or concerned about. An intervention such as this can be expected to loosen up previously clogged communication channels as well as to pinpoint a few problems that participants can solve on their own initiative. It is unlikely, however, that the many causes of intergroup problems embedded within the status quo system itself will be affected.

Characteristic of the catalytic approach is the fact that global statements rather than operationally descriptive comments were formulated in the images each group drew up. Their rationale for being general rather than specific follows.

> In general, restraints against communicating "dangerous materials" still are powerful. And the very writing-up of a global 3-D Image tends to encourage less defensiveness than, for example, a verbal and necessarily linear statement of the same content. (Golembiewski and Blumberg, 1967, p. 545)

In comparison with a confrontational approach, where the objective is to provide opportunities for defensiveness to surface in order to study and work through underlying causes, the catalytic approach facilitates communication within the status quo. This is evidenced by the parallel character of consultant-originated strategies for conducting these intergroup sessions:

- a cafeteria-selection basis so that those whose intergroup situations are "ruptured," and who may not wish to come to terms with their problems, can avoid doing so;

- a short duration, such as ninety minutes, which may be enough to get "big" images presented, but not nearly enough to work through their meanings in any detail, and certainly insufficient for operational problem solving;

- core groups for problem analysis, again composed on a cafeteria basis for self-selection, rather than intact real-life groups, composed of *all* of those who have a vested interest in the outcome of such deliberations.

The consultants called the procedure used a "confrontation" meeting, but "confrontation" translates as "catalytic" when a closer examination is made of the intervention strategies employed. Nonetheless, according to the clinical description of what transpired, an unforeseen "confrontation in reverse" did occur when the client challenged the consultants to explain or justify the values and assumptions underlying their interventions. These other-way confrontations were prompted by the managers' feelings that they had been offended by the consultants. They confronted the consultants spontaneously in a way that was not a calculated feature of the design.

Administration versus Staff

Another consultant-suggested intergroup image exchange for perceptual clarification, also premised on the catalytic intervention mode, is provided by Argyris and Bennis. The intended effect of the exchange was to reduce distrust rather than solve problem issues. Bennis provides a background of the State Department in the 1960s at the time this intervention was carried out.

> Among the recent problems facing the U.S. Department of State was unproductive divisiveness between the Foreign Service officers, sometimes referred to as "the club" or "the guild" and the administrative staff of State. The stereotyping and mutual distrust, if not downright hostility, blocked communication and reduced effectiveness enormously, for each "side" perceived the other as more threatening than a realistic overseas enemy. (Bennis, 1969, p. 4)

Rather than intact groups of top-echelon administrative and Foreign Service officers, a representative sample of officials from each of the two categories was divided into two subgroups. These two aggregates were assigned separate rooms in which to develop words and phrases that would summarize their answers to three questions:

1. What qualities best describe our group?
2. What qualities best describe the other group?
3. What qualities do we predict the other group would assign to us?

Partial results are listed below. "Prediction of the others' perceptions of us" lists are omitted.

The Foreign Service Officers saw themselves as:
1. Reflective
2. Qualitative
3. Humanistic, subjective
4. Cultural, broad interests
5. Generalizers
6. Intercultural sensitivity
7. Detached from personal conflicts

The Administrative Officers saw the Foreign Service Officers as:

1. Masked, isolated
2. Resourceful, serious
3. Respected
4. Inclined to stability
5. Dedicated to job
6. Necessary
7. Externally oriented
8. Cautious
9. Rational
10. Surrounded by mystique
11. Manipulative
12. Defensive

The Administrative Officers saw themselves as:

1. Decisive, guts
2. Resourceful, adaptive
3. Pragmatic
4. Service-oriented
5. Able to get along
6. Receptive to change
7. Dedicated to job
8. Misunderstood
9. Useful
10. Modest! [added by the individual doing the presenting]

The Foreign Service Officers saw the Administrative Officers as:

1. Doers and implementers
2. Quantitative
3. Decisive and forceful
4. Noncultural
5. Limited goals
6. Jealous of us
7. Interested in form more than substance
8. Wave of the future! [Exclamation mark theirs]
9. Drones but necessary evils

(Bennis, 1969, p. 4)

After these lists were exchanged the groups discussed them, each questioning the other with respect to what had been "seen." The discussion was intense, high-pitched, noisy, argumentative, good-humored, and finally, several hours later, thoughtful. The consultants concluded that "each side moved to a position where they at least understood the other side's point of view" (Bennis, 1969, pp. 4–6).

Many of the features of the Golembiewski-Blumberg example are duplicated in the Bennis exchange. This intergroup image exchange is of the catalytic character for several reasons. First, the participants were *representative* rather than intact or *organic* groups. As such they were in no position to authorize change, even if they had wanted to do so. Then, too, the instructions called for each group to indicate qualities rather than to formulate line-and-verse operational statements. Participants produced their images in private, thus ensuring the anonymity of individual contributions. As mentioned earlier, global, abstract generalizations instead of specific statements were formulated. A period was provided for each group to be questioned by the other group with respect to reported perceptions, producing accusations and counteraccusations of a win-lose polarized sort. Discussions apparently involved some confrontational attack-counterattack in the sense that they were high-pitched and argumentative. But resolutions of the sort that a truly confrontational intergroup experience might be expected to produce could not have occurred given the description provided. Since neither side was an intact group, no resolution of differences in any practical sense could be achieved.

Summary

The image-exchange approach to resolving morale/cohesion issues is a catalytic intervention designed to help groups better understand each other and clarify existing misperceptions. If the differences are sharp or the feelings keenly antagonistic it can prove difficult to move via this procedure into a problem-solving posture.

ORGANIZATION (F_4)

When morale/cohesion difficulties permeate an entire organization, more massive, long-term intervention strategies sometimes are called for.

The introduction of change by edict, even though perhaps justified by advancing technology, can have a demoralizing effect on organization members because it breaks up long-established patterns of work, brings an end to friendships, and so on. A consultant-based approach for improving working-group arrangements while strengthening productivity in conjunction with the introduction of complex machinery, referred to as a *socio-technical system intervention,* is reported by Trist and Bamforth (1951). Besides finding that the complex system was ineffective in terms of the technology designers' expectations, Trist and Bamforth concluded that the unintegrated three-shift system of work, which had replaced small-group "hand-got" arrangements, had shattered cohesion and mutual support among workers and was inducing unnecessary emotional strain. Through their study of the work itself—a coal mining operation—and the social relations among workers that the machinery "created," they were influential in bringing about alternative combinations of technical and social arrangements which increased productivity while facilitating cohesion and esprit de corps.

Data gathering and analysis took place over a two-year period. During the information-gathering phase, repeated discussions and interviews were conducted with twenty or so key informants who represented a cross section of occupational roles and had wide and varied experience in the industry. Similar discussions occurred on the management side, with all grades of supervisors and managers up to the area level represented. Other informants included three psychiatrists acquainted with miners' physical and emotional health problems. The work of Trist and Bamforth appears to have been of a catalytic character in that a consensus as to what constitutes a "better socio-technical system" gradually emerged as the detailed analysis took shape. There is no evidence in the report of personal interventions in the workplace by Trist and Bamforth. Their report itself *was* the intervention, bringing the morale/cohesion issue to the awareness of mine managers and engineers whose previous focus had more or less concentrated exclusively on maintaining the technical system's status quo. They had been unaware of the focal sources of ineffectiveness and "poisoned" morale inherent in the accompanying social organization of the longwall method. By the time the report was published, presumably this archetype of sociotechnical analysis had already circulated among upper levels of the client's hierarchy. At all events, in their conclusions (Trist and Bamforth, 1951, pp. 37–38), the authors comment briefly on the first changes being tried in the direction of developing better morale/cohesion through revised shift arrangements, mechanization alternatives that stressed the value of the strongly knit primary work group, and so on.

LARGER SOCIAL SYSTEM (F₅)

One of the more serious problems within larger social systems is the lack of community—morale/cohesion is at a low ebb, and citizens often seem unwilling or unable to make the contacts essential for producing a neighborhood life. Several different kinds of catalytic interventions are used to establish or restore community among neighbors. These are "enabling" interventions that recognize community participation can only arise when people want to take part on a free and voluntary basis—coercion has no place here in inducing change.

Community Development

"Spontaneous" community development, particularly when involving people with minimal education and little economic security, has been slow starting and not particularly successful in the few attempts reported. Robbins (1973) reports one such intervention that proved an effective approach to the problem in terms of the enthusiasm it generated.

The assumptions underlying this intervention are that it must

1. be based on felt needs of participants;
2. readily shift from concentrating on a planned content to dealing with an immediately sensed need that had previously not been recognized;
3. be done in an informal, give-and-take way that reduces the social distance between experts and students;

4. be characterized by friendly relations supported and maintained by informal social contacts, such as home visiting by the consultant to eat and be social with participants, and so on.

On this basis, an intervention that began with extensive interviews, particularly with opinion leaders, to identify what participants wanted, led to the following list of identified community problems.

1. A feeling of isolation and despair.
2. Poorly organized community; ineffective leadership.
3. Poor communication among the people; a lack of trust and much conflict.
4. Little confidence in their ability to influence the community at large.
5. A negative and unrealistic self-concept.

In response to these data, the consultant drew up a list of "desired outcomes" of a leadership training program he was requested to design and conduct. Included was the need within the community for its members to

1. Have more self-confidence.
2. Have a more realistic self-concept.
3. Develop and use leadership skills.
4. Be effective communicators; both in formal and informal settings.
5. Function effectively in organizational structures. (Robbins, 1973, p. 16)

Rather than establish a rigid course structure, the consultants decided to have available for presentation at any one session a number of prepared activities. Whenever participants mentioned a particular problem, relating to some aspect of community leadership presently causing them difficulty, the consultants could introduce a requisite training activity to which that day's session would be devoted. The activities were designed to give participants an improved basis of confidence in approaching community leaders. Since the consultants had to fly weekly from another city to conduct the sessions, and had a long wait for their return plane in the evenings, the custom developed of their having a meal and discussions in participants' homes. Since each "host for the week" would usually invite fellow client members also, longstanding Black-Chicano-Anglo barriers were tentatively broken. Subsequently, as the consultants continued to work with the community, they saw these kinds of interactions increasing, suggesting improved community cohesion.

Community Repair

Communities sometimes go downhill, unable to solve their problems of living and growth. Lawrence, Kansas appeared to be in such a self-defeating cycle at a point in time where collaboration between community groups had broken down to such an extent that

> this community has in recent years experienced open conflict between blacks and whites, arson, student violence and death. The town is large enough to harbor several communities with their own way of life. It is small enough for every citizen to feel the impact of colliding values. The people I met looked at events through the lens of their own personal experience and defined truth by what they saw. So fiercely had each adherent sworn loyalty to his part of the whole, that the idea of community —of a place where people exist competitively without malice—would be hard to repair. (Moyers, 1971, p. 122)

Several steps toward beginning to resolve these problems were undertaken. One involved the formation of a steering committee. In turn, the Menninger Foundation provided consultation services to a number of workshop groups composed of community members. The groups convened outside Lawrence, with consultant interventions to facilitate problem diagnosis and recommendations for change.

> The workshops produced about 80 suggestions to improve community relations. These included allowing citizens to ride as observers in police cars, continuing the workshop programs, establishing a day care center and increasing the staff in the human relations department. There were recommendations for improved police-community relations, for more involvement in the schools and their problems, for more job opportunities and in particular better relations between blacks and whites. (Auerback, 1973, p. 288)

This catalytic mode of community intervention sought to break the self-defeating cycle generating community malaise. Its operational outcomes were not evaluated at the time the report was published.

Shifting of Traditional Roles by Community Agents: The Police

Homes are sometimes the settings for violent acts, often in the midst of disputes that represent a breakdown in power relations among husband and wife, parents and children, various other family members, and erstwhile friends and visitors. Even preceding physical violence, the dispute may have been noisy enough to attract outside attention. Police are likely to arrive, either of their own accord or in response to a call.

Necessarily, such police interventions often occur "after the fact" of injury or death and are made in terms of whatever laws have been broken. Nonetheless, many severe family disputes can or might be kept from the brink of violence by timelier interventions that deal with the mental-health aspects of the problem and in this way steer the situation toward resolution. The intervention can ease violence-inducing tensions or, at the least, can forestall acts of violence.

Police officers have been trained not only in the prescriptive interventions of law enforcement but also in catalytic types of mental-health interventions involving efforts to aid protagonists in relieving tensions and restoring home-centered morale/ cohesion. Although found to produce successful outcomes, these interventions may also create legalistic dilemmas. In the United States, for example, even a foresighted catalytic intervention with a family in a situation where no violence or other law violations have yet occurred can be interpreted as unconstitutional in the sense of violating privacy: a contravention of the Fourth and Fifth Amendments. Yet, without the intervention, the conflict may be expected to culminate in physical violence. At that point, action can only be taken legally in terms of arrests, sentencings, court orders, and other law-enforcement agency/judicial-branch options and determinations. This suggests that very difficult problems are to be anticipated where a "prescriptive role person," such as a police officer, is expected also to assume a catalytic role such as is characteristic of some community casework. (Bard and Zacker, 1971, pp. 677–82)

Minister: From Prescriptive to Catalytic

Changing the function of already-established institutions is another aspect of community change. A shift in the character of the relationship between a minister and the church membership is described in the following example. The shift is from "minister as prescriptive agent of outside power" to "minister as community consultant."

Conventionally, church-centered traditions and rituals such as the sermon, the passive role of members, choral and community singing, are reinforcement mechanisms helpful in maintaining the surrender of self-will to higher authority. The minister, likewise, is the agent of this prescriptive format. How one church changed the character of such an established institution is described below.

> The University Church of Goleta worship service has emphasized movement and action in all parts of the worship. There are no pews, thus seating and movement has open-ended possibilities. People are provided opportunities to participate in all aspects of the service. During the singing, everybody sings; during the sacramental celebration itself, everybody is given the opportunity to move around and participate, even to dance if the person so desires. During the sermon opportunities for involvement are provided. Instead of one man talking, everybody participates and all persons are given the task of putting content into the worship experience.
>
> ... In the communal service, people participate in the experiencing of ideas and create the sermon for themselves. The minister becomes a catalyst for group activity and participation. During the communal sermon persons interact with other persons in groups of six or eight. They play with blocks, color with crayons, or use some other simple tool of expression in order to wrestle with theological ideas and to experience them in rela-

tion to other persons. They function in a context that encourages them to take themselves seriously.

The communal sermon as a catalyst to encounter rather than a package of truth, can open the possibility of discovering the individual self as incomplete, perhaps absurd, and human. This self-view can bring about a recovery of authentic dealing with a person's secret feelings of guilt and shame. (Kennedy, 1973, pp. 104–105)

The minister's role is one of introducing procedures and of providing process facilitation rather than that of forwarding expert prescriptions. By avoiding advocacy, the resolution of problems is left open-ended, with each member free to reach his or her own conclusions as to how personal responsibility should be interpreted under higher authority.

Destitute Social Conditions

Hallowitz (1968), in describing a neighborhood service center (NSC), indicates different contributions its paraconsultants are able to make to the client. One possibility is to expedite assistance for clients who require professional help but who are so overwhelmed with the problems of everyday living that they have little energy to invest in problem solving. For example, a request for assistance was referred to the center by a guidance counselor in a local elementary school. Johnny, a boy of nine, had been showing symptoms of behavior problems since the start of school in the fall and his schoolwork had dropped off markedly. Over the previous two months the school counselor had worked with Mrs. Jones on a week-by-week basis with the intention of having facilitating discussions with her about Johnny. However, each time this client met with the school counselor, her primary concerns related to troubles she was having with the Welfare Department. She needed to find better housing; there was a lack of heat and hot water; she repeatedly had to go to court when her husband failed to provide support payments, and so on. Such difficulties were even more salient to her than the concerns she had earlier expressed about her son.

The NSC undertook to assist Mrs. Jones. One of its paraconsultants went to the school to meet with her in the presence of the guidance counselor, who first explained to Mrs. Jones why this aide had been invited. The NSC worker then described the kind of services the neighborhood center was able to contribute. Before leaving, she said, "I'd like to see you soon. I can do it this afternoon or tomorrow morning; and if you like, I can come visit you at home." Mrs. Jones was surprised that the aide would take the trouble to visit her, but was pleased.

Issues of misunderstanding about how the Welfare Department operates were clarified and requests for winter clothing, additional bedding, and household items were expedited as the paraconsultant worked with Mrs. Jones. The probation officer at the court arranged for her support payments to be made on a full-allowance basis rather than a supplementary one so that she would not have to suffer in the event of her husband defaulting. Finally, with the paraconsultant's assistance, Mrs. Jones contacted other neighbors in the building, with the result that a multiple-building-violations complaint was filed and a rent reduction obtained. The consultant was giving procedural assistance and at the same time, through a strategy of process consultation, was helping Mrs. Jones learn how to make her needs known, how to assert herself, and how to work through the complexities of gaining the assistance welfare agencies are capable of providing. (Hallowitz, 1968, pp. 94–95)

Another catalytic intervention by paraconsultants operating out of the neighborhood service center involves *sociotherapy*. This is initiated when the mental-health paraconsultant decides that an important part of the client's development needs is for him or her to become active in community affairs. Three purposes underlie this decision. One is that an increase in socialization—the process of entering the culture of the larger social system—will reduce the client's present feelings of isolation. A second purpose is to provide constructive channels for working through aggressive tensions. A third is to offer each participant an opportunity to contribute through helping others, in itself an important source of self-esteem.

Mental-health consultants find it feasible to involve clients in such activities as organizing welfare recipients and escorting clients to health facilities, organizing tenant councils, conducting voter registration drives, and sometimes assisting with clerical chores. As the consultants work alongside their clients they have the opportunity of observing strengths and weaknesses in their everyday contacts with other people. These observations can in turn be fed back to the expert-consultant to further clarify the diagnostic picture, enabling him or her to be more precise in thinking through treatment plans and desirable interventions.

A third kind of catalytic intervention made possible by the neighborhood service center involves part-time supervised work within the center itself, an arrangement particularly helpful for referred patients who have not used their skills for a long period of time. When interest to work has been restored the client is able to test himself out at the center in a quasi-protected environment, gradually increasing the number of hours worked per week. While the client is supervised at work, he or she is still being seen occasionally by the clinic's professional consultants so there is the opportunity to discuss and evaluate the work experience. Such an arrangement permits poor work habits, attitudes, and behavior, which would be self-defeating drawbacks on a regular job, to be discussed. The client often comes to recognize what behavior must be phased out in order for him or her to compete effectively in the outside job world.

New Communities

Under certain circumstances, urban redevelopment for example, families are uprooted from their existing homes and moved to newly constructed neighborhoods. Such enforced relocation can have a destructive effect on what was previously a community by fragmenting it and placing individual families in new surroundings where they feel both ill at ease and isolated. In addition, increased geographical mobility, made possible by greater access to transportation and job opportunities, has further dissolved a sense of community in many areas.

Friendly, supportive, social and project-related activities with neighbors can be significant positive elements in the improvement and maintenance of social relations. Community mental-health consultants feel these activities are needed if positive morale/cohesion is to emerge among those who live together in a shared geographical space. The proposition is that, "people grow to their full stature when they are associated with others in warm, enjoyable fellowship, not based on artificial emotion but on intimate common interest in some aspect of being and doing" (Wilson, 1963, pp. 23–24).

These kinds of needs often are not considered by those planning new residential areas. Because of this, the negative effects associated with mobility generally work against the establishment of social relationships in the new neighborhood. Consultant-based interventions may be needed to initiate and strengthen community cohesion.

Based on experiences of the social project team in Bristol, England, the following suggestions are offered as to how a community organizer can stimulate the development of community-building relationships. Though these suggestions apply particularly to new communities, they have value for already existing communities, and are not necessarily limited to relatively poor, ill-educated, or problem-plagued citizens.

The first suggestion is for the consultant to engage in cohesion-building between community authority and citizens.

(a)   To act as a link between authority (especially the local authority) and the people—explaining and representing *both ways,* and in the process affecting the attitudes of both parties. There is a tendency for those with authority to think that, because they understand what they are doing and why, therefore this must be clear to the citizenry. In fact, this is not so; the process of explanation is an intimate one and needs continuous attention if "they" are to be felt to remain within human reach. Equally, citizen aspiration often gets lost because it has no way of making itself perceptible to those with power, usually because it does not know how to formulate its objectives. This is where the function of interpretation could contribute to the establishment and preservation of a sense of human relationship between authority and those for whose benefit authority is established.

A second contribution to community cohesion is for the consultant to be available as a rallying point through whom initial contacts between citizens with common interests can be made.

(b)   The community organizer should help people to bring to fruition constructive group intentions: that is to say where people want to get a society going for the study of railway-lore or to discuss pigeon breeding;

to start a cycling club or to push for a better local clinic or library. The community organizer should be a person to whom they know they can go, not to do the job, but to tell them how to go about it, whom to contact, where to look for a room, what forms to fill in, who might help them to keep the accounts. Middle-class organizers, active political leaders, and people used to business negotiations tend to have no idea how difficult it is for average citizens with limited contacts and experience to get started on putting ideas into practice if they range beyond the family circle.

A third aspect is for the community consultant to identify and provide for the expression of "latent" needs so they will be "felt."

(c)   The third function of the community organizer is to try to generate social groups of one sort or another where he sees promise which does not look as if it would mature by itself. This, of course, is often done at present by specialists, particularly in the field of adult and further education. Its very success in these fields is a good reason for considering whether it could not be developed in the purely recreational and informal club field, through which some people grow in stature just as much as do others through activities which have higher educational status. (Wilson, 1963, p. 24)

Interventions (a) and (b) are facilitating in nature and are responses to felt needs. Intervention (c) is not in that category, for the interventionist, after identifying latent needs, takes steps toward creating local situations in which such needs will be recognized and self-fulfilled by the residents themselves.

Families under Tension

Stresses and strains are felt within most families, whatever their socioeconomic standing may be. But it is among the poorer and otherwise problem-ridden members of the community that the impact of tensions and strains can be most overwhelming, since in many such families there is little solidarity or cohesion. Members are not sufficiently integrated to cope, and interventions are needed if family breakups are to be avoided. Sometimes the identity of these "families in trouble" is obvious and the requisite support and assistance can be provided; sometimes the need for help to arrest a deteriorating situation is totally unrecognized. How might a community consultant arrange an early-warning system to detect building family crises, rather than trying to pick up the pieces after tragedy has struck?

Based on his experience with the Bristol Social Project, Wilson (1963, pp. 28–29) suggests three community sources that are useful under such circumstances. One is the rent collector or facility manager. He or she is likely to know of particular clients who are having serious financial problems and is familiar also with the personalities and concerns of these tenants. A second source consists of teachers plus the school welfare service of counselors, attendance officers, and so on. These personnel keep informed about "unusual" behavior, such as truancy on the part of a family's children, or deeply hostile attitudes toward school and teachers which may reflect stress within the home. A third source is the general medical practitioner. He or she comes into contact with family members from time to time and if he or she has more than a physical health concept in mind, useful information as to problems needing attention can be passed on to a community organizer. By becoming aware at an early stage of emerging family crises via these unobtrusive information sources, the community organizer is able to intervene in ways that contribute to the management and resolution of such crises.

A community of any size is likely to include women whose self-confidence has fallen so low that they are unable or unwilling to mix and make friends. But if facilities exist for fostering their improved mental health through group or club activities, such women can break out of their loneliness by gradually permitting themselves to gain some of the benefits of mutual help offered by friends and neighbors. In the Bristol Social Project,

> activities included sewing and cookery, the care of the feet, darning and shoe repairing, the making of lampshades, the care of the hands, and sex instruction for girls. The children played together in an adjoining room. Competitions in the making of simple articles were held most weeks and prizes given for the best work. There were several talks from outside speakers, a councillor, a health visitor, and a marriage guidance counsellor.

> It is never easy to assess precise results, but this experiment in home-making undoubtedly fulfilled in part a real need for advice and friendship on the part of a group of mothers who did not feel able to join the established women's organization at Upfield. There is little doubt that the scope for the organization of groups of this kind is very wide, particularly among mothers whose family involvements give them little opportunity for companionship outside the home. (Wilson, 1963, p. 36)

As noted before, the role of the community consultant is to provide a rallying point for group formation, with the group able to continue once the start up has been completed.

Rumors that disturb people can have a negative effect on morale/cohesion. Rumor Control Centers sprang up in the United States during the turbulence of the 1960s. Their purpose was to fill a need felt by people who wanted to "know the score" as to what was happening or about to happen, or who wanted reassurances of some kind regarding difficult-to-track-down stories—perhaps rumors of impending violence or the shutdown of a local industrial plant.

After getting wind of a rumor, these centers first check out the factual situation and then establish standard answers based on the best judgment possible in light of presently known facts. Disseminated in response to telephoned inquiries or by other means, these serve a perception-building function. For example, they may provide an inquirer with access to social realities that otherwise might be unavailable to him. They serve a morale/cohesion need by helping the inquirer to deal with his or her fears and anxieties by determining whether they are real or imaginary (Ponting, 1973, pp. 391–401).

Integration of Mental Patients into the Community

A two-step application of the basic idea of an intermediate living situation between mental hospital and open community is described by Fairweather, Sanders, and Tornatzky (1974). It started with a training program for mental patients designed to assist them in acquiring social skills and rapidly expanded into patient government. Research evaluation demonstrated that patients in such a program improved more rapidly than would be expected under standard conditions. However, they were unable to "hold" the gain when released and therefore the rate of return to hospitalization was comparable in both groups.

The extension of in-hospital, more or less autonomous problem-solving group training involved the creation of lodges in the community where groups of patients would continue to live and collaborate after hospital discharge. Training during hospitalization as to how to solve problems after discharge was provided and lodge administration was patient-based, with nominal administrative representation or support provided by live-in hospital staff. The consultants describe lodge life as follows.

A lodge is a special kind of social organization in the community for ex-mental patients with features that make it different from any other kind of place for such patients, whether it be a family home, a boarding house, other forms of transitional residence such as a half-way house, or whatever. The essential characteristics are:

A. *The lodge depends on lodge members themselves to keep their members in the community rather than upon the support of hospital personnel.* Three basic practices help create this distinguishing feature.

1. *No live-in staff:* Unlike most other community facilities for ex-mental patients, staff persons are kept to a minimum. No staff persons reside on the lodge premises under any circumstances. Typically, only a single person or a few hospital personnel will have contact with the lodge during any eight-hour work day, and this contact will exist only because he or they have been specifically designated by hospital authorities as the staff for the lodge organization.

2. *Only lodge staff on call:* Unlike most other community facilities, the lodge staff are the medium through which lodge members contact the hospital. Only these designated staff members should be used by the members when they feel the need for assistance. The staff is available to lodge members for all 24-hours of a day, not for a "shift" or "8-hour work day." The resultant minimized contact with hospital staff should decrease the lodge members' dependence

upon hospital staff persons for direction and guidance in everyday life in the community.... (Fairweather, Sanders, and Tornatzky, 1974, p. 108)

Summary

A common theme runs through these examples of community-oriented morale/cohesion problems. Facilitative interventions that respond to immediate felt needs are helpful, particularly for community residents who are detached and, in a social sense, functioning submarginally. Such catalytic interventions are devised to help by getting isolated individuals in touch with one another, by providing the assistance they need to function as community members, or by scotching demoralizing rumors.

IMPLICATIONS

In these examples of catalytic interventions, the focal point has been either the individual-within-society or the development of a larger sense of community. Alternate forms of existing institutions as well as new and more vital ways of working within existing organizations appear to be needed if higher and more sustained levels of morale/cohesion are to result.

In interventions with individual clients, it is noteworthy that the catalytic consultant takes care not to provoke defensiveness. But if he or she finds defensiveness present or can diagnose its latency in the client, the consultant attempts to dissolve this barrier rather than confront it directly. The approach may or may not be successful, but in any case the specific effect of a particular catalytic intervention is not readily observable. By contrast, a confrontational intervention is much more likely to draw forth a discernible reaction from the individual or group client.

When the client system is at a group to larger-social-system level, a catalytic consultant may find additional possibilities for interventions directed toward improvement of the *contexts* of members' circumstances as an indirect means of heightening morale/cohesion. The Trist/Bamforth, Wilson, and Fairweather *et al.* reports contain evidence of this approach. Trist/Bamforth is a "pure" example of a detailed —and, at the time, novel—analysis and report that *itself* catalyzed the client system by indicating that its technical and social subsystems were out of joint. The Wilson and Fairweather *et al.* consultations show "context" interventions taking place in conjunction with more directly focused catalytic interventions.

REFERENCES

Auerback, A. "The Psychological Health of the City Today." In J. L. Carleton and U. Mahlendorf, eds., *Man for Man: A Multidisciplinary Workshop on Affecting Man's Social and Psychological Nature through Community Action.* Springfield, Ill.: Charles C Thomas, 1973, pp. 270–92. Reprinted by permission.

Bard, M., and J. Zacker. "Dilemmas of Community Intervention." *Journal of Marriage and the Family* 26, no. 3 (1961): 677–82.

Bennis, W. G. *Organization Development: Its Nature, Origins, and Prospects*. Reading, Mass.: Addison-Wesley, 1969. Reprinted by permission.

Fairweather, G. W., D. H. Sanders, and L. G. Tornatzky. *Creating Change in Mental Health Organizations*. New York: Pergamon Press, 1974. Reprinted by permission.

Golembiewski, R. T., and A. Blumberg. "Confrontation as a Training Design in Complex Organizations: Attitudinal Changes in a Diversified Population of Managers." Reproduced by special permission from *Journal of Applied Behavioral Science* 3, no. 4 (1967): 525–47.

Hallowitz, E. "The Expanding Role of the Neighborhood Service Center." In F. Riessman and H. R. Popper, eds., *Up from Poverty: New Career Ladders for Nonprofessionals*. New York: Harper & Row, 1968, pp. 92–105.

Kennedy, D. R. "The Church as a Therapeutic Community." In J. L. Carleton and U. Mahlendorf, eds., *Man for Man: A Multidisciplinary Workshop on Affecting Man's Social and Psychological Nature through Community Action*. Springfield, Ill.: Charles C Thomas, 1973, pp. 101–14. Reprinted by permission.

Moyers, W. *Listening to America*. New York: Harper's Magazine Press, 1971. Copyright © 1971 by Bill Moyers. All rights reserved.

Ponting, J. R. "Rumor Control Centers." *American Behavioral Scientist* 16, no. 3 (1973): 391–401.

Robbins, J. G. "Using Trainer Participation in a Community Development Program." Reproduced by special permission from the *Training and Development Journal* 27, no. 10 (1973): 14–19. Copyright 1973 by the American Society for Training and Development, Inc.

Schwartz, M. S., and G. T. Will. "Intervention and Change in a Mental Hospital Ward." In W. G. Bennis, K. D. Benne, and R. Chin, eds., *The Planning of Change*. New York: Holt, Rinehart and Winston, 1961, pp. 564–83. Reprinted by permission.

Trist, E. L., and K. W. Bamforth. "Some Social and Psychological Consequences of the Longwall Method of Coal-Getting." *Human Relations* 4, no. 1 (1951): 3–38.

Wilson, R. "Difficult Housing Estates." *Human Relations* 16, no. 1 (1963): 3–43. Reprinted by permission.

CATALYTIC INTERVENTIONS

11

NORMS / STANDARDS

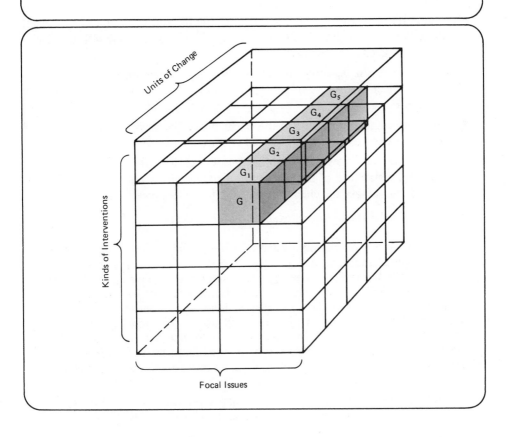

Much of the catalytic methodology appears ideally suited to deal with a norms/ standards focal issue, for norms involve shared perceptions. Since they often operate silently in influencing a client's behavior, the many and varied catalytic awareness interventions can help the client to see what norms/standards are guiding his or her behavior and to replace them when more valid alternatives are called for.

INDIVIDUAL (G₁)

Counseling that deals with a client's emotions-as-facts can be carried out through catalytic interventions relating to personal norms and standards. Although an individual may be aware of these norms/standards, if they are unacceptable to the client or others they can become the focal issue of consultation. Two prominent practitioners of this approach are Mowrer (1964) and Jourard (1971). The rationale is based on several considerations introduced by Mowrer.

1. Many emotional difficulties arise because people feel guilty about some past misdeed—that is, an instance in which they violated a norm or standard—and try to hide it from others. Yet the memory remains clear to the client. The incident has not been buried.

2. By admitting the norm violation to the consultant and to the more significant of these "others," such as husband or wife, tensions associated with norm violation are reduced or eliminated.

3. The consultant can assist the client to disclose a personal norm or standard and how it has been transgressed. This can be done by "setting a model" of such disclosure. For example,

    a. the consultant first reveals to the client his or her own past difficulties and the relief experienced from past and continuing self-disclosures;

    b. the consultant writes out a similar episode, offering the client a case study that sets a standard of self-disclosure together with a rationale that explains it, and encourages the client to engage in his or her own self-disclosure.

Mowrer provides the following example of this process.

Recently I have been seeing a talented young woman whose life situation raises many of the same issues in a little different way. The presenting picture was that she had been drinking much more than was good for her, "imposing upon" (as she put it) and embarrassing her friends when intoxicated, and not meeting her responsibilities in connection with her work. In her sober moments she realized that if this trend continued, it would be only a matter of time until she would lose her very responsible and attractive position. She was, in fact, scheduled for an important promotion soon; and instead of feeling pleased and zestful about it, she was acutely apprehensive.

During our first interview this young woman reported an accident in which she had been involved a few months ago and implied that this was what had unnerved her; but when I said it seemed to me that her symptoms bespoke a deeper source of disturbance, she acknowledged that there *"was* something," which in our second interview she courageously reported. Some three years earlier she had permitted herself to become involved homosexually with an older woman whom she very much admired and liked. Although this was decidedly against her "better judgment"— she said the excitement and enthrallment "clouded out everything else," until the affair came to an end and she was left with only ashes and remorse. She felt she did not deserve the trust people were inclined to put in her or the preferment which her very real abilities and good work had won for her in her profession; she therefore began to drink excessively, disillusion her friends, neglect her work, and to feel, as she put it, that she was fighting for her very "survival" psychologically.

As she rose from her chair at the end of the second interview, this woman remarked that she already felt *"much* better"; and she was now able, simply at my request, to leave off the drinking forthwith. She settled into her work again, and she manifested an active and sincere desire, in our ensuing talks, to find a way of further restoring her self-respect and social integrity. I explained to her my feeling that in situations of this kind "treatment" may begin with a specialized "therapist," but that full recovery is achieved only in restoration to community in the ordinary, common sense of that term. Obviously, in entering into the homosexual venture, this young woman had isolated, alienated herself from the "significant others" in her life and had created what Donald Cressey, in a different context, has called an "unsharable problem." She said that for a long time she had felt that she could "work this thing out" herself; but she had come to realize that this was an illusion, that she must have "help"; and she was now not too resistant to the idea that such help cannot come entirely from just one other person. (Mowrer, 1964, pp. 50–51)

By adhering to the standard of disclosure and telling about her past, the client was released from her burden of guilt. The consultant served as listener. Thus far, it was an instance of catharsis—the consultant's *catalytic* intervention came in his suggestions about "reconciliation," which involves information sharing.

One criterion of mental health is that a well-functioning person is able to interact freely and with spontaneity. He or she is "unburdened." In other words, the individual does not feel compelled to hide or to deny past deeds in the interest of maintaining acceptance. When such burdens exist, they reduce freedom and spontaneity and probably diminish the individual's energy to pursue daily objectives.

Mowrer's catalytic yet emotion-based counseling approach deals with these issues in a double-norm way. He says,

I find myself, more and more, guiding neurotic individuals into a two-fold strategy which involves (a) confession of past misdeeds and (b) *concealment* of present and future "good works." Instead of advising disturbed persons to continue to pay fees to a professional counselor, I urge them to take advantage of the opportunities which are always freely available for becoming honest and open with respect to past mistakes and then to take the equivalent of a fee (in time or money) and devote it to "charity by stealth."

A case example is offered in the following:

A bright young man with a history of adolescent delinquency and de-
bauchery, he had, when I first saw him, already been attracted to and
joined a religious group and had undergone a conversion of sorts; but he
continued to be ruminative, moody, unpredictable in his interpersonal
responses, and never quite certain when he might revert to his old mode
of life. At the suggestion of a mutual friend, he came to see me; and we
moved quickly and with surprisingly little resistance toward the decision
to make a clean breast of his past to two trusted members of this group,
and from this step the new policy of openness was extended to "significant
others."

The relief experienced by this young man and the personal change noted
in him by his friends were very striking; and we were soon able to start
thinking about the more positive aspects of the program. At this juncture
I began introducing him to Clive Randolph's "secret." The lad was much
interested, and presently I saw his face contort into a sort of scowl, his
eyes light up, and with some difficulty he succeeded in re-stating the idea
in a way which, to me at least, was both clarifying and novel. I am sorry I
do not have a record of his exact words; but they went something like this:
"What you seem to be saying is that when we tell or brag about some
accomplishment or favor we've done someone, we exchange the 'credit'
for immediate satisfaction, that is, we 'spend' it. And in the same way,
when we confess an *evil,* something we feel *guilty* about, we likewise get
rid of it, dissipate it . . . like those things I did and thought I wasn't
ashamed of but was. Now that I have admitted them, they aren't really a
part of me anymore—they just don't seem very important. By admitting
these things, I have 'spent' my guilt. And now the same principle seems
to work also the other way 'round. Just as the wrong kind of 'credit,' if
accumulated, will eventually destroy you, so will good 'credit,' if *not used
up,* give you strength and inner confidence. The net effect is that you *are,*
in any case, what you keep back, *save:* strong and self-accepting if what
you hide and keep back is good and weak and self-hating if what you keep
and hide is bad." (Mowrer, 1964, pp. 69–70)

The "Clive Randolph's 'secret'" referred to consists of the following consultant-
distilled double-norm rationale from a literary source: Lloyd Douglas' *Magnificent
Obsession* (1929).

Most of us live *depleted* existences: weak, zestless, apprehensive, pes-
simistic, "neurotic." And the reason is that when we perform a *good* deed,

we advertise it, display it—and thus collect and enjoy the credit then and there. But when we do something cheap and mean, we carefully hide and deny it (if we can), with the result that the "credit" for acts of *this* kind remains with us and "accumulates." A person who follows such a life style is chronically bankrupt in the moral and spiritual sense. If, at any given moment, his life were "required of him," he would be found *wanting,* could not pay out, settle up; for his "net worth" is less than nothing, negative. Small wonder, then, that a person of this kind has no confidence or zest and lacks creativity. He is too busy pretending, too "insecure," too afraid of being "found out."

So what is the alternative, the remedy for a person who had already fallen into, or wishes to avoid, such a miserable and meaningless existence? It is, quite simply, to reverse this whole strategy: admit and thus divest oneself of one's weaknesses, errors, follies, and *hide* one's charities, good deeds, virtues. This, Randolph tells Dr. Hudson, is the secret of "that mysterious power I mentioned. By following these instructions to the letter, you can have anything you want, do anything you wish to do, be whatever you would like to be. I have tried it. It works. It worked for me. It will work for you!" (Mowrer, 1964, pp. 66–67)

Characteristic of norms/standards catalytic interventions is the gathering of information additional to that already at hand to assist the client in seeing his or her situation in a broader, and therefore possibly more valid, context. Add to this the consultant's help as the client seeks to release withheld information, and the likelihood is increased that a person will view his or her situation in a richer, more objective, and more problem-solving manner.

Summary

Catalytic interventions centering on the individual-as-client are pertinent in any situation where (1) the client is involved but is not so emotionally upset that thinking is impractical; (2) the client is burdened or feeling "buffaloed" by being the sole possessor of guilt-laden information regarding his or her past. Given the client's uncertainty as to what to do, he or she is interested in exploring an acceptable course of action. The consultant facilitates these processes by "modeling" for the client "how to confess," thus helping the client to release hidden information and be freed from its negative effects.

GROUP (G₂)

In the catalytic consultant's search for an answer to how to be helpful, he or she frequently looks at norms and standards as the force holding members in an unexamined status quo position. If a group is operating according to dysfunctional norms/standards, the consultant tries to help them see how alternative norms/ standards might be more appropriate to their situation. This is a difficult feat for a group to accomplish alone, since members themselves are open to rejection if they challenge the status quo. A consultant, by comparison, can ask an "innocent" question regarding almost any topic, such as "Why is *this* done *that* way?"—and be a hero for voicing the unspoken criticisms.

Agenda Determination

The following intervention by Schein (1969) facilitated group action by focusing attention on how the agenda for meetings was determined. The consultant reports being a participant observer of barriers to effectiveness among group members who were contending with work problems.

> In the Apex company I sat in for several months on the weekly executive-committee meeting, which included the president and his key subordinates. I quickly became aware that the group was very loose in its manner of operation; people spoke when they felt like it, issues were explored fully, conflict was fairly openly confronted, and members felt free to contribute.

Nonetheless, as he listened, the consultant began to identify a repetitive cycle that constituted a worsening problem.

> This kind of climate seemed constructive, but it created a major difficulty for the group. No matter how few items were put on the agenda, the group was never able to finish its work. The list of backlog items grew longer and the frustration of group members intensified in proportion to this backlog.

Part of the problem was that members were responding to it in a "more and more of what we did before" fashion.

> The group responded by trying to work harder. They scheduled more meetings and attempted to get more done at each meeting, but with little success. Remarks about the ineffectiveness of groups, too many meetings, and so on, became more and more frequent.

The consultant could see the problem pattern more clearly.

> My diagnosis was that the group was overloaded. Their agenda was too large, they tried to process too many items at any given meeting, and the agenda was a mixture of operational and policy issues without recognition by the group that such items required different allocations of time.

Consequently, he introduced a procedural suggestion, but did not attempt to sell the group on it. Rather, he left it to them for debate and decision.

I suggested to the group that they seemed overloaded and should discuss how to develop their agenda for their meetings. The suggestion was adopted after a half-hour or so of shared feelings.

His later facilitations came in response to the eventual group-agreed decision.

It was then decided, with my help, to sort the agenda items into several categories, and to devote some meetings entirely to operational issues while others would be exclusively policy meetings. The operations meetings would be run more tightly in order to process these items efficiently. The policy questions would be dealt with in depth. (Schein, 1969, p. 106)

Thus the intervention dealt almost exclusively with procedures involved in the work discussions of this particular group.

Work Practices

An intervention by Rice (1953) in India, involving a textile weaving factory, is of a socio-technical genre similar to that reported by Trist and Bamforth (Chapter 10), but is more illustrative of consultant-client collaboration in performing an analysis of socio-technical interrelationships inherent in the factory's weaving process. It was carried out, however, not to solve a cohesion problem but one of norms/standards.

The analysis was made in collaboration with a development group in which the author worked with the Chairman, the Mill Manager, and Works Manager of the Company. (The Works Manager was the direct executive subordinate of the Mill Manager, who reported directly to the Chairman. The Works Manager also acted, however, as Technical Staff Officer to the Chairman.) The members of this group and the author collaborated closely, working as a group, in pairs or singly as the situation demanded, until each was satisfied, from his own point of view, of the validity of the analysis. They reported as a group to the other members of senior management at all stages. The decision to initiate the reorganization was taken by the Chairman at a meeting which was attended by all Senior Managers. At that meeting the Weaving Master of the mill concerned was called. He listened with evident enthusiasm to the proposals and began at once to produce from his own experience arguments in their favour. The Works Manager, as the senior executive responsible for the experimental loom shed, then discussed the proposals with the Top Supervisor of the shed. Thereafter the supervisors and workers in the loom shed took over the proposals as their own; and within a few hours, to the surprise of management, the workers had organized their own working groups. The Chairman, the Mill Manager, the Works Manager, and the author did not attend any of the discussions with supervisors or workers, nor did they visit the loom shed again until the reorganization had been implemented. (Rice, 1953, p. 298)

Rice (1953, p. 327) describes the group pattern identified by initial socio-technical analysis as "an aggregate of individuals with confused task and worker relationships and with no discernible internal group structure." Even so, the focal issue was evidently not one of morale/cohesion (as in the case of the Trist/Bamforth coal-mine study), since relationships among supervisors and workers were already quite positive. The norms/standards focal issue was basically one of traditional status quo assumptions about "who *should* do what" which were still operating within a highly automated plant. Interestingly, these were not traditional Indian assumptions but had been imported at earlier stages of industrialization and, in effect, had been sanctified by task-by-task industrial engineering practices.

The first significant norm shift occurred when higher management decided to *discuss with* lower-level managers and the workers an experimental reorganization, with an associated piecework pay offer. Taking full advantage of the newly legitimized participation/involvement opportunity, supervisors and workers themselves reorganized their work arrangements. Rice reports (1953, p. 328) that after a shakedown period productivity stabilized at a higher level than before.

Team Norms

In correctional and other settings, such as high schools, Vorrath and Brendtro (1974) offer an intervention termed "Positive Peer Culture." This is a carefully designed influencing sequence of passive, active, and general background "mood changing" steps and other initiatives to be undertaken by an adult who continuously sits in with a group during its regularly scheduled meetings. Basically the Vorrath/ Brendtro methodology involves having the leader monitor in a knowledgeable manner the more or less informal interactions between newly met members which constitute the beginnings of group process among teenagers. The adult leader exerts influence in a variety of ways ranging from overt confrontation through ostensibly passive withdrawal. His or her "behavior kaleidoscope" is chosen according to momentary readings of process events during the four successive stages of guided group process delineated by Vorrath/Brendtro (1974, p. 52): "Casing," "Limit Testing," "Polarization of Values," and "A Positive Peer Culture." The last-mentioned stage constitutes effective functioning.

In effect, the adult leader-interventionist acts as a leavening agent that, when added to the teenage group's own process, serves to convert that process to the production and enforcement of what the larger adult society views as positive norms of behavior. For this reason, the long-term, overall intervention can validly be described as catalytic even though various other interventions may be used on a moment-to-moment basis.

Family Norms of Parent/Youngster Interaction

How parents and children relate to one another is more a matter of historical precept than of thoughtful discussion between two generations. This may occur when the parent is thirty-six and the "child" eighteen or even when the parent is eighty-five and the "child" is fifty. In other words, this focal issue appears to be norms/standards related rather than age related.

An intervention concerned with norms/standards is reported by Gordon (1970). Designed to help parents and youngsters resolve impasse situations, the process is termed the divided-sheet method of "no-lose" problem solving. In the following description, parents learn the methodology and initiate its use with their children; in similar circumstances and with some rephrasing, Gordon-trained children might initiate the approach in much the same way with parents. Success is possible only when both the parents and the children "buy" the procedure.

> ...we designed a surprisingly simple method for overcoming the resistance and distrust that kids bring to a problem-solving session. All parents need is a pen and a sheet of paper divided into two columns by a line drawn down the middle. The parent can start the session by saying something like:

> "I've brought a sheet of paper divided down the middle. We'll list our problems and conflicts on this sheet as they are brought up by any of us. In the left column I'll write those conflicts we've had about behavior of you kids that really does not tangibly or concretely affect us, even though it might have bothered us. One I can think of immediately is your homework. In the right column I'll write down those conflicts we've had about behavior of you kids that really does affect us, things you do that interfere directly with our lives. An example would be your not carrying out the trash.

> "When we've completed our list, then we'll promise not to hassle or nag you about any of the problems in the left column. We'll simply throw those problems away—no more bugging you. Take the homework, for example. We agree never to mention it—it will be up to you when you do it, or whether you do it. You are capable of taking care of this yourself.

> "But all the problems in the right column will have to be worked out some way so that we come up with a solution for each that is acceptable to all of us—no one loses. Any questions about how we're going to operate here? [After answering questions] Okay, let's start listing the problems—anyone can bring up a problem. Then we'll take each one that's brought up and decide whether it goes in the right column or the left."

By adopting this newly suggested norm, parents can convert power/authority impasses into a joint search for further norms under which agreement may be approached. Following is the sheet of problems one family came up with. In this family, as in most, there were far more problems in the left column than in the right. Gordon (1970, p. 280) recommends this intervention for use "in families where parents have been authoritarian, that is, have been hassling and nagging their kids a lot about behavior that does not tangibly and concretely affect them, the parents." He does not indicate at what age levels this approach is most suitable, or what "hap-

Problems agreed to be child's responsibility (no mutual problem-solving)	Problems that must be problem solved
1. His school work—how much he studies, when he studies, whether he studies.	1. How much he contributes to the work required around the house.
2. How he wears his hair.	2. The problem of allowance and what parents buy and child buys.
3. When he goes to sleep.	3. The problem of parents not being told when child will or will not be home for dinner.
4. What he eats.	
5. What clothes he wears to school.	4. The problem of the use of the family car.
6. His choice of his own friends.	
7. How often he takes a bath.	5. The problem of the child not cleaning up his mess in the family room.
8. How he decorates his room.	
9. Where he goes when he goes out.	
10. How he spends his allowance.	
(Gordon, 1970, pp. 280–82)	

pens" to the left side when solutions to problems on the right-hand side cannot be found. Neither does he deal in detail with how parents help their children solve problems that do not affect the parent but which, if ignored or "thrown back" on the child, may adversely affect the child's very basic growth needs. Presumably the expression of felt needs followed by problem-solving discussions are expected to resolve these issues.

INTERGROUP (G₃)

Norm clarification is an approach used in helping intergroup situations that are in a state of tension because either (1) neither group is able to recognize the norms and standards that characterize the other's approach to it, or (2) the norms/standards are recognized but not accepted as legitimate. The solution is to identify existing norms/standards and help the interacting groups to shift their norms so that assignments may be carried out without stepping on one another's toes, or to promote needed collaboration while avoiding needless friction.

Pure versus Applied Research Department

Lorsch and Lawrence (1972) premise their interventions on a rationale that is explained to managers of both groups prior to intergroup problem analysis. The following are its main points.

1. Any complex social system, such as a company, is composed of differentiated parts.
2. These differentiated parts must be integrated into a unified effort to accomplish corporate purpose.
3. Any part, because of the tasks it performs, develops at least four distinctive attributes: (a) time orientation, (b) interpersonal orientation, (c) internal formal structure, and (d) goal orientation.

The more unlike one another any two interdependent groups are in terms of the four attributes, the greater the likelihood of difficulties in achieving an effective integration between them. Through questionnaires and interviews, consultants seek to understand how the two interdependent groups differ in regard to each of the four attributes, and then convene the top managers of both groups, as intact units, to explain the "cognitive map" rationale as the basis for feedback of interview-based data. Managers have the opportunity to test feedback from the other group for congruence with their own understanding of intergroup difficulties of integration. Problem solving to reduce barriers to integration mechanisms, by shifting the intergroup norms according to one or more of the four attributes, is the final step.

One intervention example involved integrating two research subunits within the same organization. One subunit was supposed to be engaged in fundamental, long-range research; the other was to be involved with applied research of shorter-range significance. The consultants collected data by interviews and questionnaires and concluded that extremely poor integration was characteristic of the intergroup relationship. Also, while their internal characteristics were highly differentiated in structure and interpersonal attitudes, both laboratories were trying to perform the same kinds of tasks and had similar time orientations. A further finding was that members of one laboratory saw the members of the other laboratory as competitors.

The consultants convened meetings of top managers and this information was fed back as the basis for presenting the following conclusions.

> We explained that the high differentiation in interpersonal and structural attributes was related to the problems of achieving integration, but that the fact the units were occupying the same task and time space seemed to be intensifying the difficulties in achieving collaboration. In this discussion the managers recognized that two things were needed; first, a clearer differentiation of the role of the laboratories and second the development of improved integrative devices. (Lorsch and Lawrence, 1972, p. 223)

The consultants comment that this information supported the laboratory managers' intuitive hunches and clarified underlying norms and standards. Discussion followed, moving in the direction of redefining operating norms and standards for each laboratory as a first step toward better integration between the two.

Staff versus Line

A variation on this theme is referred to as the *organization mirror*. This technique answers the question posed by a group inside an organization, How do outsiders see us? "Outsiders" constitute the second group and the problem is to get information from them transferred to the inside group so that insiders can see themselves more objectively and take needed corrective actions. An example of this kind of one-sided intergroup intervention is reported by Fordyce and Weil (1971). A seven-man staff organization had been working to improve its effectiveness for about a year, yet still experienced either friction or indifference from the various line groups it was supposed to aid (Fordyce and Weil, 1971, p. 101). Something in these relation-ships was out of kilter, and the consultants hoped a catalytic intervention would help the group see its own performance in a "mirror" provided by the eyes of others in the organization who were actual or potential users of its services. The mirror is composed of data: feelings, attitudes, and reactions the "consumers" groups held toward this staff group. The consultant initiated these activities by interviewing to learn something about the problem as these outside individuals, singly or in groups, saw it. Since information was collected on pertinent issues, the consultant could present it to the staff group to facilitate the feedback process.

The following steps suggest how a consultant intervenes to enhance the flow of data from outsiders. In the above example, he first reviewed interview findings. Then the outsiders, an aggregate rather than intact group, composed of two prospective "consumers" from each of the line organizations who were invited by the central staff group, met among themselves. They discussed and interpreted the interview data while the seven-man staff group listened as the audience (Fordyce and Weil, 1971, pp. 165–67).

This cycle completed, the staff group met to discuss what its members had heard the outsiders say and identify issues requiring further clarification. After a general session that focused on reviewing progress and specifying next steps, task groups were created. These were made up of members from the staff group and from among the outsiders. Working on the same tasks but independently of one another, each identified the most important changes needed to improve the effective-ness of the staff group. These findings were reported in a general session and a single priority list of items to be solved was then created. It served as the basis for each task force reconvening to develop plans and/or specific action steps for change with regard to each listed item. The remainder of the period was for summary purposes. Conclusions and assignments for further work after the meeting's close were also taken up. The following schedule outlines an Organization "Mirror" meeting.

Meeting Schedule

8:30 – 9:00	Introduction by staff director
9:00 – 9:30	Review of interview data by Third Party
9:30 – 10:15	Outsiders discuss among themselves to try to in-terpret the data while insiders listen to them

	and take notes on what they heard to use in the next step
10:15 – 11:00	Insiders discuss what they heard outsiders say and identify issues needing clarification while the outsiders observe the discussion
11:00 – 12:00	General discussion to summarize what has happened thus far (ground rule: don't start working problems)
12:00 – 1:00	Break for lunch
1:00 – 1:30	Four task subgroups, each comprising both outsiders and insiders, identify the five most important changes needed to improve the effectiveness of the organization
1:30 – 2:00	Reports from subgroups
2:00 – 2:30	Total group synthesizes lists
2:30 – 4:30	The four task subgroups develop a plan and specific action items for change
4:30 – 5:00	Meeting summary—each task group reports plans, action items, person responsible, and reporting dates
5:00 – 5:30	Staff director concludes meeting by reviewing day's work and assigning remaining action items (Fordyce and Weil, 1971, pp. 101, 103)

The intervention is implemented through a consultant-as-interlocutor. His interventions are facilitating in that they provide a procedural framework involving a sequence of steps, and his interview-based interventions produce information that can be helpful to the group in viewing itself more objectively.

Behind all this is the assumption that because it has been "asked for," the information will be received in an open and undefensive way. Under the "rational man" assumptions of this catalytic approach, arrangements are not included for confronting the staff group's underlying motivations or for working through the fundamental internal or intergroup antagonisms that often are present but unrecognized, or that surface during such periods of self-discovery.

Union and Management

Truskie (1974) reports a union-management intergroup intervention designed to generate increased mutual understanding. During ongoing negotiations, union and corporation representatives had become cognizant of the need to improve relations between their respective groups, and negotiated an agreement to arrange a joint human-relations program. This agreement became part of the overall three-year contract.

In the resulting human-relations program, which used a university extension instructor as moderator, a total of 125 foremen, general foremen, union stewards, negotiators, and grievance committeemen participated in the program which began February 27, 1972 and lasted for eighteen consecutive weeks. The eighteen sessions were divided so that six were devoted to communications, six to human relations, and six to grievance handling. Membership in each subgroup consisted of 18–23 participants. The union-management ratio of the total group—41% union and 59% management. The groups met on company time and on company premises.

Mr. Kirby was the moderator for each group throughout the entire program. His role was one of advising, motivating, and guiding. He provided the participants with the knowledge base, training aids, and discussion leadership. The participants were encouraged to interact freely on a give-and-take basis. Random observations of the groups indicated minimal group interaction during the first few sessions, but as the program progressed, interaction within the groups increased significantly.

An interesting aspect of the program was the formation of a steering committee which met biweekly during the eighteen weeks to evaluate the progress and over-all direction of the program. In some cases, slight program modifications were made upon suggestions of the steering committee. The committee consisted of the moderator, the University representative (the writer), two management representatives, and two union representatives. (Truskie, 1974, p. 278)

Also, at the program's final session, all participants were asked to complete evaluation questionnaires. Truskie reports that responses to questions posed in this survey were highly favorable regarding the program's value and essentiality in improving management-union and company-union relations, in gaining better outlooks on their intergroup problems, and in promoting proper conduct between representatives. In modified form it was continued the following year. Acknowledging that these evaluation methods cannot be taken as firm evidence that union-management relations were improving, Truskie concludes:

> The important point of this case study lies in the realization that union and management personnel can join in an extensive learning encounter to discuss substantive, job-related issues and problems—to the mutual benefit of both groups. Union-management relations in the future will improve only to the extent that both are willing to learn and appreciate each other's role. The above approach appears to be a logical step in that direction. (Truskie, 1974, p. 279)

Summary

When the focal issue between groups is norms/standards, catalytic procedures can more precisely pinpoint where differences lie than when power/authority, for example, is the focal issue. This could be because the particular units studied had more or less equal power and therefore were less threatening and more open, both to each other and to the consultants.

ORGANIZATION (G₄)

Mann (1961) provides a clinical example of the survey-research interaction, in which eight thousand employees engaged in a company-wide data gathering as to attitudes and opinions. Three sets of data were produced.

> (1) Information on the attitudes and perceptions of 8,000 nonsupervisory employees toward their work, promotion opportunities, supervision, fellow employees, etc.; (2) first- and second-line supervisors' feelings about the various aspects of their jobs and supervisory beliefs; and (3) information from intermediate and top levels of management about their supervisory philosophies, roles in policy formation, problems of organizational integration, etc. (Mann, 1961, p. 609)

These attitudes and perceptions covered several significant issues, but appeared to concentrate on norms and standards. A chain of interlocking conferences, beginning with a report of major findings to the president and senior officers and then repeated down through organizational "families," permitted each boss and his subordinates to participate in examining the data. Data made available to particular groups came from their own group or from subordinate groups for which they were responsible. Each group interpreted the data and then decided what further analyses were needed for administrative action. Finally they planned how the feedback of data to the next level down should be carried out.

Consultants took part in helping line officers prepare for these meetings according to the following:

> Usually, a member of the Survey Research Center and the company's personnel staff assisted the line officer in preparing for these meetings, but attended the meetings only as resource people who could be called upon for information about the feasibility of additional analyses ...

Mann's evaluation of this survey led him to conclude that:

> Our observations of the feedback procedure as it developed suggested that it was a powerful process for creating and supporting changes within an organization. However, there was no quantitative proof of this, for our work up to this point had been exploratory and developmental. (Mann, 1961, p. 610)

Changing organization-wide norms as a way of increasing effectiveness also is described by Allen and Pilnick (1973). Realizing that norms/standards constitute one manifestation of organization culture, their approach seeks to change norms/

standards either by discussing and comparing current norms with ideal norms, thereby pointing up an ideal/real gap and generating a desire to close it, or by participants' completing a norms profile which permits a similar discovery of norm discrepancies.

The norms profile is a sixty-item questionnaire organized into ten areas, such as (1) organization pride, (2) performance excellence, (3) teamwork, and so on. Each respondent indicates not what his or her own personal norms are, but rather, ". . . his estimation of what most other employees would do when confronted with that behavior by another employee." The instrument can then be scored in two ways. One is according to how participants perceive the actual culture of their organization or division, department, etc. Each participant can compare his or her attributed perceptions with statistical averages of attributed perceptions. The alternative, made possible by the fact that each scale has a good and bad end, is to compare perception of actual with what would be ideal: the wider the gap the greater the need for improvement.

The authors provide an example of how this norms/standards approach is used in bringing change about—pilferage among employees and customers was involved. The actual norm was perceived to be: ". . . pilferage is not my problem. It is the responsibility of security alone." A positive answer does not mean the respondent holds this attitude; rather, it is his or her perception of attitudes held by others. Allen and Pilnick do not report how the shift toward greater responsibility for reducing pilferage was brought about; presumably discussions led to widespread support of a new norm of shared and individual responsibility for reducing pilferage. However, it is reported that observed pilferage was now confronted whereas previously it had not been, and that individual and group success in reducing theft levels was positively rewarded.

At a more general level ten conditions, actually ten norms, must be embraced throughout an organization in order for this approach to achieve significant impact. These include top-management commitment to the norms-change program; top management's modeling the behavior it desires to see others embrace by adhering to these norms themselves; feedback to indicate whether norms are changing or not; reward of norm-wanted behavior; and six others.

LARGER SOCIAL SYSTEM (G_5)

Community action to solve social and other problems often cannot be taken because no real basis exists for identifying the problems, their real depth, or the amount of concern they generate. Action is blocked in the absence of shared norms or standards for perceiving issues that need attention.

Relationships between Various Ethnic Groups

The community self-survey is an intervention calculated to enable a community to arrive at shared norms and standards for community social perception and actions. Its use to investigate tensions between the established ethnic majority in a community called Northtown and two minority groups—Blacks and Jews—is reported by Wormser (1959). The survey was carried out during the 1940s, and was expected to reveal discrimination centered on employment, housing, education, public facilities and services, and community organizations. An objective was to use such survey data to increase the clarity with which community members perceived social facts to which they may not ordinarily have been exposed. Thus the survey itself became a mode of community intervention.

The survey was premised on several propositions, including

1. the importance of focusing on felt needs of community members, as exemplified by creating a broad-based community committee of actively interested persons to "steer" the project;

2. that such a committee should review each survey question and either confirm or change it according to whether it evaluated an issue they felt to be important;

3. that interviews should be carried out by local citizens;

4. that interpretation of information summaries and report writing should be carried out by representative citizens;

5. that review of findings with community action groups should be undertaken by those responsible for information summary and interpretation.

This approach is catalytic because its main aim is perception building, with focused issues relating almost entirely on felt needs or points of tension. The information, once summarized and interpreted, is assumed to be the catalyst needed to bring about desired changes in tense relationships.

Opinion Polling

Another type of catalytic intervention, quite well known to the public, involves empirical information gathering and feedback by such professionals as Gallup, Roper (1957), and Harris (1954, 1970). As consultants, each starts out with interviews designed to identify what it is the client wants to know. They then formulate opinion sampling, usually structured interviews or questionnaires, and administer these to a representative sample of the total community. Through newspapers, TV, books, and other media, reports of their findings are fed back to the community with interpretative suggestions provided through breakdowns by political party, sex, age, and so on. When the same questionnaires are used periodically, this approach permits assessment of long-term trends as well.

Alternatively, a particular client, such as the Republican or Democratic party, can commission opinion studies and use the results for action planning and program implementation. In another application, exemplified by Dichter and other motivational researchers, opinion-sampling techniques are employed for analyzing attitudes within the larger society toward commercial products of any variety. Such data can be analyzed by economic group, geographic region, and so on, and a profile of probable markets for a new product created. This can shorten the trial-and-error phases of new-product launchings (Dichter, 1960).

Police versus Minority Groups

Information used to broaden perception can also have the catalyzing effect of re-ducing rather than increasing the likelihood of a particular outcome, as shown dur-ing police and minority-group confrontations in the mid-1960s. The on-the-street encounters appear to have been significantly modified by a previously held police training session (Shellow, 1965, pp. 243–53). This intervention took the form of a six-hour seminar spread over a one-week period, undertaken in the context of a crash training program whose major activities involved drill, antiriot measures, uses of special equipment, and so on. The seminar, attended by forty-five uniformed po-licemen, began with lectures on the civil-rights movement. The origins and com-position of the Rights March, which was imminent, were dealt with.

The presentation of this kind of historical and legal perspective produced much private conversation among the police. The intervention created a common intellec-tual framework, replacing ignorance and prejudice with factual information, and promoted an exchange of points of view among them. As discussion continued, shared norms began to emerge concerning the genuine responsibilities of a police organization in the civil-rights field. The intervention bolstered "the professional image of . . . officers . . . called upon to enforce a social change not necessarily in line with their sympathies or sentiments. . . ." (Shellow, 1965, p. 252)

Summary

When the client is the larger social system, survey methods in particular can have an impact on reducing pluralistic ignorance. The very fact of "knowing where people stand," particularly if they are near agreement, can have a powerful motivating effect on behavior change.

IMPLICATIONS

Norms/standards function forcefully to hold behavior "in place" by promoting so-cially shared perceptions that discourage deviance or change. What is surprising is the apparent lack of attention to this focal issue when change is desired. There are several possible explanations. The most obvious is that the consultant is likely to share the same norms/standards and therefore "sees" them no more clearly than does the client. Or, the consultant might intuitively sense that an examination of norms/standards would promote immediate defensiveness on the part of the client.

REFERENCES

Allen, F. A., and S. Pilnick. "Confronting the Shadow Organization: How to Detect and Defeat Negative Norms." *Organizational Dynamics* 1, no. 4 (1973): 3–18.

Dichter, E. *The Strategy of Desire.* New York: Doubleday, 1960.

Douglas, L. *The Magnificent Obsession.* Grosset & Dunlap, 1929.

Fordyce, J. K., and R. Weil. *Managing with People*. Reading, Mass.: Addison-Wesley, 1971. Reprinted by permission.

Gordon, T. *Parent Effectiveness Training*. New York: Peter H. Wyden, 1970.

Harris, L. *Is There a Republican Majority?: Political Trends, 1952–1956*. New York: Harper and Brothers, 1954.

Harris, L. and B. E. Swanson. *Black-Jewish Relations in New York City*. New York: Praeger, 1970.

Jourard, S. M. *The Transparent Self*. Rev. ed. New York: Van Nostrand Reinhold, 1971.

Kinsey, A. C. *et al. Sexual Behavior in the Human Male*. Philadelphia: W. B. Saunders, 1948.

Kinsey, A. C. *et al. Sexual Behavior in the Human Female*. Philadelphia: W. B. Saunders, 1953.

Lorsch, J. W., and P. R. Lawrence. "The Diagnosis of Organizational Problems." In N. Margulies and A. P. Raia, eds., *Organizational Development: Values, Process, and Technology*. New York: McGraw-Hill, 1972, pp. 218–28. Reprinted by permission.

Mann, F. C. "Studying and Creating Change." In W. G. Bennis, K. D. Benne, and R. Chin, eds., *The Planning of Change*. New York: Holt, Rinehart and Winston, 1961, pp. 605–15. (Originally appeared in Research in Industrial Human Relations, *Industrial Relations Research Association*, Publication No. 17, 1957, pp. 146–67.) Reprinted by permission.

Mowrer, O. H. *The New Group Therapy*. New York: Van Nostrand Reinhold, 1964. Reprinted by permission.

Rice, A. K. "Productivity and Social Organization in an Indian Weaving Shed." *Human Relations* 6, no. 4 (1953): 297–329. Reprinted by permission.

Roper, E. *You and Your Leaders: Their Actions and Your Reactions*. New York: Morrow, 1975.

Schein, E. H. *Process Consultation: Its Role in Organization Development*. Reading, Mass.: Addison-Wesley, 1969. Reprinted by permission.

Shellow, R. "Reinforcing Police Neutrality in Civil Rights Confrontation." *Journal of Applied Behavioral Science* 1, no. 3 (1965): 243–54.

Truskie, S. D. "A Case Study of a Union-Management Learning Encounter in Industry." *Personnel Journal* 53, no. 4 (1974): 277–79. Reprinted by permission.

Vorrath, H. H., and L. K. Brendtro. *Positive Peer Culture*. Chicago: Aldine, 1974.

Wormser, M. H. "The Northtown Self-Survey: A Case Study." *Journal of Social Issues* 5, no. 2 (1959): 5–20.

CATALYTIC INTERVENTIONS

12

GOALS/OBJECTIVES

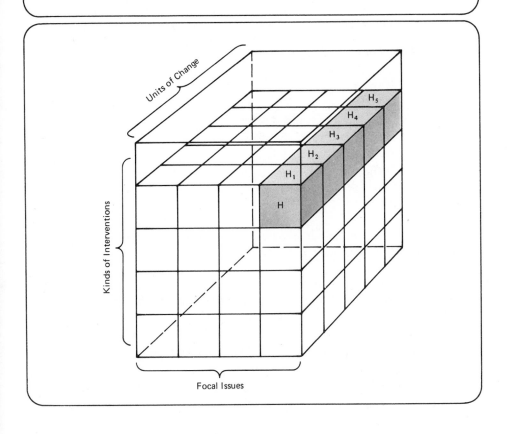

INDIVIDUAL (H₁)

When the focal issue is goals/objectives, the catalytic consultant may find it particularly difficult to penetrate a client's real problem. The exception—a unit of change in which helpful goals/objectives catalytic interventions are made—appears to be when an individual is the client. Major shifts in a person's goals/objectives oftentimes occur as part and parcel of age-, education-, or work-related changes.

Decisions about one's career may be difficult because of insufficient knowledge of opportunities, or even of one's own talents and abilities. Interventions in this area range from assisting school and college students who are trying to "find themselves," to aiding middle-aged managers who may be questioning their own career histories and searching for more rewarding kinds of assignments, to preretirement or retirement counseling.

Career Planning with a College Student

A college student seeking to improve his own unsatisfactory performance profited from a catalytic intervention in career planning. A teacher had suggested that he go to the University Counseling Bureau for further discussions of his situation. In the early phase of the interview the consultant gathered background information about the client's repeated in-school difficulties and then suggested a review of results from a series of tests administered earlier. This intervention assumes that additional data might assist the student to reach a more viable career decision. The scores could enable the client to see his current career objectives in the light of his measured abilities.

> *Consultant:* Do you remember taking that science test and the algebra test last September when you entered?
>
> *Client:* Uh-huh. Yes, I do ...
>
> *Consultant:* Those results might be the kind of thing that we're talking about. Here they are on the sheet here ...
>
> *Client:* Uh-huh.

The consultant takes the initiative by explaining *how* to interpret the data rather than telling the client *what* they mean.

> *Consultant:* In this column it indicates where you ranked ... on the percentage basis ... compared to entering agriculture freshmen. This number places you on a rank on a scale from 1 to 100.
>
> *Client:* Uh-huh.
>
> *Consultant:* If you were then at the 50 on that, that would mean that you were right at the average.
>
> *Client:* Uh-huh ... So I'm below average ...
>
> *Consultant:* The ranking there would be below average. Those tests, by

the way, have been given to quite a few students over the years in that college and they have an idea of how you might be able to handle the work in that college from how you do on these tests.

Client: Uh-huh.

Consultant: Scores...uh...like this would be the kind of scores... that persons make who have difficulty in making a satisfactory record ...in that college.

Now the client begins to see what this information might imply.

Client: The answer, I mean, I always did have a hard time and it was through my high school and...

Consultant: Uh-huh. Do you find that you have that same sort of trouble in your college chemistry?

Client: Yes, I think I do.

Consultant: Uh, huh. It's the same thing there....

Client: Uh, huh. Uh...do you think that's because of the background... that I didn't have too uh...good a background in those subjects?

The consultant presents a previously explored alternative to the client.

Consultant: Well, yes. Either that or you didn't master it well...

Client: Uh-huh.

At this point he refocuses the discussion.

Consultant: There are those two possibilities. You know there are all kinds of abilities and academic ability is just one kind of ability. It might be that you don't stand too well in that kind of ability. It may be that there are others for you. What sort of things do you think that you can do well?

Client: You mean in subjects?

Consultant: Or anything.

Client: Well, I don't know...I don't believe I understand what you mean.

Consultant: That's kind of a hard question to answer. What I mean is are there other things that you like to do better than school work or that you feel that you do better than school work?

Client: Well, I mean there isn't much else...I mean, there's...I've lived on the farm all the time... (Williamson, 1950, pp. 513–14)

The catalytic nature of the consultant's approach is clear, in several ways. He avoided expressing any personal convictions about the realism of this student's college program and career interests. What did he do? Through *procedural* suggestions he aided the student to gather and to interpret information pertinent to understanding his own performance. The consultant undoubtedly appreciated that test scores can take on unmerited proportions in the client's mind and thereby inhibit self-analysis and decision making. Scores may be interpreted as absolutes, having a prescriptive character rather than being used as indicators or "clues" of moderate or low validity. Thus the consultant serves as a sounding board to help the student clarify his current academic and career objectives.

Identifying and measuring a person's general pattern of interests and feeding back this information, with predictions as to how his or her interests will "fit" each of several vocations, is a well-known and time-honored way of assisting a client to select a career (Strong, 1943). The client fills in a standard vocational-interest blank and his or her responses are then evaluated in the light of answers given to the same questions by successful people in each of several lines of work. An additional use of such an interest questionnaire is to ask the client to answer the same questions again, but to do so according to his or her "ideal self." In this way discrepancies between "the way I am" and "the way I would like to be" become clearer, and the consultant can aid the client in exploring the implications for vocational decision making (Beit-Hallahmi, 1973).

Job Transfer

In the next situation a young man has requested a job transfer and is being interviewed as to why. The consultant is helping him review and clarify characteristics in his own self-development plans and aspirations. While the client's aspirations seem rather grandiose, the consultant does *not* brush them aside. He focuses the client on examining information as one basis for aiding him to reach his own conclusions as to what his career goals are or should be.

> *Client:*   Goal? I guess I'd like to hold an important position in the company.
> *Consultant:*   What level in the organization do you have in mind when you refer to an important position?
> *Client:*   Well, chairman of the board or president, I guess.

Now the consultant suggests a procedural strategy for information gathering.

> *Consultant:*   We could try to set down all the skills and experience we feel the president should have and evaluate just how much you'd need to do to get to that level of expertise. You could then decide whether you'd commit yourself to that kind of effort and try to estimate how successful you might be in carrying it off. But we'd also have to take a look at your competition, so let's examine that angle first. Assuming the next president will come from within the company, how many people do you figure you'd be competing with?
> *Client:*   I'm not sure.

Consultant: What thoughts do you have about the kind of person who would be more likely to be promoted? Do you feel that the next president could be someone upgraded from the wage ranks?

The client is now examining "facts" he believes to be true but that he had previously not evaluated.

Client: Oh no, the job will require a professional background.

Consultant: Then your competition will number, say, some four hundred or more people. What we have to do now is to identify what *you* have, that they *don't* have, which gives you an edge in achieving the presidency of the company.

Client: (no response)

Consultant: In view of our type of operations, how significant do you feel the level of technical or professional proficiency, broadly speaking, would be in the selection?

Client: I'd say that it would be very important.

Consultant: Well, then, how do you see yourself in this regard as compared to the four hundred people we're looking at?

Client: Smarter than some, not as capable as others.

Consultant: About in the middle?

Client: Yes.

The consultant narrows the search further. Questions aid the client to bring more information to bear and view his situation from a different perspective. Important to notice is that the consultant keeps from taking a stand on the man's career plans; decisions reached are the client's alone.

Consultant: If this kind of proficiency were the prime consideration, then we might say that the competition has been narrowed to two hundred. Now what advantage do you see yourself as having over these two hundred?

Client: (no response)

Consultant: Well, to what extent would you work harder than they would, to get there?

Client: I don't think I could say I'd work harder. I'm sure they'd all make as much effort.

Consultant: How about desire? How much more do you feel you *want* the position than they do?

Client: I couldn't truly say that I'd want it more. I really hadn't thought out very carefully what I said about the presidency. I guess that the goal isn't a realistic one for me at this stage of the game. Perhaps an intermediate goal is what I should establish. (Gould, 1970, pp. 226–34)

The interview continued, but focused on lesser, more attainable goals. He came to appreciate that there was little *realistic* possibility, at least in terms of any present evidence of progress or in his personal efforts at self-preparation, of his making it to the presidency. Accordingly, he scaled his career plans to more limited but possibly achievable objectives.

Mid-Career Changes

A career direction, once established, tends to perpetuate itself from its own momentum. Yet early or mid-career shifts into other activities may result in more gratifying and rewarding work. Retirement similarly offers another opportunity for a person to sort out his or her thinking and plan future activities, oftentimes unrelated to previous responsibilities.

The job a person takes on entering industry or government generally is related to his academic preparation, at least to some extent. He or she is considered for promotion as vacancies arise for which his or her qualifications are suitable. Under these conditions, there may be a poor fit between personal interests and goals on the one hand and organization needs on the other. If maturing talents and interests could be identified relatively soon after beginning employment, when a wide range of options are still open, but long enough after a person has absorbed initial and reality-producing work experiences, his or her career might take a different direction.

A career-planning approach intended to be helpful in the early years of managerial employment is described by Marsh (1973). The entire strategy rests on aiding participants to retest and reset their career goals. It is accomplished through:

1. participants completing information-gathering instruments prior to exercises that permit feedback. They work in self-selected trios whose members provide one another feedback regarding formal as well as informal aspects of behavior. In effect, the trio members are data sources for each participating individual;

2. clarifying and testing self-perceptions of their strengths, weaknesses, skills, and interpersonal effectiveness;

3. increasing their understandings of the contents of those jobs to which they might aspire;

4. identifying gaps between present competencies and what would be required for success in particular future positions; and

5. preparing and implementing their personal plans for acquiring the skills essential for success in qualifying for and moving into one or more targeted positions.

During a week-long workshop, self-selected participants engage in a number of activities aimed at accomplishing these purposes. Consultant assistance during the information-gathering sequence includes facilitating:

1. questionnaires that are completed as prework by each participant and by his

or her acquaintances to provide information that will enable the person to contrast self-perceptions with the perceptions held by others;

2. a "first impressions" exercise in which participants exchange initial reactions to
   other group members;
3. each participant studying his or her own past experiences with a view to identifying those work themes in which he or she has been most successful and those
   that have been most satisfying;
4. each participant studying the performance requirements of higher-level jobs. In
   this way, he or she is enabled to appreciate the knowledge, attitude, and skill
   requirements essential for success in more advanced job assignments.

All of these activities share in common a catalytic character: they provide the
participant with empirically derived perceptions calculated to increase his or her
goal clarity. Although a theory basis of self-diagnosis using the transactional-analysis
model is introduced, it is employed as a perceptual "test" for feedback rather than
as a central strategy for career planning.

An organization-simulation exercise is followed by decision-making tasks in
which participants alternate between participating as managers and as observer-
advisors. On the fourth day, the focus turns to the compilation of career development plans. Trio participants study and discuss upper-level job requirements in the
corporate structure and relate these to each person's self-perceptions and past experience. Personal obstacles to achievement are identified.

On the final day, after a briefing on criteria for setting and writing goals, participants work individually to formulate their own career development programs.
After trios critique these, participants form teams to role play career development
discussions of the kind individuals will soon be having with their supervisors. Each
team's role playing is videotaped for subsequent comparative analysis.

After the workshop, the company's facilitator gets in touch with each participant's supervisor to smooth the way by giving advance notice of the request for a
career discussion. The facilitator continues to monitor and provide background support as all or part of the plans are put into effect following the supervisor-subordi-
nate discussions. Participants convene six months later to write a commentary on
progress toward their career goals. Thereafter, annual reviews and updates of the
plan are made (Marsh, 1973, pp. 38–45).

A somewhat comparable approach to career consultation is offered by Haldane.
It attempts to help the individual identify those elements and activities in his or her
past life which have provided success and/or enjoyment, array and compare various
jobs that include some or all of these features, and evaluate the desirability of
change from a present assignment to one identified as more rewarding.

Take, for instance, the case of a brilliant man of 35, the controller of a
large corporation. He had a good salary and had worked his way up to
his present position after getting his master's degree in accounting. But
he was very frustrated and his anxieties were at a point where psychiatric

consultation was essential. The doctor referred him to us for career counseling.

The counselor asked him to recall experiences from which he had derived satisfaction. He mentioned several.

1. Raising funds for a Boy Scout drive
2. Selling magazines
3. Developing a printing business
4. Selling photographs
5. Operating concessions in college

But although he had followed his father's advice and pursued a college education and successful professional career, presently his heart was not in his job.

> ... In his free time he had volunteered for every community activity that involved selling or promotion of any type. He had sold tickets, he had organized groups to sell tickets. He had raised funds, he had organized groups to raise funds for many community activities. He had worked for community betterment projects and organized groups to promote them, then lobbied successfully to have them accepted by the city council.
>
> And, all this time, he had been becoming increasingly job-frustrated. While often commended for his controller work, he had always been glad when the week ended, somewhat resentful at having to go to work in the mornings. Because he had seen many other executives suffer the same feelings, he thought frustration was normal. Only when his home life had deteriorated substantially did he bow to his wife's insistence and discuss his problems with a psychiatrist.
>
> After he was referred for career counseling it was soon apparent that at least some of his frustrations were due to his being in a figures-and-paperwork job rather than in a selling and people-persuading job.
>
> Counseling helped him think through how he could swing within his company to an activity in the sales department where his accounting skills would be useful. He, on his own, suggested some private studies in marketing techniques and strategy. A program developed for him led to his becoming regional sales manager for the company within two years. The company had lost a man who was about to become a disaster in his controllership but gained a man who proved to be happy and highly productive in sales management. (Haldane, 1974, pp. 4–6)

The Haldane intervention recognizes and centers on the possibility that the talents an individual has and the satisfaction derived from using them may not be applicable in his or her present job assignment. To try to assist the client to find greater gratification *within* that assignment, such as by helping the person see how significantly his or her work contributes to organizational effectiveness, would miss the point. The career-planning objective is for the client to recognize those talents from which he or she can derive greater gratification, and then to set job goals within which they can find expression. This may be within his or her present career ladder or far removed.

A similar use of catalytic intervention, but at a different and usually later point in a person's career, is designed to help the individual develop "life plans" (Lippitt, 1970, pp. 2–7). The information-gathering method was pioneered by Shepard and makes use of a number of self-study and group activities. In broad outline, it involves each individual

1. reviewing past experiences that were rewarding and finding the main patterns or themes that run through them;
2. sharing one's findings with several others engaged in the same activities to obtain helpful reactions and suggestions;
3. based on conclusions reached, designing developmental goals which the particular individual can work toward so as to develop requisite competencies or find situations that permit more frequent involvement in rewarding activities.

An application of this general approach within corporate situations is described by Fordyce and Weil (1971, pp. 131–36) in the setting of a "Life/Career Planning Laboratory." This technique can be used at any critical career point, such as when a person is considering a new job opportunity, or whether to shift from a technical into a managerial assignment, or whether to accept early retirement.

These various interventions on the part of the consultant are of a catalytic character. They supply participants with procedures that permit them to explore their self-information, to gather new information, and to interpret its meaning. The consultant's participation hastens a process of self-discovery that probably could have gone on anyway, but at a slower rate and possibly on a more superficial level. He or she ensures that each member gets a "proper" share of attention and aids participants in identifying options that may never have occurred to them. Wishful thinking is separated from realistic prospects and the person may find that the cause of his present situation is not the organization, the boss, or fate—but is within himself.

Retirement Counseling

At the other end of the employment cycle is retirement. Since retirement presents a new set of problems, it also has become an important area of counseling (Beaumont and Tower, 1961; Greene, Pyron, Manion, and Winklevoss, 1969; Pellicano, 1973; Pyron, 1969). The range of new problems calling for innovative adjustments at retirement is unusually large: less income; an end to the everyday workplace relationships within which many long-term personal friendships may have been formed and sustained; the search for new activities to replace those of several previous decades; the consequences, for some, of spending most days at home and thus impacting on the wife's long-established solo routines; and, usually, the prospect of diminishing physical activity.

Preretirement, as well as postretirement, counseling may be conducted either with individuals on an interview-by-interview basis or in group settings. Whichever the case, its *educational* aim is to aid those facing termination of their careers to understand the retirement benefits their companies offer and to know more about Social Security. Its *counseling* aim is to aid retirees to anticipate and become adjusted to their new situations by selecting from the goals open to them those best suited to their needs. This kind of retirement counseling rests on a catalytic approach for problem definition, broadening perception, and making goal choices.

Summary

There are still other applications of the catalytic approach to counseling individuals. For the most part, however, they differ by subject and situation rather than involving basic shifts at the strategic or career-goals level. Included are rehabilitation, special disabilities, marriage, divorce, and so on, where the approach adopted depends to a substantial degree on whether an individual, a couple, a group, etc., can be aided best by procedural assistance, face-to-face information gathering, or through survey or aptitude and interest devices.

GROUP (H₂)

Nonexistent or fuzzy goals may be the factor causing things to be less satisfactory than they could be. Given that the client group feels the problem is in the goals area, the catalytic consultant may be able to make a constructive contribution to the situation.

Setting Objectives in Industrial Situations

An example of how a catalytic intervention occurs with boss and subordinate as they engage in "management-by-objectives" (MbO) is provided by Humble (1967). In the introduction of MbO in an organization, a third party consults with boss and subordinate to facilitate the program. In Humble's terminology, these third-party consultants are "company advisers."

> Company Advisers must be selected and trained to a highly professional standard in the various techniques. . . . An Adviser is a source of professional advice on the whole programme. He develops suitable techniques and methods with managers; counsels each individual manager in the Key Results Analysis preparation; is present at first Reviews; helps to analyse training plans. He is an "educator" and "catalyst," *not* a man who states what the standards should be, nor what the priorities are and how the problems should be solved. That is management's task. (Humble, 1967, p. 60)

Humble sees the consultant's role in a catalytic way when he maintains that this role is to "stay out" of the issues, limiting participation to what Schein (Chapter 11) would probably refer to as "process consultation."

Redefinition of Objectives in Nursing Services

A catalytic intervention with a view to providing a basis for management-by-objectives within a hospital department is described by Pearsall and Kern (1967, pp. 243–66). Although the final solution was actually not the one planned, its development offers useful insight into the catalytic process.

The hospital had opened nearly a year earlier and, as its first anniversary approached, the director of nursing services was becoming increasingly concerned about discrepancies she sensed between her department's stated goals and some of its actual practices. She formulated a proposal to make the anniversary a target date for evaluating and recharting departmental policy and practice. The administrative staff of the hospital endorsed this proposal. As the nursing director had raised the question of objectivity, they and she agreed that she was much too personally involved to provide objective leadership of this analytic undertaking. Instead, they decided to tap the resources of their affiliated college of medicine's department of behavioral science by asking for a "skilled discussion leader."

The nursing director put this initial request to an anthropologist in a college department, who commented that discussion leadership seemed an inadequate way of providing the nursing director with detailed feedback about staff functioning. Instead, she proposed and the director agreed to a limited observational study being undertaken. Accordingly, the anthropologist interviewed the nursing organization, observed and took notes at departmental meetings, and so on, maintaining a friendly, though still rather distant, demeanor. Trust and other indications of acceptance were accorded her by the nurses who would later be recipients of her findings.

The thrust of the intervention was to assemble, on the basis of the anthropologist's findings, hypothetical organization charts to mirror *actual* behavior. In this form, the findings were readily comparable with the hospital department's present organization chart and job descriptions.

In her intervention some weeks later, the anthropologist, rather than describing her findings in conventional organization-theory terms, used simple and picturesque allegories such as "tribal territories," contrasts between "emerging into an open mountain meadow" and staying within organizational "neat and bounded woods," and so on. The audience of nurses listened with interest but remained passive.

The nursing director and the anthropologist had no prior arrangement as to who would lead the discussion after the report. On the spur of the moment, the director seized the initiative. She "translated" the report's generalizations into detailed and specific nursing-service language. Thus, before she knew it, *she* had become discussion leader rather than turning that job over to the anthropologist, as the hospital administration had advised. At the same time, the objectivity issue had been resolved by the director's acting as translator and illustrator of the anthropologist's report.

In effect, the two principals had found their way to a consultant-client relationship rather than, as had been the case initially, the nursing director needing to "pass the torch of leadership" temporarily to an outside person. Pearsall and Kern indicate that this series of evaluation meetings evolved into lively policymaking and planning staff meetings, with the anthropologist as "sideline resource person." In this way the consultant took a more catalytic rather than directive role in the goal/objective-setting process.

Unclear Goals in a Community Agency

Grambs and Axelrod (1953) describe an intervention with a professional staff of a community center which typifies in several respects the catalytic mode of intervening. In this example, the consultant was unsuccessful in several respects. One was in failing to aid the group to reformulate its goals/objectives in such a way as to make progress; another was in not dealing with the existing power/authority structure in order to grapple with the problems presented by it. Both are representative of difficulties faced when the consultant seeks to work *within* the status quo situation.

> For example, the consultant presided at the first two meetings. He tried to find out about the center's program and problems, and the staff tried to explain what the center was really trying to do for its members. In these discussions, they began to see that the key factors in the kind of program that would lead to these goals were volunteer leaders.
>
> Before the end of the second meeting they reached the seemingly inescapable conclusion that the supervisors themselves were responsible for recruiting and training, guiding and helping the volunteers—who actually carried on the program.
>
> In an outburst of self-confession the staff members admitted that they had been more concerned with materials, membership drives, the appearance of the building, and recruiting more volunteers—than they had been in doing their best with the volunteer leaders.
>
> In fact, they admitted, only a minimum of attention was being given to those aspects of the volunteer's job most closely connected with what the center was trying to give its members.
>
> The group felt good following this self-revelation of shortcomings. The director thanked the consultant for not having criticized the admitted inadequacies of the staff. She ended by hoping that the future training sessions would be "a shot in the arm." (Grambs and Axelrod, 1953, p. 17)

The approach helped participants redefine their development goal and this in turn resulted in a review of past deeds as "emotional" facts and "misdeeds." How a consultant may "cooperate" with the status quo problem-solving atmosphere rather than challenge it is evidenced in the following.

> The consultant chatted informally with those who were there until the director and the last staff member arrived, 15 minutes late. Then it was discovered that arrangements for the coffee-break had been forgotten, so two staff members rushed out to handle this detail. As the meeting was called to order, the director leaned across to the consultant and said, "Well, so far we've been having fun—but today, maybe we can get down to work."
>
> The consultant had planned to ask one of the staff members to summarize the agreements reached at the end of the last meeting and restate the problem that was to be explored. But pressed "to get down to work," he felt he had better do it himself. (Grambs and Axelrod, 1953, pp. 17–18)

Just as the third session was ending the following happened.

> Suddenly, as the members were moving toward the door, the director called out, "I forgot to tell you that I will be obliged to miss our next training meeting since I must be at the state AASW conference. I'm sorry, because it promises to be an interesting one. We've got the ball rolling now. We've got it rolling." (Grambs and Axelrod, 1953, p. 18)

Rather than the consultant directly raising for group attention certain identifiable issues of its operating effectiveness, the fourth session reveals the same basic acceptance of the group's status quo and the effort to work within it. Other aspects of the consultant's efforts to catalyze change without challenging are revealed in the study's final summary.

> ... the consultant's behavior points up some interesting aspects of the training leader's role in leadership training. For instance, when the members started listing desirable qualities of volunteer leaders on the blackboard in the third session, he probably could have predicted a letdown when they realized they didn't know and hadn't planned what, if anything, to do with their list. He could have anticipated this and perhaps prevented it by urging them to carry out some other activity (and this might have helped make that session run more smoothly and accomplish more tangible results). But this is a program to help them learn to be better leaders. How much should he protect them from making their own mistakes? If they can learn more about leadership from making mistakes and evaluating the results than they can from following his directions, he should probably let them venture. This may be an acceptable principle to govern the leader's judgment. But the actual judgment is never an easy one for any training leader to make. (Grambs and Axelrod, 1953, p. 20)

Each of these episodes exemplifies the meaning of "cooperating" with the status quo, one of the key features of the catalytic mode of intervention. What *may* change as a result of the consultant's interventions are those aspects of group functioning that identify their felt needs. Other matters, even though they may be barriers to effectiveness in the consultant's eyes, are bypassed as inappropriate for examination. By not questioning the felt-needs aspects of the staff group's definition of goals/objectives, the consultant appears to have lessened the prospects of change.

INTERGROUP AND ORGANIZATION GOAL SETTING (H_3, H_4)

The lack of examples available in these two categories probably is attributable to two different sources. Rarely do two groups perceive their problems as goals/objectives issues—each tends to view the other's distinctive goals with disapproval and generally ignores similar or superordinate goals that might be achieved by cooperation. At the organization level there is likely to be the feeling that the organization must already *have* a purpose—otherwise, why would there be an organization? Although more and more organizations are beginning to question their traditional goals/objectives, particularly when faced by external economic or social threats, the entry issue is unlikely to be formulated in goals/objectives terms.

LARGER SOCIAL SYSTEM (H_5)

Community problems abound, often because citizens who might join together to reach community-oriented goals don't know how to get started. Unable to get together, they are unable to identify goals they might reach in concert. As often as not the community consultant initiates and supports group formation in order to move into goal achievement through community problem solving. The first two examples are of this character; the third involves an antagonism felt toward the school by community residents. The latter was approached in a catalytic manner since feelings by residents were sufficiently crystallized to enable them to take confronting actions on their own initiative.

Community Action Groups

Creating an urban *block organization* for concerned community action is a development-oriented program dating back to at least World War II. The idea is pertinent mostly in socially and economically deprived neighborhoods plagued by untenable conditions requiring united action. The social-worker approach for stimulating group formation and action usually is catalytic, but the resultant organization may later come to rely on political confrontation as a way of forcing corrective action. One method involves finding "indigenous" leaders, around whom other residents can mobilize. Suggested leader criteria include:

1. the ability to articulate community needs,
2. some degree of stability as evidenced in family, marital, or employment relations,
3. some previous demonstration of activity on his or her own behalf,
4. an awareness of the potential value of group action,

5. an ability to look at reality with a degree of objectivity,

6. an ability to understand cause and effect in relation to immediate problems,

7. some evidence of a degree of independence of thought and action from people in positions of authority,

8. evidence of physical and mental health,

9. a genuine feeling for, and interest in, people,

10. evidence of willingness to assume some concrete responsibility. (Bowens, 1954, pp. 19–20)

The second approach involves interventions with a group of individuals who have shown interest but lack the knack of getting together on their own initiative. The following describes a typical early meeting and shows how the consultant adopts a catalytic role.

> The group was busily engaged in perusing literature and pictures from other blocks. It was suggested that 8:30 p.m. would be a more convenient meeting time since Mrs. Ring had left home without eating; Mrs. Blake had had to return home to put the children to bed.

The consultant initiates discussion by putting a task-oriented goal before them.

> I told the group I had discarded a letter I had prepared to go to all block members at such time as we decided to hold our general meeting since I felt this was something we might all work on together. They agreed. After several unsuccessful attempts at wording by Mr. Feld and Mrs. Ring, Mrs. Bough's suggestion that we make a leaflet instead was picked up eagerly by the group.
>
> I wondered how we wanted to word it. They felt the heading should be something striking, compelling. Mr. Feld suggested, "Look." This seemed acceptable. Mrs. Bough asked for pencil and pad: "I can write better than I can talk." I asked how we wanted to continue. Mrs. Mack suggested, "Dear Neighbor, We are trying to get something done for the betterment of the neighborhood." Mrs. Ring suggested, "To the people of Fifth Street, we are trying to get together to better the conditions of our homes and neighborhood." This was a combination of Mrs. Mack's and her own contributions and was accepted by the group.
>
> Mrs. Bough suggested "Calling Fifth Street" instead of "Look" as a headline. This was agreed upon with enthusiasm. Mrs. Ring continued, "We are calling a meeting to discuss clean halls, hot water, plumbing, rat holes, steam heat, ceiling plaster, etc."
>
> *Mrs. Bough:* "Don't forget painting." *Mrs. Fox:* "All who are interested, and we are sure you are..." *Mrs. McGirk:* "...come to the meeting to discuss these problems." *Mrs. Fox:* "United we stand, divided we stand!" Some wondered when we fell. All laughed, and the correction was made.

I read the completed leaflet, adding that this was their own creation, made by their own efforts.

A discussion followed about the next meeting. Mrs. Rubin felt it should be a general one of the block. Mrs. Ring cautioned, "We are getting the cart before the ox. This group must plan for the next big meeting." I gave her support here. It was agreed to meet the following Thursday.

I felt we might want to consider everything that would go into getting out our leaflet. The Center could do the mimeographing but would need assistance in delivering. Mr. Feld volunteered to handle the distribution in 309 and 311. Mr. Blake, Mrs. Bough, and Mrs. Fox would take 303 and 305; Mrs. McGirk, 301.

Earlier, Mrs. Fox volunteered to act as temporary chairman and Mr. Feld, temporary secretary. (Bowens, 1954, pp. 30–31)

The social-work rationale for such intervention is summarized as follows:

1. Encourage voluntary and self-developing interaction of members toward the group by using the common interest (project or program) as a catalytic agent
2. Permit the release of hostilities and aggressions without damaging the group process
3. Meet the dependency needs of members while enabling them to move toward more independent action
4. Offer constructive opportunities for sublimation
5. Enable individual members of the group to function better inside the group and their block
6. Lead the group through the natural leader toward a successful achievement of their project.

It is not possible to delineate all the basic group work principles used. Some are implicit in the foregoing material; four other principles enunciated were:

1. The necessity of choosing as a project one that will unite all members of a group rather than identify with a subgroup
2. The necessity of keeping the leadership group geared to the larger block group and to develop program after organization is ready for it
3. The necessity of doing things with people, not for people, in order to develop independence
4. The necessity of having programmed clearly the means, not the end, in order to enable individuals to grow within and toward one another. (Bowens, 1954, pp. 22–23)

Often the action sought by the block organization involves confrontation of elements in the larger community. An example is their request for additional police protection. After a meeting on the subject, the group went to the precinct station with Mrs. Hink leading the delegation and with the consultant present as backup spokesman.

> Mrs. Hink served ably as spokesman. She told who we were, where we were from, and our purpose in being there. We spoke to Captain Merrill, who seemed duly impressed with the number of people and the vigor of their statements. Mrs. Hink said that we had come before with no results and now wanted action.
>
> Everyone participated. They told how many windows were broken and in which apartments, the dangers of flying glass and missiles. They listed the names of boys they had seen on the roof. Mrs. Ring said, "We're human beings, not dogs. We pay taxes for protection and want it."
>
> I told the captain this was our second visit. We had seen no policemen on the block; this was our last trip. If we got no action, we would go to the Police Commissioner. The Captain winced; he would see that we got action; he knew nothing of our previous visit; he would send plainclothesmen to the block. He spoke of the man shortage. Mrs. Hink felt this was the Captain's problem; all indicated approval. The Captain flushed, cleared his throat, and said we would get action this week. He rose, shook hands— the conference was over.
>
> All filed out with a dignified air of importance. They had accomplished something together. Participation was well distributed. This positive experience of concrete accomplishment will serve as encouragement for further forthright action on other issues. (Bowens, 1954, p. 37)

A negative aspect of this catalytic approach to community development is found in a gradual tendency toward reacceptance of the status quo situation, with diminishing hope of improving it, if the consultant is no longer available to act as catalyzing agent.

> The group seemed disappointed when I reminded them that I was leaving. When they said, "We'll have no worker of our own," I told them that the Director would be available whenever they needed him. They said, "But we'll have to go to him. He won't be able to come to us."
>
> Mrs. Ring said that this was really their organization and they would have to prove that they could run it themselves. The worker would hear that things had not fallen apart.
>
> The consensus was that there should be no meeting during the summer. They would meet again during the fall to determine what path their organization should take.
>
> After the worker left, leadership could not be provided by the Center. Actually, the people never met again as a group. Some members remained quite active by joining Blocks United. However, this group's activity was truncated by the termination of the project. (Bowens, 1954, p. 48)

Protecting Property Values

Thelen (1954) describes a series of interventions aimed at assisting a long-established residential community to identify and tackle its economic and social problems. The interventions took place in Chicago, beginning in 1950 when a rumor that exploiters planned to purchase a house in the area and pack it with several black families was sweeping the neighborhood. Everybody in a row of fifteen owner-occupied homes was invited to a meeting organized by a small planning group.

The meeting got off to an unexpected start when an elderly resident began badmouthing blacks. The chairman and other participants let his remarks pass without comment. Then the consultant formulated objective possibilities that block residents might consider.

1. It could form a pitchfork mob to try to drive the Negroes out.
2. It could attempt to ignore them.
3. It could attempt to establish communication with them with the idea of explaining the block's determination to prevent physical deterioration and to make the block a pleasant place in which to live. (Thelen, 1954, pp. 10–11)

Here is what happened.

Posed in this way, looking toward alternative possibilities for action growing out of a real situation, the group quickly decided to begin talking to people. A committee, combining the features of investigation team and friendship group, was appointed to go calling on the new neighbors. The Negroes, fortunately, could see the committee's embarrassment and were mature enough to help them establish communication. The fact that members of the committee did not have strong feelings either way about Negroes undoubtedly made matters easier.

Three other actions were taken at the first meeting; and the second meeting started with a report of these actions, the introduction of new people, and the setting-up of an agenda consisting of the things people on the block thought were problems to be looked into.

As the neighbors left the first meeting they felt considerable relief from anxiety. The meeting had not yet done anything very important by way of taking action but the neighbors had found out something that they knew intellectually but could never have really felt if they had not been called together to enter into action. They had found out that there were a lot of people just as concerned and just as frustrated as they were. Instead of feeling that "everybody else is perfectly able to cope with the situation, but I am not," the individual found that everybody was equally unable to cope with the situation, so that the feeling of inadequacy dissolved and was replaced by the much more objective perception that the group as a whole had problems. Thus the feeling of being out of the group, of being a helpless spectator on the sidelines—feelings which had led individuals

> to turn inwardly on themselves and feel lonely—these were replaced by a complete reversal of the relationship of the group. The group of neighbors was felt now to be supportive; one was no longer alone. Under these conditions of establishment of communication and support the individual could feel free to act intelligently rather than out of anxiety. (Thelen, 1954, p. 11)

This intervention resulted in a widening of social perception; participants now felt more of a sense of community than had previously existed. Such sharing appears to have had secondary cathartic effects. Feeling relieved of anxiety, residents could turn their thoughts toward action.

> Thus there arose spontaneously from the meeting a demand for subcommittees to get busy. The group identified a wide range of practical problems: the moving of abandoned cars, the installing of porch lights to dispel darkness, the prompt reporting of movements of materials into houses so that the plans for conversions could be checked, the development of tot-lot and recreational space, the collective buying and sharing of garden implements. Working committees arose from volunteers who felt strongly about one or another of these problems. And committee action, supported, encouraged, and supervised by the block group, resulted in positive acts of neighborhood improvement.

> The actions resulting from working together had their effect on the physical community. In addition, during the processes of co-operation, neighbors began to make some highly significant personal discoveries about themselves and each other. They learned that the things they used to worry about don't need to matter. A Negro worker or a low-income renter can have just as useful ideas, make as many phone calls, dig out just as valuable facts, and be just as helpful as anyone else. Through these discoveries, the neighborhood as a community of people became stabilized. The block began to feel like home; life in the block acquired new richness of meaning and satisfaction. The neighbors learned that the physical and social communities are inextricably linked: actions are taken to maintain and improve the physical community, but it is the way in which neighbors participate to take action that maintains and improves the social community. (Thelen, 1954, p. 12)

This suggests how a catalytic intervention to help formulate agenda and procedures can enable people, who have not interacted previously, to take the first steps in social organization—a process of perception-building, sharing, and action.

Thelen summarizes principles of block leadership for goal-oriented community action. Each is amplified in the original source.

1. *Participation depends on reward.* For the neighbors to remain involved and interested over a long period of time, they must receive rewards at a sufficient rate. . . .

2. *The block works on "felt" problems.* The only matters on which people will expend energy are those which they feel are problems, things about which people have feelings which they must deal with. . . .
3. *Leadership is by team.* The kind of leadership required encourages free expression of feelings and opinions, sifts these to help diagnose problems realistically, and guides the group into action. . . .
4. *Movement spreads through friends.* A component of the initial attitudes of people in disorganized areas is the feeling of lack of trust; they are suspicious of each other. Meetings can be organized most successfully when friends call on friends so that the initial hurdle of distrust does not have to be overcome.
5. *Membership is based on willingness to work, not on ideology.* The basis of participation in block meetings is merely that one lives on the block. There is no test of ideology because it is not what people say they believe that is important so much as their willingness to work on problems. . . .
6. *Discussion focuses on concrete problems.* Arguing about "ideologies," making grand generalizations which take in all the territory from here to Alaska—these behaviors are gratifying to some individuals, but they are irrelevant to the action part of the block meeting. When the group is trying to select problems, define them, and work on them, it gathers steam and enthusiasm through being able to see more and more clearly what the problem is and what acts will be appropriate. . . .
7. *All decisions are subject to revision as a result of taking action.* A "good" decision results in action which remedies the situation. A "bad" decision results in action which makes people even more uncomfortable, apathetic, or frustrated. It is possible for a group to make the wisest decision of which it is capable and then find that when it acts on the decision matters get worse. The value of a decision cannot be known at the time the decision is made; it can be known only through study of what happens during action. . . .
8. *Each block group determines its own autonomy.* The fact is that the existence, success, and prospects of most block groups are in no small measure owing to the efforts of the Conference organization. Block groups, however, react in different ways to this fact. Some will deny it; others will accept it gladly and look to the parent organization for much help; still others will feel little concern one way or the other. Some block groups develop jealous loyalty to themselves; others, to the community. (Thelen, 1954, pp. 14–17)

The above suggest, then, that interventions with those community members who have a significant vested interest—homeowners in this case—can catalyze a situation and result in community-based problem solving.

An approach to community action useful in dealing with any existing problem and relying almost solely on the use of a catalytic facilitator is offered by Strauss and Stowe. Examples of its application include community problem census and community growth goal setting that cut across the conventional power structure, solving parent and youth problems, finding jobs for the hard-core unemployed, and establishing effective communication between the local community and state legislators.

The catalytic agent is a facilitator, who can

1. help the participants explore a problem and improve their understanding of it;
2. help them integrate their thinking and work together to reach a decision on which they can agree and which they will carry out with zeal;
3. help them plan and organize the process for carrying it out, including the assignment of responsibilities to individuals;
4. help them plan evaluation of progress, review the findings, and replan and reassign responsibilities as necessary. (Strauss and Stowe, 1974, p. 193)

This approach goes beyond reliance on the professional consultant by training local community leaders to acquire catalytic-oriented discussion skills. This training is completed in three two-and-one-half hour training sessions throughout one day or evening. Central to this training is discussion of the elements quoted below, the requisite skills of an effective discussant.

HOW GOOD A DISCUSSANT ARE YOU?
HOW OFTEN DO YOU—

To Facilitate Progress of the Discussion:

1. Question what a statement means
2. Ask about an overlooked viewpoint
3. Question the course of the discussion
4. Summarize
5. Test for consensus

To Make Discussion More Penetrating:

6. Ask a pertinent question
7. Initiate thinking
8. Use logic in attempting to find a solution
9. Try to separate facts from opinions and assumptions
10. Try to integrate separate ideas

To Improve Both Discussion and Group Solidarity:

11. Listen
12. Draw others into the discussion
13. Build on others' contributions
14. Bring discussion out of chaos
15. Support others, give others recognition
16. Change position when clarification is made
17. Under tension make conflict reducing remarks
18. State your thoughts or opinion for clarification
19. Give needed information
20. Seek clues to acceptable solutions

To Improve Group Solidarity:
21. Show approval by gestures, posture, or facial expression
22. Show politeness or friendliness
23. State your feelings about others usefully

To Satisfy Your Personal Needs:
24. State your feelings destructively
25. Ask non-pertinent questions
26. Attempt to sell your viewpoints, regardless
27. Interrupt unnecessarily
28. Talk excessively, reminisce, tell stories, talk with neighbors
29. Try to impress others
30. Repeat yourself or others
31. Backtrack when opposed
32. Become antagonistic
33. Read
34. Be apathetic, preoccupied, withdrawn, hurt
35. Show boredom or tension by doodling, nail-biting, shifting in chair, etc.
(Strauss and Stowe, 1974, p. 216)

Considerable success from using this mode of intervention for community development is reported.

School and Community Goal Discrepancies

Goals embraced by one group may be at variance with those favored by another group that is serviced by the first. Resolution of such conflict is possible through goal clarification. However, when a catalytic approach leads toward goal clarification but mutual agreement as to shared goals is not reached, the effort may lead nowhere and result in a worsening of the situation. Caplan (1970) presents an example of such an episode in which the consultant sought, by catalytic interventions, to help a school system during an intense school/community cleavage. The consultant, whose contractual duties involved being available at the school one half-day per week for mental-health problem solving with individual students, was discussing related matters with the school's principal when a deputation of black parents came into the principal's office.

They told the principal that they were not satisfied with the way in which the school was being run, and they complained aggressively about the quality of education their children were getting, as well as about the deplorable conditions of the school building, with its broken windows, inadequate heating, peeling paint work, and unsanitary toilet facilities. They said they had been complaining individually about these things for years without results. Now they had banded together into a committee and were demanding immediate action. (Caplan, 1970, p. 359)

The principal was shaken by this unanticipated challenge.

> ... The consultant supported him during the ensuing discussion; and after the parents had temporarily withdrawn into the outer office, he helped him review their demands and work out a reasonable reaction. The principal discussed the problem over the telephone with his district superintendent. He then called the deputation back into his office and informed them that their grievances would be brought to the attention of the school administration and that something concrete would be done about the matter. (Caplan, 1970, pp. 359–60)

After the parent group had left, discussion between principal and consultant continued. The consultant helped him to discern the legitimacy of certain of the goals-for-change that had been placed before him and to recognize that it was actually the hostile manner in which they were presented that caused the principal's initial upset. Furthermore, the consultant offered to come as a "resource person" to a parent-teacher meeting scheduled for two weeks away.

The consultant made this offer, and the principal accepted it, prior to discussing its implications with the director of the mental-health center where he was a staff member. When he did mention it the director pointed out that this mode of intervention brought the center into a new area altogether: intergroup tensions between school and residents. Furthermore, it could cause residents to see the consultant as the school's ally or even as one of its staff members. However, it was decided that this principal did need support; and coincidentally, that the center itself needed to learn more about racial tensions within the community. This situation afforded an opportunity for the center to serve both interests, the client's and its own. But it was also decided that the consultant should as far as possible avoid taking an active role in the meeting; rather, his interventions could well be limited to post-meeting consultation with the principal.

When the meeting took place—the first time that such an interchange had occurred between parents and teachers in many years—it was well attended by both groups. The principal led off by stating that the parents' demands had been passed up to higher levels of the school system and that certain building repairs had already been authorized while other demands, particularly those involving additional budget, were deferred because actions could not be taken on them until they had been reviewed by the city board of education. As they were expecting specific and concrete actions and had little use for promises, several of the parents were angered by his remarks.

At this point, nonparent militants began speaking in hostile and insulting terms, and by attacking the principal and his staff succeeded in stirring up audience support. The principal and two teachers tried to rebut the accusations with logical counterarguments but were shouted down. The meeting ended in disorder.

The consultant did not get directly involved in the confrontation and tumult, but in a post-meeting session he intervened with the principal and some of the teachers to help them recover their composure and gain some understanding of what had happened. As the consultant saw it, the parents' proper concerns for the school's effectiveness and the well-being of their children were being pushed out of focus by the more diffuse racial tensions existing within and outside the neighborhood. Militants were exploiting the circumstances, with a view to publicizing and perhaps amplifying black/white conflict. He suggested also that since the situation's scope extended beyond the school's immediate jurisdiction, it would be appropriate to refer the matter to the school system's higher levels, and offered the center's assistance as a specialized resource for dealing with these larger issues. Caplan describes the events that followed.

> On the consultant's return to the center, the director concurred with his position and offered to attend a meeting with the district superintendent and perhaps to try to bring in some of the local black leaders for a behind-the-scenes discussion. The consultant phoned the principal and conveyed the director's offer, and the principal said he would discuss the matter with his district superintendent.
>
> The following week, the principal reported to the consultant that the district superintendent did not wish to open up this matter in the manner suggested by the center and that while he appreciated their offer, he would not accept it at this time. If he felt the need for the center's help, he would get in touch with the director. (Caplan, 1970, p. 361)

Thus community tensions were approached catalytically by aiding the school group's representatives to clarify goals and by offering procedural suggestions. When this proved insufficient for bringing group protagonists into any sort of problem-solving harmony, contacts between the consultant and the school were discontinued. By the beginning of the next school year tensions had worsened to a significant degree. Now a confrontational approach was attempted by the consultant, to be discussed more completely in Chapter 15.

Peacekeeping between Nations

Peacekeeping activities by the United Nations initiated during the Hammarskjöld era appear to have been premised on catalytic assumptions. This catalytic approach was implemented in several situations where (1) vital interests of leading Security Council members were *not* at stake, and where, therefore, the Secretary-General could exercise his good offices according to personal discretion; and (2) both sides in the controversy gave their explicit consent that the UN peacekeepers could employ measures short of armed force to dampen local violence, to reduce the likelihood of escalation, and to create a climate conducive to negotiations (Fabian, 1971). Such initial consensus between the contending factions was prerequisite to intervening in this manner. Additionally, as a means of defusing hostility, the UN took no actions of a sort that would specify one party or the other as guilty of aggression; far less, use force against one or more states. Finally, it made no attempt to sketch or explore potential areas of political settlement.

Inferentially at least, the Hammarskjöld-directed UN interventions were geared to produce information that would aid both parties in seeing the problems existing between them and in finding the means to improve mutual understanding of national interests, particularly as these bore upon issues that were or were not open to future negotiation. As a third party, the UN representatives stepped away from confrontation or arbitration in preference to providing catalytic consultation, helping protagonists to identify both nonnegotiable and negotiable goals.

REFERENCES

Beaumont, R. A., and J. W. Tower. *Executive Retirement and Effective Management.* New York: Industrial Relations Counselors, Inc., Industrial Relations Monograph No. 20, 1961.

Beit-Hallahmi, B. "Counseling with the SVIB: The 'Ideal Self.' " *Personnel and Guidance Journal* 52, no. 4 (1973): 256–61.

Bowens, M. G. "The Neighborhood Center for Block Organization: An Experiment in Self-Help at the Neighborhood Level." In C. E. Murray, M. G. Bowens, and R. Hogrefe, eds., *Group Work in Community Life.* New York: Association Press, 1954, pp. 13–67. Reprinted by permission.

Caplan, G. *The Theory and Practice of Mental Health Consultation.* New York: Basic Books, Inc., © 1970. Reprinted by permission.

Fabian, L. L. *Soldiers without Enemies: Preparing the United Nations for Peacekeeping.* Washington, D.C.: The Brookings Institution, 1971.

Fordyce, J. K., and R. Weil. *Managing with People: A Manager's Handbook of Organizational Development Methods.* Reading, Mass.: Addison-Wesley, 1971.

Gould, M. I. "Counseling for Self-Development." *Personnel Journal* 49, no. 3 (1970): 226–34.

Grambs, J. D., and J. Axelrod. "Time Out for Training: A Record of Staff Training in a Community Center." *Adult Leadership* 2, no. 2 (1953): 17–20. Reprinted by permission.

Greene, M. R., H. C. Pyron, V. V. Manion, and H. Winklevoss. *Preretirement Counseling, Retirement & Adjustment, and the Older Employee: An Experimental Study Measuring the Interrelationship of Factors Affecting Retirement Adjustment, Resistance to Retirement, and the Effectiveness of the Older Employee.* Eugene, Oregon: Graduate School of Management and Business, College of Business Administration, University of Oregon, 1969.

Haldane, B. *Career Satisfaction and Success: A Guide to Job Freedom.* New York: AMACOM, 1974. Reprinted by permission of the publisher.

Humble, J. W. *Improving Business Results.* Maidenhead, Berks.: McGraw-Hill, 1967. Reprinted by permission.

Lippitt, G. L. "Developing Life Plans: A New Concept and Design for Training and Development." *Training and Development Journal* 24, no. 5 (1970): 2–7.

Marsh, P. J. "The Career Development Workshop." *Training and Development Journal* 27, no. 7 (1973): 38–45.

Pearsall, M., and M. S. Kern. "Behavioral Science, Nursing Services, and the Collaborative Process: A Case Study." *Journal of Applied Behavioral Science* 3, no. 2 (1967) 243–66.

Pellicano, D. "Retirement Counseling." *Personnel Journal* 52, no. 7 (1973): 614–18.

Pyron, H. C. "Preparing Employees for Retirement." *Personnel Journal* 48, no. (1969): 722–27.

Strauss, B., and M. E. Stowe. *How to Get Things Changed.* Garden City, N.J.: Double day, © 1974.

Strong, E. K. *Vocational Interests of Men and Women.* Stanford, Calif.: Stanfor University Press, 1943.

Thelen, H. A. *Dynamics of Groups at Work.* Chicago: University of Chicago Press 1954. Reprinted by permission.

Williamson, E. G. *Counseling Adolescents.* New York: McGraw-Hill, 1950. Reprinte by permission.

CATALYTIC INTERVENTIONS

13

SUMMARY
AND
IMPLICATIONS

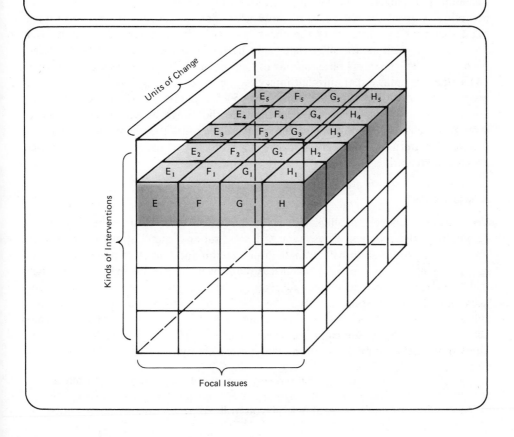

Catalytic interventions, whether the client is an individual, a group, two or more groups in an intergroup situation, an entire organization, or a larger social system, have recognizable common features. First, and most important, are the three basic assumptions on which the approach rests. The consultant can offer help in dealing with each of these.

1. Deficiencies of perception are the cause of malfunctioning. The "solution" is to strengthen perception of problems through improving the flow of information.

2. Barriers to improved information flow include inadequate procedures and processes used by the client.

3. Mutual isolation of member components within the client system prevent them from coming together. This may be observably true of clients consisting of two or more individuals. For the individual as single client, it may be inferred that an analogous "separatedness" is associated with his present lack of integrated awareness of a focal issue.

TECHNIQUES

Techniques of catalytic consultation include: (1) working within the status quo by accepting as given the felt needs of those who operate it; (2) serving as a rallying point that enables members of the client system to get together; (3) offering (a) procedural suggestions for steps that might be taken in seeking to satisfy those felt needs, and (b) "process" observations to help people see how to be more effective; (4) gathering data, either through interviews, survey research, group meetings, or instruments—or aiding the client to do so; (5) feeding the data back to those who are in a position to take action; (6) helping in the design of implementation steps through which resolutions are possible; (7) building into the client's mechanisms a repetition pattern so that regression can be avoided and the possibility of further progress increased.

LIMITATIONS

To consultant and client alike, felt needs may seem close to or even identical to definition of the problem. Consonant with the "rational man" approach, they may presume that information will strengthen perception and that clear perception is the key to solving many if not all problems. A major weakness of the catalytic approach is that information deficiency is more likely to be a symptom than a cause of problems. A pertinent question is, *Why* is "available" information unavailable? The consultant may ponder this question, but he does not raise it with the client. A certain kind of institutionalization can occur when reliance is placed on consultants operating within the broad ambience of a catalytic orientation.

> In TRW Systems, we are now moving in a number of directions, some of which I would like to describe. We are now moving more toward day-to-day coaching—on-the-job feedback, if you will—with or without consultants

and without calling special meetings, but just as we work together. We are paying continuing attention to process as a way of doing business. We are moving more and more toward using third-party facilitation as a standard operating procedure. (Davis, 1967, pp. 18–19)

A risk is that, given heavy reliance on "third-party facilitators," this may become "standard operating procedure." The need for an organization to have effective managers who can solve problems without "artificial" help is disregarded.

When the consultant is permitted free access to all parts of the organization certain problems can arise in determining which issues are worked on when and by whom. Caplan pinpoints the consultant's difficulty as follows.

> . . . the consultant may intervene at an individual, group, or organization level. His interventions are of a time-limited, circumscribed nature; and whether or not they are prompted by his own awareness of an issue or initiated in response to a feeling of need for consultation by a member of the organization's administrative staff, they must be limited by the boundaries of what the consultees feel are salient current predicaments. This means that although the consultant may be visiting the organization on a regular weekly basis for several years, and having continuing contacts with particular individuals and groups with whom he develops stable relationships of a gradually evolving character, his consultation interventions continue to be of an *ad hoc* type focused on temporary intercurrent episodes. This is so even though the consultant may recognize in his own mind that certain repetitive issues are linked to major continuing difficulties in the organizational structure. From time to time he may choose an opportunity for focusing discussion on these major problems; but on the whole, his strategy is to help the consultees handle them piecemeal in relation to the crisis and social system disequilibria they produce. (Caplan, 1970, p. 283)

The catalytic consultant's task, then, is subject to a fundamental dilemma. As he or she relies on the client to voice felt needs, to move toward defining the problem, and to become an active participant in its resolution, the consultant can lose his or her own perspective. Yet to the degree the consultant retains responsibility for definition and resolution, he or she is likely to meet with client resistance to imposed views. Carried further, the latter course would become prescriptive intervention, the consultant assuming full responsibility for the project.

APPLICATIONS

When the client's current problems appear to be related mainly to power/authority, the consultant attempts in a low-key manner to bring the client to an awareness of this as the focal issue. He or she is careful not to intervene in ways that would suggest to the client that "consultant power/authority" was being employed.

If the issue, however, is one of morale/cohesion, the consultant may suggest at least the rudiments of some procedure by which the client can initiate activity to "dissolve away" the present problem and its prevailing effects. The consultant may be able to select any one or more of a number of options open for intervening in the problem-related context, thus helping indirectly to improve the client's morale/cohesion.

If norms/standards constitutes the focal issue, a catalytic intervention may be more precise in the sense of instituting procedures whereby related problems of pluralistic ignorance can be resolved. Survey research is a prime example of such a technique.

The catalytic approach to a goals/objectives focal issue seems particularly helpful with individual clients; it is seldom applicable to problems at the group, intergroup, organization, and larger social system levels except to the extent that some external threat to such a unit of change is already facilitating the formation of interest groups that, in turn, can be aided in their goal-setting processes by this mode of intervention.

REFERENCES

Caplan, G. *The Theory and Practice of Mental Health Consultation.* New York: Basic Books, © 1970. Reprinted by permission.

Davis, S. A. "An Organic Problem-Solving Method of Organizational Change." *Journal of Applied Behavioral Science* 3, no. 1 (1967): 3–21. Reprinted by permission.

3

CONFRONTATIONAL INTERVENTIONS

14

CONFRONTATIONAL INTERVENTIONS: AN INTRODUCTION

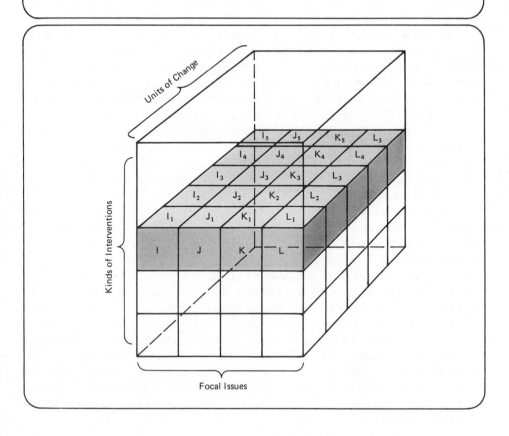

Units of Change

Kinds of Interventions

Focal Issues

Values direct behavior not only in a general way but in specific terms as well. Sometimes guidance from a particular set of values is sound—things go smoothly, results are good. Sometimes values cause problems—they are inappropriate, invalid, or unjustified under the circumstances. Often people who must work in concert hold different values; failure to achieve unanimity in such situations results in antagonisms, disorder, or outright chaos.

Many deeply held values are related to *authority/power* dynamics: "Rank has its privileges," "It's not what you know, but who you know that gets you ahead," "The boss is always right," are but a few examples. *Morale/cohesion* focal issues between individuals and among groups, organizations, and larger social systems often relate back to unreconciled differences in basic values that people in the situation have embraced or are currently emphasizing. For example, loyalty to a national ideal or to an historical image may form the basis of an older generation's morale but have no relevance for a younger generation. With regard to *norms/ standards,* values that individuals either have at the outset or are induced to adopt fuse into group or organization-wide enforced norms—whether "official" or not— that define "right" and "wrong." Those who subscribe to them are in good standing; those who do not are either ostracized, thrown out, or excommunicated in some form. Living on a day-to-day, "come what may" premise might be an example of a short- versus long-term time horizon with respect to life *goals and objectives.*

To successfully break out of self-defeating cycles, the individual must first explicitly identify and understand the values he or she presently embraces. Confrontation is one way of helping a client explore the consequences of acting in accordance with these values, a first step toward implementing change. A consultant who operates in a confrontational mode pinpoints for the client inappropriate, invalid, or unjustified values and gets him or her to face up to a *reality* in the values domain which was previously unrecognized, ignored, disregarded, or rejected. The confrontational consultant seeks to create a discrepancy between values generally considered valid, either in the light of behavioral-science findings or in terms of a sound philosophy of life, and the self-defeating values and assumptions actually operating within the situation.

Many values that undergird human activities are deeply embedded, often constituting second-nature "truisms" not subject to introspection. But value scrutiny is what a confrontational intervention is calculated to produce. Initially it could seem a poor choice of intervention, since when "confronted" people often engage in defensive practices. Defense mechanisms of the kind described in psychoanalytic literature are best understood as strategems for protecting deeply held, sometimes "unconscious," values, often those related to maintaining self-esteem or decreasing feelings of weakness and inadequacy. Rationalization, justification, projection, denial, and reaction formation are examples of such mechanisms. Prejudices that influence the way people "see" also have the character of embedded values—if they are challenged, the client ordinarily adopts a defensive posture, unable to acknowledge that some of his or her deeply held beliefs may be unjustifiable. By the same token, of course, certain personal values are fully consistent with mental health and effective interpersonal functioning.

Confrontational interventions are among the most effective in reducing the efficacy of defense mechanisms. A well-designed confrontation literally faces the client with a contradiction between his or her stated values and those—as yet unrecognized by the client but evident to the consultant—on which his or her behavior *actually* is founded. Once the contradiction becomes apparent the client is better prepared to investigate the consequences of failing to manifest his or her "merely mouthed" values. Usually such consequences are less desirable than the consequences of behaving in terms of values already preferred at the cognitive level, and so the client may next decide to shift his or her behavior accordingly. The following summary of confrontational intervention ground rules is useful in understanding what the confrontational consultant seeks to do as he or she intervenes with individuals, groups, and so on.

A confrontational consultant's strategy takes into account the likelihood that the client will rationalize and justify his or her present behavior as consonant with "mouthed" values, thereby explaining away difficulties rather than facing them squarely. The underlying assumption is that the client can be helped to see his or her actual values in a more objective manner if challenged to explain the "whys" of present behavior.

The consultant avoids, however, telling the client in a prescriptive way what he or she has inferred these values to be. Rather, the consultant asks questions that push the client to recognize them independently, and then zeroes in on inconsistencies the client may have missed. For example, "You said you expect candor from your subordinates, but how can you expect that when you are not even being open and honest with me?" If the client responds defensively rather than giving open thought to the question, the consultant picks this up as further evidence of reality-avoiding attitudes that need attention. The impact of a confrontation is increased when the behavior or attitude it identifies is occurring at the moment, rather than being some historical reconstruction of long-gone events. The client is unlikely to be able to reconstruct in accurate terms what feelings propelled him or her into some past action or attitude, and as such it becomes much more difficult for the client to sense the contradiction that the confrontation seeks to identify and resolve.

A confrontational consultant might proceed in the following manner. He or she:

1. takes nothing for granted as the client describes his situation. In answering questions the client either shows that he understands the situation, or that he doesn't. If the client doesn't, the consultant keeps asking questions that "force" him to face up.

2. presents facts, counterarguments, and logic to help a client test his objectivity.

3. challenges the client's thinking regarding different courses of action, once the client understands his own actual values and assumptions.

4. probes for reasons, motives, and causes that will give the client a clear and possibly different perspective on his present situation.

5. gives the client his or her own thinking, particularly when these differ from the client's values and assumptions, but in such a way that the client doesn't feel personally attacked or put down.

A confrontational consultant deals with individuals in a somewhat different way than he or she deals with larger social units, such as teams or organizations. In working with an individual, the consultant necessarily has less input on which to base judgments and therefore is often slower to pinpoint the real issues. Also, when working with teams or larger units, he or she may find collusion—i.e., several members unwittingly working together to deny the possibility that they might be operating on the basis of unjustifiable values. Since these client members reinforce one another they create additional difficulties, but at the same time provide the consultant with richer data to use in formulating a confrontation strategy.

The "richer" the data, however, the more complex—and therefore the more difficult to unravel. In addition to reinforcing one another's shared but inappropriate values, group members are likely to be motivated by unique values, more privately held. Thus it becomes more difficult for the consultant to frame confrontational interventions that are not subject to rejection by *some* members as being "unfair criticism" or ". . . your misperception of what's really going on in *our* situation." Eventually, however, the group's value pattern may become clear to the consultant, and from that point on he or she is prepared to intervene with a jolt.

CONFRONTATIONAL INTERVENTIONS

15

POWER / AUTHORITY

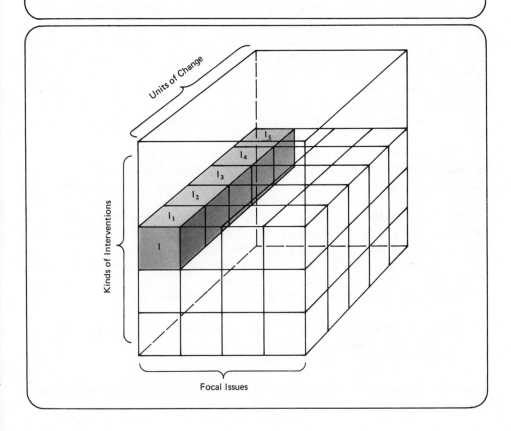

Confrontations that deal with behavior or attitudes in the power/authority area are themselves based upon the power/authority relationship between the consultant and the client. If the consultant can be regarded by the client as junior to him or her in age or experience, or comes through as weaker—say, by signs of reluctance to stand by the confrontations and "force" the client to give them self-analytical consideration —then the client may reject more or less out of hand what the consultant has to say. While dynamics such as these are likely to weaken any mode of intervention, confrontation in the power/authority area is perhaps the most susceptible to risk of failure.

INDIVIDUAL (I₁)

Confrontations related to power/authority issues can aid an individual client to understand the assumptions presently underlying his or her own conduct. As mentioned before, these assumptions often arise from deeply embedded personal values and the client may strongly resist facing and evaluating them.

Authority-Obedience as Boss's Managerial Style

Argyris (1971) describes a confrontational intervention with the chief executive officer of a large company. The chief was interested in getting his top forty executives, who were stationed throughout the world, involved in a Management-by-Objectives (MbO) program and wanted the consultant to attend a one-day meeting to help him sell them on the idea. His underlying value premise was that the boss-subordinate relationship is one of authority and obedience. However, he saw the impending situation as one in which he needed to bolster his authority to push the program through and was anxious to enlist the consultant's independent "authority" in support. The consultant responded by indicating that success for any such program results from the personal commitment rather than the knuckled-under compliance of those who must carry it forward, the kind of commitment that could hardly be generated during a one-day meeting. He pointed out, too, that MbO has its own value system and that unless the operating values present in the broader organizational context are congruent with and supportive of the MbO value system, the strain of contradiction will cause the effort to crumble. He also remarked that one aspect of an MbO program is performance appraisal, and that in his experience many performance review sessions are inconsistent with and sometimes antagonistic to the objective of helping executive development.

These points having been made, the conversation continued.

> *Client:* I know there are these problems and that is why we need you to be there. I am sure that you can sell the executives on the importance of interpersonal relationships and dealing with people.

The client has not yet sensed that the consultant's reaction is based on a difference in value orientation.

Consultant: Even if I were effective in selling such programs to top management, little internal commitment would be generated. The initial enthusiasm soon would become a vivid memory while behavioral change, or even a modest increase in sensitivity, on the part of the executives would not emerge. Therefore I appreciate the invitation, but I best not accept, for your sake and for mine.

That the consultant had not yet been successful in getting the client to face his power/authority values is seen in the latter's rejoinder.

Client: But this meeting is important. I think that you have much to offer us. Many of our officers have heard of you. Surely, there must be something useful you can do in a day. (Argyris, 1971, p. 28)

The consultant had challenged the value orientation of the client by pointing to discrepancies between the value system espoused in the Management-by-Objectives program and the authority-obedience values inherent in this client's leadership of the organization. An extended discussion followed and some conclusions were reached. The consultant indicated that a positive basis for his participation with the top forty executives would be in helping them diagnose the potential problems they saw in the MbO program and in identifying and evaluating factors that would help or hinder their effectiveness in implementing it. He suggested he could confront them with the possibility that certain leadership styles currently being employed were adverse to, or at least not congruent with, the value system essential for an effective Management-by-Objectives program. Such a meeting did occur; it is commented on in the Group (I₂) section of this chapter.

Combining research procedures with interventional practices has led Argyris (1974) to formulate a change strategy actually developed for management but pertinent to change interventions in professional education. Concentrating on the uses and misuses of power, his contention is that most current hierarchical situations are premised on setting goals unilaterally, which leads to win/lose, which creates defensiveness and the need to "be rational." This kind of behavior leads to closed, growth-stultifying relationships. Though other features are involved, he calls this Model I behavior.

By contrast, Model II relationships are premised on resolution of differences based on valid information, free choice of alternatives, and internal commitment. Confrontation within a group is the characteristic intervention strategy for assisting an individual to shift from Model I to Model II behavior. The client produces two structured written protocols involving genuine past situations. One of these situations was easy for the client, the other was difficult. These protocols are reviewed in a group environment where the intent is to assist the client to (1) check out the extent to which his or her espoused "theory"—what the client thinks he or she was doing—corresponds with the theory-in-practice—the theory on which he or she was actually operating, and (2) as a derivative, establish the relationships that exist between these two theory positions, known as Models I and II. These theories are not made explicit in advance of the confrontation, however, but emerge as a result of a succession of confrontations.

Each such intervention to evaluate these protocols also has its own structure. A designated segment of behavior is specified and then the client (1) looks forward to predict consequences of the behavior, (2) looks backward—to see what in his or her own "theories" caused it, and (3) tries to spot the feedback that maintains resistance to change. Personal insights thus produced arise from valid information and permit the client to freely decide whether he or she wishes to change and under what conditions.

Overcontrol by Boss

The Kuriloff and Atkins report of the incompany T-Group, introduced in Chapter 3, also has a confrontational aspect. Helen had said some things about her deteriorated work relationship with Bob, her former boss, and an acceptant intervention had induced cathartic release on her part. Soon afterwards, the consultant confronted Bob about power/authority attitudes that also seemed to underlie his participation in the ongoing discussion.

> I asked Bob why he felt so responsible for everyone—Helen, the men in the field, production, engineering. Giving my further impression, I said to Bob that it appeared to me that he had a strong fear of failure and shouldered responsibility that was not rightfully his. "Why do you try to make everything perfect?" I asked.
>
> "That's enough, laddie. I've said my piece," Bob concluded with finality. "No more. I have to leave for school in a few minutes and now I'm all upset." (Kuriloff and Atkins, 1966, p. 78)

The value-oriented intervention had pointed out that Bob appeared to exercise too much control and shouldered excessive personal responsibility for whatever happened. The consultant made an interpretative linking to what might be one of Bob's basic values, in the comment about his seeming to have "a strong fear of failure"— the other side of an "I highly value being a winner" orientation. Adding a confrontational point, "Why do you try to make everything perfect?" brought the issue to a head. Bob did not accept the consultant's reality-testing challenge. The consultant says he (the consultant) then "backed off," as a retreat strategy. Assuming that Bob was resisting hearing an accurate portrayal of his approach and its value-based rationale, backing off was the only option available. The confrontational intervention had failed to penetrate existing defenses sufficiently to open two-way discussion of the pros and cons of alternative values and the personal commitments founded upon them.

Less-than-Frank Clients

Uses of survey research, primarily in a catalytic frame of reference, have already been described. If the topic to which the survey research is addressed is relatively noncontroversial, little difficulty is encountered in obtaining clients' cooperation in furnishing requested data. However, if the area being evaluated through survey-research techniques is personally significant to the client, or embarrassing to him or her, or in other ways constitutes a topic that motivates or stimulates defensiveness, then either the catalytic consultation fails or the consultant shifts the basis to confrontation. Confrontation is calculated to cut through the client's defenses in order to make it possible to gather the needed data, which in turn will be treated in the catalytic manner.

The use of confrontation by survey interviewers is demonstrated in the following:

> In instances where lack of cooperation was felt to be of [the] spoofing kind, good-humored bluff-calling tended to create a release of tension and subsequent cooperation. For example, one woman stoutly insisted she had no partners other than her present one. The interviewer put down her notebook and, with a broad grin, said "Get off it honey. I'm not that innocent!" The respondent laughed and gave a detailed history. (Back and Stycos, 1973, p. 259)

Still other techniques were used by these interviewers to encourage participation, often with boomerang effects. Efforts to manipulate, such as through compliments or flattery, appear to be less effective in getting to the heart of the matter than is readiness of a consultant to confront the behavior or attitudes of the client and thereby relieve him or her of the defensiveness presently blocking candor and cooperation.

Authority Exercised by Parents

Power/authority is basic in parent-child relationships. One approach for strengthening family ties involves a process through which adults learn to be more effective parents by "hearing themselves talk." It is described by Gordon (1970, pp. 121–25) as a component of Parent Effectiveness Training (PET). One of the many facets involved deals with the kind of "message" the parent communicates, particularly when some tension-producing situation has arisen with the child.

Of the many messages parents communicate to children, two are of particular importance. An "I-Message" is authentic and does not cause a child to feel that parents are rejecting him. When a mother or father communicates the feeling being experienced, the parent is sending an authentic message. For example, "I'm very tired!" is a *statement of fact*. A "You-Message" is an inaccurate expression of a parent's momentary frustrations. By contrast a "You-Message" says to the child, "You're a pest!"

"You're a pest" and other "You-Messages" are likely to be received by the child as an *evaluation* from a person with power/authority, which comes through as meaning "I am bad." The "I-Message," on the other hand, simply conveys "Dad is tired," thereby enabling the child to gain a fuller perspective and deeper understanding of the momentary situation, and to adjust his or her behavior accordingly.

Interventions during PET sessions offer a way for parents to study their unexamined power/authority values, how these are conveyed to their children in such situations, and what the consequences for the child are. In the following episode, mother and daughter had agreed that the latter would return home from a movie date no later than midnight. However, the daughter came in at 1:30. Mother had missed sleep while worrying that something awful might have happened. The mother and another person enact the incident.

> *Mother:*   I'm angry at you.
>
> *Daughter:*   I know I'm late.
>
> *Mother:*   I'm really upset at you for keeping me awake.
>
> *Daughter:*   Why couldn't you sleep? I wish you'd go to sleep and not worry.
>
> *Mother:*   How could I? I was mad at you and worried sick that you might have been in an accident. I'm really disappointed in you that you didn't stick to our agreement.

Most "You-Messages" are saturated with power/authority attitudes and not all "I-Messages" are devoid of power/authority value assumptions either. For example, at this point the consultant interrupts to confront this mother, saying something like, "Not bad—you sent some pretty good 'I-Messages,' but only the negative ones. How did you *actually* feel when Linda walked in the front door? What was your first feeling?" The mother answered, "I felt terribly relieved that Linda was home safe. I wanted to hug her and tell her how glad I was to see her in one piece."

The consultant then asked this mother to repeat the incident.

> *Mother:*   Oh, Linda, thank God you're home safe. I'm so glad to see you. What a relief. *(Hugs the instructor).* I was afraid you'd been in an accident.
>
> *Daughter:*   Gosh, you *are* glad to see me, aren't you. (Gordon, 1970, p. 123)

The replay differed significantly from the mother's actual handling of the incident. This second set of messages was more expressive of true person-to-person feelings of intimacy, and in the power/authority sense less evaluative, judgmental, and rejecting.

Authority Exercised by Teachers

As mentioned in our discussion of acceptant consultation, classroom problems between teacher and student may "belong" to the student, causing no one else difficulty, in which case an acceptant intervention is called for, as desired by Gordon (1974). On the other hand, the problem may impede the teacher or classroom learning, in which case the intervention for dealing with it relies on *confrontation* with I-Messages, which show the client consequences of his behavior for others, rather than You-Messages, which make him feel wrong and guilty. In the following example the teacher is the consultant. The intervention begins with a confrontation and quickly shifts to an acceptant basis.

Teacher: Allan, your being late to class is causing me a problem. When you come in late I have to stop whatever I'm doing. It's distracting to me and I'm frustrated.

Student: Yeah. Well, I've had a lot to do lately and sometimes I just can't get here on time.

Teacher: I see. You're having some new problems of your own lately. *(Active listening)*

Student: Right. Mr. Sellers asked me to help in the chem lab after third period—you know, setting up for fourth period. It's a good deal.

Teacher: You're really pleased he asked you. *(Active listening)*

Student: Right on! I can probably get to be the lab assistant next year and I could sure use the job.

Teacher: There may be a good payoff for you and that's pretty important. *(Active listening)*

Student: Yeah. I know you're upset about me being late. I didn't think it would be such a problem. You know, I've tried to sort of slip in quietly.

Teacher: You're a little surprised that it's such a problem to me even when you try to be quiet. *(Active listening)*

Student: Well, not really. I can see your point. You do have to stop and change the attendance record and stuff. Mostly I'm late because Mr. Sellers and I get to talking too long. I'll tell him it's a problem for you and I'll just split a few minutes earlier, okay?

Teacher: That would sure help me. Thanks, Allan.

Student: No sweat. (Gordon, 1974, pp. 146–47)

By shifting to a different consulting mode, in this case an acceptant one, the consultant can help the client take responsibility for solving the problem.

Summary

These interventions demonstrate how deeply held and difficult to bring into the focus of attention personal assumptions about power/authority may be. The hidden aspect of authority seems to involve feeling "responsible" for someone else. The person with the power/authority knows "what they need," or "what they should do." Confrontations may bring these assumptions to the surface, but confrontation *per se* may be insufficient to change them.

GROUP (I₂)

One of the central questions of modern society relates to authority and its uses. In boss-subordinate relationships, an authority-obedience value orientation demands group loyalty and compliance without regard for understanding, and denies the pertinence of participation, involvement, and commitment for effective problem solving—compliance based upon obedience is presumed sufficient for putting into effect the boss's wishes. These and many other facets are significant for understanding the role of a confrontational consultant in the power/authority area. It is his or her purpose to bring clients face-to-face with the impact that power/authority assumptions are having on their effectiveness in resolving problem issues and on personal satisfaction.

The consultant is more likely to embrace values congruent with behavioral-science research findings than are his or her clients, a value system premised on *involvement, participation,* and *commitment.* In terms of these values, leader-member relationships are sound when work problems are identified in such a way that everyone involved in solution finding is engaged participatively. Shared "ownership" of the problem can lead to team-wide commitment to reach effective solutions.

Authority Unilaterally Exercised by Boss

An example described by Argyris and reported earlier illustrates how a confrontational consultant resisted accepting the power/authority assumptions under which a chief executive was inviting him to help sell a Management-by-Objectives program. By confronting, the consultant shifted the chief executive and some forty key executives toward an examination of the value orientations underlying their behavior. The consultant requested a meeting of all top executives to provide an opportunity to question and confront their boss, as well as for the consultant to confront them all.

An initial hour-and-a-half meeting was held with twelve of the officers present. The agenda focused on what they wanted to accomplish with regard to the introduction of a Management-by-Objectives program and what their reactions were to the interventionist's views on the matter. Following this meeting the officers met without the consultant to decide whether he should be invited to the later meeting. Their session on this matter was taped and sent to the consultant for evaluation.

Then a third meeting was held to discuss whatever conclusions the consultant had reached from the tapes in regard to the values and assumptions revealed in that second meeting.

> *Consultant:* I listened to the tape and found it fascinating and helpful. I should like to attempt to accomplish two objectives during this meeting. One is to answer some substantive questions raised about the proposed session. The other is to develop a better undertanding of my relationship with you. I should like to start with this objective first, unless someone prefers differently. *(pause)*

I heard on the tape such comments as, "The benefit will come when he criticizes us publicly;" "He may say, 'your attitude is wrong';" "Are we ready to take criticisms publicly, to have someone get to the nerve?"

I should like to ask a question. What did I do or say that led you to believe that I would make such comments? (Argyris, 1971, p. 39)

Since in the subsequent discussion no one in the client group could identify the source of such an impression beyond "Just looking at you!", Argyris was able to demonstrate that at least one assumption they had used as a judgmental basis was somewhat less than reliable (pp. 40–41).

Argyris provides another example of a confrontational intervention in which his observations are of here-and-now events occurring within the group. What is demonstrated is how the authority-obedience dynamic operates in structuring boss-subordinate relationships.

The consultant had asked the marketing vice-president, "Is there anything you do that may make it more difficult for marketing people?" Before he could reply, the president cut in and said, "I'm sure that A [the marketing vice-president] can answer that better than anyone, but let me try." The consultant listened. When the president had finished, the marketing vice-president partially agreed, then the president and he explored their differences. The event was over. But not for the consultant, who said:

"May I ask why you felt that you had to answer for A even though you stated A could answer it better than anyone else?"

President: "I don't know. That's a good question. I do it an awful lot with A."

A: "Yes, you do."

Consultant: "How did you feel when he answered for you?"

The marketing vice-president recounted how he had felt and concluded that he was angry at himself whenever this happened. The president asked if this was dominating behavior and went on to say:

President: "I wonder if others feel that way. No, I don't think so because they know me well and would say so."

Interventionist: "I can't confirm or disconfirm your view. Perhaps you can check your view some day by asking them directly." (Argyris, 1970, p. 168)

This episode is useful for understanding confrontational interventions. The president was acting on an authority-obedience premise: his value-based, probably implicit, assumption was that it was his prerogative to cut off any subordinate by whom the question might best have been answered in order to answer it himself. Not only was this one of his hierarchical "rights"; he undoubtedly thought that important questions got answered quicker and—despite his compliment to A—*better* that way. Furthermore, the president's presumption of prerogative is matched by subordinates' presumption of obedience: one lets himself be cut off. One of the "costs," though, was the anger and lack of creative involvement felt by A, and probably by other subordinates as well. But the president seemed unaware of this until the consultant intervened to produce some evidence.

Another episode reveals the values and assumptions this president held as structuring the authority-obedience character of his relationships with A and the others. Later in the meeting the consultant asked the president how he felt.

> *President:* "Exhausted, but I have a lot to think over."
> *Consultant:* "Do you feel the spotlight has been on you?"
> *President:* "Hell, yes!"
> *Consultant:* "How do you feel about that? For example, do you feel ganged up on? Are you wondering if A, B, C, and D maybe got together and planned this session?"
> *President:* "Well, as a matter of fact, I felt that way during the meeting."
> (Argyris, 1970, p. 169)

The discussion continued. One issue considered was how people may become defensive when they feel others are out to "get" them; another was concerned with how trust, as well as some ground rules, can be developed among group members so that the probability of subordinates ganging up against the boss would be reduced.

Not all client-held values are equally susceptible to confrontational interventions. Among the most resistant to change are attitudes of paternalism on the part of the client in which the authority/obedience value is one component of orientation and the other is warm feelings toward "good" (i.e., outwardly respectful and obedient) subordinates and kindly treatment of them. Confrontational interventions that focus the client's attention on paternalistic behavior and attitudes are likely to be rejected because the client emphasizes in his or her own thinking the "good things" that he or she does for people. Accordingly, he or she expects them to be grateful and compliant and tends to be insensitive to those coercive actions and attitudes likely to promote subordinate frustration and anger. If this is the case, the consultant's intervention does little more than provoke righteous indignation—which itself is another defensive way for the client to avoid facing the consequences of the consultant's confrontation.

Paternalism

An example of team-based confrontation that produced unsuccessful results is described by Levinson.

A rigid, authoritarian company president, who built his organization into international prominence, was disappointed by the fact that he could not seem to retain a corps of young managers who had top management executive potential. While he hired many, they left after two or three years with the organization, usually moving up into higher level roles in other companies. He himself attributed this loss to an inadequate management development program and sought the help of a social scientist well versed in the concept of confrontation. Certain that the problem was the president himself, and equally certain that he would profit by attack from his subordinates, the social scientist arranged an organization development program whose first steps included just that kind of confrontation. In the course of the experience, the president became livid with frustrated rage, angry that his paternalism was unappreciated, and abandoned his efforts to develop the company further. In impulsive anger, he sold it, a fact that ultimately cost him dearly and enmeshed his management in the adaptive problems of a merger which made his company merely an appendage of a larger organization. (Levinson, 1973, pp. 162–63)

The strategy of confrontation did not break through the authority-obedience-love basis of paternalism, but instead provoked greater resistance and anger on the part of the president, who could not understand why his subordinates would want to bite the hand that had fed them so well. This confrontational approach should be compared with the acceptant mode of intervention (reported in Chapter 4), which is a way of relieving the frustration-dependence feelings of subordinates who have experienced paternalistic supervision. In this case the target of frustration was not dealt with directly. Instead, he and others listened to recordings of subordinates' disguised voices. In the recorded session these subordinates had been induced to pour out their genuine resentments, grievances, and criticisms. Then, in separate session, the boss heard the messages without being able to identify his critics by voice.

Therapist as Focus of Power/Authority Attitudes

Confrontations are basic in psychoanalytic group therapy. However, the rationale of the psychoanalytically oriented consultant needs to be understood in order to appreciate what he or she concentrates interventions on and what he or she ignores as of no importance. In this medical context, the focal issue parallels closely the focal issue in the business context; that is, authority-obedience as a sickness-producing rather than health-giving set of value assumptions.

The following selection is from Ezriel, a psychoanalyst whose confrontational interventions deal with people in groups. The thesis is that each participant brings his or her own tensions to the meetings, tensions that may cause the person to react to other participants in something less than objective terms. These tensions are not necessarily in the ambit of the person's self-awareness and in that sense are uncontrolled by the client. Ezriel's view is that each person tries to move others into roles that will relieve that person's unique unconscious tensions.

Initially, most group members accept, without question, the authority of the consultant under an authority-obedience convention. They have come to obtain his or her expert advice. If, instead, the consultant acts passively, a "Rorschach card" situation results where each person's reactions to the consultant *not* giving the expected advice tells something of that person's underlying tensions toward authority. By eventually identifying these reactions, participants come to comprehend their tensions about authority, and thenceforth to get control over them.

When the consultant acts passively, the group is thrown on its own resources and must find something to talk about. Whatever the content of discussion turns out to be, a common underlying problem develops which is shared by all in varying degrees. Ezriel refers to this as an "unconscious group tension." Confrontations are intended to make clear to participants what their unconscious group tensions are, and to help them understand how they are affecting each person's characteristic way of dealing with the dilemma.

This conception of group behavior is illustrated in the following, a recounting of a group's first session (Ezriel, 1950). It occurred after the consultant had introduced group members to one another and had stated that the purpose of the group was: "for people to find out the causes of their difficulties." He indicated also that no topic was barred from discussion. A silence of three minutes was ended by:

F2*: I suppose we are all waiting for somebody to say something.

M4: What do you want us to do? Do you want us to get everything off our chest, explain our own problems, our own difficulties, or should we not do that? If so, as a first thing, one of my problems is to be able to speak to a lot of people, to lecture. Do you want us to explain our difficulties, or are you already familiar with them? Does anybody else experience difficulty in speaking in front of a number of people?

M2: I think it is fairly common in most people—you don't like to push yourself forward.

M2 had come up with a value proposition, whether or not this was an accurate commentary about "most people" or was more in the nature of a personal norm of his own.

M4: But you must admit it is a very bad thing. For certain jobs you have to master it somehow or else you don't get very far.

M2: Is there not a difference between talking about a technical subject and talking to people personally?

M4: I don't think the subject matters, as long as you know what you are talking about. If you don't know what you are talking about, it is more difficult. A person who is inclined to be a bit nervous in front of people does not really think of what he is saying. He is inclined to get a little bit confused—as I am doing now.

---

* *F* and *M* are female and male respectively; 1, 2, 3 and 4 indicate different group members.

At this point, one of the group's members seems to feel that M4 needs help from an authoritative source.

> *M2:* Is your part, Dr. Ezriel, passive, or are we allowed to draw you in?
>
> *Dr. E:* What do you think?
>
> *M2:* I think it would be a good idea if you acted as a reference point. Then if we come to blows we can get you to arbitrate.
>
> *M4:* It might ease the situation.
>
> *F2:* I don't think he wants to. I think that if there are going to be any blows, he wants us to fight it out among ourselves.
>
> *(Somebody):* Why should there be blows? This is the Peace Conference.
>
> *M2:* I take it that in this group no subject is barred. Therefore we are likely to talk on subjects people don't normally discuss—subjects in which you are likely to get more disagreement. *(short silence)*

Here is a second value proposition coming from M2. It is quite consonant with the first one, and the two may be seen from the outside as facets of a particular value system. Again, M2 has phrased it as what "people" don't do—but others in the group will have had their experiences of what people do, and perhaps they believe otherwise. Indeed, M2 could be a minority of one.

> *M2:* I'm sorry. I have turned the discussion off.
>
> *M4:* No, it all leads on, I presume.
>
> *M2:* I don't want to alter it from the point of the difficulty of talking. I still think it makes a difference what one is talking about.
>
> *F5:* No. Because you don't really think about what you are talking about. You are thinking about yourself all the time, then you come home and think of all the things you should have said.
>
> *(Somebody):* A sort of inferiority complex.
>
> *M2:* Can we ask Dr. Ezriel what an inferiority complex is?
>
> *Dr. E:* What do you think? (Ezriel, 1950, pp. 64–65)

As participants continue jockeying to find an acceptable basis for their discussions with one another and for their relationships to the consultant, even greater focus is placed on the role of the person who "should" be in authority. Different reactions and attitudes toward the consultant, ranging from working to please him to being resentful of his nonresponsiveness, come to the fore. The consultant can then confront any participant with that person's particular way of dealing with the common group tension.

> (By refusing to answer the questions put to me and referring them back to the questioner I had prevented the group from pushing me into a role which they wanted me to play, i.e., that of a person in authority.)

> I pointed out to the group that they apparently wanted the presence of such a person who would take responsibility for what happened, since they feared that without such a safeguard the free expression of their problems might lead to dangerous quarrels in the group. I added that they resented my not playing the part of this controlling figure. I then pinpointed M2 who seemed to fear the consequences of his hostile impulses even more than the rest of the group. (Ezriel, 1950, p. 65)

The confrontation identified a common group tension related to authority and obedience: the members of the group were expecting the consultant to act as an authority—as arbitrator, information giver, and so on—and when he resisted doing so, tension built up. The confrontation focused attention on what had been happening and each participant's particular reaction to it.

A parallel use of confrontation strategies based on Ezriel's psychoanalytic formulation but applied in the context of "businessmen as students" is described by Rice. Its character is revealed in the following excerpts from the first meeting of such a study group. Someone said, "Let us introduce ourselves." But after the introductions an embarrassed silence fell on the group. While Rice was pondering what to say, one member commented, "Well, we didn't learn much from that—in fact I've forgotten most of the names already. I seldom pick them up the first time." This remark stimulated another round robin of mutual introductions which ended again in embarrassed silence. Someone slapped his hand on the table and exclaimed, "Well, that's cleared the decks."

In the nautical spirit of the moment, Rice weighed anchor and sailed in with a confrontational intervention, referring first to the "clearing of the decks." He commented that the decks may have been cleared for a fight directed against him for not giving the kind of leadership expected. He pointed to their hostility to others who had tried to take a lead, shown by lack of support. The members individually and collectively denied they had any such feelings:

> "I don't feel hostile, but I do feel afraid of what is going to happen. If only we had a clear purpose."
>
> "We need to establish formalities to enable us to discuss."
>
> "We're trying to find a common denominator. This is an unnatural situation. The trouble is that nothing is happening. There is nothing to study. We're not competing for a job or anything . . . *(a pause, in which tension in the groups could be felt to mount).* We all look at Mr. Rice . . . *(then another pause).* For God's sake somebody else talk!"
>
> And then the tension was broken by laughter. (Rice, 1965, p. 60)

Rice's intervention focused attention on his nontraditional leadership behavior. He indicated that in his view his "refusal" to engage in the typical implicit rules of cooperation had put members on the spot, and they reacted with hostile feelings toward him. This is the same reaction subordinates have to a boss whose unfamiliar "leadership through delegation" leaves them nonplussed. Rather than critical fingers being pointed inward, they tend to be pointed at the boss as cause of their trouble.

Rice comments upon aspects of his role as a confrontational consultant working with a group.

> The consultant's job is to confront the group, without affronting its members; to draw attention to group behavior and not to individual behavior; to point out how the group uses individuals to express its own emotions, how it exploits some members so that others can absolve themselves from the responsibility for such expression.

> As a group fails to get its consultant to occupy the more traditional roles [authority-obedience relationship] of teacher, seminar leader, or therapist, it will redouble its efforts until in desperation it will disown him and seek other leaders. When they too fail, they too will be disowned, often brutally. The group will then use its own brutality to try to get the consultant to change his task by eliciting his sympathy and care for those it has handled so roughly. If this manoeuvre fails, and it never completely fails, the group will tend to throw up other leaders to express its concern for its members and project its brutality onto the consultant. As rival leaders emerge it is the job of the consultant, so far as he is able, to identify what the group is trying to do and to explain it. His leadership is in task performance, and the task is to understand what the group is doing "now" and to explain why it is doing it. Drawing attention to interesting phenomena without explanation is seldom used. (Rice, 1965, pp. 65–66)

In the above example, the medical model of confrontation has been "transferred" to the industrial context in order to create a learning situation. Confrontational interventions can be made with the object of helping business, government, and other leaders to study the extent to which values and assumptions regarding authority-obedience are embedded in their group behavior. Such examination, in turn, often points toward alternative possibilities—e.g., supervision based on participation, commitment, and involvement.

Summary

These confrontational interventions provide insight regarding the depth and pervasiveness of power/authority-related assumptions in group life. Confrontation is likely to be successful when the consultant can mobilize enough indications of the client's unrecognized behavior or unexpressed attitudes to counteract denial. In addition, the consultant may be able to focus attention on issues of unexamined behavior or unexpressed attitudes by *himself* serving as a model of certain behavior and attitudes opposite to those that the consultation seeks to intervene upon. This is possible, for example, when the client's values are carefully hidden but the consultant counters with openness and spontaneity. Such interventions also give an indication of existing defenses—sources of resistance to change which prevent present assumptions from undergoing significant alteration.

One of the easiest ways for a consultant to reduce intervention effectiveness is to allow the client to provoke him or her into win-lose attitudes of argument. Such attitudes are relatively easy for the confrontational consultant to fall into, and once this has happened the ability to force a reexamination on the part of the client is greatly reduced. Indeed, the core problem the client may need to reexamine is a readiness to create win-lose situations. Thus if the client is successful in maneuvering the *consultant* into such behavior, the very attitudes involved become, from that moment, unavailable to identification because each person—client *and* consultant—is unwittingly acting them out in their own interactions.

INTERGROUP (I₂)

Confrontational interventions may be necessary when an intergroup relationship has become "set" or "frozen" in ways that make needed cooperation difficult. This is particularly true when the frozen state is characterized by hostility, antagonisms, and mutual disrespect. If the frozen state is one of indifference, it is unlikely that consultative assistance will be sought as there is little motivation to change.

When groups are of unequal power, each is likely to regard the other in a different light. Students and faculty relations involving power/authority tensions were approached by confrontational intervention in a New Jersey high school workshop. The confrontation was based on the assumption that each group—students and faculty—has its own motivations and, in addition, may be seen by the other quite differently than either group sees itself. Clarifying these values and assumptions about one another while preserving the integrity of *both* sides is basic to the intervention.

Volunteer students and teachers were separated into their respective groups and were each asked to develop a list of ways they saw the other. Here are some of the results.

How Students Perceive Teachers

Unaware, think they are correct because they are older, putting on a big show, some making honest effort, think they are more mature because they are older, less outspoken, passive when the principal is there, take things personally, don't really listen, are prejudiced, some willing to listen even when they don't agree, curious about students' views.

How Teachers Perceive Students

Cherish individuality, hopelessness, confusion, self-confidence, frustration, sensitivity, eagerness, resistance to seeing both sides of the question, clannish, irresponsible, candid, bored, angry at inequities, powerless, flexible, racially polarized.

They then exchanged basic attitudes towards one another and tried to explore the meanings behind them. Subjective aspects of these descriptions were emphasized on the presumption that resolving mutual misunderstandings is a prerequisite if realistic problem-solving collaboration is to replace an authority-obedience basis.

The initial response was positive. As the school year wore on, however, collaborative efforts ended for reasons that are not explained except that "separation" pressures were greater than the bond of cooperation developed during the confrontation sessions. This may have been because neither students nor faculty involved their constituencies to any significant degree, with the result that participating teachers might have been seen by their colleagues as "soft," and participating students as "traitors" by their peers (Chesler and Lohman, 1971, pp. 201–202). If so, this would indicate the significance of the *intergroup* nature of the client system. Because only a representative portion of the total population was included and no efforts made to spread the strategy throughout the respective student and faculty populations, the former reference-group norm was sufficiently strong to reestablish authority-obedience relations and dissolve the desired basis of collaboration.

ORGANIZATION (I₄)

The use of power/authority throughout an organizational system is most likely to be experienced by members lower in the organization as a reflection of signals received from the top. Unless the top leadership is interested in changing, it is unlikely that major shifts in the use of power/authority will be initiated at lower levels.

Under these circumstances, when the real key to change, from the consultant's perspective, is to confront power/authority as the focal issue, his natural inclination is to start with the top man or group. This may have been the circumstances of the interventions by Argyris described earlier under "Individual as Client" and "Group as Client" (Chapter 9). Unless successful at the pinnacle, a consultant is seldom provided opportunities to set up situations of confrontation throughout the organization.

LARGER SOCIAL SYSTEM (I₅)

It is more probable that power/authority differences rather than equality exist among segments within larger social systems. Sometimes this is because of real or presumed power differences; or frictions may arise because people are not satisfied with the status quo situation and attempt to shift it in a direction more favorable to their self-interests. Consultant interventions that aid a confrontation of differences with the final objective being a mutually satisfactory resolution are described in this section.

Border Disputes between Nations

Confrontational interventions have been attempted as the basis for dealing with border disputes between nations. One such intervention, described by Walton (1970), involved Ethiopians, Kenyans, and Somalis. The handful of participants in this workshop were checked out and "green-lighted" by their respective governments, but were not empowered to act as official representatives. They met on neutral territory.

After an initial period of developing contacts among members and practicing teamwork skills in crisscross groups, national groups were assembled as units to list "...key grievances or disputes your people have with each of the other countries...." On a second sheet they listed their predictions of the grievances or disputes the other two countries would come up with. This intended confrontation was not successful, possibly because the consultant compromised when resistances appeared rather than assisting clients to gain insight into their reservations about moving forward. Two of the three national groupings resisted using the design as structured by the consultants. Being unable to reach agreement on issues that were in conflict, the workshop was unable to reach consensus regarding proposed solutions. Nonetheless the approach is suggestive of an alternative to conventional win-lose and bargaining approaches to intergroup solutions existing in larger social systems and to "shuttle diplomacy" as well.

Police-Community Relations

In the following example, confrontational techniques were used to reduce the perceived arbitrary exercise of power by the stronger group. It involves a police-community intervention in Houston, Texas, described by Bell, Cleveland, Hanson, and O'Connell (1969), in which 1400 members of the police force participated. Police officers met with community members, 200 each for six different times over a six-week period. Each week subgroups of officers, 20 or so, were scheduled into three-hour sessions with an equivalent number of community members. Police participants were required to attend; citizens attended voluntarily and did not ordinarily participate in each successive session for all six sessions. Invitations for citizens involved efforts to ensure participation by a cross-section of the community, but especially of representatives from (1) minority groups, (2) poverty groups, and (3) dissidents. Consultants provided leadership.

During initial sessions, police and community groups first met separately to develop images of themselves and of the other group. Then the two groups convened in a general session where images were compared and discussed. During subsequent sessions efforts were made to diagnose causes of disagreements, to correct distortions, and to identify key issues, as well as to devise better methods of conflict resolution. The flavor of what was accomplished is provided in a consolidation of image elements, summarizing the key factors of many such sessions.

Police Self-Image

"As officers we are ethical, honest, physically clean and neat in appearance, dedicated to our job, with a strong sense of duty. Some officers are prejudiced, but they are in the minority, and officers are aware of their prejudice and lean over backwards to be fair. We are a close knit, suspicious group, distrustful of outsiders. We put on a professional front; hard, calloused, and indifferent, but underneath we have feelings. We treat others as nicely as they will let us. We are clannish, ostracized by the community, used as scapegoats, and under scrutiny even when off duty trying to enjoy ourselves. We are the blue minority."

Community Image of Police

"Some police abuse their authority, act as judge, jury, and prosecutor, and assume a person is guilty until proven innocent. They are too often psychologically and physically abusive, name-calling, handle people rough, and discriminate against blacks in applying the law. Police are cold and mechanical in performance of their duties. We expect them to be perfect, to make no mistakes and to set the standard for behavior. The police see the world only through their squad car windshield and are walled off from the community. Our initial reaction when we see an officer is 'blue.' "

Self-Image of Citizens as Members of the Community

"We lack knowledge about proper police procedures and do not know our rights, obligations, and duties in regard to the law. There is a lack of communication among social, geographical, racial, and economic segments of the community. We do not involve ourselves in civic affairs as we should, and we have a guilty conscience about the little crimes (traffic violations) we get away with, but are resentful when caught. We relate to the police as authority figures, and we feel uncomfortable around them. The black community feels itself second class in relation to the police. The majority of the community is law-abiding, hard working, pays taxes, is honest and reliable."

Police Image of Community

"Basically the public is cooperative and law-abiding, but uninformed about the duties, procedures, and responsibility of the police officer. The upper class, the rich, support the police, but feel immune to the law and use their money and influence to avoid police action against themselves and their children. The middle class support the police and are more civic-minded than upper or lower classes. The major share of police contact with the middle class is through traffic violations. The lower class has the most frequent contact with the police and usually are uncooperative as witnesses or in reporting crime. They have a different sense of values, live only for today and do not plan for tomorrow. As police officers we see the Houston Negro in two groups, (1) Negro—industrious, productive, moral, law-abiding, and not prone to violence; (2) 'nigger'—lazy, immoral, dishonest, unreliable, and prone to violence." (Bell, Cleveland, Hanson, and O'Connell, 1969, pp. 242–46)

Assessment of the effectiveness of this intervention is difficult but indications point in a positive direction. It is reported that the Houston police characterized the summer that followed these interventions as a "cool" summer in contrast with 1967. Another sign is that there was a reported 70 percent drop in citizen complaints about police behavior for the seven-month period following the program. The consultants saw this kind of a confrontation as the beginning of a development endeavor rather than as an intervention capable of removing the effects of years of rancor and distrust (Bell, Cleveland, Hanson, and O'Connell, 1969, p. 246).

School Administration versus Community Residents

In Chapter 12 a consultant's approach to a worsening relationship between residents of a black community and their school system was presented. That intervention was insufficient to bring the outstanding issues of controversy into focus and, as a result, problems were not resolved. Tensions increased further during and after the period when the consultant was participating with the school authorities in a catalytic way. At the beginning of the next year these heightened tensions came into the open.

> On the first day of school, there had been some disorder in the school yard, sparked by black community leaders and parents who had come unannounced to confront the principal and who were apparently not seen by him. The police had been called to remove "unauthorized persons" from the school building. The following day, a group of community organizers descended on the school and marched most of the students, together with some of their teachers, to a nearby community recreational building, where they set up a "Freedom School." The sponsors of this overt act of rebellion were the parents' committee, aided by a number of black community militant organizations. (Caplan, 1970, p. 363)

Even though the mental-health center's previous school consultation had been inadequate, a new opportunity was created when five professional community workers called upon the center director.

> ... They gave him a more detailed story of what was happening, and they emphasized the dangers of a serious community conflagration if the impasse were not quickly resolved. They felt that the main problem revolved around the school authorities' refusal to meet with the parents and to discuss their legitimate demands; and they placed particular blame on the new school principal, who was making matters worse by his highhanded authoritarian approach to the parents. They said that the parents' committee represented the moderate leadership of the ghetto community, which wanted to resolve the conflict peaceably and were interested only in improving a very bad school. They also said that the black community contained a group of extremist militant leaders who intended to use this situation to wrest power from the moderates and to provoke a bloody confrontation with white authorities, particularly the police, whose brutality they wished to expose publicly. Press, radio, and television reporters were continually on the scene, and the stage was set for a major battle.

The group of community professionals, which included both white and black workers, said they had come to ask the center staff to intervene in this situation because the center's consultation contract with the school system gave it direct access to the superintendent. The center must use its influence to persuade him of the absolute necessity of reinstituting communication with the black parents so that the problems might be handled quietly and rationally. Otherwise, they would become a cause of racial strife, in which people would be injured and possibly killed and property would be damaged. (Caplan, 1970, p. 363)

An interesting episode from the standpoint of how colleagues from another discipline saw the felt-needs aspect of earlier consultation came about when

... the director gave a brief report on their consultation activities in the school and said that they had not yet begun their program for the new school year. The visitor [a black professional] asked somewhat aggressively, "How can you justify this passivity and slow routinized style of operations, when people's lives are at stake?"

The director replied with some heat that he saw no need for them to justify their style of consultation on these grounds; their program with the school system was in its early stages and the beginning relationships had to be developed gently lest the school staff feel that the center was infringing on their internal domain. It was center policy that no moves should be made into new problem areas until the school board staff asked the mental health workers to help them. This meant that inevitably the consultation program would develop slowly and at a rate dictated by the consultee institution. The alternative could easily be the disintegration of the center program and their ejection from the school system—a fate that had befallen many other mental health workers in the past, who had come in with missionary zeal to reform that institution.

The community organizer was not convinced. He apologized for his vehemence but said he was concerned about the immediate dangers to his community and to the school system. He accused the center of "fiddling while Rome burned." He admitted that the center approach to its consultation program was in keeping with the latest and best theories of mental health consultation, but he asked whether the center had no concern for basic issues of community life that had clear implications for the mental health of wide sections of the population. He urged that such concern should convince the director to set aside, at least temporarily and as an emergency measure, his slow, deliberate professionalized style of operations. He also questioned the wisdom of the center's decision several months earlier to retire from the community action approach in the ghetto school. (Caplan, 1970, p. 364)

This confrontation by the consultants was sufficient to break through the catalytic assumptions on which the center previously had been working and to bring a new set of forces into play.

The next day the center director and some of his staff had an emergency meeting at school headquarters with the deputy superintendent and the district superintendent. The director described his discussion with the community workers and offered his help in resolving the communication impasse with the parents of the ghetto school.

At first the superintendents were rather surprised to discover the center's interest in this matter. The deputy superintendent said he could not see what this administrative issue had to do with problems of emotionally disturbed or subnormal children, which he thought was the center's area of interest.

The director replied that his center was concerned with all community issues that might affect the sense of well-being of children and their families and that might be conducive to mental health or mental disorder. He felt that racial tensions and lack of consonance between parents and educators must inevitably affect the feelings of security of many families, and might have a deleterious effect on the emotional stability of schoolchildren. Moreover, problems of communication between individuals and groups were a topic of special interest to mental health specialists and one in which they had developed some expert knowledge.

He also told the superintendents that his visitors had predicted a more dangerous community upheaval if the local problem between the ghetto school and the parents' group was not quickly resolved. He said that the center staff, like all citizens, had a fundamental interest in preserving public order and preventing damage to property and lives, such as had recently occurred in other cities as a consequence of similar racial conflicts in the schools.

The superintendents' immediate response was very positive. They freely admitted to being at their wit's end and warmly welcomed this offer of help. They then gave a detailed account of their problems in dealing with the parents of the ghetto school. The parents were making a series of outrageous demands, most of which could not be dealt with in practical terms. For example, they wanted complete community control over the school, with power to hire and fire its personnel. They demanded a black principal. They wanted several of their number to be put on the school payroll as "guardians of discipline" in the school. (Caplan, 1970, pp. 364–65)

Center personnel now proceeded to make their resources available in the context of this deep-seated community tension.

The center staff offered two types of assistance. First, they promised to consult with the district superintendent, whenever he felt the need, about the day-to-day tactical problems of managing the crisis. He accepted this offer with alacrity and set up the first consultation appointment for that afternoon. Second, they offered to make informal contacts with leaders of the black community to explore how and where the two sides could get together for a behind-the-scenes discussion outside the orbit of the public media. (Caplan, 1970, p. 366)

What transpired next is complicated by a variety of secondary issues. Eventually meetings were arranged that were attended by high-ranking school authorities and by three or four members of the parents' committee as well as a black leader. The center director was able to act as chairman. The meeting ran smoothly until, close to its end, one of the parents' committeemen drew from his pocket and read a provocative written statement that had been composed by several parents. Of particular interest is how the consultant intervened.

> The amicable atmosphere immediately gave way to tense hostility. The school administrators showed signs of barely suppressed anger, and the parents began to speak provocatively and with raised voices. The center director broke into this discussion and pointed out that the meeting had been progressing well until the inflammatory words "local control" had been used. He felt that such "fighting words" should be ruled out of order, because they probably meant completely different things to each side and because they were more like battle cries than attempts to convey information. He called on all participants to return to the spirit of cooperation which had brought them together. (Caplan, 1970, p. 370)

A further series of meetings was held. Though characterized by numerous ups and downs, it is reported that eventually the inflammatory situation cooled and basic problem-solving relationships were restored.

This has been an instance of a confrontational intervention complicated by the interplay of ever-widening *community* variables. The example is imperfect in many respects, yet it offers an indication of how confrontational methods can be employed in defining, confronting, and resolving community-based disputes. It also demonstrates the difficulties encountered by the community organizer as he tried to confront the real issues needing attention. By trying to go against the established status quo collusion between the administration and the conventional mental-health approach to following the felt needs of clients, he was eventually successful in surmounting seemingly impregnable barriers.

Should the Social Worker Confront on Behalf of the Client?

Social-work practice is geared to helping clients, usually individuals and families, solve problems they are unable to resolve independently. Many times the fundamental problem needing solution is not amenable to the social worker's direct efforts. But the solution either exists within the Establishment, which itself may presently be unresponsive, or can only be brought into existence by changing the Establishment.

To deal with the client's problem, the social worker may feel personally committed to intervene *on the client's behalf* in the agencies and systems of the Establishment itself. Such interventions often challenge the power/authority system, and in effect say, "This is what the agency should do." This kind of unsought consultation is likely to be interpreted as insubordination because the consultant is also an employee. Such interventions often take on the character of *advocacy* by a member of the official establishment who is seen as "going against" the Establishment.

Dilemmas often arise for the social worker who undertakes confrontational advocacy for his or her client vis-à-vis institutions of the Establishment. Even though they are not a direct employer, they come within the same "family" of governmental or other agencies. It is a situation where Establishment representatives stand against institutions of the Establishment. For example, the social worker's voice carries little weight unless his or her skills of confrontation are particularly effective, or the issue happens to be one the Establishment is disposed to resolve goodnaturedly with perhaps the initial response, "Now, let's not get all heated up about this. . . ." Then the social worker may gain a resolution without creating antagonism.

However, this result is by no means assured. As far as the Establishment is concerned, the social worker who intervenes in a confronting way may polarize into a win/lose orientation one or more issues that previously had been "sleeping dogs." To curb such confrontations, the Establishment may threaten or take reprisal measures against the social worker's agency, thus reverse-confronting the agency with risk to its continued capacity to function. Next, to remain acceptable to the Establishment, the agency itself might apply counterpressures against the social worker. As a self-protective response, social workers may then organize in protest, possibly through professional associations, so the area of conflict is widened. Even though issues and areas of professional integrity may receive better definition as an outcome of the controversy, this does nothing to solve the client's problem.

This dilemma of confrontational intervention has been studied by the National Association of Social Workers' Ad Hoc Committee on Advocacy. The Committee's report (NASW, Ad Hoc Committee on Advocacy, 1969) and a subsequent paper (Sunley, 1970) have described difficulties encountered from attempted intervention, both in terms of dealing with the Establishment and from the standpoint of providing needed reforms through legislation.

IMPLICATIONS

Confrontational interventions ranging from the individual to the society level share a significant feature when the focal issue is power/authority: the consultant usually takes a stand that challenges unilateral or arbitrary use of power/authority. He or she may, for example, lend outside support to the weaker of those represented.

However, if this stance is taken there is a high probability that the consultant will be seen by those on the stronger side as biased and opinionated in favor of the weaker, thus reducing the likelihood that his or her interventions will be effective. If the consultant enters the situation on the stronger side, success in bringing about a confrontation of power differences is far more likely. But the stronger side may not see the need for such an intervention, since the difficulties it experiences are viewed as difficulties of the weaker component, unrelated to its own behavior.

One of the most basic issues of confrontational consultation in the power/ authority area is the power ratio in the client/consultant relationship. If the consultant is "weaker" than the client, he or she is unlikely to be listened to, no matter how valid his or her interventions may be. If his or her own power/authority is equal to that of the client, then a successful basis of intervention may be established. However, if the consultant is significantly "stronger" than the client, interventions are likely to be responded to as though they were prescriptions and taken at a level of absoluteness that they in fact do not deserve.

REFERENCES

Argyris, C. *Intervention Theory and Method*. Reading, Mass.: Addison-Wesley, 1970.

Argyris, C. *Management and Organization Development: The Path from XA to YB*. New York: McGraw-Hill, 1971. Reprinted by permission.

Argyris, C., and A. Schön. *Theory in Practice: Increasing Professional Effectiveness*. San Francisco, Calif.: Jossey-Bass, 1974.

Back, K. W., and J. M. Stycos. "The Survey under Unusual Conditions: Methodological Facets of the Jamaica Human Fertility Investigation." In D. P. Warwick and S. Osherson, eds., *Comparative Research Methods*. Englewood Cliffs, N.J.: Prentice-Hall, 1973, pp. 248–67. Reproduced by special permission of the Society for Applied Anthropology, Monograph No. 1, 1959.

Bell, R. R., S. E. Cleveland, P. Hanson, and W. E. O'Connell. "Small Group Dialogue and Discussion: An Approach to Police-Community Relationships." *Journal of Criminal Law, Criminology and Police Science* 60, no. 2, pp. 242–46. Reprinted by special permission of the *Journal of Criminal Law, Criminology and Police Science*, © 1969 by Northwestern University School of Law.

Caplan, G. *The Theory and Practice of Mental Health Consultation*. New York: Basic Books, © 1970. Reprinted by permission.

Chesler, M. A., and J. E. Lohman. "Changing Schools through Student Advocacy." In R. A. Schmuck and M. B. Miles, *Organization Development in Schools*. Palo Alto, California: National Press Books, 1971, pp. 185–212.

Ezriel, H. "A Psycho-Analytic Approach to Group Treatment." *British Journal of Medical Psychology*, 1950, pp. 23, 59–74. Reprinted by permission.

Gordon, T. *Parent Effectiveness Training*. New York: Peter H. Wyden, 1970. Reprinted by permission.

Gordon, T. *T.E.T.: Teacher Effectiveness Training*. New York: Peter H. Wyden, 1974.

Kuriloff, A. H., and S. Atkins. "T Group for Work Team." Reproduced by special permission from *Journal of Applied Behavioral Science* 2, no. 1 (1966): 63–93.

Levinson, H. *The Great Jackass Fallacy*. Cambridge, Mass.: Harvard University Press, 1973.

NASW Ad Hoc Committee on Advocacy. "The Social Worker as Advocate: Champion of Social Victims." *Social Work* 14, no. 2 (1969): 16–22.

Rice, A. K. *Learning for Leadership.* London: Tavistock Publications, 1965. Reprinted by permission.

Sunley, R. "Family Advocacy: From Case to Cause." *Social Casework* 51 (1970): 347–57.

Walton, R. E. "A Problem-Solving Workshop on Border Conflicts in Eastern Africa." *Journal of Applied Behavioral Science* 6, no. 4 (1970): 453–89.

CONFRONTATIONAL INTERVENTIONS

16

MORALE / COHESION

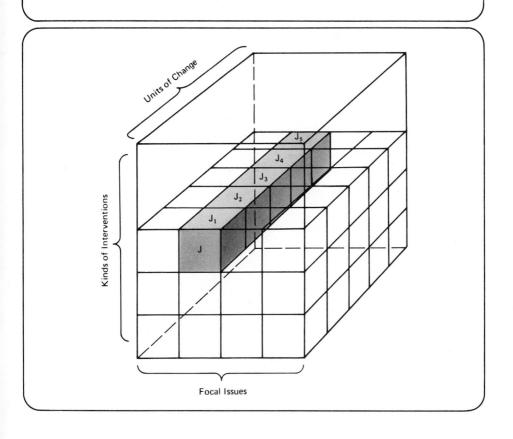

Units of Change

Kinds of Interventions

Focal Issues

When morale/cohesion is on the plus side, even to an excessive degree, it is rare for a client to request consultation of the sort that will test the validity of these feelings in real-world terms. However, when morale/cohesion is low, it becomes more likely that a consultant will be invited to help. It is a generally accepted convention that the consultant will refrain from "kicking a client when he's down," i.e., such remarks as, "It's stupid of you to feel so sad . . . unhappy . . . desperate . . . dependent . . ." will be avoided. For the moment at least, the consultant does not challenge or confront whatever underlying values he or she discerns as associated with the present state of low morale/cohesion. It is more probable that he or she would adopt an acceptant orientation that would promote the expression and discharge of unpleasant feelings and tensions. This may account for the absence of published examples of confrontational interventions in the morale/cohesion area.

To focus on the basic problem: how could confrontational interventions be of use when low morale/cohesion is related to failure? In principle, it would seem appropriate to challenge the client in regard to a perceived lack of goals; or for setting objectively unattainable goals; or for not reaching them due to morale/cohesion-related deficiencies along the way. These three possibilities, as well as others that are conceivable, clearly are ones in which earlier states of low morale/cohesion are probably the cause. Another possibility is that real circumstances exist which are adversely affecting the client's well-being. Many instances could be conceived in which a current state of morale/cohesion on the client's part is a result of some other dimension going awry.

Confrontation may be indicated in a morale/cohesion situation when a client has the *capacity* to solve the problem but is unwilling to face those in positions of power/authority who are responsible for the situation. Under these conditions, a confrontational intervention can have sufficient "arousal impact" to push the client into actions that can lead to resolution of problems associated with his or her morale/cohesion downturn. Such a confrontation, in other words, has a trigger value for activating a person to approach rather than avoid problems requiring attention if real-world resolution is to be achieved.

CONFRONTATIONAL INTERVENTIONS

17

NORMS / STANDARDS

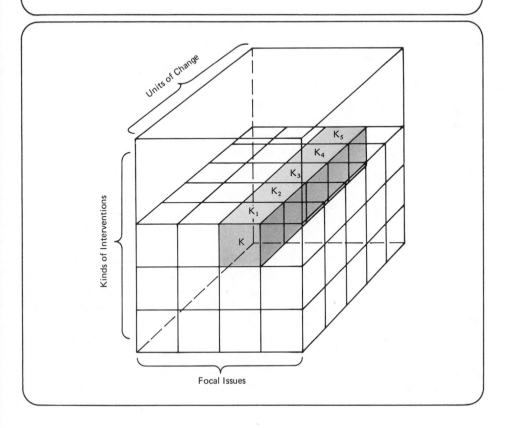

Norms/standards can operate so subtly that many times those whose behavior is affected by them are unaware of the impact on their actions. Thus outsiders may be in a better position to discern how norms/standards are influencing behavior. In addition, to the degree that norms/standards are relevant and central to a membership unit, those who might challenge their appropriateness are subject to conformity pressures and the risk of sanctions, such as various forms of rejection. Both features suggest that a consultant who is intervening in a confrontational way may have less to lose than an insider consultant should the interventions prove unsuccessful.

INDIVIDUAL (K_1)

Welfare Dependency

How a confrontational approach can be used to aid a physically mature adult break out of continued welfare dependency and achieve a norm of autonomy and self-reliance is presented in a casework study by Robinson (1948). Earlier, Joseph Marks, an unemployed 32-year-old at the time consultation began, was being provided financial support and a variety of reassurances that had the effect of causing him to jump from one job to another without really trying to be successful at any one. After two and one-half years of this pattern, circumstances caused a change of consultants handling his case. Rather than picking up and continuing what had become regular support procedure, the new consultant studied the pattern and saw Marks as "leaning on the agency." In a variety of ways the new consultant confronted Marks with this possibility. These confrontations included:

1. questioning whether the agency was of any worth since there was little evidence that in two and one-half years it had been of help to him;

2. challenging his motivation to put forth the effort to work at a job on a continuing basis;

3. pushing him to face his dependent outlook and habitual need for reassurance and support.

As a result, Marks began to face up to prospects of *constructing* reality rather than letting reality be a situation specified by other people and otherwise shaped by the drift of circumstances through his own default. He accepted a job to prove that he could take initiative and stick with the effort and succeeded in maintaining constructive work relationships after several attempts.

These interventions focused Marks' attention on the weak, non–self-reliant crutches that he had been leaning on to get by. Being able to reject them made it possible for him to act in terms of increased self-reliance and he was eventually able to terminate the consultation since it no longer offered him anything he could not provide on his own.

Personal Growth

Ellis (1962) presents a confrontational approach to personal growth based on the idea that people make problems both "for" and "of" themselves because they embrace norms that are irrational, superstitious, or senseless—ones that inevitably lead to personal difficulties. The solution is to "unlearn" these invalid norms and standards, and to replace them with others that provide a more reality-addressing basis for living. Ellis indicates that each of the following norms for self-evaluation are inculcated in Western societies but are unjustified by fact:

1. It is a dire necessity for an adult human being to be loved or approved by virtually every significant other person in his or her community.
2. One should be thoroughly competent, adequate, and achieving in all possible respects if one is to consider oneself worthwhile.
3. Certain people are bad, wicked, or villainous and should be severely blamed and punished for their villainy.
4. It is awful and catastrophic when things are not the way one would very much like them to be.
5. Human unhappiness is externally caused and ... people have little or no ability to control their sorrows and disturbances.
6. If something is or may be dangerous or fearsome one should be terribly concerned about it and should keep dwelling on the possibility of its occurring.
7. It is easier to avoid than to face certain life difficulties and self-responsibilities.
8. One should be dependent on others and needs someone stronger than oneself on whom to rely.
9. One's past history is an all-important determiner of one's present behavior and that because something once strongly affected one's life, it should indefinitely have a similar effect.
10. One should become quite upset over other people's problems and disturbances.
11. There is invariably a right, precise, and perfect solution to human problems and that it is catastrophic if this perfect solution is not found. (Ellis, 1962, pp. 61–87)

Knowing and rejecting these absolute norm-based statements in a cognitive way is one thing; seeing how they apply to one's own behavior is another. The consultation technique described by Ellis involves confrontation to bring this about.

The effective therapist should continually keep unmasking his patient's past and, especially, his present illogical thinking or self-defeating verbalizations by (a) bringing them forcefully to his attention or consciousness; (b) showing him how they are causing and maintaining his disturbance and unhappiness, (c) demonstrating exactly what the illogical links in his internalized sentences are, and (d) teaching him how to re-think, challenge, contradict, and re-verbalize these (and other similar sentences) so that his internalized thoughts become more logical and efficient. (Ellis, 1962, pp. 58–59)

Ellis' confrontation strategy makes a concerted attack on the client's illogical norms and standards in two main ways: The consultant

(1) . . . serves as a frank counter-propagandist who directly contradicts and denies the self-defeating propaganda and superstitions which the patient has originally learned and which he is now self-instilling.

(2) . . . encourages, persuades, cajoles, and occasionally even insists that the patient engage in some activity (such as his doing something he is afraid of doing) which itself will serve as a forceful counter-propaganda agency against the nonsense he believes. (Ellis, 1962, p. 95)

In this particular approach, the consultant has a well worked out alternative set of norms/standards that "make sense" on rational grounds. Through being confronted time and again in terms of these, the individual can be persuaded that it is in his own best interests to calibrate his thinking according to these more rational standards.

GROUP (K₂)

Groups whose memberships are relatively stable quickly develop norms/standards to regulate members' conduct. These norms/standards have been looked at from the point of view of a work group, yet there are other more intimate groups where faulty norms/standards are the core issue. One such unit is the family—either the husband-wife pair or the more extended family.

Communication

Valid communication among members is critical to effective family functioning. When communication is free and open, members are able to understand each other's intentions and expectations, and family goals of intimacy and love and of personal educational development for each member can be pursued with greater confidence and prospects of success. One aspect of therapy aids families in replacing invalid communication norms with sound ones.

Satir (1967) presents an approach that treats family-wide problems, or problems of any one member, as group-centered communication problems. One or more sessions are conducted with the several family members present.

. . . Here is an example of how the consultant confronts the communication processes of interaction within a family:*

---

* The client family members are (H) husband, (W) wife, and (S) son.

Consultant: (to husband) I notice your brow is wrinkled, Ralph. Does that mean you are angry at this moment?

H: I did not know that my brow was wrinkled.

Consultant: Sometimes a person looks or sounds in a way of which he is not aware. As far as you can tell, what were you thinking and feeling just now?

H: I was thinking over what she [his wife] said.

Consultant: What thing that she said were you thinking about?

H: When she said that when she was talking so loud, she wished I would tell her.

Consultant: What were you thinking about that?

H: I never thought about telling her. I thought she would get mad.

Consultant: Ah, then maybe that wrinkle meant you were puzzled because your wife was hoping you would do something and you did not know she had this hope. Do you suppose that by your wrinkled brow you were signalling that you were puzzled?

H: Yeh, I guess so.

Consultant: As far as you know, have you ever been in that same spot before, that is, where you were puzzled by something Alice said or did?

H: Hell, yes, lots of times.

Consultant: Have you ever told Alice you were puzzled when you were?

W: He never says anything.

Consultant: (smiling, to Alice) Just a minute, Alice, let me hear what Ralph's idea is of what he does. Ralph, how do you think you have let Alice know when you are puzzled?

H: I think she knows.

Consultant: Well, let's see. Suppose you ask Alice if she knows.

H: This is silly.

These questions confront the husband with explaining his personal communication norms and standards. His answers to these questions suggest he and his wife do not have a shared norm of understanding. The consultant continues.

Consultant: (smiling) I suppose it might seem so in this situation, because Alice is right here and certainly has heard what your question is. She knows what it is. I have the suspicion, though, that neither you nor Alice are very sure about what the other expects, and I think you have not developed ways to find out. Alice, let's go back to when I commented on Ralph's wrinkled brow. Did you happen to notice it, too?

W: (complaining) Yes, he always looks like that.

Consultant: What kind of a message did you get from that wrinkled brow?

W: He don't want to be here. He don't care. He never talks. Just looks at television or he isn't home.

> *Consultant:* I'm curious. Do you mean that when Ralph has a wrinkled brow that you take this as Ralph's way of saying, "I don't love you, Alice. I don't care about you, Alice."?
>
> *W: (exasperated and tearfully)* I don't know.
>
> *Consultant:* Well, maybe the two of you have not yet worked out crystal-clear ways of giving your love and value messages to each other. Everyone needs crystal-clear ways of giving their value messages.

The consultant has summarized for the couple the fact that they do not have shared norms and standards for communication. She has also emphasized the importance of having such norms and standards within the family if mutual understanding and intimacy are to prevail. Next, she checks out the son's communication norms as these apply in communicating with his parents.

> *Consultant: (to son)* What do you know, Jim, about how you give your value messages to your parents?
>
> *S:* I don't know what you mean.
>
> *Consultant:* Well, how do you let your mother, for instance, know that you like her, when you are feeling that way? Everyone feels different ways at different times. When you are feeling glad your mother is around, how do you let her know?
>
> *S:* I do what she tells me to do. Work and stuff.
>
> *Consultant:* I see, so when you do your work at home, you mean this for a message to your mother that you're glad she is around.
>
> *S:* Not exactly.
>
> *Consultant:* You mean you are giving a different message then. Well, Alice, did you take this message from Jim to be a love message? *(to Jim)* What do you do to give your father a message that you like him?
>
> *S: (after a pause)* I can't think of nothin'.
>
> *Consultant:* Let me put it another way. What do you know crystal-clear that you could do that would bring a smile to your father's face?
>
> *S:* I could get better grades in school.

Here the consultant confronts the mother to check out what the son's communications sound like to her.

> *Consultant:* Let's check this out and see if you are perceiving clearly. Do you, Alice, get a loving message from Jim when he works around the house?
>
> *W:* I s'pose—he doesn't do very much.
>
> *Consultant:* So from where you sit, Alice, you don't get many love messages from Jim. Tell me, Alice, does Jim have any other ways that he might not now be thinking about that he has that say to you that he is glad you are around?

W: (softly) The other day he told me I looked nice.

Consultant: What about you, Ralph, does Jim perceive correctly that if he got better grades you would smile?

H: I don't imagine I will be smiling for some time.

Consultant: I hear that you don't think he is getting good grades, but would you smile if he did?

H: Sure, hell, I would be glad.

Consultant: As you think about it, how do you suppose you would show it?

W: You never know if you ever please him.

Consultant: We have already discovered that you and Ralph have not yet developed crystal-clear ways of showing value feelings toward one another. Maybe you, Alice, are now observing this between Jim and Ralph. What do you think, Ralph? Do you suppose it would be hard for Jim to find out when he has pleased you? (Satir, 1967, pp. 97–100)

Numerous consultant-induced confrontations occur between members of the family as they attempt to explain to one another what each is thinking and feeling, and the discrepancies between what they intend to communicate and what the receiver actually "gets." In addition, the consultant sets up confrontations between family members in the interest of testing understandings and clarifying intentions and values. The common denominator of the consultant's interventions is challenging communication norms and standards among family members which come through as incomplete, provocative, or distorted, and therefore difficult for the other family members to respond to in a problem-solving manner. In this way, unrecognized distortions are brought into view.

Sexual Inadequacy

Consultant interventions to solve sexual-inadequacy problems of married couples as a unit were expanded in the 1960s through the work of Masters and Johnson. Their working hypothesis was that, regardless of which member of the pair has the major problem, the difficulty is couple-based and can be resolved most successfully by dealing with the couple-as-group rather than with either member separately.

This usually two-week, rapid-treatment intervention takes place in a medical setting under the supervision of a man and a woman as coconsultants. Four steps are involved. One is routine physical examinations. Another involves case history–taking, with the male consultant interviewing the husband, and the female the wife. The third and fourth intervention steps are unique features of the Masters and Johnson approach, and therefore are described here in more detail.

The third step, often lasting several hours, is called a Roundtable, and is attended by both consultants and husband and wife. Using primarily case-history data, the purpose of the Roundtable is to compare the client pair by holding up a "professional mirror" in such a way that the pair can see their respective sex-pertinent norms and standards—spoken of as attitudes, values, myths, misunderstandings, and so on —through the consultants' eyes. This is approached in a manner that permits discrepancies between soundly based medical knowledge about sexual norms and standards and personally held or couple-shared beliefs to be recognized for what they are. Since these confrontations are carried out in an objective, nonjudgmental manner, the Roundtable makes it possible for couples to face their actual situation in a more reality-oriented way. Weaknesses and vulnerabilities, when brought to awareness, can be talked about; needed but previously unavailable facts can be presented; accompanying behavioral problems can be resolved in a way that puts the couple on a sounder conceptual footing about sex. According to Masters and Johnson this is a necessary but not sufficient basis for achieving sexual adequacy.

The fourth step is prescriptive in character and represents a type of consultation to be dealt with in greater detail in Chapters 20–25. The couple is provided with guided "skill practice" in how to become more sexually effective. Though the sequence of skill-practice experience varies with the couple, it (1) advances from undemanding, mildly erotic interactions to more consummatory sexual activity; (2) concentrates first on the husband and next on the wife; (3) shifts from mechanical exercises to functional performance.

Major differences exist between this approach and other strategies for solving sex problems in marriage. Among the more significant are that it is (1) brief; (2) involves nonpsychoanalytic and nonpsychiatric confrontations regarding the sexual norms and standards held by either partner or shared by both; and (3) engages the couple in concrete exercises for the purpose of aiding a husband to gain adequacy, and the wife to become more spontaneously responsive and pleasure seeking. Other problems that hinder sexual adequacy are also dealt with, but the aforementioned are the more central (Masters and Johnson, 1970).

Summary

The family-as-unit is likely to be the focus of many emotionally charged experiences. Both minor and major violated expectations can result in unhappiness, frustration, and anxiety. Interventions to aid family members in examining their norms/standards and in replacing them when invalid are likely to be confrontational in character, particularly when the norms/standards have become frozen and habitual, so that people are unable to shift them merely by talking with each other.

INTERGROUP (K₃)

In an intergroup situation confrontational interventions are likely to be successful when the component groups holding different norms/standards share some degree of common organization membership. These conditions are present in many industrial and government situations.

Union-Management

In the following union-management episode conflicting norms and standards had created a never-ending win-lose battle. The circumstances leading up to it were described in Chapter 3 in connection with a group confrontation. The consultant already had helped management become more aware of its own underlying antagonisms toward the union and had challenged them to shift fundamental attitudes from a win-lose to a problem-solving basis. That confrontation had led senior managers to arrange a conference with the international union's business agent to propose a "union-management laboratory," to be conducted by behavioral science consultants. The union officers eventually agreed but actually felt that management's intention in proposing this approach was to "get them," one way or another. So the question remained, How could such a meeting be of any real merit?

On the agreed-upon day, the nine most senior union officers and nine ranking managers met with the two consultants. The union group included the international union's business agent, the local's president and vice-president, secretary, and others; the nine from management included the general manager, the head of administrative services, the employee-relations manager, and others down to first-line supervisors. At the outset management and union got together for a brief orientation in a general session. Consultants outlined the purpose, the ground rules, and the background involved. One consultant began by saying, "During these next two days, we wish to explore the problems that are blocking your relationship, to identify them and, if possible, to plan constructive steps for their elimination. Therefore, we are not concerned with issues of bargaining, problems of grievance handling, or attitudes about problems now being arbitrated. Nor are we concerned with personalities. The key concern is with the *character* of the relationship between your two groups and with the shifting away from the unproductive strategies which have characterized relations between the two of you in the past."

One consultant worked with management, the other with the union. At certain times the groups met separately. During these periods the consultants' interventions were primarily designed to challenge the power/authority assumptions each held toward the other, as well as to aid each group to see its own win-lose posture. Meeting separately, each group prepared a description of how it saw its relationship with the other group and developed an image of how it saw the other group's behavior toward itself. These images were written on newsprint for use when the two groups reconvened as a General Session.

The union got off to a false start. They were unable to distinguish between the *process* of behavior as characterized by actions, feelings, and attitudes and the content problems they were arguing about on a day-by-day basis; consequently, they began discussing issues that had been in controversy at a recently completed bargaining session. After several minutes the consultant intervened to redefine their task. "The present task is to describe the *character,* the quality, of the relationship; that is, typical behavior and attitudes. The task is *not* to debate technical, legal, or operational issues."

The Local's secretary, addressing the business agent, said, "I think we should caucus before we go further."

The consultant immediately commented, "Look, if this cannot be discussed in my presence, then there is little hope that anything can be achieved in the next two days."

There was silence for some moments. Union members exchanged glances, but no one spoke. Finally the business agent began again. Gradually, tediously, the discussion shifted toward a detailed picturing of the union's behavior and attitudes relative to their relationships with management. Participation gradually spread to include all members.

Meeting in a separate room, management launched into the first task with greater assurance, confident that they could quickly put their finger on the real problems. Examining "process" didn't come easy for them either, but from prior training they had grasped the basic concept and were able to develop a strategy of work and move into the task. Then they, too, ran into trouble. Their relationship with the union was so antagonistic that discussion of their own attitudes repeatedly slipped into a discussion of union personalities. The consultant intervened. "As I understand it, you plan to develop your own image first, and then to develop your picture of the union. You are having difficulty doing this. Your own image is repeatedly forgotten and union behavior and personalities keep coming into the picture. Everyone wants to get something off his chest." The consultant recognized the need for an emotional unloading and said, "Let me suggest that you might table your own image for the time being and begin on that of the union. If this moves easier, then stay with it. Having done this, you may find it easier to talk about your own behavior. Alternatively, you might work on both images simultaneously as thoughts about either occur to you, or when parallel behavior is seen by both groups."

This intervention caused management to examine how it was working. "Let's admit it. They are no angels, but neither are we. Let's get a mirror up here where we can see ourselves, and put down what we see, whether we like it or not." Eventually both groups managed to complete this initial "image" task. The results are shown below.

Management

Image of Itself	Image Created by the Union
1. Concern with running the business effectively	1. (an issue not considered)
2. We show equal concern for production and people	2. Management is concerned only with production
3. Autonomous decentralized decision-making body	3. They follow all headquarters' policies and dictates
4. Want to learn to work better with international	4. Opposed to all organized labor
5. Prefer to deal with independent unions	5. Prefer to deal with independent unions

6. Strive continually to upgrade supervision

6. ....

7. Goal is to establish problem-solving relationship with the international

7. Their goal is to drive us out of the plant

8. Maintain flexibility in areas concerning our "rights to manage"

8. Management wants power and control over every aspect of a worker's life—they are "fatherly dictators"

9. We are inconsistent in how we treat independents and the international

9. They treat the independents one way and us another

10. Honest and above-board in our dealings

10. They are underhanded and they lie

The Union

Image Created by Management	Image of Itself
1. Little concern shown for the profit picture of the company	1. Concerned primarily with *people*
2. They are skillful and have intense pride	2. Proud of our craft and skills
3. Controlled by a scheming professional leader and a minority clique	3. We are governed by the will of the total membership
4. Legalistic and rigid in interpreting contract	4. Approach problems and contract with open mind
5. The union pushes every grievance to the point of arbitration. When they want to establish a precedent, they want to arbitrate	5. Do not want to have to arbitrate every grievance. We want to work them out with management
6. They want to prove they can "win"—they don't care what, just so it is something	6. We want good relations and to solve our problems with management
7. They want to co-manage. They want a say in every decision we make	7. We want a voice in those areas that directly concern us
8. The union wants the training of their people back under their control	8. We want joint control of the training and apprenticeship program
9. The union does not communicate internally. Their people don't know what is going on	9. Our people always know what is going on and what important union business is coming up
10. Union is concerned only with seniority and job security. They are not concerned with our problems	10. We want greater consideration for our skills and what we can contribute to the plant

Many hours were spent working from these two sets of images toward a diagnosis of causes of (1) basic attitudes and (2) the discrepancies existing between them. The consultants intervened frequently to challenge participants' readiness to find explanations based upon feelings of hostility and tension rather than to search for understanding based upon a more objective view of the situation (Blake, Mouton, and Sloma, 1965, pp. 25–57). Eventually these confrontations produced a "controlled" explosion, after which a problem-solving basis of cooperation was possible.

Headquarters-Field Interrelationships

A second example of confrontation, also at the intergroup level, involves a company headquarters' Division of Manufacturing and those responsible for running one of its major plants, located thirty miles away. The headquarters' division was headed by a vice-president; a general manager ran the plant. These two had gotten increasingly out of "tune" with each other over the years until they had reached nearly total impasse. The problem of their relationship might mistakenly have been seen as a power/authority standoff bogged down in interpersonal difficulties, a clash of personalities. Rather, the problem was thought to be of another kind. Their differences arose from two quite distinct ways of life, two sets of norms and standards for guiding action. The headquarters "culture" valued efficiency, modernization, youth-in-management, and competitive spirit while the plant "culture" rested on tradition, seniority with loyalty, compliance, and discipline based on a deeply rooted organizational paternalism, with managers expected to pursue a lifelong plant career rather than using it as a ladder into headquarters management.

The vice-president of manufacturing and the ten headquarters people who reported to him, and the plant's general manager and the twelve who reported to him convened for a three-day period at a neutral location to study their relationship. The first task was for each group to describe what a "really good" relationship between headquarters and the plant would be like. After recording their thoughts on newsprint, the groups reconvened and posted their results on the wall. The two descriptions of a sound relationship were quite similar; differences were discussed and resolved.

Thereafter, each group described what the relationship was *really* like as seen from its vantage point. Newsprints were again posted. The relationship being described, as viewed from the headquarters, was "totally" different from the relationship pictured from the plant point of view. These dramatic divergences stimulated heated exchanges. The consultants, one working with each group, had constantly to intervene in confrontational terms to focus issues and to identify rationalizations, justifications, denials, and projections. The consultants created a "controlled" explosion by keeping the discussion focused on issues rather than personalities. Only by working through these defense strategems was it possible to puncture the status quo and unfreeze the relationship sufficiently to shift it toward mutual problem solving. A more accurate picture of the present relationship gradually emerged which permitted both groups to identify the many truly deep problems that constituted barriers to cooperation and progress (Blake, Shepard, and Mouton, 1964, ch. 11). Task forces and other arrangements were set in motion to concentrate effort on solving each of these.

Summary

For a confrontational intervention to have a significant impact, it is insufficient merely to challenge existing norms and standards that serve to regulate actions between groups. Even though both groups may agree that they have an unsatisfactory relationship, change is unlikely to occur unless current behaviors are replaced by more cooperative ones. Thus it is important to suggest "new" norms/standards as possible replacements for the old ones. Both groups are then in a position to evaluate the likely consequences, in terms of mutual benefit, of shifting over from one to the other.

ORGANIZATION (K₄)

Myths, known to have influenced world history, are no less influential within organizations. Ill-founded and untested beliefs influence behavior just as do any other organization-based norms and standards. They may have detrimental effects on individuals' as well as on an organization's functioning, unless they are identified and rejected as unfounded explanations.

Bradford and Harvey (1970) present several examples of organization myths and outline a kind of *discrepancy* intervention useful in eliminating them. The following is an example of what later was proven to be a myth.

> *Consultant:* "What are some things that block you from getting your job done?"
>
> *Client:* "Well, for one thing, it's no use trying anything new here, because somebody would block it. It's just not allowed."
>
> *Consultant:* "Is this what others think? Have you talked to other people about this belief?"
>
> *Client:* I'm sure everybody thinks the same thing. I've never talked to anybody about it because it's so obvious that everybody thinks the same way."
>
> *Consultant:* "What makes it obvious?"
>
> *Client:* "Well, you don't see many new things tried here."
>
> *Consultant:* "Have you tried something different, or have you seen someone else try something new?"
>
> *Client:* Well, yes. So and so installed a whole new process of working in her department."
>
> *Consultant:* "Did it work and was it allowed?"
>
> *Client:* "Yes it did. But I'm sure that was an exception." (Bradford and Harvey, 1970, p. 2)

Other examples include the presumed high risk of asking questions, the dangers of being caught short when asked a question, and so on.

The authors recommend the use of external consultants to help identify myths, or of insiders who are sufficiently skeptical as not to embrace myths without questioning their veracity. The external or inside consultant's particular usefulness is in being able to identify myths through an open-ended interview survey, carried out through several successive organizational levels. Such interviews involve two steps: (1) questions designed to aid individuals in describing positive and negative aspects of the organization, and (2) questions to check out whether what has been reported as true can be subjected to verification or disproof.

Once in hand, interview findings that point to the existence of a myth are returned to small groups of interviewees, preferably in boss-subordinate family groupings. The myths can then be discussed with those who presently either accept them or by those who dispute their validity. For example, the proposition "Bosses don't want to be asked questions" can be directly tested when subordinates who believe this are grouped with the bosses who can prove, if they have the evidence, that this is a myth. If the myth is convincingly shown to be false, this is one kind of success. If, however, the "myth" is shown to be true, a problem is identified to those who are in a position to begin solving it.

LARGER SOCIAL SYSTEM (K₅)

The norms and standards that people adhere to can also be a cause of maladapted behavior. Our first example occurs in an organized work setting in which forces from the larger society are key in confronting internal problems. The studies that follow show how such norms of conduct can be changed via "temporary" communities, in which individuals reveal their norms and standards through interactions with others and then learn to live by new, more satisfactory ones.

Remedying Poor Service

Confrontational interventions are employed in the community-building processes of Albania: elected representatives of the consumers are allowed to confront those responsible for the delivery of services to them. Confrontations focus upon shortcomings that have occurred and corrective actions that should be taken.

The selection below involves some machine-shop mechanics who have been assigned in a consultant capacity to investigate and rectify unsatisfactory service at the local hospital that machine-shop personnel and their families can use as needed.

> The workers of Hospital No. 2 in Tirana, which was our first objective, extended a good reception to our group and did their best to create all the necessary facilities for us to discharge the task we were charged with. We had not come there to find anyone at fault but to help make the service towards patients as good as possible. Since the work in the

hospital has a specific of its own, we were helped by the workers in carrying out our control. This was, in fact, a joint control. This helped us to take up key problems and draw valuable conclusions both as regards serving the patients as well as behaving in a cultured way towards them. We discussed our tasks and conclusions with all the workers employed by the hospital. They expressed many valuable opinions and helped us delve deeper into the causes of the shortcomings we had observed. Together with the collective of the hospital we drew up a very detailed program of work with dates and names of persons who would carry out these tasks. On this occasion, the group of worker control drew up a number of suggestions and remarks for the Health Sector of the Executive Committee of the Regional People's Council and for the Public Health Department of the Ministry of Public Health and Sanitation.

All tasks left behind by the worker control team are binding to the administration of the institution which has been controlled. Therefore, at the end of the time limit set, another group of worker control went to the hospital again to verify how the tasks left behind by the first group have been carried out. (Lalmi, Romana, and Hoxha, 1973, p. 22)

The authors also describe how they and other group members intervened in a catering-supplies enterprise and a creche, both of which had been performing below par in servicing their plant and the wider community. As in the hospital, their approach here was basically confrontational in focusing the attention of administrators and others on problems producing inconvenience to consumers. While the mode was confrontational, there are also prescriptive elements in Albania's control mechanisms to ensure that "recommendations" are in fact put into operation.

Drug Addiction

Synanon, a live-in-community approach for dealing with drug addiction, is an intervention strategy designed to further personal growth and social effectiveness, thus making dependence on drugs unnecessary. Part of the reason that Synanon works is because of its insistence on self-responsibility as an important aspect of change. The program is based on two different sets of norms and standards: one set applies in the "Game"; the other applies in doing the work expected of all members.

The Synanon Game's confrontational character and its basic assumptions are illustrated in the following. Imagine several people coming together for the game. While this is a group setting in a broader institutional culture, what is studied is the distinctive reactions of each individual.

The position of the game seems to be that anything a person already knows about himself is probably false and irrelevant and is certainly misused to maintain his narrow, unchallenging, and less than completely satisfying life. ... Any valid self-knowledge will survive the acid bath of doubt the game will put him through. We want to shake his assumption about life and himself, to test and question, not justify and excuse. The usual manipulations just won't work. . . .

The game's norm is "take nothing for granted; challenge anything and everything a person does or says." This norm violates many customary social-convention norms, such as "be polite, friendly, and keep your distance," behind which members may be hiding. Breaking through protective self-deceptions is a basic feature of the game.

> We want people in the game to examine what they actually *do* in their lives, not what they think they do, and examine the *values they actually live by,* not the ones they mouth. Rationalizations, cover-ups, "I forgot" are spotted as lies by the world's greatest experts in lying and are probed and examined until the person is forced to see what he is really doing. . . . (Enright, 1971, p. 164)

Enright describes how the game operates. Ten to fifteen members from the larger Synanon community meet for up to three and a half hours. The membership is rarely the same in any two sessions. Two ground rules are employed: 1) no physical violence, and 2) no drugs. Players are expected to try to tell the truth about themselves and others. Attempts are made to strip away every mask that is put on, to clear away self-deception and, in a sense, to drive a person out of every less-than-authentic position he or she assumes. Even friendships which a person might use to find support are left at the door.

Compared with this direct confrontation of personal and group norms, the broader Synanon community operates in accordance with different norms and standards. As a community person each Synanon member is expected to be cooperative, civil, responsible, constructive, positive, and self-controlled. He or she is expected to act in a mature manner at all times; in other words, the community norms are "ideal." Thus the game and the community pull in opposite directions, both of which support growth and development.

Although Synanon started as a strategy for coping with problems of drug addiction, it is important to realize that its game sessions are sometimes attended by people for whom participation involves self-learning for its own sake, rather than learning for help with a drug problem. The game's mental-health value is seen in the following.

> From this point of view, the game is to emotional life what exercise is to physical life; a place to challenge and push myself beyond the relatively low demands of life. Because I jog or play tennis regularly I feel better in normal daily physical activity and have an extra reserve of stamina available for emergencies such as running for a bus. If I play the game weekly, hold my own against its spirited and exaggerated attack, and give as good as I get, I am readier for the emotional emergencies of life, and the usual emotional demands are child's play. (Enright, 1971, p. 165)

The power of the game is in assisting an individual to recognize his or her own values and assumptions as to rules for living.

Alternative Culture Norms/Standards

The term *alternate culture* generally describes a culture that is destined—or so its proponents believe—to replace the established culture. Values within the two systems are quite different. At many critical points they are incompatible in the sense that even though the people holding them may coexist, they don't blend.

Radical therapy (Clark and Jaffe, 1973) denotes an approach to consultation calculated to bring about a shift from establishment to alternate culture. Radical-therapy groups are found in various cities and maintain a loose association with one another.

At any point in time, problems that clients bring center on three main issues: need for legal help in dealing within the established culture, help with drug problems, and matters relating to sex. The underlying thesis of radical therapy is that these problems arise from faults inherent in the establishment culture. Only by changing this culture can such problems eventually be prevented.

> ... The old culture relies on drug use, confinement, coercion, and punitive conditioning to force people out of deviance, drug use, depression, or confusion. Thus, when a person in transition comes under the control of a conventional therapy center, the results are apt to be brutalizing and to aggravate the initial anger and confusion as a result of the conflict of values and goals between the individual and the treatment center. Alternate services are needed because support for personal growth, temporary shelter, and alternative living and working arrangements are a means of avoiding such dehumanizing treatment.

> The collective for alternative service, crisis intervention, or radical therapy is important not only to the people who come for help. The structure and process of the alternate group also act as a laboratory for the basic issues of how a new culture deals with its day-to-day business of working and living. Staff members can use their personal sensitivity and experience of crises to help in defining and establishing guidelines for relationships within a new culture. The social change movement received its earliest lessons in the structure of our society and government by confronting them directly, and now we have turned some of our energies to defining and practicing fair and human relationships among ourselves. Psychedelics and new therapies have led to a new psychological sophistication, to go with the movement's economic and structural critique of our culture. Communes, group marriages, consciousness-raising groups, extended family living, and great mobility under extreme pressure have also exposed problems, even created some new ones, as well as building new methods for dealing with them as they arise. Intimacy and openness elicit fears and conflicts which traditional families rarely experience, and our upbringing in such families has given us few tools with which to face

these situations. Radical therapists are called on to help communities learn to incorporate such experiences into their lives.

Although radical therapists may only be a half a step ahead of their brothers and sisters, that half-step may be crucial to a new community racked with personal pain. The role of a radical therapist or alternate service is thus to be both explorer and educator, seeker and helper. (Clark and Jaffe, 1973, p. 4)

Some aspects of the alternate culture's value system and how it would change the fabric of the larger social system include:

The myth of one love, for example, forms the basis for such monogamous systems as marriage and going steady. It is also a metaphor for the basic independent relationship, where appropriate behavior by one leads to the fulfillment of all needs by the other. To question this myth, to assert that there can be many loves, or at least a few, perhaps even simultaneously, and that a dependent relationship is unnecessary and ultimately frustrating, implies that marriages are unnecessary, even undesirable. Living with someone, or living alone, even the raising of children by one parent instead of two or in a small communal situation, all become viable alternatives. Whatever the counter-culture is, it is a discussion of the moral issues of our time, and the search for new alternative modalities for self-expression.

As the individual examines the social obstacles to moral growth, the relationship between personal and social changes will become evident. Young people are close to the truth. To question the dependency assumption, to challenge the internalized authority-parent figures, to violate the social authority of the family and school in an attempt to survive—these actions threaten the viability of the entire social system at its roots. Economics, the political structure, attempts to remove moral examination of the self and to institutionalize morality through laws and the legal system are all extensions of the basic structure of the society, the family.

Why interventions help in bringing about this form of escape from the establishment culture is suggested by the following.

The usefulness of therapy to young people must come through its ability to assist in their struggles for liberation. When therapists accept young people as their clients, they are making a political move. To view their problems from the fragmented and incoherent perspective of the society— that is, as problems of the individual, who must have some basic deficiency or inadequacy—is to do them an injustice. Granted, young people's behavior (strategies) may be self-defeating and destructive, and the first step may be to help the youth regain some sense of self and personal power and responsibility; this is no more than helping him regain what the society is trying to take away. But if therapy stops with the attempt to help a person adjust his behavior to his social situation as it is, then the root of the problem will persist, and more young people will appear with "problems." Eventually this minimal treatment will fail of its own impoverishment. Young people will find it meaningless and irrelevant, just as they have many other forms of mystification and obfuscation. Therapy must make radical social changes, as well as radical personal ones. Support groups must be developed, consciousness raising processes for the young must be started, alternative institutions must be examined carefully and thoughtfully for their potential contributions and detractions to the gradual development of political and economic bases for young people.

Effective therapy will move the individual beyond the narrow confines of his own internalizations toward new alternatives in his life style and new possibilities in the social institutions he will help to form. The internalization of the family and dependency assumptions will be the two issues confronting psychotherapists working with adolescents. The demystification of love, sexuality, and aggression will only come about when the internalized punishment-and-reward system is destructured; otherwise the individual will not "understand" what is meant. Avoiding the tendency to atomize adolescents and their problems will make the therapist aware that, as with members of other politically oppressed groups in therapy, successful change implies radical social change as a necessary outcome, and that the problems of young people are indeed the unresolved moral questions of the entire society—the questions of what is right, and what is wrong. (Clark and Jaffe, 1973, pp. 24–25)

Delinquency

In contrast, the underlying strategy of an experimental intervention calculated to reduce what is legally defined as "delinquency" is described below. The setting is Provo, Utah.

... Although a "bad" home may have been instrumental at some early phase in the genesis of a boy's delinquency, it must be recognized that it is now other delinquent boys, not his parents, who are current sources of support and identification. Any attempts to change him, therefore, would have to view him as more than an unstable isolate without a meaningful reference group. And, instead of concentrating on changing his parental relationships, they would have to recognize the intrinsic nature of his membership in the delinquent system and direct treatment to him as a part of that system. (Empey and Erickson, 1972, p. 4)

Fourteen- to eighteen-year-old boys who had repeatedly been offenders lived at home but became members of the reformation project in preference to incarceration. The program relied on complex strategy features, several aspects of which are unique. Under the supervision of an adult leader, boys met in ten-person discussion groups once a day and on weekends. A premise underlying the use of peer-based discussion groups is described as follows.

A treatment system will be most effective if the delinquent peer group is used as the means of perpetuating the norms and imposing the sanctions of the system. The peer group should be seen by delinquents as the primary source of help and support. The traditional psychotherapeutic emphasis on transference relationships is not considered the most vital factor in effecting change. (Empey and Erickson, 1972, p. 6)

The core of the intervention methodology involves the peer group in defining norms and setting standards which, when adhered to, lead away from self-defeating cycles of delinquency toward nondelinquent behavior.

. . . A successful program must be viewed by delinquents as possessing four important characteristics: (1) a social climate in which delinquents are given the opportunity to examine and experience alternatives related to a realistic choice between delinquent or nondelinquent behavior; (2) the opportunity to declare publicly to peers and authorities a belief or disbelief that they can benefit from a change in values; (3) a type of social structure which will permit them to examine the role and legitimacy (for their purposes) of authorities in the treatment system; and (4) a type of treatment interaction which, because it places major responsibilities on peer group decison-making, grants status and recognition to individuals, not only for their own successful participation in the treatment interaction, but for their willingness to involve others. (Empey and Erickson, 1972, p. 7)

Adherence to nondelinquent norms was reinforced in several significant ways. One was that boys were expected to live by the wider society norms and standards and function as responsible community members.

. . . During the winter, those boys who were still in school continued to attend. Those who were not in school were employed in a paid city work program. On Saturdays, all boys worked. Late in the afternoon of each day boys left school or work, came to Pinehills, and attended a group meeting. After the meetings were completed, they returned to their own homes. During the summer every boy attended an all-day program which involved work and group discussions. On rare occasions a boy might work apart from the others if he had a full-time job. (Empey and Erickson, 1972, p. 9)

Another major reinforcement mechanism was that a program member who resisted the reformation group norms was rejected by either his peers or the staff, depending on the severity of the resistance. Rejection was through extra work, detention over weekends, or being exported from the program to a reform school. Power/authority constituted an important backup to ensure the development of new norms and standards as a method of cycle breaking.

The consultant strategy in the Pinehill meetings was to provide a model for members to confront each other regarding their problem behavior. When they were doing this effectively, the consultant would not comment but remained ready to do so at any pertinent moment. This is demonstrated in the following:

Sam: Mr. G. [group leader] pisses me off. I keep askin' him what I should do an' he won't tell me.

George: Isn't that what your mother does—always front for you? You want him to do that?

Phil: Yeah, that's somethin' Sam has to decide.

Sam: What do you mean?

George: Can't you see that you don't think for yourself?

Sam: (Shouts) Well, fuck! If you want me to do something different you got to tell me what to do. If I don't know how, how the fuck can I change?

Leader: You want me to be your mama? I'm trying to tell you that you're somebody and should learn to think like somebody.

Phil: You're Sam, not some punk that everybody tells how to live.

Even though the exchange was painful to Sam, it revealed attention to him as a person and respect for his individuality—responses he had obviously not had in the past. His remarks, even though emotional, may also have revealed a desire to learn more about himself. The responses of the other boys, in turn, indicated a respect for that desire. (Empey and Erickson, 1972, pp. 114–15)

The significance of peers engaging in constructive learning from one another is revealed in the following comments from boys who were interviewed concerning crucial aspects of the program.

One sentiment that was especially pronounced was the idea that peers were of greater help than staff:

"Boys know more about themselves than grownups do. The first couple of months don't do any good. Then you find out that the meetin' knows you better than you know yourself. They can tell when you're lyin'. They can tell you things about yourself, an' find out what your problems are."

"What can the group leader do that helps the most?"

"To shut up an' let the boys figure things out."

"Mr. ____ suggested a lot of things that helped, like we should check each other out when we're workin'! An' he made an overall summary so that you got the main thing of what the meetin' was about. But I jus' don't like to listen to adults lecturing . . . it is boring as hell."

"All the help I got, I got from other guys in the meetin'—nine other guys instead of one stupid adult talkin' to you. I felt they done the same things I done, an' know exactly how I feel, an' why I do them things." (Empey and Erickson, 1972, pp. 58, 61)

Key to understanding the Provo intervention are the following:

1. Prior to delinquency most individuals have learned socially responsible norms as a basis for self-conduct.

2. Once delinquent acts appear, the person is unlikely to think of himself as delinquent.

3. Through reformation-group confrontation discussions, the person is "forced" to recognize his antisocial assumptions.

4. Such discussions also provide positive alternative models for socially responsible normative behavior that can help the person avoid future delinquency.

5. Reformation-group sanctions reinforce the readiness to achieve according to prosociety norms.

6. Being successful in work or school reinforces personal effectiveness in meeting legitimate social expectations.

Unlike a classroom-type of learning situation or a clinical-treatment situation, the Provo program enabled the boys to identify and reject their old self-defeating patterns of behavior as well as to acquire insight and skill in practicing and internalizing new behavior patterns. The consultants point out that for many progress was made toward socially effective behavior, although the program was not universally successful.

An experiment similar to the Provo experiment is reported by Stephenson and Scarpitti (1974). The strategies of this intervention had been unfolding since 1951, although the particular version described occurred in the early 1960s. Delinquents, sixteen to seventeen years old, living at home, were placed on probation, predicated on their taking part in the Essexfields Program. They engaged in "total" work and group-discussion activity. Since all worked together in a yard maintenance project, work behavior was relevant for examination in the daily ninety-minute group discussions. These discussions were each centered on a particular boy—either self-nominated or nominated by others—who became the agreed topic.

A new boy would be introduced to the group meeting by reviewing his personal delinquency history. Other boys would question, cross-examine, and probe to uncover the unvarnished truth. The thrust of the meetings was to create the kind of environment that would lead each boy to give up his antisocial ways and accept the norms of established society. When evidence was available that he was doing this, as well as helping other boys do the same, he became a candidate for release from the program. A fundamental characteristic in this intervention as well as in the Provo experiment was the deliberate decision by those in charge not to rely directly on their own power/authority as the means of enforcing obedience to established norms. In place of it, the power/authority to exercise initiative and to enforce norms and standards was in the hands of the boys themselves. Staff interventions of an authority-obedience character were rarely needed. Occasionally graduates of the program returned as consultants to the group either as catalytic facilitators or for confrontation or prescription.

Mental Illness

In the "therapeutic community" described by Jones (1953) for treating patients severely disturbed by anxiety, patients are subjected not only to catalytic interventions but also to significant confrontational and acceptant interventions by members of the entire hospital community: psychiatrists, social workers, nurses, occupational instructors, and resettlement counselors, as well as other persons who have been admitted for therapy. Such interventions are intended to foster a shift from social norms that project weakness drawn from disabling anxiety toward norms promoting a self-reliant capacity for work and family-oriented relationships. As at Synanon, one norm of the therapeutic community is that everyone works. Each participant's attitudes toward work, toward supervision, and toward other members of the community, are commented on in discussion groups.

In addition, participants may choose to prepare a written psychodrama which is later acted out with the help of other participants. This last-mentioned activity is more in the direction of cathartic tension-releasing to improve morale/cohesion than in the uncovering and working through of unexamined norms and standards for living.

Confrontations may be initiated by the consultant or, modeling him, by any participant. For example,

> Dr. Baker now asked the new patients in the group to stand up and introduce themselves. All six had arrived the day before and had been shown around the workshops and had met their doctors for an initial interview. One of these new patients was asked to take the place of Mr. S. Mr. W., a patient with a long record of unemployment, did so. Dr. Baker now turned to the patients and asked what sort of questions he should put to Mr. W. Having been briefed he asked Mr. W. what his last job had been. Mr. W. said he had done heavy work in the engineering trade but had had to give it up.

Was the "why" of his giving up on heavy work related to being *physically* incapacitated or not?

> "Why did you find it difficult?" asked the doctor. Mr. W. replied that it had been dull and boring so he had tried other work but it had always been the same story.

So it was a value-related reason. The consultant and other members of the group began gathering data from this "area" of Mr. W. and relating his responses to possibilities they saw for placing him as a working member.

> Dr. Baker asked again, "Well, what would you like to do here?" Mr. W. replied, "I don't want to do anything." Dr. Baker then turned to the patients one of whom suggested that Mr. W. should be allowed to wander around the workshops where he would probably settle down in one. An-

other, however, pointed out that Mr. W. had been around once, and if after further wandering he still did not settle, we had the same problem. Another suggested that the community should find out what his interests were because maybe he wanted a job where he could use his brain as well as his hands. So Dr. Baker put these questions to Mr. W. who replied, "Yes, I've been a fur dresser and I liked that." "And why did you give that up?" asked Dr. Baker. Mr. W. replied, "Because I liked night work and when that ended I did not like the same job on the day shift, I don't like mixing with people."

By now Mr. W. had expressed what presently was of key personal value to him. This value might be summarized as "Touch Me Not." As group members discussed further how Mr. W. might fit into the therapeutic community, *their* contrasting value —which, as a norm, might be expressed as "People who live and work together should mix together," emerged.

A patient then suggested that we should place him in one of the work-shops in the morning and send him to the local Government training centre at Waddon in the afternoon where he could be tried out in a trade. Dr. Baker remarked, "But we don't yet know if he is suited for a trade." A patient now stated, "We don't usually send new patients to Waddon— he might not be suited for it temperamentally." Another patient suggested that physical training was the best activity we had. Dr. Baker asked Mr. W. about physical training but the latter replied that he would not last an hour at this. Dr. Baker then asked another patient, Mr. C., who had been in the hospital for some time, to come out and explain the work therapy to Mr. W. The latter was told that he ought to mix more with other people at work. Mr. W. replied, "But I don't want to mix with other people." Mr. C. answered this with, "You meet people at the local, don't you?" "Don't go to pubs," said Mr. W. bluntly. Mr. C. responded with, "Well, I suggest that you just go and look at the occupation shops for a week." "I always keep myself to myself," Mr. W. stubbornly replied. Mr. C. said in explanation, "That's part of your neurosis. You must give things a trial and try to change, for after all you can keep yourself to yourself even in the work-shops." Dr. Baker thanked Mr. C. who returned to his seat in the audience.

Other members of the group, who do not share Mr. W.'s "Touch Me Not" value, discuss its rationale and certain of its consequences with him in a way that points up the contrasts between their norms and the ones he is trying to "import" into the community. Even though Mr. W., at this moment, may be a long way from adopting the norms and standards he is hearing, the confrontation at least sets up a comparison basis for what until then had been his nonsocial private world of personal values.

A patient now queried, "Does he want to mix with people?" Mr. W. replied, "I'll mix but I won't talk, but if an argument starts then I'll join in."

A patient questioned, "Is he afraid of talking in case he makes a fool of himself?" Dr. Baker suggested, "Well, go ahead and ask him." Mr. W. agreed that there might be something in this. "Perhaps he's learnt he gets people's backs up when he talks," suggested another patient. Dr. Baker agreed that the discussion related Mr. W.'s work difficulties to his personality defects and that if these could be remedied it would be much easier for Mr. W. to find satisfactory employment. He went on to point out that Mr. W. had already taken an active part in the community life of the Unit by his performance, that he had been given an opportunity to talk without being misunderstood or being laughed at, and that perhaps he would go on improving.

The hospital consultant, addressing the group as a whole, makes his own concluding points. While this is an intervention calculated to lend perspective rather than a confrontational intervention, Mr. W. may "hear" part of it, particularly if these general comments connect, for example, to what he is able to remember experiencing as a child.

In conclusion Dr. Baker pointed out that there was general agreement that no one liked the idea of being compelled to work. Indeed, many patients were over-sensitive to any suggestions of compulsion. This was related to experiences in their early lives when compelled to do things to please an aggressive father or over-anxious mother. The patients were encouraged to review their past work history and their patterns of behaviour which had led to failure, and then to use our workshop facilities to try and create new and healthier patterns. (Jones, 1953, pp. 61–63)

To illustrate the pertinence of Dr. Baker's comment on patients' earlier life experiences, here is an instance of an "aggressive father" *and* "over-anxious mother" reacting in contradictory fashion to an action by their young son. The incident is described by a group-therapy client in another setting. He is now aged twenty-four and the incident that he recalls is said to have occurred when he was of preschool age.

Consultant: ... Spell it out.

Henry: It's like ... everything Mother says is irrelevant ... and most of what Father says is frightening. So where are you?

I was playing with some matches once. I set some leaves on fire in the backyard. Father said the police would come and take me away. He said they would take me to Juvenile Hall. Then Mother came and put her arms around me and told me I was her darling angel. Then Father began yelling. I think he got mad at her and forgot all about me. I remember, later that evening, he gave me a present. I never understood it. He was smiling and cheerful like what happened earlier had never happened.

But I couldn't stand all the shouting in the house. There was always shouting, and my mother was always afraid, always crying and talking about heaven and Jesus and hugging me and looking off into space and not even knowing she was holding me.

Consultant: You must have felt terribly frustrated.

Henry: Frustrated, yes. And afraid. I felt afraid of people. I've always been very shy. (Branden, 1970, p. 21)

Jones' strategy of creating a community in which all members, professionals and participants alike, accept responsibility for intervening confrontationally is to help client-members to recognize and to reject norms and standards of conduct that run counter to health. Group-norm pressures coexist with the supportive character of the community when an individual reveals his or her "real" problems, whether in discussion groups or in psychodrama.

SUMMARY

The Synanon game, radical therapy, the residential approaches to delinquency, and the therapeutic-community strategies appear to be based on similar approaches for inducing change. The underlying proposition is that change is unlikely to occur unless the norms and standards upon which personal behavior rests are brought sharply into focus and invalid aspects of one's orientations are modified or replaced by new norms and standards that permit more productive living. In each of these approaches, confrontation is the tool used to help the client identify these invalid aspects and explore alternative systems and their possible consequences.

REFERENCES

Blake, R. R., H. A. Shepard, and J. S. Mouton. *Managing Intergroup Conflict in Industry*. Houston: Gulf Publishing Company, 1964.

Blake, R. R., J. S. Mouton, and R. L. Sloma. "The Union-Management Intergroup Laboratory: Strategies for Resolving Intergroup Conflict." *Journal of Behavioral Science* 1, no. 1 (1965): 25–57.

Bradford, L. P., and J. B. Harvey. "Dealing with Dysfunctional Organization Myths." Reproduced by special permission from *Training and Development Journal* 24, no. 9 (1970): 2. Copyright by the American Society for Training and Development, Inc.

Branden, N. *Breaking Free*. Los Angeles: Nash Publishing, 1970. Reprinted by permission.

Clark, T., and D. T. Jaffe. *Toward a Radical Therapy: Alternate Services for Personal and Social Change*. New York: Gordon and Breach, Science Publishers, 1973. Reprinted by permission.

Ellis, A. *Reason and Emotion in Psychotherapy*. New York: Lyle Stuart, 1962. Reprinted by permission.

Empey, L. T., and M. L. Erickson. *The Provo Experiment: Evaluating Community Control of Delinquency*. Lexington, Mass.: D. C. Heath, 1972. Reprinted by permission of the publisher.

Enright, J. B. "On the Playing Fields of Synanon." In L. Blank, G. B. Gottsegen, and M. G. Gottsegen, *Confrontation: Encounters in Self and Interpersonal Awareness*. New York: Macmillan 1971, pp. 147–77. Reprinted by permission.

Jones, M. *et al. The Therapeutic Community: A New Treatment Method in Psychiatry*. New York: Basic Books, Chapter IV, copyright © 1953 by Basic Books, Inc. Reprinted by permission.

Lalmi, D., T. Romana, and N. Hoxha. "Worker Control." *New Albania* 27, no. 2 (1973): 22.

Masters, W. H., and V. E. Johnson. *Human Sexual Inadequacy*. Boston: Little, Brown, 1970.

Robinson, V. P. "A Discussion of Two Case Records Illustrating Personality Change." In J. Taft, ed., *Family Casework and Counseling: A Functional Approach*. Philadelphia: University of Pennsylvania Press, 1948, pp. 150–64.

Satir, V. M. *Conjoint Family Therapy*. Rev. ed. Palo Alto, Calif.: Science and Behavior Books, Inc., 1967. Reprinted by permission of the author and publisher.

Stephenson, R. M., and F. R. Scarpitti. *Group Interaction as Therapy: The Use of the Small Group in Corrections*. Westport, Conn.: Greenwood Press, 1974.

CONFRONTATIONAL INTERVENTIONS

18

GOALS / OBJECTIVES

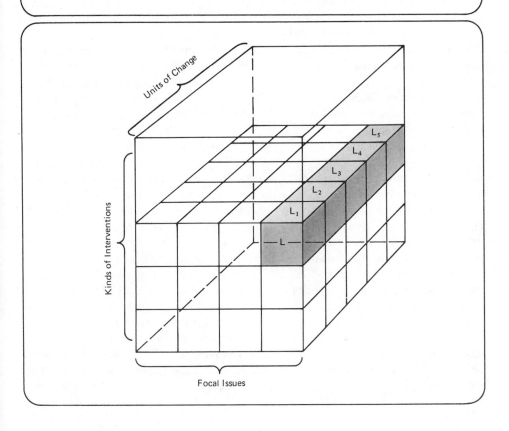

No published accounts of confrontational interventions calculated to solve goals/objectives problems have as yet appeared, and the absence of such identifiable examples needs to be accounted for. In many settings conduct as perceived "from the outside" often seems controlled more by norms/standards than by personal goals/objectives. Whether or not this is actually the case in specific circumstances, the consultant encounters difficulty in determining whether or not the situation is best evaluated as a norms/standards or as a goals/objectives focal issue. For practical purposes of intervention, especially when the client is more than one person, addressing the situation as a norms/standards issue provides a readier entrance into problem areas susceptible to some degree of quick-action resolution.

An example of the difficulty can be drawn from the Alcoholics Anonymous approach to the problem of alcoholism (Chapter 23). As a norm/standard the rule of abstinence constitutes a means of aiding an individual to regulate what otherwise would be an uncontrolled drift into downward-spiral behavior. The social-support system of Alcoholics Anonymous in itself reinforces the norm, and the extended-group aspect of being able to call upon other members of Alcoholics Anonymous under trying circumstances provides further norm strengthening.

Looked at in another way, the pursuit of abstinence is a goal/objective that an individual member of Alcoholics Anonymous commits himself to seeking. Viewed as a goals/objectives issue, however, it is more difficult to see how actual interventions of Alcoholics Anonymous in that mode might work as compared to the efficiency of those interventions premised on having the client try to adopt and hold a norm/standard of abstinence. In time, despite possible setbacks, everyday compliance with that norm can become habitual. In any event, the norm/standard intervention focuses the issue on "making a beginning *right now* by not taking the next drink." Given adherence to that norm, the clock-and-calendar goal of sobriety is or is not achieved from one day to the next.

There are circumstances where the most practical intervention might be a goals/objectives confrontation. But even here, the entry consultation is likely to be concerned with confronting the client to examine his or her current norms/standards. Once he or she has done so and found them wanting, then the consultation may proceed in the direction of identifying alternate goals and objectives to be pursued. The confrontational aspect is in challenging the client to recognize and then commit himself or herself to the attainment of goals/objectives that otherwise would not be recognized; or, if they previously had been, were not classified as attainable.

The above remarks are no less valid for analyzing situations confronting groups, organizations, or even larger social systems. A group or an organization may at its point of formation have clear-cut goals/objectives; but soon, behavior in pursuit of such goals becomes repetitive and mechanical, coded into a bureaucratic set of formal rules that regulate what individuals do and how they interact with one another. When organizations take on such a ritualized character, the problem of change is initially and centrally a problem of challenging existing norms/standards prior to confronting the client system to examine the goals and objectives it *should* be striving to accomplish. Even here, although the client system may become aware of its problems from a norms/standards point of view, it is likely that if the focal issue shifts to one of goals/objectives the intervention will take on a prescriptive rather than confrontational character.

CONFRONTATIONAL INTERVENTIONS

19

SUMMARY
AND
IMPLICATIONS

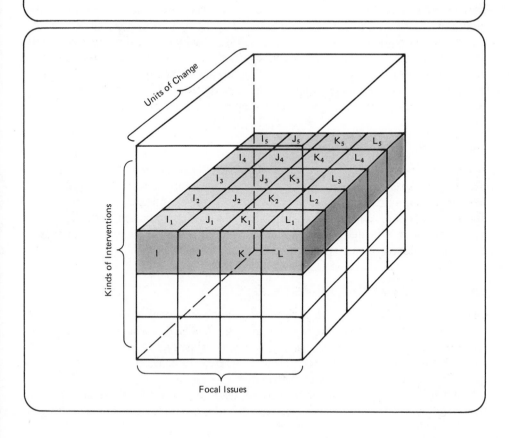

Some values and assumptions lead to self-defeating cycles of behavior. By becoming aware of these, a client has the possibility of reorienting his or her behavior in terms of more valid and justifiable ones and of escaping from unproductive behavior patterns. The strongest confrontation presents the client with facts that reveal his or her values and assumptions in ways that are undeniable and indisputable. This kind of feedback brings into focus a contradiction between expressed beliefs and operational values: the president says he respects the rights of others, but then ignores their rights by using rank to interrupt; management claims to respect the union, but the union can identify endless examples of disrespect that management cannot dispute. The client is faced with either changing behavior to be congruent with more valid values or continuing it in the face of recognized inconsistency.

WHAT THE CONSULTANT DOES

The confrontational consultant does not take the problem situation at face value, nor does he or she respond to the client's felt needs. Rather, it is the consultant's objective to highlight the client's underlying value system in such a way as to enable the client to become forcefully aware of how present value orientations control present behavior. At the same time the consultant may assist the client in examining alternative values, more legitimate or justified in the light of existing circumstances. Under ideal conditions, this value reexamination is achieved by directing the client's attention to here-and-now behavior rather than past-and-gone events that can only be indirectly observed by the consultant through the client's reports. The client finds it more difficult to rationalize and thereby explain away the implications of value-based behaviors observed in his or her contemporary situation.

LIMITATIONS

A major limitation of this approach is the possibility of client resistance to participating in the kinds of interactions described. Many clients sense that confrontational interventions may reduce their ability to "control" the situation and thus feel it safer not to throw open Pandora's box. In addition, it is a common tendency for a challenge, even if it is in the form of a question, to be sensed as criticism and thus to generate win-lose arguments regarding the facts themselves.

WHY CONFRONTATION CAN BE HELPFUL

One of the main benefits to be derived from confrontational modes of intervention is that the client is enabled to examine aspects of behavior which otherwise might go unrecognized. While operating on the client "silently," these aspects have uncontrolled influence on his or her conduct; therefore, a confrontational intervention can make a consciousness-raising contribution.

When the client is composed of a group, team, or organization, challenging less-than-valid values becomes even more crucial and more difficult—the values may be silent or may be well known and shared in common, in which case they are not subject to challenge within the membership itself. Shared values produce norms and conformity, and a person transgressing the norm or even speaking against it must be willing to oppose values the entire group holds. This opens up the possibility of rejection, and in the face of such a threat a momentary deviant may go back to accepting the norms as given.

As an individual, the reader may readily role play himself or herself as recipient of a confrontational intervention coming from an unfamiliar "outside" source —a consultant. An "outsider" may be defined as anyone who, in everyday life, is assumed to have no legitimate reason to be interested—far less, interfere—in what you are feeling, thinking, and doing. So in everyday life situations, if and when someone is confronted by an outsider who makes a comment that zeroes in on the most sensitive nub of whatever you hold dear—your present values—your immediate reaction might be a dramatic and colorful expression of indignation. At the other extreme, you might retreat "back into your shell" and say nothing. Either way, it is probable that you would feel hurt.

But what is hurting? A variety of intervention situations have been illustrated in Chapters 15–18, some *not* from everyday life, but all intended to improve the everyday life of some particular client, whether one or an aggregate of individuals. In each of these situations, then, the outsider *does* have a legitimate interest in confronting "you," however painful for the moment, in areas where you are sensitive. In each case, "what's *really* hurting" is more likely to be obvious to the detached consultant than to the client or member of client group.

Value-based assumptions are as basic to understanding behavior of groups, teams, committees, or families as they are for comprehending patterns of individual behavior. While an almost endless variety of values related to power/authority, morale/cohesion, norms/standards, and goals/objectives can be identified in the individual, a more limited range underlies the behavior of people in groups. Other episodes in Chapters 15–18 demonstrate that confrontational interventions at the intergroup level can be useful when norms and standards of one group clash with those of another and produce rationalizations, defensiveness, justification, projection, and a number of other very deep-seated defense mechanisms. The aggregate effect of these mechanisms at the intergroup relationship level is to preserve self-defeating cycles of interaction. A consultant usually employs two different points of intervention, both important to success. The first is to intervene in terms of identifying assumptions regarding the character of the relationship; the second is to get each group to identify the stereotypes it has of the other and then to challenge the other's stereotype of itself if perceived as "inaccurate." Each group justifies its posture of win-lose, withdrawal, apathy, and so on, by "protecting" the stereotype it has of the other. It can only break out of its own defensiveness by reexamining and discarding implicit and possibly destructive values and attitudes. With awareness of these and their past influences, possibilities open up for each group's membership to seek a more objective basis of interaction.

Consultants can intervene with a total organization in a confrontational manner by challenging assumptions that are hampering organization effectiveness. Two general considerations underlie the large variety of confrontational organization interventions: one deals with the specifics involved in making an intervention; the other has to do with how a confrontational consultant builds his or her relationship with the organization. Blake and Mouton (1964, pp. 282–83) have identified nine specific approaches to confrontational interventions that are used in here-and-now problem solving within an organizational framework for issues of power/authority, morale/cohesion, norms/standards, and goals/objectives. These are:

1. *Discrepancy.*   This intervention calls attention to a contradiction in action or attitudes and is useful for keeping the organization on a new course rather than allowing it to shift unwittingly into old and less satisfactory behavior patterns in response to momentary pressures.

2. *Theory.*   A type of intervention in which confrontation draws on behavioral science concepts and theory to throw into bold relief the connection between underlying assumptions and present behavior.

3. *Procedural.*   A challenge of various steps in problem-solving efforts that may not in fact lead to the most effective action.

4. *Relationship.*   This kind of intervention focuses the attention of participants on issues that arise between people, by virtue of different value orientations, as they work together.

5. *Experimentation.*   An intervention that involves introducing experimentation as the basis of testing and comparing two or more courses of action *before* a final decision is taken, particularly when the way to proceed has become institutionalized or tradition-bound.

6. *Dilemma.*   A dilemma intervention aids in accurately identifying a choice point in managerial actions. It often can help members reexamine outworn assumptions and search for alternatives other than those under consideration.

7. *Perspective.*   Many times in the intensity of the effort applied in production settings, it seems almost inevitable that individuals or teams will lose their sense of direction. A perspective intervention permits present actions to be challenged by providing a background of broader historical orientation.

8. *Organization Structure.*   The fabric of the organization itself can prevent communication, decision making, and the application of effort from being as effective as it might be under different organizational arrangements. An organizational intervention focuses on issues that confront the total organization membership or its various subcomponents.

9. *Cultural.*   A cultural intervention challenges traditions, precedents, and established practices which constitute properties of the organizational fabric itself. Challenging the appropriateness of organization culture is difficult, because culture permeates actions in such a silent way. The intervention that lifts up culture for examination may indeed be one of the most critical.

Not all confrontational consultants utilize all of these to focus attention on implicit values and attitudes. Probably the most common are *discrepancy, procedural,* and *relationship* interventions.

Jaques' (1951) approach to work in organizations parallels, in certain respects, that of psychoanalysis with individuals or groups. He calls it "social analysis," but the mode of intervention is based on confrontational assumptions. His account is noteworthy because he has been specific about what a consultant should and should not do as he intervenes in organizations. According to Jaques, the consultant should steadfastly avoid developing social relations with any member of the client organization. He stays away from off-the-job contacts that might conceivably be interpreted as a "special relationship" with any one of the organization's individuals or groups. Under this ground rule, he refuses invitations to members' homes, to "have a drink with us," and so on. This rule is to ensure that the consultant's capacity for intervention is in no way compromised.

Other rules aimed at preserving this necessary independence include:

1. complete confidentiality of the consultant-client relationship,
2. participation in the analysis of problems without entering into recommendations that would cause the consultant to "share" responsibility,
3. remaining free to accept other consultation opportunities, thus avoiding dependence on any one source of livelihood,
4. an understanding that his participation in the analysis of problems must be initiated by the client. (Jaques, 1951, pp. 11–16)

These contractual arrangements with an organization-as-client do not prevent Jaques' participation from being confrontational. He concentrates on assisting organization members who seek his help to go deeply into organization questions, to get behind facades, to discard behavioral clichés, and to seek reality-based solutions, even though these may require dramatic shifts away from current modes of thought or operational practices.

The substantive issues that organization members of the "client" bring to the consultant extend over a wide range of concerns, including structure, policy, pay, products, personnel practices, training, and even fundamental matters of finance. The consultant confronts the particular person with whatever assumptions underlie the latter's convictions, assumptions ranging from the most empirical to the most philosophically abstract.

Because of the barriers of client defensiveness, confrontation is a more difficult intervention mode for the internal consultant than for an external consultant. Given that a client may be provoked to "lash back" under confrontation, catalytic interventions are inherently safer.

Confrontational interpretations can introduce insights that result in resolution of a problem, but such results are seldom predictable. In contrast, the theory-oriented mode of intervention is less likely to provoke dependency or hostility reactions toward the consultant. Thus, under that mode of consultation, it is unnecessary to deal with such reactions except as they are the cause of blockages within client-system relationships.

REFERENCES

Blake, R. R., and J. S. Mouton. *The Managerial Grid*®. Houston: Gulf Publishing Company, 1964.

Jaques, E. *The Changing Culture of a Factory*. London: Tavistock Publications, 1951.

PART

4

PRESCRIPTIVE
INTERVENTIONS

20

PRESCRIPTIVE INTERVENTIONS: AN INTRODUCTION

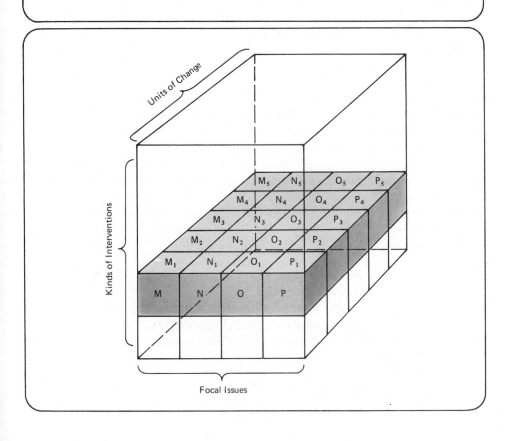

Prescription is probably the oldest approach for dealing with problems. In the field of medicine a physician usually listens to what a patient has to say about symptoms —his or her felt needs—and then conducts an independent examination to establish the nature of the problem—the client's real needs. Once the physician's diagnosis is completed he or she tells the patient the conclusion: what the patient faces; what he or she needs to do or what needs to be done, including what treatment, if any, will help in the restoration of health.

The prescriptive consultant in nonmedical fields relies on skills acquired from a body of knowledge or from years of practical experience, also acting on the premise that he or she is sufficiently expert to discern the client's *actual* needs as contrasted with *felt* needs. The presumption is that the client lacks the necessary knowledge or objectivity to make a sound self-diagnosis and design a plan of corrective action. A prescriptive consultant not only identifies what the real need is but also specifies the actions necessary if the client is to escape from self-defeating behavior cycles.

A prescription-oriented consultant creates a relationship with the client that in many respects parallels that of doctor and patient. A significant feature is that prescriptions are possible even when the client is at his "wit's end" or has thrown up his hands in despair. The consultant's aim is to give the client needed guidance or the convictions he lacks in order to take action. The prescriptive consultant's recommendations may have the greatest impact when the client surrenders his self-will and unquestioningly accepts and follows the consultant's expert recommendations. The prescriptive consultant may or may not offer a rationale for what he or she recommends. When one is provided, the "answer" may become even more acceptable because the client understands the problem-solving strategy involved. But readiness of the consultant to explain his or her answer makes it no less prescriptive— a prescriptive consultant operates on the assumption that the client, by coming to him or her, either does not want or is unable to act on personal initiative.

A useful distinction that highlights a significant aspect of prescription can be drawn between a client on the one hand and a customer in a selling situation on the other. A customer acts on the assumption that he knows what his needs are and has sufficient knowledge to be able to make a choice between alternative possibilities for satisfying these needs. By contrast with the client, therefore, he does not want to be "told" but rather wants to be informed about the various available possibilities. The exercise of an option is his. Seeing the client as a "customer" is more typical of the catalytic approach.

The prescriptive consultant listens to the client's remarks and while he or she does not reject them, he or she does not necessarily take them at face value; in other words, they serve as a useful point of departure for the consultant in initiating diagnostic activities. The consultant then interrogates, observes, interviews, and investigates. After satisfying himself or herself that the real problem has been identified, the consultant says something like, "Here is your problem," and "This is the best thing for you to do . . ."

The prescriptive consultant:

1. interrogates for what he or she needs to know about the client's situation and in a businesslike manner cuts through to the heart of the matter, sometimes without much concern for social delicacies. Unless they are in a power position, he or she is unlikely to explain much to interviewees as this can color their reactions to answers;

2. controls the situation by telling the client how he or she perceives the problem;

3. tells the client in a confident, authoritative way the "best" solution to implement;

4. expresses confidence in the plan and often offers to supervise its implementation;

5. if the client procrastinates, or tries to avoid acting on recommendations, the consultant may say, "I don't think we can presently work together, but feel free to call for an appointment whenever you feel seriously committed to having your problem resolved";

6. weakens the client's defensiveness through undermining his or her claims or explanations, or establishes a relationship based on positive transference which can result in the client doing what he or she has been told in order to enjoy the consultant's appreciation.

The basic premise of prescriptive interventions is that the consultant is an expert authority and the client is prepared to accept the answers the consultant provides. This situation of authority/dependency is fraught with difficulties when selected as the intervention strategy for certain types of problems, for even though the consultant may know what is best for the client, the client may not be prepared to introduce those behavior or attitude changes into his or her life. This could be partly because the client feels incapable of implementing the recommended actions, and partly because if he or she does implement them this may result in controversial situations with others who, unlike the client, are unprepared to accept the recommendations of an outside expert. It should be noted that the prescriptive approach may prescribe *what* to do in solving a technical problem of operations, as well as how to behave in the "process" sense.

Another common feature of the prescriptive mode of consultation, particularly as it relates to group, intergroup, organization, or larger-social-system applications, is that answers are directed to the top of the system so that the system's power/authority-obedience structure can be used to implement the changes called for. Under these circumstances, although implementation is likely to occur, resistances may be generated, ones that eventually cause the changes to become distorted, watered down, or merely ignored.

The prescriptive mode of intervention is found to be particularly effective when the client has reached "the end of his rope" and, though action is imperative, is unable to select from the options available to him the one best suited to solving the problem at hand. This inability may be due to emotional turmoil, or to having reached a hopeless impasse, or to the client's deep ignorance of the variables operating in his situation. Under any of these conditions, the client's dependency has reached a sufficient degree to result in his being ready to trust and be governed by the consultant's expertness. Yet because the consultant provides his or her client with a ready-made solution, the client may not gain enough competence to solve the same kind of problem in the future or related problems as they arise unexpectedly.

PRESCRIPTIVE INTERVENTIONS

21

POWER/AUTHORITY

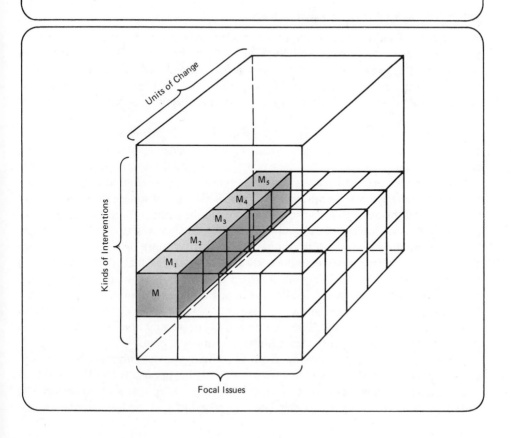

Prescriptive interventions are frequently pertinent when the focal issue is one of power/authority. The intervention might be to aid a person to exercise his or her power/authority more effectively over another person, such as a consultant trying to help a parent manage a child. Or, in situations where the exercise of power/ authority is carried out through the hierarchical arrangements of organization structure a consultant may be the first to identify the problems in a faulty structure. Having done so, he or she prescribes how the power/authority relationships should be changed in order for the organization to work more efficiently.

INDIVIDUAL (M₁)

A major use of prescriptive consultation with individuals is to bolster the client's assertiveness. For whatever reason, the individual is presently weak in the power/ authority area. In some cases, the person expected to exercise power/authority is weak in the sense that his or her actions need strengthening; in other cases, the "natural" subordinate is the one who should increase his or her power in the particular situation.

Ineffective Performance by a Subordinate

An example of individual prescription to bolster individual effectiveness in exercising power/authority is described by Flory (1965, pp. 158–59). The consultant involved was asked by his client for help in dealing more effectively with a "problem" subordinate. Responding to this invitation, the consultant first diagnosed the client's problem and then offered a behavioral prescription for boosting his use of power/authority.

The client was a plant manager who had been having trouble with his chief accountant, a "cold and formal" individual. To obtain better results than he was presently getting from this man, the plant manager—a genial fatherly person who liked to develop warm personal relations with his subordinates—was told to take a forceful, direct, and impersonal approach with him. This, the consultant predicted, would resonate much better with the accountant than did the manager's more typical "soft" approach. On the matter of delayed reports the manager was to say the following, "I want your report on my desk at nine o'clock Friday morning, complete in every detail, and no ifs, ands, or buts about it." Having delivered that ultimatum, he was to turn around and leave. The plant manager did just that, although, being the kind of person he was, it was hard sledding for him. But the new approach brought striking results. The report came in on schedule and was one of the finest the plant manager had ever received. The client had been told specifically how he should act and he followed through in accordance with the consultant's plan.

A similar kind of prescription given to individuals, but this time by a group-as-consultant, is described by Cohen and Smith (1972, pp. 84–106). This intervention is said to be most suitable toward the end of a group learning experience. At that time the total group is divided into subgroups of four or five members each.

They are given instructions and one person from each subgroup leaves the room for ten minutes or so. Those who remain,

> will first diagnose this person's typical style of interacting with others, and secondly try to pinpoint definite, specific, helpful suggestions as to how he might be helped to engage in atypical but productive behavior both for himself and the group. I must stress the terms 'definite' and 'specific' . . . give him definite and specific prescriptions to carry out that are generally atypical but productive. Thus, one person might be told to express anger toward the group more directly and verbally instead of remaining quiet. (Cohen and Smith, 1972, p. 103)

At the end of this session, in other words, each person has a prescription for what he should do to increase his effectiveness.

Daughter-Mother Conflict

One of the roots of prescriptive behavioral-science interventions is in the work of J. L. Moreno on psychodrama, an approach patterned in some respects after Greek tragedy. The method uses dramatic portrayals to help a client deal with some significant situation in his or her life. This may relate to feelings of being rejected by parents, issues of marriage, concerns about work, or other emotion-provoking situations that can block effective action.

Psychodrama takes place on an open, often circular, stage around which ten to thirty or more people may be seated. Lighting arrangements can either turn the stage into a kind of "room" where the audience is "set apart" from participants, or can create a setting where actors and audience interact with one another. The psychodrama proceeds through three phases: warmup, enactment, and wrap-up. During the warmup, the consultant-director provides background information, such as how the Greeks built their plays around a central protagonist whose contest with his circumstances—the tragedy—purged the audience of violent and overpowering emotions. Then someone in the audience is invited to volunteer to be the actor of his circumstances. Others in the audience participate by taking roles of significant persons in the actor-client's life. There are many terms for supporting-cast members, such as "alter ego" ("other self") or "auxiliary ego," and for the processes that take place, such as role reversal, soliloquy, etc., but knowledge of these is not essential for understanding how psychodrama works in practice.

The following is an account of the opening of the enactment phase of a psychodrama conducted by a psychodramatic consultant. Judy is the volunteer client.

> "What do you do, Judy?"
> Judy shrugged. "Nothing . . . I guess."
> "Nothing?" The director's voice had a hint of sarcasm. "You mean you sit around all day and stare at the walls?"

The girl smiled. "Well . . . no."

"Do you go to school?"

"No."

"You graduated?"

"I went to art school for six months and dropped out," Judy revealed.

"How did your parents feel about it?"

"They didn't like it very much."

"Show us," the director said.

A table and a couple of chairs were brought on stage and, under Judy's direction arranged in an approximation of her family's living room. Then the director invited a woman from the audience to come up on the stage and portray Judy's mother.

"All right, Judy," she said. "Now show us what happened."

Judy looked self-conscious as she walked into the make-believe room, but she made her announcement in a strong clear voice. "Well, I've done it," she said, "I've told them I'm not going back to art school."

Before Judy's "mother" had a chance to reply, the director stepped in and suggested that the two characters switch roles. Now Judy stood in her mother's place; the volunteer from the audience walked in and repeated Judy's announcement.

"How do you feel, Mother?" the director asked Judy.

The girl seemed confused. Her voice faltered. "I'm angry, I'm disappointed. I'm hurt," she said.

"And what are you going to say to your daughter?"

"How could you do such a thing?" Judy said sharply. "Your father and I have worked hard to give you the things we never had. But you won't take them. You keep refusing our kindness."

"How do you feel about that, Judy?" Mrs. Moreno cut in. "This time answer her as yourself."

"You aren't very kind. You're selfish!" Judy cried. "You don't care about me at all. You just want your children to go to school and graduate because it makes you look good to the neighbors." (Fleming, 1969, pp. 46–47, 73–74)

This episode suggests the richness of expression made possible through a psychodramatic presentation. The director supervises the entire process and both stimulates and supports the expression of emotions that have been aroused under client "protagonist" circumstances. Moreover, the director supervises the expression of feelings by *others* who represent "real life" people. The prescriptive nature of the consultation is in the *process* interactions. That is, the consultant tells the client what to do to release feelings and how to set up a situation, rather than giving answers to specific problems. Prescription comes from the outside but impacts upon interior or subjective problems the consultant judges to be of central importance.

During the wrap-up, reactions toward the protagonist's problem and toward one another are shared between audience members and actors. Participants often describe their feelings toward the circumstances enacted and sometimes relate their own similar or different-but-pertinent experiences for reactions and comments. This third give-and-take step, usually in the catalytic but also in the acceptant vein, permits the central character to see his or her situation in the perspective of similar problems experienced by others. While the outcome for the client may be *cathartic,* the prescriptiveness inherent in psychodrama makes it a very different kind of approach than an acceptant intervention. A critical difference between the two is related to what the client learns. In an acceptant intervention the client learns *how* to express his or her emotions and feelings, and, at least theoretically, this learning can be transferred to real-life situations. But the client is only able to express what becomes evident to him or her through *self*-discovery as the consultant does not "push." In a prescriptive psychodrama the consultant pushes the client into discoveries the client might not have faced on his or her own initiative.

Wife-Husband Conflict

In addition to relying heavily on psychodramatic techniques of the sort pioneered by Moreno, Gestalt therapy has as one of its guiding assumptions the central concept and goal of "wholeness" or "completeness" of a client. Lack of completeness is characterized as a personality "hole" produced by an impasse at some point along the way to maturity. The purpose of therapy is to find the hole and to identify and solve the impasse. This cannot be done as well, according to Perls (1971), by a talking approach (such as psychoanalysis) as it can be by an active and directed approach. The impasse must be confronted actively by the client, with the consultant skillfully directing as well as sometimes frustrating the client by keeping him or her focused on the impasse.

Two chairs are used to facilitate this procedure. One, where the client sits, is the "hot seat." The other is empty except when the client shifts over to sit on it while enacting another person or even another part of himself. The consultant may be standing at a podium before the assembled audience.

The Gestalt consultant aims at preventing rather than permitting a client to rationalize or in other ways escape from the here-and-now activities. Then, some aspect of a client's personality that has never been completed can move toward closure. In this sense, Gestalt therapy somewhat resembles Frankl's "logotherapy" (Frankl, 1955, 1967) or Wolpe's (1965, 1973) desensitization techniques. Relief results from doing the thing that is feared in fantasy and which, therefore, has been shied away from in fact.

The Gestalt therapy approach also parallels psychodrama in certain of its aspects. One of these is role reversal. The client enacts his or her own subjective reactions and then taking the role of his or her adversary (boss, wife, husband, etc.), "answers" by reacting from the adversary's point of view. A series of such reversals provides a client the basis for seeing the way he or she has been projecting ideas and attitudes onto the adversary and, in turn, how he or she experiences the adversary reacting to these projections. Each step along the way is directed in a prescriptive, "Now do this," "Now do that," manner by the consultant who, in addition, may apply pressure on the client to intensify a reaction or to experiment with a different solution to the problem.

A consultation Perls had with a client illustrates the prescriptive character of these interventions. For a decade Carol had been trying to decide whether or not to divorce her husband. Carol begins in the "hot seat," expressing herself. Then, at the consultant's bidding, she switches over to an empty chair and talks for him. Her husband appears to be present in the conversation they have, but this is not so. This back-and-forth reversal continues, with her going from being herself to "being" her husband, interrupted only by the consultant.

> *Client:* I'm trying to decide whether to divorce my husband or not, and have been for ten years.
>
> *Consultant:* It's a real impasse, yah! A real unfinished situation. And this is typical of the impasse. We try *everything* to keep the status quo, rather than to get through the impasse. We keep on with our self-torture games, with our bad marriages, with our therapy where we improve, improve, improve, and nothing changes, but our inner conflict is always the same, we maintain the status quo. So talk to your husband. Put him there."
>
> *Client:* Well, I feel like I've been—I've found out some things, Andy, and I found out who you—who you are to me, and I love you in some ways. You know, I didn't love you when I married you, but I love you now, in some ways, but—but I feel like I'm not gonna be able to grow up if I stay with you, and I don't want to be a freak.
>
> *Consultant:* Change seats.
>
> *Client* (as husband): That's not fair, Carol, because I love you so much, and we've been together for so long . . . and I want to take care of you . . . I just want you to love me, and—
>
> *Consultant:* I don't understand. First, he says he loves you, and now you say he wants—he needs love.
>
> *Client* (as husband): Yes. I—I really need—I guess I do need love.
>
> *Consultant:* Is it a trade? A trade agreement—love vs. love? . . .
>
> *Client* (as husband): I need you.
>
> *Consultant:* Ah! What do you need Carol for?
>
> *Client* (as husband): Because you're exciting . . . I feel dead without you.
>
> *Client* (herself again): You're a *drag,* Andy. I can't *feel* for *both* of us . . . I'm—I know, I'm scared too, I'm really scared of leaving. I'm scared of leaving, too, but—we're just scared. We both need love. I don't think I can give it to you.
>
> *Consultant:* Can we start with resentments. Tell him what you resent about him.

Client: Oh, I resent your being such a burden on my back. I resent—every time I leave the house, I have to feel guilty about it. I feel guilty for—

Consultant: Now that's a lie. When you feel guilty, you actually feel resentful. Scratch out the word guilty, and use the word *resentful* instead, each time.

Client: I resent not being able to feel free. I want to move. I want—I resent . . . I resent your nagging at me . . .

Consultant: Now tell him what you appreciate in him.

Client: All right. I really appreciate—your taking care of me, and your loving me, 'cause I'm—I know nobody else could really love me like you do. I resent you—

Consultant: Now let's scratch out the word "love," and put in the real words instead.

Client: Oh, I resent your smothering me. I resent your keeping me a little girl. (Perls, 1971, pp. 167–68)

At the end of the session, with Carol still present, the consultant responds to a comment from the audience.

Consultant: . . . I can tell you only this much: It is possible to get through the impasse. If I would say how, I would be "helpful," and it would be of no avail. She has to discover it, all on her own. If she really gets clear, "I'm stuck," she might be willing to do something about it. She is pretty close to realizing it, at least, that she is stuck in the marriage. She doesn't realize yet that she is stuck with her self-torture, in her game. "You should/you should not; you should/you should not; yes/but; but in case this happens/then; why doesn't Prince Charming come/but Prince Charming doesn't exist." All this verbiage, what I call the merry-go-round of the being stuck whirl, the real whirl. I think you got a good example. The only solution is to find a magician with his magic wand. And this doesn't exist . . . (Perls, 1971, pp. 171–72)

The consultant has sought, through prescribing in a step-by-step way, to help Carol grapple with her impasse. The prescription here relates to how she should explore her problem rather than what she should do to resolve her situation. In contrast, the manager-accountant example described earlier in this chapter involved *content,* in the sense of a consultant telling the client "what to do."

Child-Parent Conflicts

A prescriptive strategy is offered in the following description of behavior modification as an approach that has emerged from the work of Pavlov (1927), Hull *et al.* (1940), and Skinner (1938). A rationale that applies to behavior modification was stated by E. Stanley Jones some years ago when he said, "It is easier to act yourself into a new way of thinking than to *think* yourself into a new way of acting" (Jones, quoted by Mowrer 1964, p. 68). Thus the field of behavior modification is premised on the idea that if you can get people to change their behavior, changed attitudes will follow. Other approaches, particularly the acceptant mode of consultation, are based on the opposite: get people to change their attitudes and changes in behavior will follow.

In the behavior-modification approach the consultant selects the goals to be achieved and intervenes in the client's life to make sure he or she moves in that direction. The purpose of the intervention is to build new skills or strengthen desirable behavior through defining the client's problem in terms of learning needed and stating the goals to be achieved in terms of specific behavior changes (Krumboltz, 1966). The fact that the client is expected to enter into a mutual agreement is an element in the prescriptive character of this kind of intervention. In the contract the client acknowledges an authority-obedience relationship in which he or she agrees with the regimen designed. The carrying out of such an approach with a particular client can involve a variety of techniques.

An intervention to reduce the frequency of objectionable behavior by a child is described by Zeilberger, Sampen, and Sloane (1968). The approach relies on behavior-modification techniques to structure the child's environment so as to reward behavior that the consultants and/or parents consider desirable and to discourage unwanted behavior.

Rorey, who was nearly five years old, repeatedly screamed and told other children what to do and how to play. He would enforce his demands with punches, kicks, and slaps. The consultant's diagnosis was that these undesirable behaviors were being reinforced by Rorey's mother. In play situations they had seen her giving him excessive attention, as well as not following a consistent pattern of providing discouraging "consequences" for his objectionable behaviors. Instead, she would try to correct Rorey by going into lengthy explanations, the overall effect of which was to give him attention after each one of his temperamental episodes, while failing to make any connections between the act and her discouragement clear to him.

The consultants prescribed a program to replace what they saw as this mother's self-defeating strategies with Rorey. They suggested she arrange a one-hour play period each afternoon, with neighborhood children present. This daily one-hour session served as a training phase, during which the consultants coached and corrected Rorey's mother until she was well practiced in following these instructions:

1. Immediately after Rorey acts aggressively or disobediently, take him to the time-out (TO) room. One of the family bedrooms was modified for this by having toys and other items of interest to a child removed.

2. As Rorey is taken to the TO room for aggressive behavior, say "You cannot stay here if you fight." As Rorey is taken to the TO room for disobedient behavior, say "You cannot stay here if you do not do what you are told." Make no other comments.

3. Place Rorey in the TO room swiftly and without conversation other than the above. Place him inside and shut and hook the door.

4. Leave Rorey in the TO room for two minutes. If he tantrums or cries, time the two minutes from the end of the last tantrum or cry.

5. When the time is up take Rorey out of the TO room and back to his regular activities without further comment on the episode, i.e., in a matter-of-fact manner.

6. Do not give Rorey explanations of the program of what you do, of his behavior, or engage in discussions of these topics with him. If you desire to do this, have such discussions at times when the undesired behaviors have not occurred, such as later in the evening. Keep these brief and at a minimum.

7. Ignore undesirable behavior which does not merit going to the TO room. "Ignore" means you should not comment upon such behavior, nor attend to it by suddenly looking around when it occurs.

8. Ignore aggressive or disobedient behavior which you find out about in retrospect. If you are present, treat disobedient behavior to other adults the same as disobedient behavior to you.

9. Reinforce desirable cooperative play frequently (at least once every 5 min.) without interrupting it. Comments, such as "My, you're all having a good time" are sufficient, although direct praise which does not interrupt the play is acceptable.

10. Always reward Rorey when he obeys.

11. Special treats, such as cold drinks, cookies, or new toys or activities, should be brought out after periods of desirable play. It is always tempting to introduce such activities at times when they will interrupt undesirable play, but in the long run this strengthens the undesired behavior.

12. Follow the program twenty-four hours a day. (Zeilberger, Sampen, and Sloane, 1973, pp. 228–29)

The consultants furnish data which make it clear that this regimen had the desired effects of diminishing the frequency of Rorey's disruptive behavior.

Student-Teacher Conflict

Another series of interventions, similar in character but involving a ten-year-old child in a classroom situation, is described by Whitley and Sulzer (1973). The fourth grader, normal except for being hyperactive, was disrupting class by talking out of turn and leaving his seat. The intervention strategy was for the teacher to use her authority by taking notice of the child only when he was *not* talking and was in his seat. When he met these conditions she was to give him encouragement. When he asked for permission to talk, she was to call on him to speak as soon as possible. If what he then said was to some degree correct, she voiced approval. Furthermore, he was to be responded to when he requested permission to be out of his seat for a good reason, such as to pass books out to others.

When he behaved inappropriately she moved away from his desk, ignored his calls when his hand was not raised, and did *not* respond to any of his behavior that interfered with the desired learning circumstances. The teacher-as-consultant was able in this manner to cause unwanted behavior to become less frequent and desirable behavior to increase.

Aggression in the Classroom

The disruptive effects of disturbed relations with people in positions of authority can be observed in the learning disabilities of even very young children, children who are acting like delinquents in preschool. Prescriptive interventions, themselves based on exchange theory, have had productive effects in terms of shifting such predelinquent behavior into more tolerable classroom conduct (Hamblin *et al.*, 1969). The rationale of the approach was explained in the following way.

To establish a preintervention basis to be used for comparison purposes later, the consultants hired a trained teacher and put her in with five four-year-old boys who had been carefully selected by psychiatrists and social workers as the cream of the hyperaggressive crop. Her customary techniques of classroom control were futile—the boys were easily able to get her goat by behavior such as refusing to give up Playdoh, turning over chairs and throwing them at her, kicking and spitting at the teacher, or fighting with each other.

> What Miss Sally did not realize is that she had inadvertently structured an exchange where she consistently reinforced aggression. First, as noted, whenever she fought with them, she *always lost*. Second, more subtly, she reinforced their aggressive pattern by giving it serious attention—by looking, talking, scolding, cajoling, becoming angry, even striking back. These boys were playing a teasing game called "Get the Teacher." The more she showed that she was bothered by their behavior, the better they liked it, and the further they went. (Hamblin *et al.*, 1969, p. 23)

Next the consultants provided the teacher with a mode for rewarding desired behavior: giving the children tokens for attending to lessons, putting up supplies, and so on. These tokens could then be exchanged for desirable activities such as seeing movies, snacks, nature walks, and playing with desired toys. The teacher was also instructed to ignore disruptive behavior. She was helped to do this by being "wired" to observers behind a one-way screen who could inform her as to what was going on and suggest what actions would be appropriate to take.

> First, the teacher had to be instructed in how *not to reinforce* aggression. Contrary to all her experience, she was asked to turn her back on the aggressor, and at the same time to reinforce others' cooperation with tokens. Once we were able to coach her and give her immediate feedback over a wireless-communication system, she structured the exchanges

almost perfectly ... [there was]: a gradual increase in cooperation—from about 56 to about 115 sequences per day, and a corresponding decrease in aggression from 150 to about 60 sequences!

What this meant in terms of changed behavior is illustrated as follows.

Here is an example of their new behavior patterns, taken from a rest period—precisely the time when the most aggressive acts had occurred in the past:

All of the children are sitting around the table drinking their milk; John, as usual, has finished first. Takes his plastic mug and returns it to the table. Miss Martha, the assistant teacher, gives him a token. John goes to cupboard, takes out his mat, spreads it out by the blackboard, and lies down. Miss Martha gives him a token. Meanwhile, Mike, Barry, and Jack have spread their mats on the carpet. Dan is lying on the carpet itself since he hasn't a mat. Each of them gets a token. Mike asks if he can sleep by the wall. Miss Sally says "Yes." John asks if he can put out the light. Miss Sally says to wait until Barry has his mat spread properly. Dan asks Mike if he can share his mat with him. Mike says "No." Dan then asks Jack. Jack says "Yes," but before he can move over, Mike says "Yes." Dan joins Mike. Both Jack and Mike get tokens. Mike and Jack get up to put their tokens in their cans. Return to their mats. Miss Sally asks John to put out the light. John does so. Miss Martha gives him a token. All quiet now. Four minutes later—all quiet. Quiet still, three minutes later. Time: 10:23 A.M. Rest period ends. (Hamblin *et al.,* 1969, pp. 23, 24)

Prescriptive interventions based on giving tokens in exchange for wanted behavior and withholding them and other forms of reinforcement when unwanted conduct occurs produced a significant reduction of predelinqent behavior. Similar applications of token-based interventions with comparable results are reported by the Hamblin team with regard to ghetto and autistic children.

Help in Unexpected Circumstances

Since the consultants and clients involved are unacquainted and are interacting in a remote and anonymous relationship, the value of intervention-by-telephone might be thought to be very limited, particularly with regard to prescriptive interventions. The following example indicates the contrary.

A unique problem, with features common to most emergency calls, occurred recently. A telephone counselor was called at his home, by a girl who reminded him of a call she had made two months previously, when she suspected that she was pregnant. His warm, nonjudgmental attitude at that time, combined with his willingness to be helpful, had stuck in the girl's mind—even though her call had escaped his. The situation was unbelievable. The girl had carried a baby to term without her parents becoming aware of the fact. She was sixteen and had only had intercourse once. At the time of the second call, she was at a friend's house, having just completed a Christmas shopping trip with her mother, who, in turn, was upstairs having coffee with the girlfriend's mother. Meanwhile the pregnant girl had begun to have labor pains; her bag of water had broken. She was crying and feeling helpless, yet neither she nor her friend could summon up the courage to tell her mother.

Rather than expressing cynicism and suspicion, the counselor acted on the face-value statements of the caller, despite their highly unusual nature. He insisted that the girl call her mother to the phone. When the mother answered (still upstairs, while her daughter was downstairs), he explained briefly and to the point who he was and what was happening to her daughter. He concluded with a specific instruction to go downstairs and take her daughter to the hospital. Then the counselor went to the hospital himself. The girl had already been admitted to the delivery room, and the mother wanted to be left alone. However, the counselor discovered that no social worker or psychiatrist in the hospital would be informed of the peculiar situation, and fearing for the girl's emotional difficulties in having to confront intimidating parents (the father put his hand through a wall upon his arrival at the hospital), he called someone himself. After explaining the situation to the head social worker in the hospital—who was grateful that the affair had been brought to his attention—the phone counselor went into the waiting room, where the girlfriend, a fifteen-year-old, was sitting shaking. She had been sent down to wait for her friend's father but had not wanted to tell him exactly what was happening to his daughter. Despite the man's angry and hostile attitude, the girl had ridden the elevator up to the appropriate floor without saying anything. Now she was terrified, uncertain about what would happen to her friend and upset because of her own involvement almost from the beginning. The counselor calmed her down; when the social worker arrived, he left.

The girl telephoned again the next day to tell him she had had a seven pound, three ounce boy. Further developments occurred. The counselor found the girl willing to call and talk with him with more honesty and feeling than she was able to bring to contact with the hospital staff or the social workers assigned to her case. He communicated freely with them about the content of her calls, after receiving the girl's permission to do so. Her deep and reassuring trust in him grew out of his quick and decisive intervention. It is doubtful whether any other agency would have ever been called; no family work would ever have been done, and the girl would have continued on without any intervention if it were not for this crisis line. As it was, he continued to give help (always over the phone) to the girl as she dealt with her grief and her unwillingness to give up her baby—issues very important in her life if she is to ever trust relationships with men again. (Clark and Jaffe, 1973, pp. 160–61)

This prescriptive intervention had an impressive measure of success because the consultant told the client the specific steps necessary to avert tragedy and took immediate concerned responsibility, in a foresighted way, to protect his client and her girlfriend from what might otherwise have been traumatic effects of ungoverned parental "aftershock." The mother's self-isolation and the father's putting his hand through a wall confirm how predictively accurate was the consultant's rapid diagnosis of the impending situation at the hospital. Over the ensuing period, and still without meeting face to face, the client trusted the consultant more than anyone around her. This permitted additional interventions, apparently of a more acceptant character.

Increased Assertiveness

Interventions designed to help clients express themselves more authentically and competently in situations where they ordinarily experience fear of criticism or rejection have been described by several practitioners. Wolpe (1973) sees this as a sound approach to behavioral change whenever a client is blocked from saying or doing things that would seem reasonable to an unbiased observer. Here is an example.

> *Consultant:* What do you do if you are standing in line for theater tickets and somebody gets in front of you?
>
> *Client:* I don't do anything.
>
> *Consultant:* Well, how do you feel?
>
> *Client:* I feel mad. I boil up inside.
>
> *Consultant:* So, why don't you do anything?
>
> *Client:* I'm afraid of making a scene.
>
> *Consultant:* People are taking advantage of you. Here, this person is taking advantage of you. You cannot allow it. You must say to him, "Will you kindly go to the back of the line?" In doing this, you will be expressing your anger in a way that is appropriate to the situation and socially acceptable. (Wolpe, 1973, pp. 84–85)

It is expected that when the client acts in his or her own behalf and is successful, confidence for repeating this behavior in the future will be increased and his or her habitual fear of undesirable consequences will be commensurately reduced.

Summary

Prescriptive interventions in the power/authority area are generally employed for either of two purposes: (1) when the client is abusive of those in positions of power/authority and needs to learn more constructive and compliant behavior; and (2) to aid those who are presently blocked in the exercise of legitimate power to become more effective in using it. Usually this client holds the weaker position in some present relationship. No basis is available for estimating how much transfer of learning occurs from the intervention situation to other parallel circumstances.

GROUP (M₂)

When a prescriptive consultant works with a group, he or she most often accepts and works through the existing power/authority system. He or she may do so in either of two ways: the first way is to tell the group's top man what he should do that he is not now doing in order to achieve needed results; the second is to literally step into the top position in the power/authority system and enact the role requirements of that position until a sufficient basis of collaboration permits the consultant to return the formal system to its ordinary operating mode.

Boss's Withdrawal when Challenged

An example of Gestalt therapy in work groups illustrates how this kind of prescriptive intervention is applied when the focal issue is the top man's faulty use of power/authority. Herman (1972) describes the character of a Gestalt-based intervention in the setting of a corporate team. The boss, a high-level manager, had developed a strong commitment to what he called "OD Values"—to be fair, rational, and helpful. Being a man of great personal forcefulness as well as occasional moodiness—personal characteristics said to be not consistent with "OD Values"—he was in conflict with himself. This was made clear by his conduct of staff meetings. For the most part they proceeded satisfactorily, but from time to time the manager would "blow his stack" and pin several of his staff to the wall. His logic was not faulted, but his vehemence led to subordinates' feeling themselves steamrollered. Some defended by presenting counterlogic; one reacted in humor; another felt he had been punished. Regardless of the individual reaction, the boss's response was to "clam up." This in turn led to work issues remaining unresolved.

On a particular occasion the consultant observed the kind of go-around described. A proposal for a policy change had been suggested by one of the team members and received some support from two others. The boss's immediate reaction was negative. He accused the proponents of being unrealistic and, after some back and forth, went glum.

How did the consultant deal with this? He could have focused attention in a confronting way on the deadening response the top man's reaction had produced. In a catalytic way he might have encouraged the team to collect and analyze data on steps to take so as to start moving again. Instead, he intervened in a prescriptive way by pushing the manager to follow through, to get it all out. The manager acted on the recommendation, at first clumsily, but, as he warmed up, with gusto. He tore into his subordinates. Those whom he attacked, counterattacked. Soon everyone was shouting back and forth.

At a later time these participants critiqued what had transpired and concluded that these and more recent but similar episodes of explosiveness had resulted in a greater sense of vitality, excitement, and relatedness than had been experienced previously. Subordinates had learned not to buckle under but to stand their ground and fight back. The top man had achieved a new respect for both them and himself.

Herman's prescription rested in the Gestalt concept of wholeness. The top man needed to "complete" himself rather than cut himself off half way. By rejecting his typical impulse not to follow through he could further unleash his frustrations. This got others stirred up to the point where they too could respond in ways that made them more "whole."

Parent Abdication of Responsibility for Teenager

Parents are ordinarily expected to exercise supervision over their children, particularly in the teen years. The notion, if not always the actuality, is that in this way positive growth can be stimulated and traumatic situations either averted or reduced. Sometimes such supervision breaks down, leaving a power vacuum; as a consequence, teenagers may engage in many kinds of activities, some of which might set up self-destructive cycles.

Sometimes what first appears to be "the problem" is merely a symptom rather than the problem itself, as illustrated in a situation where the consultants tried to deal with an individual case of heroin addiction with only momentary success. Eventually they recognized that Jim, an intelligent youngster, was using drugs to act out his resentments, particularly against his father who had failed to supply much guidance or to set limits. The consultant decided to intervene upon the family itself, thus redefining the "client" to be both parents and their son.

> Three experienced staff members made an appointment to meet with the family, in their home, one evening shortly after the second episode with heroin. These two men and one woman had not consulted with each other about what they would do beyond thoroughly exploring the family structure and system of interrelationships. They entered the home respected and trusted to an extent, because of our organization's previous work with the family, and because the parents were desperate, afraid, and angry, looking for a kind of help they had never received.

The session began casually, but soon,

> Jim began to rationalize his use of drugs, saying that it was his business. He felt he had a right to do what he wanted, as long as he knew of the possible effects of the drugs. He said he did not know whether he would use drugs again, but there was no attempt to promise. He left the possibility clearly open.

Before long the consultants had heard and seen sufficient evidence on which to diagnose Jim's behavior and its consequences within the family group. Jim was displaying

> defensiveness, an irritating disregard for the feelings of his parents, an arrogant self-centeredness, a subtle intellectual game being played of overt reasonableness camouflaging a deep disinterest in anyone but him-

self. The counselors began to feel more confident about what was going on. An example is sufficient. Jim wore his hair shoulder length, and frizzed out, and he was often mistaken for a girl by his family's friends, to the embarrassment of the parents. They had tried to point out the pain he was causing them (humiliation, embarrassment), and he had listened to them carefully, saying he would take what they had to say into careful consideration; then he let his hair grow even longer. This irritated his parents, but they depended on reason to communicate and to convince. His father was a liberal, who felt that reason was the only appropriate way to deal with the situation. His desperation came from the sinking feelings he got when his son played at being reasonable but continued acting in a selfish way, which hurt his parents deeply.

From this point on the consultants began actively intervening in a prescriptive way.

As the session focused on the parents' feelings, the counselors began to treat Jim as a four-year-old, interpreting this to both his parents and to him as the only appropriate way to deal with his actions and his defensiveness. He denied he was being defensive, but the counselors cut him off several times, telling him to be quiet, they were talking to his parents. As his parents talked, their feelings of helplessness were clearly evident. It was interpreted that Jim seemed to have all the power in the house, able to do whatever he wanted, even if it hurt himself or them. The counselors refused to believe that it had to be that way, pointing out that they did not let Jim control their behavior by either threats or actions.

As the threat to his means of power became clearer, Jim became uncomfortable and attempted to threaten the counselors: "This isn't helping," "I'll probably take drugs just to show you I don't have to do what you say," "Who are you to come in here and do this?" Finally he simply got up and walked out, saying, "I don't have to put up with this bullshit!"

At this point two of the consultants intervened on the parents, telling them that as adults they did not have to accept being abused and manipulated. Also, as the consultants saw it, Jim's father and mother were "allowing him to use drugs." Meanwhile, the third consultant went to bring Jim back by compulsion if necessary. The interventions took effect as

several facts clicked in the father's head. He was the father; he was the one with the power; he could prevent Jim from growing his hair long or from taking drugs; he was the boss. And he had surrendered all of this, threatening only to send the boy to where someone else would be powerful and would make him mind. He could also see Jim's incredible anger and resentment, how it was directed at himself through drugs and indirectly at his parents through his hair and his drug abuse. Jim's father got up and went after the counselor and Jim.

For the first time the father used physical force to bring the boy around to doing what the father wanted him to. He realized that, if the boy could not act in a reasonable, adult manner, it was absurd to treat him as an adult. The boy was acting like a four-year-old; so the father tried to pull him back, though he was still indecisive.

The second counselor walked over to where the three were struggling and picked the boy up and carried him back, where he sat quietly. The father then decided that the boy must cut his hair. Immediately the boy protested, saying he must talk to his father alone. The clear implication was that he could control his father, but not them—something the father could not miss. He refused and insisted the boy cut his hair to a respectable length. He said to Jim, "You have been punishing us with your hair, and we are merely stopping you from continuing to do this." After his hair was cut, by himself, with no use of force, Jim ran out of the house. His father ran out after him. He had only walked a block away, to see if he still cared. He returned without a struggle.

Thus, in effect, the focus of power/authority had shifted from son to father. The consultants sum up the results and some subsequent outcomes.

Jim's father had learned that he had to set limits and, more importantly, that he had to enforce them. By being strict with Jim he gave Jim an opportunity to act like a little boy, which Jim needed, expressing anger through swearing, crying, and yelling, instead of shooting heroin. As Jim acted in this new way he was able to relax more, and his personality began to change. He became much more friendly, convincing, open, honest, and stopped playing games. He was a different person. (Clark and Jaffe, 1973, pp. 194–96)

Although the problem as initially presented appeared to be the problem of an individual, its dynamics involved intense though indirect reactions against a father who had failed to meet his son's unexpressed expectations for close and personally concerned guidance. Recognizing this as they surveyed the family's interaction, the consultants prescribed to Jim's father and boosted his confidence to act in such a way as to give his son the kind of structure and framework needed.

Gang Fights

Consultants who work with juvenile street gangs in a general endeavor to reduce delinquency by encouraging alternative and more constructive activities rarely make use of the prescriptive approach. However, Christie (1966) describes one situation where prescriptive methods were employed to resolve a power struggle between two gang members contending for gang leadership.

The consultant was approached on the street by Blackie who said, "Manuel wants to fight me and I hear he's got a gun. I've got a gun too." Christie managed to "park" him at the local Boys' Club director's office before going to locate Manuel.

After checking whether Manuel had a gun yet (he hadn't), the consultant invited him to come over to the Boys' Club so that "we [can] all sit down and talk about it." As they talked, the actual cause of these youths' bad feelings toward one another surfaced.

> "Manuel felt that Blackie, a relatively new member, had challenged his position as the toughest guy in their group. Manuel remarked, "The other guys consider me the bad boy," and when Mr. Simon asked, "What do you mean?" he said, "I'm the toughest guy in the group, and Blackie, being new, plays the role of the tough guy. I've let him push me around in school and other places, but I'm not going to anymore." (Christie, 1966, p. 110)

This dialogue was intended by the consultant to increase mutual understanding, but it soon became evident that both Blackie and Manuel felt a need to fight it out. So they fought, but with gloves on in a boxing ring. Other members of the Wildcats were spectators as the two slugged at each other wildly, with Blackie getting the edge in the sixth round. Then Manuel wanted to go on fighting, gloves off.

Christie's next intervention was to take Manuel and Blackie in his car, ostensibly to find an alley where they could fight it out according to bare-knuckle tradition, but actually to get a period of time for more talking. He got them to agree to stop for Cokes and then drove them around for another thirty minutes before driving into an alley and parking. The three sat for about five minutes, not saying anything. Then Manuel said, "Fight."

At this point Christie made his prescriptive intervention. He spoke of the "model" they had set for others back at the club by fighting in the ring rather than on the street, thus implying that they could both respect themselves and be respected by others to the degree that they continued to act in terms of this model. He also told them that some gangs get along well enough with two or more equally matched tough guys. If "you two" now fought, there would be a winner-and-loser outcome that could split the club into Manny and Blackie factions.

Neither of these interventions was sufficient. Manuel still wanted to fight, but as the three of them headed for the alley Blackie capitulated. Manuel then insulted Blackie. Christie immediately faced Manuel with what the consultant saw as his real reasons for being antagonistic toward Blackie. Then, acting as angrily as he knew how, Christie—making another prescriptive intervention—ordered them back into the car, slammed the door as he got in, and took off in a hurry. Along the way Manuel and Blackie decided to go home and the threat of a fight ended.

Christie's earlier more or less administrative or supervisory efforts with the two rivals may have set the atmosphere for the final successful outcome. But only after he had dramatized some irritation that he did not actually feel was a successful outcome reached. By prescribing a "forced" action, he successfully broke their will to fight.

Power Vacuum

Crises occur among group members whenever an unexpected event prevents the realization of important objectives. When crises with potentially disastrous results arise they leave those affected with a sense of being powerless to respond; in such cases, prescriptive intervention can provide a basis for restoring the capacity of members to react in a problem-solving way. The consultant, who is not involved in the crisis as a participant, can prescribe by exercising initiatives and direction that group members are unable to exercise upon themselves.

A case study of such a crisis intervention is reported by Thomas, Izmirian, and Harris (1973). For some time they had been working with an organization's training team to help it strengthen its own competency. The training team had recently scheduled its work for the year ahead when it learned that necessary funds for implementing the program would not be forthcoming. Talking with one another the day after the announcement, as well as with others in the organization, had the effect of further blurring whatever facts were available and left team members feeling victimized and hopeless. Under these conditions the consultant's prescriptive interventions were based on the following assumptions:

When the Client is	*The Consultant Should*
1. The group is unable to provide leadership.	The consultant assumes group leadership.
2. The group is unable to stay with any one task.	The consultant keeps the group on the task.
3. The group assumes it knows less than it really does know.	The consultant provides a method for the group to look at things clearly.
4. The group assumes all power has been taken away.	The consultant provides a method for the group to look at reality.
5. The group therefore doesn't know what it is doing or how to function.	The consultant tells rather than asks the group how to function but not what to function on.
6. Conflict will erupt internally unless movement/success occurs rapidly.	The consultant speeds up the movement.

(Thomas, Izmirian, and Harris, 1973, p. 1)

So the consultants intervened prescriptively to:

1. stop the reactive and self-destructive behavior,
2. lead the evaluation of what the current situation actually was,
3. focus attention on new goals,

4. identify steps—within the "new" circumstances—by which these goals could be reached,

5. "supervise" the step-by-step actions needed for movement,

6. ensure that these steps were taken.

In the situation described, confusion, anger, frustrations, and fear led to emotional contagion, which in turn prevented members from focusing on a task and coalescing around it. The consultants stepped in to impose an agenda topic dealing with how planned and previously scheduled activities would now have to be changed and new goals formulated. With this meaningful and pertinent agenda focus, the consultants were thereafter able to lead a team analysis and evaluation of the situation which permitted members to collect current facts and analyze them in the light of their altered circumstances. With these new findings it was possible to consider resources available for initiating steps and to set concrete priorities for taking these steps. With a problem-solving basis restored the consultant could then return to its rightful owner the leadership he had taken.

Success was largely a result of the timeliness of these interventions, which took place the day after the fund-cut catastrophe occurred while participants were evidently aroused and before despair had set in. Because of its prescriptive character, relying on consultant-based direction and initiative to fill the power vacuum left by the "natural" leadership's demoralization, the group was provided with the power/authority needed to rally its forces.

Summary

The general significance of crisis viewed from the standpoint of inducing change is commented on by Klein and Lindemann (1964).

Brief work with predicaments has been likened to the situation of exerting a gentle push against someone standing upon one leg. The "disequilibrium" can be maintained only temporarily. The other leg eventually will come down, whether or not one pushes. The opportunities for direct intervention during the predicament period, as implied in the analogy, are twofold: first, to ensure that the psychological "other leg" comes down on firm ground; second, to exert pressure in such a fashion that the individual is encouraged to move in a desirable direction as the foot descends and equilibrium is re-established.

The analogy also suggests that in working with a crisis a maximum of change may be possible with a minimum of effort, as compared with intervention in a noncrisis situation when, so to speak, both feet are planted firmly on the ground. At the very least, it may be possible to carry out primary prevention by helping to restore the equilibrium existing prior to the crisis before the situation leads to some form of emotional pathology. Beyond this goal, however, is the opportunity in some cases to foster a more desirable equilibrium between an individual and his immediate human environment than had existed before. It is the second, in many

ways more ambitious goal that heads to a form of preventive intervention that can be differentiated from the several brief psychotherapies or
ego therapies that have been developed over the past few decades. Preventive intervention shares with such remedial efforts the need to make a
careful assessment of the intrapsychic structure and dynamics of personality. However, it extends the assessment to an equally important appraisal of the individual's social role and of the significant role relationships in which he is involved. Hence the weight of emphasis shifts from
the individual alone to the individual enmeshed in a social network. The
unit of inquiry, planning, and intervention is, therefore, not the individual
patient alone but rather the individual and one or more of the social orbits
of which he is a member. The essential difference is one of emphasis and
focus. (Klein and Lindemann, 1964, pp. 286–87)

Prescriptive interventions with groups characteristically involve the consultant in
substituting his or her personal power/authority for the group's natural leadership.
Authority may be turned over to the consultant, as when he or she prescribes group
structure or job descriptions; or the consultant may impose himself, as in the Herman and Clark/Jaffe examples, by telling the nominal power/authority person to
do something that he or she ordinarily would not do. Stronger degrees of consultant
authority in place of rational leadership helped to solve a gang-leadership power
struggle and to refocus a group when a crisis had thrown it into confusion. Concentrating as it does on more or less severe situations of authority breakdown, prescriptive consultation is itself a radical approach. Without follow-up interventions of a
nonprescriptive character its impact on the group's longer-term capacity for dealing
effectively with problems remains questionable.

INTERGROUP (M₃)

Prescriptive intergroup interventions are uncommon, probably because both sides
need to agree in order to utilize a consultant who "takes over" from them. Since
intergroup difficulties needing consultation are usually of the win-lose variety, the
needed cooperation is generally lacking. An important exception is the third-party
arbiter in union and management relations. He or she functions to mediate differences, but only when both sides have previously agreed to submit their disagreement to binding resolution. Two groups—say, management and a union—reach an
impasse. The arbitrator, an expert in the subject but a disinterested outsider, hears
evidence or otherwise studies the case and renders a decision. This usually takes the
form of a prescription that both sides in the dispute are obligated to implement
(Lazarus, 1965; Linke, 1968).

Thus in intergroup situations the use of prescription exhibits many of the same
characteristics identified in prescriptive consultation with a single group. The win-
lose power struggle is not solved; rather, power/authority is handed over to a neutral outsider who assists in solving the problem the disputants are incapable of
resolving themselves.

When groups are unable to agree on engaging a consultant to prescribe a co-ordinated "solution," either may decide to base its approach on the formulations of "how-to-negotiate" texts (e.g., Walton and McKersie, 1965; Nierenberg, 1968, 1971) or to retain its own consultant for advice on strategy and tactics in what continues to be essentially a win-lose dispute. Such "consulting to win," involving as it usually does an expert "quarterback" calling the plays, frequently takes on the character of prescription. It usually affects the intergroup situation, but its unilateral character can aggravate rather than cure the "disease."

ORGANIZATION (M₄)

Prescriptive consultation with organizations dates back to the emergence of the Mc-Kinsey consulting firm. A large number of present-day consultants continue to rely primarily on prescription as their mode of assisting organizations to solve problems.

There are three primary areas of organization-based prescriptive consultation. The first is concerned with the organization's power/authority system, where consultation frequently takes the form of recommended changes in organization structure. These are the kinds of changes that lead to either greater centralization or greater decentralization, or to a regrouping of functions. The other two primary areas will be considered in Chapters 23 and 24 respectively.

Restructuring a Marketing Division

A classical published example (Thompson, 1959) involved the Arthur D. Little consulting firm and the top management of Philco. The corporation had engaged A.D.L. to study its organization and to propose needed changes. A several months' study was concluded and reports of findings had been prepared and were about to be presented to Philco's top man. The problem was diagnosed as involving a change in the existing power/authority system. Here's how the crucial intervention was set up to report the conclusions these consultants had reached.

> James M. Skinner, Jr., president of Philco Corp., [arrived] for a momen-tous meeting that had been six months in the making. Waiting for Skinner in Suite 1808 were the nine somewhat apprehensive men from Arthur D. Little, Inc., the technical consulting firm of Cambridge, Massachusetts.
>
> . . . Donham spoke first, outlining in general terms what A.D.L. hoped to accomplish with its reorganization plan. What he was proposing, in brief, was a massive reorganization of Philco's marketing setup, which would: make the job of marketing all of Philco's consumer products the responsi-bility of one division; fix profit responsibilities at precise points in the company; get day-to-day pressure off the backs of men who should be doing long-range planning; and provide much closer support for Philco's independent distributors and dealers. (Thompson, 1959, pp. 113–14)

Rather than reacting submissively, however, Skinner resisted the plan and an intense "battle" between consultants and client followed.

Reducing Bureaucratic Layers

The State Department was identified earlier as an organization seeking change by consultant intervention during the late sixties and early seventies, and A. J. Marrow has been one of its major consultants throughout this era. Though each major intervention is described separately, he has brought the several together and presented them as a coherent whole in *Making Waves in Foggy Bottom* (Marrow, 1974).

One of the most significant interventions resulted in an attempt to make the State Department a "Theory Y" organization, using "Theory X" methods to accomplish this. In other words, authority was relied upon to invoke a more participative problem-solving client.

In June of 1965, Crockett announced what was called a major reform designed to reduce bureaucratic stratification. It was the formal word of the cutting out of six supervisory layers between Crockett and the operating managers. The announcement signaled the elimination of 125 positions and the transfer of 160 employees to other parts of the Department. Some of the operating units were to be broken up and some relatively powerful unit managers were about to be stripped of some of their former powers. The new program was to follow McGregor's Theory Y managerial approach. Crockett expressed the hope that the reorganization would replace the spirit of authoritarianism in the Department. The announcement was couched in Theory Y concepts—openness, participation, self-management, decentralized responsibility, management by objectives.

Interviews held at a later date with program managers by a research team from the University of Michigan found that the staff perceived the reorganization as an order. They were dismayed at the inconsistency of the preemptory way the reorganization was announced in contrast to the constant references to the new participative management concepts.

It is instructive for the record to see how Crockett outlined the rationale for his proposed changes. In July 1965, Crockett spoke to some 450 managers and employees of the administrative area (known as the "0" area). Here is the essence of his remarks.

...Our challenge is to find a structure—one which releases people from the obstacles and inhibitions of our highly centralized organization, thus permitting them to feel they are their own managers, with their own operations. Is there a way of organizing ourselves so that each of us can feel that we are a vital part of the whole?

I believe that our present concept of decentralized management by objectives and programs will accompilsh these objectives by: decentralizing our management into self-contained, semi-independent, and semi-autonomous programs, each with a manager; eliminating *every* intermediate supervisory level: delegating almost complete authority for daily operations to the program managers: ensuring that each program manager has the resources, the tools, the people, the money, the authority, the regulations, the means, and the conviction for attaining our mutually established goals.

Of course, there are both objections as well as problems that we must face in getting this concept into being. What are some of the objections that have been raised?

1. Existing managers, within the hierarchical structure, will lose part of their operations. (Absolutely true. This is one of the reasons for the new plan.)
2. Many intermediate supervisory jobs will be abolished, and not all of these people like the idea. (Absolutely true. Again, this is one of the basic objectives of the plan.)
3. It is really not decentralization but supercentralization, since all of the managers will report to the top man. (Not true. Each manager will be given almost autonomous operating authority with self-defined policies and mutually agreed-on objectives.)
4. The head man has too long a span of control; he can't supervise so many people. (Not so. Each manager will have his *own* program, and report only as he needs assistance. He will be freed from the usual concept of the old hierarchical control.)

Naturally, there will be some problems. The things you and I must do together are the following:

1. We must define the general purposes and concepts of your program.
2. We must state the general objectives and goals of the program as we see them. What do you think we can achieve next year? What will it take?
3. We must establish what kinds of authority you need to get the job done.
4. We must decide about whom you serve. Is your service really fulfilling your needs?
5. How can I be most helpful? How can you use me to accomplish your purposes and your goals?

Now what do I really expect of each of you managers? These are some of the main things: to achieve the goals we have set; to operate as if you were running your own business; to keep your operations, procedures, and regulatory materials up to date.

And now, what are the things that you can expect from me? This is a two-way street and you'll need assurances and help. The following things come to mind:

1. Full understanding and concurrence with the goals, and the resources and requirements for their attainment.

2. Availability in person or by phone when you need advice or counsel.

3. Support for the things we are agreed that you will need to attain your goals.

However persuasive seemed Crockett's brief for his changes, the old climate of suspicion, fear, and anger was only slightly improved. Grumbling, complaints, and fears were evident among those who had no opportunity to participate in the decisions about the new system. The resistance these people created helped to limit Crockett's original objectives. (Marrow, 1974, pp. 19–22)

The resistance to these changes eventually resulted in their being rescinded and the State Department returning in significant ways to its traditional mode. Change by edict, no matter how well intentioned, is likely to provoke resistances that lead to a restoration of the status quo.

Strengthening Manufacturing Operations

Another prescriptive intervention, in which Marrow's own organization was the client, involved the Weldon Co., introduced earlier in Chapter 4. As described by Roberts (1967), his firm, Norris & Elliott, Inc., had been asked to conduct a fact-finding survey of the Weldon Company and to recommend a program for strengthening cost control and production quality in its manufacturing operations. The survey and analysis identified the need for strong action. Weldon owners and plant staff reviewed the recommendations and authorized the consultants to implement the proposed program, which included changes in incentive rates, production planning, work study methods, and other classical approaches intended to strengthen the "task" side of the organization by centralizing power/authority. Correspondingly, these changes had the effect of breaking up the status quo and reducing the autonomy of managers and supervisors. All the new techniques had to be brought in because, as the consultants commented, the supervisors and their assistants

... lacked ... an understanding of the principles and methods of controlling work flow and the use of work study in keeping operation performance high. At first, the supervisors reacted to the consulting engineers and their training efforts stoically, as if lining up for an inoculation they did not want or need. (Roberts, 1967, pp. 83–84)

According to Roberts, after a period of resistance the supervisors came to accept and even to solicit the consulting engineers' assistance. One of the consultants says,

By the end of 1963 the great majority of employees felt that management wanted them to improve their production and earnings and that they were prepared to provide a great deal of attention and practical aids in getting their earnings up to the level considered favorable in the community. Their morale improved a great deal, and this helped to speed up the later phases of the earnings development program. (Roberts, 1967, p. 86)

Viewing the situation from a behavioral-science-practitioner orientation, however, David (1967) says that in May of that year, about nine months after the first consultant had begun, another set of interventions was necessary to build cooperation and trust into the Weldon organization. He comments that the progress possible from technical improvements was not being realized because of "hostilities, suspicions, and fears of the Weldon managers and supervisors in their work relations with one another. Not that these had become worse, but just that they had not become better" (David, 1967, pp. 95–96). As a result, acceptant interventions were introduced with beneficial results (see Chapter 4).

Realignment of Power/Authority Structure

Another example of a prescriptive organization intervention is described in step-by-step terms by Levinson (1972), a consultant operating in the psychoanalytic tradition. The consultant gathers data for his own diagnostic use through interviews, questionnaires, by examining financial and performance data, and in other ways. The approach appears to be prescriptive in character, as demonstrated in the following excerpted recommendations. First is a summation of how he sees the present status of the company.

> Claypool Furniture and Appliances is now in a tenuous position both financially and psychologically. Profits have fallen steadily during the last 3 years while sales have continued to grow. Because of the falling profits and their aversion to long-term debt, their expansion plans cannot be financed through retained earnings. Their choice is either to forego the plans for expansion or to give up part of the financial control to get the necessary money. The employees have lost confidence (if they had any) in their role in, and impact on, the organization. They see themselves as mere observers of a process that is slowly passing them by. They are angry at the organization and the management for not including them in the plans for growth, either by informing them of the plans or by training them to be an important part of them. They feel that the organization exploits them for its customers. Conversely, management feels that it is losing control of those factors which, in the past, were responsible for the success of the company. The personal relationships with the manufacturers and the other retailers are disappearing. The confidence of the line management is deteriorating because many see themselves as being unable to handle their positions. Robert Claypool and Michael Samson see themselves as being required to assume more of the managerial responsibilities, even though they are already overburdened. Management also feels that it is losing control over the employees. No longer can they manipulate employees freely. As a result, management places more pressure on itself to resolve the apparent conflicts by refusing to delegate responsibility, tightening its control, and increasing its competitive effort. (Levinson, 1972, pp. 485–86)

In the following excerpt a colleague, Spohn, provides the flavor of recommendations included in a Levinsonian diagnostic report. The various recommendations impinge at numerous points on the existing power/authority system and in effect "tell" the Claypool management what the new power/authority system should do to increase its effectiveness.

> *Personnel Practices.* The company should establish descriptions and standards and objectives for all positions. It should develop orientation and training programs to properly prepare people for their jobs and provide appraisal devices by which personnel and their superiors can assess progress and training needs. Positions and training in supervision and management are to be included in this process. A procedure for identifying prospective managerial talent should be evolved. The representative council should be abolished, and it should be replaced by employee task forces appointed to solve specific intraorganizational problems. Such groups, to include stock personnel, would end the isolation of the stock people and contribute to organizational identification and group cohesion. (Levinson, 1972, p. 491)

The prescriptions above assume that executive management is ready to follow the conclusions the consultant has reached, pretty much on an authority-obedience basis. This is seen also in Levinson's feedback strategy: first report conclusions to the top man, then to the next echelon down, and so on to the lowest level involved. The feedback approach seeks to overcome resistance to the report's content.

To feed back his findings and recommendations the consultant convenes with the executive who first retained his services. In setting up an appointment, the consultant asks him to allocate two hours of an afternoon for a one-to-one meeting. The executive is asked to listen as the consultant reads the report and to jot down any notes he may wish to discuss. The consultant makes clear that, even if the client disagrees with it, he cannot change the report's substance. Nonetheless, says the consultant, he wants assistance in expressing things in the most advantageous way. The client executive is then given the report and asked to read it overnight and set aside two additional hours for discussion the next morning. The intention is to provide an opportunity for cathartic release of hostility felt toward the report and the consultant—feelings that, unless worked through, could lead to total rejection of both report and consultant (Levinson, 1972, pp. 497–98). This feedback procedure is repeated with lower-level individuals and groups until the report has been presented to all involved with this aspect of the diagnosis.

At least two features of this approach go beyond the classically prescriptive. One not emphasized here is that individual behavior variables approaching the psychoanalytic level of influence are included in the diagnostic study. The other involves the consultant's effort to work through the feelings and emotions, as well as any rationalizations, projections, etc., that such a report arouses, rather than giving his diagnosis and prescription on a "take it or leave it" basis.

Power Reduction

The unsuccessful use of another consultant's strategy to promote organization development via prescriptive intervention is described below by Levinson.

> A major consulting organization undertook to advise on the drastic reorganization of a client firm. The consequence of this drastic reorganization was that many people who had previously held power were successfully emasculated of their power although they retained their positions. The firm traditionally had insisted on and rewarded compliance so these men did not openly complain, but there was widespread depression and anger among them for which the consulting firm assumed no responsibility. In fact, it is doubtful whether their developmental efforts included any recognition of the psychological consequences of what they did. (Levinson, 1973, p. 164)

This strategy, which relies on the consultant's being able to overcome resistance, can be contrasted with Levinson's own approach. His "organization diagnosis" methodology uses prescription, but couples it with confrontational methods for working through hostility and other forms of resistance that prescriptions often induce.

Summary

Prescriptive interventions at the organization level are premised on the idea that the consultant assumes complete responsibility for defining the problem and recommending solutions to it. Therefore his or her inclination is to present recommendations pretty much as though they were final. As a consequence, the client organization, perhaps unwittingly, is expected to surrender whatever independent initiative it might otherwise have exercised, in accordance with the authority-obedience formula inherent in the relationship.

The use of prescriptive consultation to change an existing power/authority system is fraught with difficulties. Its major limitations seem to be that:

1. The entire system of power/authority relations is shifted by edict. Those who lose power cannot be expected to support changes that weaken their positions.
2. Changes proposed may go against ingrained beliefs and traditions regarding "how things should be done."
3. Insufficient provision is made to assist those who must implement the prescriptions in understanding—even less, agreeing with—the changes they are expected to initiate.

In a sense, the shock wave of change recommendations produces numerous individual, group, and intergroup problem situations that could well use the help of other consultants who are neutral regarding the earlier prescription.

LARGER SOCIAL SYSTEM (M₅)

Sometimes the focal issue identified is not only one of power/authority; it may reflect an individual-based problem: incompetence of the top person to perform effectively his or her executive functions. While this misuse of power can have reverberations throughout the entire system and beyond, it is unusual for a top executive to nominate himself or herself as the problem for consultative intervention. Rather, the consultants are more likely to enter the system under some other definition of the issue.

Arbitrary Actions from the Top

A series of prescriptive interventions, initiated as an organization-oriented consultation but resulting in a larger-social-system intervention in the city of Cincinnati, Ohio, are described by Goodstein and Boyer (1972). The Health Department of that city was the initial client, but the "ultimate" client was the mayor. As first defined, the purpose of this consultation was to help the department with its internal management problems as well as in its relationships with certain segments of the community.

Internal Health Department problems had reached the point where unhappy employees were holding meetings to discuss their situation and employee discontent had been communicated to the public at large. These expressed grievances concerned the tone of administration in the department, particularly that of the Commissioner, who was thought to have been arbitrary in some past firings. At about the same time, citizen groups were voicing their concerns regarding the poor quality of health services and were demanding greater involvement in departmental decision making. Newspaper and television coverage of the issues had become extensive.

The Commissioner and others at his level wanted to approach a solution through a leadership and communication workshop and consultants were contacted in connection with this desire. Based on their initial knowledge of the expressed grievances and widespread employee distrust of the Commissioner, and considering the fact that this workshop decision was made by a very few top-level individuals, the consultants rejected the invitation to collaborate with the client within the status quo and according to his felt needs. They felt that a sounder approach would be to engage in their own independent diagnosis and evaluation of the situation without any prior agreement regarding next steps. This led to a sixty-day consulting contract, which was to result in a written report of findings and recommendations.

As they attempted to get started, a high amount of distrust toward them as "lackeys" of the Commissioner and the board made interviewing difficult; they were viewed as tools or henchmen rather than as sources of credibility and help through whom complaints could be voiced. Yet by virtue of their listening skills and capacity to paraphrase grievances and tensions—thus "proving" that they understood what they were being told—the consultants slowly earned credibility and were able to gain access to information, largely through demonstrating their independence of the Commissioner. Thus "acceptant" interventions were used here not as a way of helping one or more individual members of the client's organization (see Dickson and Roethlisberger, 1966, excerpted in Chapter 3), but to gather data for a farther-reaching purpose. The consultants made known to interviewees that one of their findings might very well be that ". . . the Commissioner should resign his position." The prescriptive character of the consultation is revealed in the following.

> Through the course of the consultation it became increasingly apparent to the consultants that the Commissioner, because of his management style, had lost his creditability, both in the Department and in the community. This point was made in interviews even by supporters of the Commissioner and it became clear that, regardless of any recommendations which the consultants might make and regardless of the talents the Commissioner had for improving health care, his tenure in office was drawing to a close. Further, the press and other news media had helped create a climate of opinion in the community in which the Commissioner was seen as the one primarily responsible for the current situation.
>
> During the two-week data-collection phase, as this conclusion became even more clear, the consultants met on several different occasions with the Commissioner in order to share this conclusion with him. After several meetings, the Commissioner was convinced that his resignation would be necessary and the question arose concerning the timing of this critical act. The consultants were concerned that his resignation might so defuse the situation that the other issues which were very much part of the current problems would go unexamined in the delight and exultation following the Commissioner's decision to leave. The consultants worked closely with the Commissioner, the president of the Board, and members of the Board, with whom a number of feedback sessions were held during the week, in the timing of the announcement of the resignation in order to preserve the impact of their report. (Goodstein and Boyer, 1972, pp. 333–34)

Recognizing that even after the Commissioner had left many of the problems would remain, the consultants expanded their concept of responsibility in the following way.

> The consulting team had decided that the simple issuance of a final report probably would not have the desired effect of initiating real changes in the Health Department and, further, the consultants had decided that their responsibility in this matter was to the broader community of the City, which was represented officially by the City Council. Therefore, the consultants decided to present their findings to the Council informally, through the Human Resources Committee. The president of the Board of Health was asked and agreed to arrange an informal meeting between the consultants and the Mayor. The consultants' tentative findings were shared with the Mayor and, while he was concerned about the extent and severity of the problem, he was positively impressed with the way in which the

report was presented. He recognized that there was a strong data base for the findings and that the recommendations were a natural consequence of the findings. The Mayor was eager to move ahead into the action steps necessitated by the recommendations but first wanted the consultant to share the same feedback with the two other members of the Council's Human Resources Committee. (Goodstein and Boyer, 1972, pp. 334–35)

The remaining Board of Health members also resigned and consequently the department was restaffed and charter amendments created that altered the administrative structure of the system.

Because of the impasse quality of this situation—i.e., the Commissioner was unable to function because he had lost community confidence, and other members of the organization and wider community were so antagonized that their cooperation was difficult to elicit—a power vacuum existed. Under these circumstances the prescriptive interventions of the consultant were like line-manager decisions which, when approved at the level of the mayor, could become operating decisions. The circumstance here is similar to that previously reported in connection with prescriptive interventions in a group (Zeilberger, Sampen, and Sloane, 1973)—in that situation, crisis had so debilitated the group's capacity to function that the consultants moved in and prescribed actions during the period of impasse in order to restore the group's capacity to function independently.

Health Delivery System

One of the advantages of prescriptive consultation is that an outsider often can recognize what others are unable to see, as clearly demonstrated in a report by Caplan (1970). His conclusion in the following case study is that the problems being encountered in the health delivery system in Alaska related to differences in goals between what the Health Department wanted for the villages and what the villages embraced as health objectives for themselves. In his work with the Alaska Native Health Area (A.N.H.A.), which comprised a number of Eskimo and Indian villages, Caplan prepared a final report from which the following excerpts are taken.

Problem 1.1. Low Salience of Health Issues for Villagers and Leaders

The outstanding problem in the village is the low importance ascribed to health matters by the villagers and their leaders. This is mirrored in their ignorance of fundamental health issues, their inconsistent and ineffective practice of communal and personal hygiene, and the relatively low prestige and influence of the local representative of the Area Native Health Service, the Health Aide. This person is usually unpaid and is often a woman or a young man, who works at a technician level in relaying information about sick villagers by radio communication to the doctors at the Service Unit and then in dispensing the prescribed medication.

Recommendation 1.1.

I suggested a revolutionary change in the approach of A.N.H.A. to the villages—mainly with the goal of making the promotion of health and the prevention and early treatment of illness a matter of immediate importance to the villagers and their leaders, so that they will actively collaborate with the A.N.H.A. and other professionals in implementing programs in which the improvement of health will be seen as an integral part of total village development, economic, social, educational, cultural, legal, and political.

(a) *Generalist Village Workers.* As the spearpoint of this new approach I recommended the organization of a network of Village Workers, similar to the community development workers of India, Pakistan, and the Philippines. A Village Worker should be a mature Native man, or occasionally a woman, of prestige and influence in the village. He should continue these occupations to some extent in order to remain identified with the day-to-day life of his neighbors.

His main duties should be broad community development and adult education, within which the promotion of health and the prevention and control of disease would be integrated. As a village leader, he would have special skills derived from his knowledge of local culture, politics, and personalities. In addition he would be given extra knowledge and skills by A.N.H.A. and other interested Federal and State organizations, such as B.I.A., O.E.O., the State Department of Health and Welfare, the Court System, etc., who would wish him to act as their collaborator and agent at the village level. According to the size of the population, he would recruit and supervise full-time or part-time assistants, one of whom might be similar in role to the present Health Aide, and assist him at a technician level to collect and relay information about sick people and to dispense drugs in line with the orders of doctors and public health nurses.

The prescription not only specifies broad directions but also contains detailed recommendations for new norms of collaboration between government-agency professionals and Eskimo and Indian members of the proposed network.

The Village Worker should be treated as a *non-professional collaborator,* and not as a sub-professional agent, by the A.N.H.A. and other Federal and State agencies. He should be given a certain amount of technical orientation by each of them, but his development should mainly arise on the job as he collaborates with representatives of the agencies in his day-to-day operations. Rather than lengthy systematic training in Anchorage or Juneau, he should be involved alongside small groups of Village Workers from neighboring villages in repeated seminars of a few days' duration at Service Units or other regional centers, or in representative villages. These seminars should focus on greater understanding of specific issues and not upon acquiring professional frames of reference and techniques. The community development work of Fred and Carmen Wale in the Division of Adult Education of the Department of Agriculture in Puerto Rico can be used as a model.

The Village Worker should operate under the control of, or within the framework of, the Village Council, or some other accepted representative governing body of the village. In certain villages one of his main tasks would be to revitalize such a Council, so that through its operations the villagers would improve their self-respect and their ability to exercise greater control over their own destinies. (Caplan, 1970, pp. 251–52)

During both the surveying and recommendation-forming stages Caplan believes the consultant should keep in touch as much as possible with the head of the client organization (1970, pp. 254–55). This strategy has several advantages: (1) the consultant can constantly monitor this and other key persons' preoccupations so as to gauge the acceptability of particular recommendations; (2) he or she can receive guidance from client members, those best able to view their organization as a functioning unit interacting with external systems; (3) the consultant is provided an entree via the top man's influence; and (4) he or she can keep tabs on the executive's responses to consultant recommendations during daily discussions, *before* these are written up. Although the final report is in the format of a prescription, Caplan argues (1970, p. 255) that it is really the product of extensive prior collaboration between himself, client members, and other persons and groups; accordingly, its acceptance is to some extent preassured.

Delinquency

The way in which individuals are assigned for group living—such as in reformatories, prisons, and other institutions where people are compelled to stay—can either promote greater social health or bring out socially negative, destructive, and pathological behavior. How can assignments to promote social health be accomplished? Assignments according to inmates' choices may amplify the institution's problems by bringing antisocial individuals together. Administrative assignment, on the other hand, may be either (a) *happenstance,* in the sense of refilling dormitories as some inmates leave on release or parole and others arrive to begin their terms of confinement, or (b) *tactical,* in the sense of separating "troublemakers."

There is a possible alternative. By means of sociometric methods, Moreno (1934, pp. 304–320) devised an assignment/reassignment system that can serve comprehensive social health–promoting strategies. In a correctional institution for girls, this involved having inmates record the preferences they currently felt for social proximity to or distance from other girls. Each girl was asked to complete a scale of preference, a "sociometric test," applying to the institution's cottage-residence and work-group arrangements respectively. When this information was tabulated by the consultant, it also indicated the extent to which any individual who had been chosen or rejected by another was reciprocating such degrees of preference. This method also was employed to determine the girls' orders of choice for housemothers and, conversely, the degree to which each of them was chosen by a housemother as a desirable or undesirable resident in her cottage.

From these sets of information the consultant was able to assess the contemporary overall social structure of living and work arrangements within the institution. Thus new living assignments, based on the consultant's integration of sociometric evidence from these several sources, could be made. His objective was to provide each resident favorable circumstances for "mental catharsis" induced through relationships with peers, housemother, and so on. Mental catharsis refers to cumulative effects occurring in the individual during a fairly long period, at least three months and sometimes two years or more, spent within these assigned arrangements. It is not a catharsis brought about directly by the consultant through a brief acceptant intervention.

A still different approach for reducing delinquency rests on in-situation prescriptive interventions rather than in prescriptive grouping. It makes an effort to alter how delinquent boys view and respond to situations in which power/authority is exercised upon them by engaging them in competition and other game-induced excitements.

At a boys' correctional institution, a specially trained staff executed the prescriptive activities designed by the consultant, Dr. H. C. Quay. Twenty boys were selected to take part in the program.

> The problem involved a hard core group, difficult to manage youths who obviously were not reached positively by the institutional program. A new approach for coping with these offenders was needed as they were not benefiting from rehabilitative efforts being made and their disruptive behavior drew a disproportionate amount of staff time from the rest of the population. Correctional personnel were placed in the position of spending less time with the more amenable inmates in order to cope with the intractable ones.

> The base for the research was provided by a theoretical statement by Quay relating extreme acting out (psychopathic) behavior to the need for seeking more varied sensory inputs than the environment usually provides.

> The nature of this pathological stimulation seeking also was investigated in experimental studies in which the more psychopathic delinquents were shown to be more susceptible to the effects of boredom, to prefer complexity to simplicity in usual form, and to choose the incongruous over the more everyday type of situation. Thus a program which would provide change, varied activities, and would avoid unfilled time intervals leading to boredom was hypothesized to reduce the necessity for the psychopathic individual to create his own excitement through acting out behavior. (Kerish, 1973, pp. 162, 164)

In order to provide excitement and novelty, designed recreations included games and competitive activities among the boys and between them and staff members.

One activity that holds a great deal of interest for most adolescents is auto racing. With points earned in other activities of R.E.A.D.Y., the youths purchased slot car kits which they assembled themselves. Once they had their own cars they were allowed to run them on a slot car track during specified times. This became a very popular activity for most of the boys. In this instance a chaining of positive consequences for appropriate behavior was established. In order to engage in a highly desirable activity a number of preliminary steps were spelled out. This was one attempt to counter the high P's (psychopathic's) conception of his environment as a haphazard world in which everything depends on luck or getting the breaks and has little to do with one's own behavior.

. . . Another type of activity which proved to be popular was competitive endeavor with staff. A team of staff members challenged the youths to a softball game. This was received with much enthusiasm and proved to be very successful (the boys won). Although the students also prided themselves on their basketball ability they were shocked to find the staff won this second kind of sports encounter. It was obvious to most observers that team work was more important than physical condition in this game, because the staff had the former but definitely lacked the latter. The R.E.A.D.Y. boys immediately demanded a rematch which was accepted. In a hard-fought, well-played game the staff again won and everybody seemed pleased. (Kerish, 1973, pp. 168–69, 169-70)

Staff retained control of the time, sequence, and other aspects of the activities. Games included bingo, basketball, softball, weight lifting, swimming. Other program activities such as psychodrama, and movies and debates on topics such as premarital sex, drugs, and so on, were calculated to help the boys in gaining insights into specific problems, but these were not successful. Nonetheless, in comparison with control groups, the subsequent behavior differences of program members seemed on the positive side, though not significantly so.

To the extent that it can be conducted effectively by a single consultant or a number of them working in a coordinated manner, prescriptive intervention in larger social systems (as compared to similar types of intervention with an individual, a group, or an organization) requires relatively vaster magnitudes and depths of comprehension. Such insight is needed to identify, span, and interrelate major dimensions of the existing social system and whatever inbuilt inadequacies may be amenable to the mutually strengthening "changes for the better" that the consultant eventually prescribes.

IMPLICATIONS

In prescriptive consultation the subject-matter expertise of the consultant is relied on as an authority/obedience premise for the purpose of solving problems in the power/authority area. The most common application is to assist those *appointed* position-holders of power/authority to exercise it more effectively in their relationships with subordinates. While prescriptive consultation has been used also to aid those in subordinate positions to strengthen their effectiveness in resisting the arbitrary use of power, this is far less frequent. The reason may be that when a "weak" subordinate is acting strong (based upon consultant instructions), his or her strength is perceived by those in a power/authority position to be both out of character and out of line.

The greater the consultant's degree of control over the situation, the more successful the prescriptive intervention. This tendency is revealed in two different contexts. In behavior modification the client from the outset is in no position to resist and the consultant's power is augmented by the technique-related fact that a particular step from point B to point C is not significantly different from an A to B move. Consequently, the client is not aware of the change and is not prompted to react negatively. Prescriptive consultation is also particularly effective when the client situation is one of total weakness, as in those examples where a hopeless impasse has been reached and the client is prepared to accept whatever recommendation the consultant offers.

REFERENCES

Caplan, G. *The Theory and Practice of Mental Health Consultation.* New York: Basic Books, © 1970. Reprinted by permission.

Christie, F. W. As cited in I. Spergel, ed., *Street Gang Work.* Reading, Mass.: Addison-Wesley, 1966, p. 110. Reprinted by permission.

Clark, T., and D. T. Jaffe. *Toward a Radical Therapy: Alternate Services for Personal and Social Change.* New York: Gordon and Breach, Science Publishers, Inc., 1973. Reprinted by permission.

Cohen, A. M., and R. D. Smith. "The Critical Incident Approach to Leadership Intervention in Training Groups." In W. G. Dyer, ed., *Modern Theory and Method in Group Training.* © 1972 by Litton Educational Publishing, Inc. Reprinted by permission of Van Nostrand Reinhold Company.

David, G. "Building Cooperation and Trust." In A. J. Marrow, D. G. Bowers, and S. E. Seashore, eds., *Management by Participation.* New York: Harper & Row, 1967, pp. 95–109.

Fleming, A. "Psychodrama." *Ingenue,* January 1969. © 1969 by Dell Publishing Co., Inc. Reprinted by permission.

Flory, C. D., ed. *Managers for Tomorrow.* New York: The New American Library of World Literature, 1965.

Frankl, V. E. *The Doctor and the Soul.* New York: Bantam Books, 1955.

Frankl, V. E. *Psychotherapy and Existentialism.* Harmondsworth, England: Penguin Books, 1967.

Goodstein, L. D., and R. K. Boyer. "Crisis Intervention in a Municipal Agency: A Conceptual Case Study." *Journal of Applied Behavioral Science* 8, no. 3 (1972): 318–40. Reprinted by permission.

Hamblin, R. L., D. Buckholdt, D. Bushell, D. Ellis, and D. Ferritor. "Changing the Game from 'Get the Teacher' to 'Learn.'" *Trans-action* 6, no. 3 (1969): 20–31. Reprinted by permission.

Herman, S. M. "A Gestalt Orientation to O.D." In W. W. Burke, ed., *Contemporary Organization Development: Conceptual Orientations and Interventions*. Washington, D.C.: NTL Institute for Applied Behavioral Science, 1972, pp. 69–86.

Hull, C. L. *et al. Mathematico-Deductive Theory of Rote Learning*. New Haven: Yale University Press, 1940.

Jones, E. S. Quoted in O. H. Mowrer, *The New Group Therapy*. New York: Van Nostrand Reinhold Company, Litton Educational Publishing, 1964. (Original source not cited.)

Kerish, B. "Toward a New Phase in Correctional Management." in J. L. Carleton and U. Mahlendorf, eds., *Man for Man: A Multidisciplinary Workshop on Affecting Man's Social and Psychological Nature through Community Action*. Springfield, Ill.: Charles C Thomas, 1973, pp. 162–76. Reprinted by permission.

Klein, D. C., and E. Lindemann. "Preventive Intervention in Individual and Family Crisis Situations." In G. Caplan, ed., *Prevention of Mental Disorders in Children*. New York: Basic Books, 1964, pp. 286–87. Reprinted by permission.

Krumboltz, J. D., ed. *Revolution in Counseling: Implications of Behavioral Science*. Boston: Houghton Mifflin, 1966.

Lazarus, S. *et al. Resolving Business Disputes: The Potential of Commercial Arbitration*. New York: American Management Association, Inc., 1965.

Levinson, H., with J. Molinari, and A. G. Spohn. *Organization Diagnosis*. Cambridge, Mass.: Harvard University Press, 1972.

Levinson, H. *The Great Jackass Fallacy*. Boston: Harvard University, 1973.

Linke, W. R. "The Complexities of Labor Relations Law." In R. F. Moore, ed., *Law for Executives*. New York: American Management Association, Inc., 1968.

Marrow, A. J. *Making Waves at Foggy Bottom*. Washington, D.C.: NTL Institute, 1974. Reproduced by special permission.

Moreno, J. L. *Who Shall Survive?: A New Approach to the Problem of Human Interrelations*. Washington, D.C.: Nervous and Mental Disease Publishing Company, 1934.

Nierenberg, G. I. *The Art of Negotiating: Psychological Strategies for Gaining Advantageous Bargains*. New York: Hawthorn Books, 1968.

Nierenberg, G. I. *Creative Business Negotiating: Skills and Successful Strategies*. New York: Hawthorn Books, 1971.

Pavlov, I. P. *Conditioned Reflexes*. London: Oxford University Press, 1927.

Perls, F. S. *Gestalt Therapy Verbatim*. New York: Bantam Books, 1971. Originally published by Real People Press, Moab, Utah, © 1969. Reprinted by permission.

Roberts, E. E. "The Technical Change Program." In A. J. Marrow, D. G. Bowers, and S. E. Seashore, eds., *Management by Participation*. New York: Harper & Row, 1967, pp. 76–87.

Skinner, B. F. *The Behavior of Organisms: An Experimental Analysis*. New York: Appleton-Century-Crofts, 1938.

Thomas, A., B. Izmirian, and J. Harris. "Federal Cutbacks: An External Crisis Intervention Model." *Social Change* 3, no. 2 (1973): 1–3.

Thompson, E. T. "The Upheaval at Philco." *Fortune* 69, no. 2 (1959): 23, 113–116ff. Reprinted by permission.

Walton, R. E., and R. B. McKersie. *A Behavioral Theory of Labor Negotiations.* New York: McGraw-Hill, 1965.

Whitley, A. D., and B. Sulzer. "Reducing Disruptive Behavior through Consultation." In J. Fischer, comp., *Interpersonal Helping: Emerging Approaches for Social Work Practice.* Springfield, Ill.: Charles C Thomas, 1973, pp. 294–302.

Wolpe, J. *The Case of Mrs. Schmidt: An Illustration of Behavior Therapy.* Nashville, Tenn.: Counselor Recordings & Tests, 1965.

Wolpe, J. *The Practice of Behavior Therapy.* 2d ed. New York: Pergamon Press, 1973. Reprinted by permission.

Zeilberger, J., S. E. Sampen, and H. N. Sloane, Jr. "Modification of a Child's Problem Behaviors in the Home with the Mother as Therapist." *Journal of Applied Behavioral Analysis* 1 (1968): 49. © 1968 by the Society for the Experimental Analysis of Behavior, Inc. Reprinted by permission.

PRESCRIPTIVE INTERVENTIONS

22

MORALE / COHESION

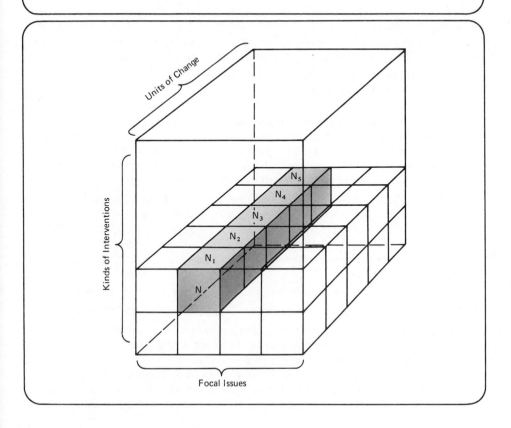

Many times people feel down without being precisely aware of the source of their depression. If frequent or even continuous, such circumstances may approach chronic conditions and a prescriptive intervention can have powerful ameliorative effects. In effect, the consultant pushes the client to overcome his or her inertia and begin active steps toward solving the problem(s) associated with the focal issue. With still other clients, blind acceptance of the necessity to carry out recommended actions is the key to personal change.

INDIVIDUAL (N$_1$)

Morale or personal cohesion is reduced or even disintegrates with loss of loved ones, with oversensitivity to events, or in the face of serious challenges to one's self-esteem associated with an inability to cope with overwhelming difficulties. In trying to stop themselves from coming apart any further, people may avoid tackling their problems, even when these issues grow larger the longer they are neglected.

Low Self-Esteem

Prescriptive consultation is one approach employed to help individuals grapple with problems that threaten or defeat their self-esteem. Psychiatric interventions involving short-term therapy often are of this prescriptive character. The consultant first attempts to diagnose as accurately as possible the underlying cause of the client's problem and then maps out an action strategy for the client to implement. His or her thesis is that action, not insight, will clear up the difficulty.

Viscott tells of the following:

> I remember a young woman, Karen Wells, who changed drastically after three weeks. Before therapy she was barely existing in a cold-water flat while her rich, widowed mother was living it up around the world. Dr. McKee, who sometimes supervised me, said after I discussed the initial hours, "Viscott, you go back and tell that girl to cut the crap."
>
> "Tell her to get on the phone and call her mother and ask for some money to help her out. She thinks she has to be in mourning for her father forever. The mother is probably worried about the girl and upset because she can't get her to take any money. This girl is just overdoing her grief reaction for her father. She thinks if she stops grieving that her father's memory will disappear."
>
> "I'll tell her that her father left something more for her than a memory."
>
> "You just do that, Viscott," said McKee. "I'd belt her with the facts."
>
> I did. Karen called her mother the same day and they got together between Karen's second and third visits. They went shopping together and her mother helped furnish Karen's apartment. At the third visit Karen was no longer depressed, no longer felt that her father had left her nothing, and she could believe that her mother had also loved her father and also remembered him. It was an incredible change. (Viscott, 1972, p. 308)

In this instance a poorly functioning client, after being given a prescription, was able to take a decisive step that cleared up her difficulty.

Wife-Husband Conflict

Not all interventions involving prescriptive psychiatry are centered on the type of brief therapy that turned Karen around. Viscott recounts the following advice he gave to Roberta, who had been a client of his for a year or more. She was married to Gary and having an affair with Roy.

> "Roberta, I think it'd be a mistake to base your decision to get a divorce on your feelings about Roy."
>
> "Why?"
>
> "You have to decide whether or not you want to stay married to Gary, independent of your feelings about Roy or anyone else. It's your decision alone and one that Roy really can't help you make. If you decided to get a divorce just because you wanted Roy more than Gary, it would put a terrible burden on Roy, on you, and on the relationship. Roy might feel obligated to love you after all that you gave up for him, and he might even resent you for it. If you want to divorce Gary, you have to divorce him because you don't want to live with him, not because you want to live with someone else. To use Roy as the reason to leave Gary only avoids dealing with the problems that you and Gary have. And that just opens the door for trouble in the new relationship."
>
> "I never thought of that. . . . Maybe you're right, maybe I *am* using Roy to make Gary look worse." (Viscott, 1972, pp. 244–45)

This prescription, which shed a new light on her situation—that of the morale/cohesion focal issue—effectively prevented Roberta from acting on the basis of momentary emotions. After considerable thought, she summed up her new insight.

> "I have to admit to myself what's missing in my marriage and decide if I can get along without it. If I can't, I'll just have to leave." (Viscott, 1972, p. 247)

Depression and Crisis Interventions

The depth of lowered morale is depression. Use of prescription in psychiatric treatment of deeply depressed patients has proven to be effective, as illustrated in the following case (Taulbee and Wright, 1971, pp. 53–92). The patient, put in a closed ward, spends his waking hours in a drab, sparsely furnished room. He receives a series of assignments that he is compelled to carry out to a high degree of perfection. Activities might include sanding a small block of wood with fine-grain sandpaper. If the client is so severely depressed that he will not even respond to instructions, the consultant may take his hand and guide him. Other monotonous, nongratifying repetitive tasks include floor mopping, bouncing a ball on a small surface, counting tiny seashells, and so on. Shortcomings in the client's performance are quickly pointed out and conversation is discouraged by telling him he is there "to work, not talk." He is never ridiculed or belittled.

Within three to four days the patient is expected to blow up and refuse any further cooperation. At that point, after he has successfully expressed his hostility, he is shifted to other treatment activities. The prescription has achieved success in the sense that the self-defeating cycle is broken and the client is now responding rather than maintaining a pattern of passive withdrawal.

A crisis exists whenever someone in serious trouble is unable to manage the situation. A promising approach, slow in emerging but which now appears to have many positive implications, is that of crisis intervention calculated to help the client hold himself together while living through the difficult period. The client, rather than worsening to the point of needing hospitalization, weathers the storm and emerges intact or in even better shape than before the crisis hit.

These interventions usually are prescriptive since in crisis circumstances the client is unable to direct himself in a socially or self-responsible manner. Attempted suicide, threatened violence, and psychotic breaks are among the most common of these crisis situations. The strategy is usually to quiet the client by sedation and to help him resume his prior life pattern as quickly as possible. Psychotherapy is *not* relied upon: the client is treated as a *medical,* not psychiatric, patient. Quick recovery and dismissal after a few days or rarely more than two weeks is a part of the basic procedure. Dismissal without complete recovery is often made possible by arranging for the client's family to offer needed posthospitalization support. The rationale underlying crisis intervention is that steps should be taken promptly to arrest what otherwise would be either a process of deterioration or a repression of the traumatic experiences which could subsequently have a negative impact on adjustment.

Acceptant interventions to aid more normally adjusted clients in coping with grief reactions related to external or situational stress have already been discussed. The following cases deal mostly with crises arising "inside" the person. The interventions are carried out in medical settings and have been effective with patients who are manic or schizophrenic, acute or chronic, or in drug-induced psychosis. Also involved have been suicidal and homicidal clients, and others exhibiting a wide range of symptoms.

An example of prescriptive intervention with a manic patient illustrates how an excessive degree of high morale was brought within manageable bounds.

M. P., a 32-year-old white, Protestant, married father of two children, was admitted from the emergency room where his wife and three neighbors had taken him after he had told her he intended to buy an expensive sports car and drive to the West Coast to close a business deal; the patient was a salesman for a small electronics firm. Ten days prior to admission he had begun to talk animatedly about "a tremendous opportunity for expansion" that only he could negotiate. He told his wife that the consummation of the deal would bring in millions and that he would be able to retire within a few years. He began to stay up all night making elaborate plans for what he intended to do with his riches and reacted to his wife's questions with scorn, jocularity, and occasional outbursts of abusiveness. Mrs. P. recognized that he was in the midst of an exacerbation but was unable to persuade him to go to the emergency room. She was eventually able to enlist the aid of neighbors to bring her husband in for treatment.

On the ward the patient was restless, excitable, and argumentative. This, combined with his rapid shifts in thought, made history-taking impossible. . . . he was totally sleepless the first night despite adequate doses of haloperidol. He was extremely disruptive to the ward partly because the other patients were fascinated by his infectious enthusiasm. The day following admission a medical evaluation for lithium was performed (EKG, serum electrolytes, serum creatinine, blood urea nitrogen, and a urinalysis), and within 48 hours of his admission lithium carbonate therapy was instituted in addition to the paloperidol. The lithium was raised by daily increments to 2.4 gm/day.

By the sixth day he began to sleep more than six hours a night, and his grandiose delusions began to dissolve. He gradually regained a normal mood and by the twelfth day was ready for discharge. Interviews with him and joint meetings with his wife failed to reveal any obvious stress in his recent life to account for the manic break. Both were impressed by the rapid clearing of his symptoms and agreed with the staff that he should remain on lithium indefinitely.

Mr. P. called his employer and his return to work was arranged without any difficulty. He was discharged home to be followed by a nearby clinic which specializes in the administration of lithium to outpatients.

Patients with manic-depressive illness are often free of the major social deterioration characteristic of schizophrenia. It is thus of major value to maintain their social adaptation by attempting to treat them without sending them out of the community to state hospitals. This requires experience with lithium and the ability to handle the patient skillfully while he is on the ward. It is often necessary to make certain adjustments when such patients are on the unit. They should not be over-stimulated and should be allowed to remain out of meetings or alone, if necessary, when they are in an excited phase. The usual gathering of information, social assessments, and interventions characteristic of crisis treatment should be postponed until the patient is able to tolerate them. (Lieb, Lipsitch, and Slaby, 1973, pp. 89–91)

Fears

Frankl's concept of *paradoxical intention* is a prescriptive approach to overcoming fears. One feature distinguishing it from similar approaches is the notion of self-detachment.

The patient was a bookkeeper who had been treated by many doctors and in several clinics without any therapeutic success. When he came to my clinic, he was in extreme despair, admitting that he was close to suicide. For some years, he had suffered from a writer's cramp which had recently become so severe that he was in danger of losing his job. Therefore only immediate short-term therapy could alleviate the situation. In starting treatment my associate recommended to the patient that he do just the opposite from what he usually had done; namely, instead of trying to write as neatly and legibly as possible, to write with the worst possible scrawl. He was advised to say to himself, "Now I will show people what a good scribbler I am!" And at that moment in which he deliberately tried to scribble, he was unable to do so. "I tried to scrawl but simply could not do it," he said the next day. Within forty-eight hours the patient was in this way freed from his writer's cramp, and remained free for the observation period after he had been treated. He is a happy man again and fully able to work. (Frankl, 1967, pp. 15–16)

Frankl points out the importance of humor in interpreting why paradoxical intention is sometimes effective.

A sound sense of humour is inherent in this logotherapeutic technique called paradoxical intention. This is understandable since we know that humour is a paramount way of putting distance between something and oneself. One might say, as well, that humour helps man rise above his own predicament by allowing him to look at himself in a more detached way. So humour would also have to be located in the noetic dimension.

After all, no animal is able to laugh, least of all at himself. (Frankl, 1967, p. 16)

Thus prescription can be an intervention mode for dealing with specific anxieties and fears that reflect a lack of self-confidence and result in lowered morale. Two further examples (Wolpe, 1965; and Wolpin, 1968) follow. The idea underlying both is that a person first does in imagination what he or she fears doing in real life. In the process of experiencing his or her fears imaginatively, the individual is freed from them before actually engaging in the activity.

In the Wolpe approach the client is first taught how to relax. After a degree of relaxation has been achieved he or she is instructed, for example, to imagine some real person whom he or she fears. In the example reported there were two such real people—Mrs. Benning and Selma. The client feared rejection from both of them but feared more the rejection by Selma. In describing his approach the consultant first points out the importance of teaching the client how to relax deeply. It's the "let go" of ordinary relaxation, carried to a fuller degree. After practice for fifteen minutes twice per day the client gains the skills necessary for relaxation and is now moved toward dealing with a focal problem.

Consultant: Now, I want you to imagine that you're walking along the sidewalk and you see, walking toward you from the other side, Mrs. Benning. Now, as you pass Mrs. Benning, you see she is looking toward you and you get ready to greet her, and she just walks past as though she didn't recognize you. Now, stop imagining that. Now, if imagining that disturbed you even a very small bit, I want you to raise your right index finger now. If it didn't worry you, don't do anything. *(no finger movement)* OK, that's fine, now just keep on relaxing. (Wolpe, 1965, pp. 7–8)

The consultant then "increases" the problem in the client's imagination.

Consultant: Now, I want you to imagine again that you're walking on the sidewalk and you see, moving toward you, Selma and you get ready to greet her, and she seems to see you but she walks right on—she doesn't greet you. (Wolpe, 1965, p. 8)

After a series of such imaginings, the hypnotic quality of the situation is seen in the following:

Consultant: ... Now, I'm going to count up to 5 and then you will open your eyes and feel calm and refreshed. 1-2-3-4-5. How do you feel?

Client: I feel like, I wouldn't feel like doing any more work today anymore. The last time when I seen her I just didn't care whether she said hello or not.

Consultant: How did you feel the first time?

Client: I was very mad. At least, the least she could do was say hello when I live just across the way from her. The last time it was, if she didn't think enough of me to say hello, then let her just go.

Consultant: Very good. (Wolpe, 1965, p. 9)

In this series of prescriptive interventions the client had for all practical purposes surrendered her will to the consultant. By permitting him to instruct her in relaxation methods step by step at the beginning of the interview, she relaxed as much as possible in preparation. Then, under the prescriptions assigned, she was able to experience and eventually control situations that she would otherwise have prevented herself from experiencing. The Wolpe approach begins with those anxieties and fears that the client reports to be least intense, and moves progressively through a hierarchy of more intense fears until finally the client is imagining the most intense anxiety-arousing experiences without demoralization.

In the strategy of Wolpin (1968), another prescriptive consultant also dealing with desensitization, the client imagines himself as actually engaged in his most feared activity—from the beginning and without relaxation. While doing this, the client is encouraged and supported by the consultant. A clinical example involves a married woman whose symptoms included a fear of the dark and of being attacked and raped if out at night or even at home alone watching TV. What she wanted to do, in the abovementioned sense, was to move around outside confidently at night and to feel at ease inside her house. The first four sessions were devoted to interview, and in this period of time she was also given tests and questionnaires to fill out and return. In the following six sessions she was asked to imagine herself in the feared situation. The first session was broken into a series of scenes, each lasting several minutes, during which her prescription was to visualize unsuccessful rape attempts upon herself. In later sessions she imagined herself up late at night watching TV alone, investigating unaccounted noises in the house and garage, and going outside at night. At a followup interview session months later she reported full mastery of the problem, except at times of excessive fatigue (Wolpin, 1968, pp. 40–41).

Even more severe personal problems involving intense fear or anxiety can sometimes be dealt with by "flooding." The consultant creates a situation where the client must "live through" the situation he or she shuns in real life. Once in the situation the consultant has created for him or her, there is no escape; the client literally must go through it. A girl who feared being in a car was subjected to riding in the back seat of a car for four hours, with no way to get out of it. For many, but by no means for all, the dreaded situation may quickly lose its capacity to arouse crippling anxieties in the future.

Agoraphobia means an intense fear of open spaces.

> *In vivo* flooding is exemplified by the case of Mrs. C., a woman with agoraphobia so severe that she was unable to go on her own more than two blocks by car without anxiety. Attempts at systematic desensitization had failed—apparently because she was unable to imagine scenes realistically. After other measures had also proved ineffective, I decided to persuade her to expose herself to flooding, which had to be *in vivo* because of the demonstrated inadequacy of her imagination. After resisting strenuously for some weeks, she agreed to take the plunge. Plans were made for her husband to place her, unaccompanied, on a commercial aircraft one hour's flight away from the airport where I would await her. When Mrs. C. in due course alighted from the plane, she walked toward me smiling. She had felt increasing anxiety for the first fifteen minutes of the flight, and then gradual subsidence of it. During the second half of the journey she had been perfectly comfortable. She flew home alone the next day without trouble. This single experience resulted in a great increase in her range of comfortable situations away from home. She was now able, without anxiety, to drive her car alone three or four miles from home and to make unaccompanied trips by plane without any anxiety. Plans to build up this improvement by further treatment were foiled by distance plus other practical obstacles. (Wolpe, 1973, pp. 198–99)

Explanations are unclear as to why a single exposure to a dreaded situation might produce such constructive results. But these situations of flooding, along with other related approaches such as "paradoxical intention" (Frankl, 1955, pp. 178–203) or systematic desensitization (Wolpe, 1973) leave little doubt as to the validity of conclusions reached. Dramatic relief from otherwise uncontrollable fears and anxieties have been reported for a varied range of circumstances.

Sexual Attractiveness

Other prescriptive approaches to personal problems share elements with a variety of "pure" approaches, such as Moreno's psychodrama, Perls' Gestalt therapy, Frankl's logotherapy, and Wolpe's desensitization. A clinical example is drawn from a marathon group situation reported by Mintz (1971). Claire had come to the session on the suggestion of her psychotherapist. She told the group that whenever men asked her for dates she did not know how to act. She thought of herself as unfeminine, felt awkward, and was not often asked out a second time. She seemed unaware of her natural attractiveness and made no effort to take advantage of it. The prescriptive approach presumed that Claire needed the directive encouragement and support of a mother-type person. When Elizabeth Mintz, the marathon leader, suggested that Claire go around the group and speak in a seductive and flirtatious way to each of the men, Claire responded as follows.

"I couldn't," Claire said.

"I'll go around with you. Come on."

Claire arose, and I put my arm around her shoulder. She was shaking violently. I stood embracing her while she spoke to the first two men.

"I like your necktie."

"You're getting bald, but that's all right. I like bald men."

Our progress around the circle was slow. After the first two encounters, Claire's trembling diminished. I took my arm away from her shoulder and held her hand as she continued.

"You'd probably be a good dancer."

"You've got such curly hair—I'd like to touch it." She reached out and touched the curly-haired man, and I relinquished her hand. For the next two encounters, I walked beside Claire but did not touch her.

"I know you're married. You have trouble with your wife, you told us, but I'll bet you're one great daddy to your kids."

"I'd love to date you if you weren't from out of town."

I returned to my chair. Claire went on by herself to the last two men in the circle.

"Hi." She touched the face of the man she was greeting. He took her hand, clasped it lightly, and let go.

"Hi to you." She looked at the last of the men in the group, and he reached out his arms, and Claire settled comfortably into his lap. She remained there for a few moments, then arose, her face glowing. She went back to her chair and said, with complete spontaneity and unconscious humor, "Oh, flirting's really fun, it's not so scary!" (Mintz, 1971, pp. 20–21)

The consultant concluded that Claire's problem with men was inhibition. By telling her what to do and by offering support while she did it, the consultant helped Claire become more confident. The prescriptive intervention was sufficient to push Claire into taking actions which she otherwise would have avoided, thus demonstrating to her that her fears were ungrounded. She had been helped in "reality-testing" as the consultant steered her around the circle of men in a "Try it—you'll like it" experiment. Before very long the consultant was able to phase out of the physical steering as Claire became increasingly relaxed.

A significant dynamic underlying successful prescriptive counseling is illustrated in the following telephone counseling situation.

> 4:30 p.m. . . . Girl named Marty called. Hung up about going out with an ex-boyfriend's best friend. She still likes the first boy, but he won't go out with her now for fear of hurting his best friend's feelings. Told her to talk to the present boyfriend and make that relationship more flexible than going steady. Then she could date the boys she wanted to more easily. She'll call back. Phone log July 1970.

Explaining why the advice was accepted and acted upon, the consultants conclude:

> The Ann Landers variety of personal problems is the most common type of a call a center receives. Such calls demand advice, even though giving advice is against standard psychotherapeutic theory and practice. Attempts to engage a caller in conversation often lead to the caller's hanging up angrily at being ignored. After hearing the advice callers commonly hang up quickly, with a sincere but short "Thank you." The suggestions which are most effective coincide with the caller's own inclinations so a counselor is not so much asked to tell the person what to do as to support an unstated but implicitly made choice or to argue effectively against it. To avoid being considered wrong or stupid, the caller states the situation in the form of a question to avoid being held responsible for the decision. (Clark and Jaffe, 1973, p. 157)

The risk, then, is that the consultant might be induced to "okay" via prescription what the client desires, thus engaging in "felt needs" counseling, which may do little more than confirm the client's injudicious wishes.

Physical Illness Related to Low Morale/Cohesion

That physical illness can have demoralizing mental effects is a well known and widely accepted truth. But claims of similar mind-body correlations, in the absence of physically demonstrated illness, are suspect—except for the claim by extremely fit people that they feel better and have consistently higher morale than their less healthy colleagues. In between these extremes there appears to be a developing awareness that bodily conditions can have negative behavioral effects and that mental effort can be applied to changing physiological facts.

The several approaches to mind-body correlations share similar properties. One example, "bioenergetics," was developed by Lowen.

> The principles and practices of bioenergetic therapy rest on the functional identity of the mind and the body. This means that any change in a person's thinking and, therefore, in his behavior and feelings, is conditioned on a change in the functioning of the body. The two functions that are most important in this regard are breathing and movement. Both of these functions are disturbed in every person who has an emotional conflict, by chronic muscle tensions that are physical counterparts of psychological conflicts.

> In the therapy, the patient is helped to get in touch with his body, with the ground on which he stands and with the air around him—through passive stress positions, active voluntary exercises and by the active intervention of the therapist who places physical pressure on chronically tense muscles to free their blocked energy. This intervention often precipitates dramatic expressions of feelings such as sadness, terror, fear and longing that have long been held back by chronically tensing the musculature. Spontaneous memories and insights often follow these expressions and they can be dealt with psychologically, through verbal interchange. (Feldman, 1974, p. 26)

Lowen (1970) describes an intervention using this method.

> ... I treated a young woman, Lucy, about eighteen years of age, who was markedly retarded in both her emotional and intellectual development. In addition her muscular coordination was severely impaired, a condition that is typical of retarded people. Superficially, Lucy was a very agreeable and pleasant person who made a slight effort to do the exercises and movements I suggested. Her movements, however, were very limited in duration and represented a gesture of cooperation rather than a serious commitment to the activity. She would, for example, kick her legs against the couch several times while saying "No" in a quiet voice that carried no conviction. Then she would stop, after only a few moments of activity, and look at me to see if I approved or disapproved of her. It was obvious that Lucy needed my approval, and I gave it to her at the same time that I encouraged her to let go more fully to these expressions.

Thus, in an acceptant mode within the encompassing prescriptive strategy, the consultant encouraged Lucy to "protest." As he worked with her, some aspects of the "inner" Lucy started to become apparent.

> During the treatment I would catch an occasional glimpse of an alert intelligence behind her mask of retardation. There were moments when Lucy's eyes would meet mine with a look of understanding. When this happened, her eyes temporarily lost their dullness and became bright and sensitive. I had the impression that she was studying me to see how far

she could trust me. On other occasions, when I asked her to open her
eyes wide in an expression of fear, she froze and became completely im-
mobile. Once when I pressed with my thumbs on the muscles alongside
the nose that activate the smiling reflex in order to block the smile, her
eyeballs rolled up into their sockets and her face became twisted in a
gargoylelike expression. She looked like a complete idiot, and I realized
that she had cut off her contact with me and had withdrawn into uncom-
prehension because of some deep inner fear. It was an unusual defense
but also a very effective one.

Having now developed a more precise diagnosis, the consultant continued his program of prescriptive interventions.

... My treatment of Lucy aimed at strengthening her ego through her as-
serting opposition and at the development of better muscular coordination.
Her kicking became more forceful and sustained, and her no's became
louder and stronger. She also hit the bed with a tennis racket repeatedly,
saying, "I won't." Bioenergetic exercises were also used to deepen her
breathing and loosen her body.

... Her ability to express her feelings was blocked by the extreme physical tensions in her body. The muscles at the back of her neck were contracted into hard lumps. The attempt to loosen them by massage was
painful, and I always stopped when she became frightened. At each session, however, I could work a little more strongly with her. At first Lucy
could not tolerate any stress for more than a few moments. Her tolerance
slowly increased as her tensions eased and her breathing became freer
and deeper. Initially she moved her arms and legs like a puppet, without
rhythm or feeling. As she gained a sense of freedom in expressing herself,
her movements became more charged with feelings. She hit and kicked
with more vigor, and her voice rose in pitch and intensity as she voiced
her no's and "I won'ts." The result was a consistent improvement in her
coordination.

Lucy's therapy ended when her family moved to another part of the country. We had worked together once a week for about two years. At the end
there were times when a casual observer would have taken Lucy for a
normal person. She had made considerable progress, and I hoped that
with encouragement and support it would continue. (Lowen, 1970, pp.
173–77)

"Rolfing" was created by Ida Rolf (Rolf, 1974). As is true of bioenergetics, it is a
way of attempting to change subjective feeling-states in directions of well-being of
the morale/cohesion variety. This is accomplished by first changing the body's muscular tone, posture, or functions such as breathing. By comparison, "biofeedback"
(Brown, 1974) is concerned with shifting physiological states that have an effect
on morale. Possibilities include decreasing heartbeat rate, decreasing skin tempera-
ture, and shifting the frequency of various forms of brain waves.

IMPLICATIONS

Prescriptive interventions with individuals when the focal issue is morale or cohesion are calculated to correct either lowered or excessive self-confidence, usually the former. They are not of the "buck up" or "pep pill" variety, but attempt to push the individual into an action where anticipated fears are unrealized, where rewards are experienced, or where contact replaces withdrawal. Such approaches may be useful when lowered morale is caused by a particular situational crisis or is related to some very specific, easily identifiable factor. Manic reactions, involving excessive and unfounded self-confidence, represent the other end of the morale continuum. One strategy involving physical intervention was introduced to suggest how prescriptive interventions may be useful when morale has exceeded the "normal" range on the up side.

Examples of morale/cohesion prescriptive interventions involving a multiperson client are infrequent, perhaps because the depressed feelings in such cases are not usually thought of as the underlying cause of a difficulty but rather as a symptom of some other focal issue. For example, the unilateral exercise of authority in an organization may generate low morale throughout the membership. Yet to concentrate on morale/cohesion would be to work on the wrong problem.

REFERENCES

Brown, B. B. *New Mind, New Body*. New York: Harper & Row, 1974.

Clark, T., and D. T. Jaffe. *Toward a Radical Therapy: Alternate Services for Personal and Social Change*. New York: Gordon and Breach, Science Publishers, 1973. Reprinted by permission.

Feldman, S. "Alexander Lowen." Copyright © 1974. *Human Behavior Magazine,* June 1974, pp. 24–29. Reprinted by permission.

Frankl, V. E. *The Doctor and the Soul*. New York: Bantam Books, 1955. (Originally published, 1946.)

Frankl, V. E. *Psychotherapy and Existentialism*. Harmondsworth, England: Penguin Books, 1967. Copyright © 1967 by Victor Frankl. Reprinted by permission of author and Simon & Schuster, Inc., Washington Square Press Division.

Lieb, J., I. L. Lipsitch, and A. E. Slaby. *The Crisis Team: A Handbook for the Mental Health Professional*. Hagerstown, Maryland: Medical Department, Harper & Row, 1973. Reprinted by permission.

Lowen, A. *Pleasure*. New York: Lancer Books, 1970. Reprinted by permission of Coward, McCann & Geoghegan, Inc., New York. Copyright © 1970 by Alexander Lowen.

Mintz, E. E. "Marathon Groups: Process and People." In L. Blank, G. B. Gottsegen, and M. G. Gottsegen, *Confrontation*. New York: Macmillan, 1971, pp. 9–31. Reprinted by permission.

Rolf, I. "Introductory Lecture-Demonstration of Structural Integration." San Rafael, Calif.: Big Sur Recordings, 1974.

Taulbee, E. S., and H. W. Wright. "Psychosocial-Behavioral Model for Therapeutic Interventions." In C. D. Spielberger, ed., *Current Topics in Clinical and Community Psychology,* Vol. 31. New York: Academic Press, 1971, pp. 53–92.

Viscott, D. S. *The Making of a Psychiatrist.* Greenwich, Conn.: Fawcett Publications, 1972. Reprinted by permission.

Wolpe, J. *The Case of Mrs. Schmidt: An Illustration of Behavior Therapy.* Nashville, Tenn.: Counselor Recordings & Tests, 1965.

Wolpe, J. *The Practice of Behavior Therapy.* 2d ed. New York: Pergamon Press, 1973. Reprinted by permission.

Wolpin, M. "Guided Imagining in Reducing Fear and Avoidance Behavior." In California Mental Health Research Symposium No. 2, *Behavior Theory and Therapy.* State of California, Department of Mental Hygiene, Bureau of Research, 1968, pp. 40–41.

23
NORMS / STANDARDS

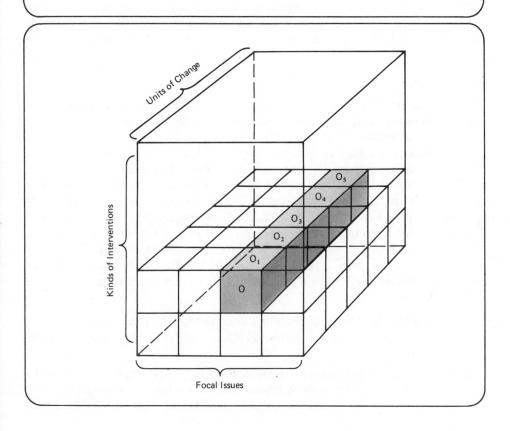

The earliest industrial example of a prescriptive intervention involving norms/standards is reported by Frederick Winslow Taylor. He recounts, for instance, that "As soon as a careful study had been made of the time elements entering into one class of work, a single first-class workman was picked out and started on ordinary piece work on this job. His task required him to do between *three and one-half* and *four times* as much work in a day as had been done in the past on an average" (Taylor, 1911, pp. 49–51). Taylor notes that it took about two years to extend this pilot individual intervention to the group level. So to an outsider who notices that numerous rules, habits, particular work practices, and so on need changing for greater work productivity, it might appear that prescriptive interventions bearing directly on the focal issue of maladaptive norms/standards should be employed from the outset. Actually, however, the first problem encountered seems to be not in diagnosing the client's situation and devising a needed solution, but in gaining the client's acceptance of the need to change and commitment to doing so.

INDIVIDUAL (O_1)

Client difficulties may result from a disregard or violation of the norms and standards felt to be essential for integration and acceptance in a given community. Intervention strategies calculated to pressure individuals into embracing such norms are discussed in the following examples.

Delinquency

Delinquency can be viewed as a special case of irresponsibility, behavior that flagrantly disregards accepted social norms and standards. Intervention in such cases is intended to enable those presently exhibiting delinquent behavior to change through actively learning to behave differently—that is, in accordance with the norms/standards a community exacts as "dues" for full membership.

"Reality therapy," as it is called by Glasser (1965), is an approach calculated to solve behavior problems by increasing the client's "responsibility." One of its most successful applications has been in the context of delinquency. As defined, responsibility is "the ability to fulfill one's needs, and to do so *in a way that does not deprive others of the ability to fulfill their needs*" (Glasser, 1965, p. 13). The reality-therapy intervention parallels both Synanon and the Therapeutic Community, described in Chapter 17. Several features of delinquency-directed reality therapy are indicated below.

1. Delinquents are congregated together in an institution (either for daytime education or round-the-clock supervision) where authorities retain physical control over them.

2. They are expected to behave in good, sound, right, valid ways as they study and work with other community members. Consultants have no reluctance to specify what, in concrete terms, constitutes "good, sound, right or valid behavior."

3. Those not cooperating are segregated into, say, a discipline cottage where they are deprived of membership in the broader community. Return to the broader community results only from improved, more responsible behavior in the discipline cottage; interventions to help the person become more responsible are implemented.

4. Those cooperating become eligible for individual or group therapy sessions.

The consultant, who is ready to pressure the client into acting more responsibly, seeks to involve the client in problem solving. Once established, the relationship permits consultant and client to engage in joint planning, with the consultant providing direction and advice if that will produce desired behavior. As clients come to accept and live according to more responsible patterns of personal behavior they become eligible to leave the institution.

Significant in this mode of intervention are the consultant's prescriptions. He or she promulgates norms for sound behavior and specifies activities designed to produce that kind of conduct. To a significant degree, this means withholding privileges when norms are violated and specifying the specific norms and standards that will be judged acceptable and rewarded by restoration of freedom.

Destitution

A variety of circumstances can result in a person becoming destitute, but whatever the particular "cause," the individual is likely to increasingly disregard the social norms and standards essential for cooperation and collaborative living. Mental-health consultation often helps the destitute person to reestablish self-respect and to reconnect with the world of work by adherence to established norms and practices. One such approach, described by Robinson (1948), relies on prescriptive intervention.

A 35-year-old woman whose 85-year-old father was still working as a mechanic, was referred for counseling. Of her two brothers, one held a responsible position; the other was barely making it due to alcoholism. Miss Lee had stopped working and had drifted into heavy drinking and quasi prostitution. She was living with an unemployed man, whom she had no intention of marrying. Her situation came to the attention of the caseworker through a government official who asked the caseworker to make contact and help her out of her current situation. The consultant shifted the responsibility for making the contact back to Miss Lee through the government official, who then arranged for her to come in for an appointment.

Nine interviews were conducted over a period of several months. During this time the consultant provided financial help that permitted Miss Lee to move to another place where she could fix meals and so on. The caseworker advised Miss Lee to stop drinking and take better physical care of herself, and offered assurance of continued support while she was reestablishing a more healthy way of living. These kinds of directions and support were continued throughout the transitional period until the client was successful in finding employment as a typist (Robinson, 1948, pp. 133–50).

The success of this prescriptive approach is at least partly due to the situation —i.e., for all practical purposes the girl had come to the end of her rope. Her gradual disregard of norms and standards had become so excessive that she could find no foothold to begin a process of reconstruction. For some two years she had been repeating the destitution cycle, and the financial help, advice, and cautions introduced by the consultant provided a sense of direction which she could embrace as a far more attractive alternative. Also, she was beginning to experience transference emotions towards the consultant through the strength, protection, and support offered her. No particular insights were suggested by the consultant regarding her "unconscious" motivations and so on. Once the client had regained a mature adult role she was able to adhere to social norms and standards in a way that permitted her to function as a self-sustaining adult.

Disorientation

Whenever a person shows significant signs of *psychotic* ("He's losing contact with reality!") behavior, the classical approach is to arrange for admission to a mental hospital. As a patient the person is no longer confronted with the need for self-responsible functioning in a house/job/community situation. As a patient he or she can be observed, supervised, and treated. In the process, however, the individual is given a diagnostic label whose legal and social significance may severely hamper future endeavors, no matter how soon he or she is released from the institution. Unlike the Ancient Mariner's albatross, psychiatric labels—for most practical purposes —don't eventually drop from around one's neck. From the still widespread lay viewpoint, the person is merely on furlough from a padded cell and "needs watching." Even to professional psychodynamicists the person's "had it" and at any moment is liable to "get it again." In addition, the hospital care offered the client-as-patient can cause a dependency reaction as the client ceases feeling a sense of responsibility for helping himself.

A strikingly different definition of the "sickness" and how to resolve it has resulted from viewing the psychotic individual in a somewhat different light. Any episode of disoriented or psychotic behavior is viewed as a crisis reaction to an intolerable situation. Without inferring as yet any cause-effect connections, this viewpoint acknowledges that other people and accompanying circumstances impact on any person's current situation. Thus hospitalization of a person constitutes an escape that can have a self-fulfilling prophecy effect by "proving" to the patient that he or she is "crazy," while contributing little or nothing to help the person cope with current realities. However, by *remaining in the "real" situation,* the client may be able to retain or regain an ordinary level of functioning and work with others toward resolving the crisis (Flomenhaft, Kaplan, and Langsley, 1973).

The Family Treatment Unit, which approaches psychotic behavior in this way, includes a psychiatrist, social worker, and nurse. The approach is prescriptive. The client is expected to keep functioning according to previous norms and standards of conduct. For a housewife this means continuing the sustaining routines of housework and family living. Medication such as drugs may be provided for the individual client and/or other family members to help them over the crisis period. After it has passed and the individual client has regained normal functioning, additional help involving counseling, welfare assistance, job retraining, and so on may be provided to increase the likelihood of successful continuance of the normal pattern.

Evaluation data for randomly selected patients treated according to this kind of crisis therapy versus psychiatric hospitalization suggest that prescription crisis therapy helps the patient to hold himself together and return to "normal" functioning more rapidly. From each of the two groups studied an approximately equal number needed to be hospitalized subsequently for psychotic episodes. However, those who had been hospitalized previously required approximately three times longer subsequent hospitalization than did those who had formerly undergone crisis therapy.

In the Soviet Union one intervention for dealing with mental-health problems having a norms/standards focal issue is called "pathogenic psychotherapy." As described by Ziferstein (1968), it is prescriptive in nature.

> This attitude was demonstrated in all five Soviet psychotherapists whose work I observed. They were all very active in giving their patients emotional support and reassurance, advice, and guidance. They vigorously engaged in reeducating their patients and presenting to them values and standards of behavior. And the doctors had no doubts as to what values and standards are realistic, correct, (the word *correct* is frequently used), and socially desirable.

> These psychotherapists would often intervene quite actively in the patient's reality situation. Where they considered it necessary, they manipulated the patient's environment, his work, occupation, place of work, or residence. One example: the doctor concluded that the patient, a young factory worker, had the capacity to be a good engineer, and that the unchallenging, unfulfilling nature of his present work contributed to his emotional illness. The doctor wrote out a prescription which was addressed to the director of the factory in which the patient worked, requiring that the patient be enrolled in an engineering institute and that the factory pay his full salary during the entire period of his schooling.

> The Soviet psychotherapists whom I observed did attempt in their psychotherapeutic work to elucidate the psychogenesis of the patient's symptoms, of his disturbed interpersonal relations, of his distorted perception of reality, and of his pathological character traits. But they took a dim view of the practice of directly interpreting to the patient and bringing to his consciousness his unconscious negative feelings and actions. (Ziferstein, 1968, p. 262)

The nonconfrontational but prescriptive nature of the approach is illustrated at another point in his description. Ziferstein recounts prescriptive strategies that parallel those of certain Western psychotherapists.

> In the course of my observations of the work of this therapist and of the other therapists, I came to realize that they were often quick to recognize the latent meaning of patients' verbal and nonverbal communications, in-

cluding dreams. However, they believed that making such unconscious negative material conscious would produce a counter-therapeutic effect. To use their Pavlovian terminology, they maintain that the words of the authority figure, the therapist, serve as powerful stimuli through both the "first signalling system" (nonverbal) and the "second signalling system" (verbal). Negative ideas expressed by the therapist, therefore, reinforce the "unhealthy stereotype" (pathological reaction patterns) already existing in the patient. The therapist, instead of making the negative unconscious feelings conscious, gives the patient a countervailing suggestion or advice, without verbalizing the latent negative content. (Ziferstein, 1968, p. 264)

Walled-Off Emotions

A. Salter's prescriptive approach to individuals when norms and standards are involved is premised on the notion that personal problems originate from a common cause, namely, an inhibition of emotions. Therefore, the intervention strategy is designed to facilitate free expression of emotions. This approach shares with others the fact that the intervention is not directed at changing thoughts and feelings but rather toward changing the norms and standards of conduct the client adheres to. The proposition is that whenever behavior changes, feelings and thoughts also change in ways that are congruent with and support the new behavior.

Salter (1949, pp. 97–100) suggests six techniques for increasing the expression of emotions. Since the strategy encourages clients to do the six different kinds of things they avoid doing, it parallels other desensitization techniques. These to-be-learned standards and norms of conduct are:

1. *Feeling-talk:* practice in being emotionally outspoken, indicating likes and aversions, annoyances, love, and other feelings. The goal is to tell the emotional truth, expressing emotions as they are experienced.

2. *Facial talk:* deliberate effort to portray one's emotions facially.

3. *Contradict and attack:* learning to disagree with others rather than to feign agreement.

4. *"I"-ness:* using the first person, "I did this . . . I did that . . . ," to learn to identify oneself with activities.

5. *Praise:* if this comes from others, it is to be expressly agreed with. Additionally, one can offer praise of oneself.

6. *Improvisation:* the goal here is to be spontaneously existential; to react out of feeling, without plan or premonition.

Salter summarizes the prescriptive character of the intervention.

The therapist uses advice, instruction, suggestion, persuasion, logic, and commands to encourage the client to practice excitation. The client is told: "Don't be so agreeable. Tell people what you think at all times, regardless of whether it's polite or impolite." He is instructed in how to do this in various situations in his life, and is given assignments. He is told that it may seem unnatural, but that "if you do the opposite of what you have been doing all your life, you will probably feel the opposite of the way you feel now . . ." (Salter, 1949, p. 61)

Summary

Since behavior that stays within the "normal limits" established by a community ensures an orderly basis for social interaction, it is not surprising that individuals who disregard or reject such norms/standards suffer personal frustrations. The prescriptive solution is to aid individuals to establish or reestablish such norms and standards as guides for their personal conduct. Correspondingly, as Salter's interventions illustrate, behaviors that presently seem too far "within" norms/standards boundaries can be aided by prescription to "expand to the limits."

GROUP (O₂)

Prescriptive interventions for solving group problems are less frequent than those directed toward individuals, partly because cooperation among several persons is necessary for the prescription to take effect. Yet an *absence* of cooperation may already be a deficiency in the group's situation. To prescribe "cooperation" gives no assurance of attaining it; yet the focal issue the client has identified has been considered sufficiently serious to justify consultation. It often follows, however, that the consultant retained to work on a group's "lack of cooperation" problem will intervene in some mode other than the prescriptive and/or upon a different though related focal issue. Nonetheless, several approaches to solving problems of group action through prescriptive consultation are conceivable. Most of them deal with norms/standards as defined by the rules of conduct among group members.

Prescriptive group development may focus on content issues or on interaction process, or on both. Formal content matters may include individual job descriptions, the boss's span of control, frequency of meetings, what the agendas of these meetings contain, and so on; process has more to do with how members interact with one another, how authority is used, how problems are solved, etc. Most often the underlying issue is in some way related to how the top person presently is using his or her authority and how better results could be achieved.

From observation or inquiry the consultant may conclude that the team has too few meetings or too many. He or she may find deficiencies related to "loose" job definitions that result in problems being overlooked, or "tight" ones that pose barriers to needed cooperation. Or the consultant may find a "lack of definiteness" evidenced by the group's chronic failure to approach problems in a focused fashion. The group may be excessively concerned with triviality, or too hemmed in by policy, or have insufficient policy guidelines. Beyond these diagnostic areas the consultant may also evaluate each member as to individual competence and potential. If the "problems" are of a process character, the consultant will recommend changes in the organization calculated to separate warring factions, etc.

Whatever the findings, the prescriptive consultant usually prepares a report for the top person giving both a diagnosis of problem causes and solution prescriptions. He or she may present these conclusions to other members, individually or together, and may recommend specific steps that need to be taken to increase effectiveness. Additionally, the consultant may offer assistance in seeing to it that the recommended plan is executed.

INTERGROUP (O₃)

The prescriptive approach to resolving norms/standards or working rules and procedures between groups is most frequently a structured one—that is, power/ authority is generally addressed as the focal issue. The inherent assumption is that a realignment of power/authority will lead to changes in the ways groups relate to one another.

ORGANIZATION (O₄)

In the following example a prescriptive consultant listens for the client's symptoms —*without* accepting the client's own conclusions regarding work practices in the company's training division. The episode also reveals how a prescriptive consultant offers a client step-by-step recommendations as to how to solve the problem at hand.

> Dallmeyer talks about one assignment he handled for a Midwest consumer company. The company boasted a hot-shot sales training director. He used every known device—booklets, seminars, training courses—in teaching his men how to push their products, yet profits had stalled. Finally the company's president hired a management consultant. "If there's one thing you won't have to improve," boasted the president, "it's our sales training. We have one of the top men in the country."
>
> It is one of the duties of the management consultant to listen to the suggestions of the client president, but also to ignore his conclusions. Obviously if the client had all the answers before calling the consultant he never would have called him. Dallmeyer spent several weeks scrutinizing the consumer company with the care of an archeologist uncovering lost relics. Finally he made his recommendations.
>
> "Your training director is doing a good job," he said. "In fact, he's doing *too* good a job. You're spending four weeks a year training your salesmen when two weeks should be enough. Get your salesmen out in the field where they can do some good." The consultant also rearranged the sales territories, balanced the work load, and advised pushing certain neglected products. Sales soon increased. (Higdon, 1969, p. 71)

That clients often resist prescriptions offered them is almost too well known to need documentation. The following is typical.

Even when a sick or dying company obtains accurate advice on how to save itself, it may be unwilling to accept the advice—just as the patient threatened by a possible heart attack refuses to quit smoking or lose weight. I spoke with Carl Devoe, president of Executive House, Inc. As a member of a group of investors, he had purchased control of a once successful auto supplies manufacturing company whose business had been sliding steadily downhill. The new investors discovered that various management consultants had attempted to advise the company. Gathering dust in its files were two or three extensive reports, any one of which if applied might have arrested the company's decline. The reports had gone unimplemented.

"These reports required such massive doses of treatment," Devoe explained to me, "that the people in the judgment area were overwhelmed. As a result they did nothing." The new investors began to apply the recommendations of the consultants one step at a time. Soon the company began to show a profit again. (Higdon, 1969, pp. 47–48)

When such a client reaction occurs it is reasonable to conclude that the consultant either failed to identify the real causes of inertia, or else failed to motivate the client sufficiently to bring about the change.

One of the most complete descriptions of behavior-modification methods for improving the performance of employees on an organization-wide basis is provided by Feeney (1972). His thesis is:

When you try to create a more positive environment where people are supportive, helpful and looking at what you do well, people feel better. Attitudes and all these inner feelings are really caused by consequences. You don't try to change them directly, you change the environmental consequences, which change the feelings so if the consequences are positive for what one does, one feels better. (Feeney, 1972, p. 9)

Emery Air Freight has concentrated on a program of productivity improvement that has four basic sequential steps for each focus of application:

1. *Identify the problem.* As Feeney points out, in many situations those who are closest to the problem are unaware that a problem exists. Since outsiders are more likely to notice problem areas, the Emery program uses outside consultants to audit particular individual and group performances. Feeney believes that the highest profit-improvement potential is to be found in areas of performance deficiency. Therefore, rather than helping people to do better what they already do well, efforts should be directed toward correcting major performance shortfalls.

2. *Set standards* for what is acceptable and *measurements* for evaluating actual performance.

3. *Feed back* "how they are doing" to those who produce results.

4. *Reward* satisfactory performance *or* improved performance—no matter how slight the improvement—preferably through personal commendation by the individual's superior. This should be done frequently in the beginning, less often after performance standards are regularly being reached or surpassed.

As described, the Emery program is a prescriptive intervention. Consultants diagnose problems, set up standards, and then advise reinforcement schedules under which people are induced to step up performance. The description does not provide an indication of how—if at all—chronically substandard performance, which cannot be rewarded but which also cannot be ignored, is dealt with by a system that is geared solely to positive reinforcement.

LARGER SOCIAL SYSTEM (O₅)

Norms/standards prescriptive interventions in larger social systems generally focus upon various disintegrative processes, such as alcoholism, drug addiction, or delinquency, which occur within or are linked to particular social contexts and circumstances. These maladies are regarded as being induced by the larger social system rather than by individual psychodynamic factors, maladies related to the stresses, strains, and strivings created within the larger social system.

Alcoholics Anonymous can be considered a truncated larger social system; a social system, in other words, which is incomplete because it does not solve or support the solution of food, clothing, and shelter issues. And yet it does support individuals as they seek to cope with alcoholic motivations in specific situations. Thus Alcoholics Anonymous is an "interest group" in the sense of convened meetings where members come together to strengthen one another's individual adherence to sobriety norms/standards. Also, an individual member of Alcoholics Anonymous who is finding it hard to abstain from drinking in social or solo settings away from Alcoholics Anonymous can quickly get supportive help from other members in adhering to AA's norms/standards. While perhaps a majority of the interventions are norms/standards related, a variety of other kinds of interventions are utilized in the total program. There are confrontational aspects to AA in that members may challenge one another in a straightforward way regarding their attitudes, as in the Synanon Game (Chapter 17). Cathartic elements are present in the sense that each member is expected to select someone as a confidant with whom he or she can talk in a very private way about past problems (*Alcoholics Anonymous*, 1955).

REFERENCES

Alcoholics Anonymous. New and rev. ed. New York: AA Publishing, Inc., 1955.

Feeney, E. J. "Performance Audit, Feedback and Positive Reinforcement." Reproduced by special permission from *Training and Development Journal* 26, no. 11 (1972): 8–13.

Flomenhaft, K., D. M. Kaplan, and D. G. Langsley. "Avoiding Psychiatric Hospitalizaion." In J. Fischer, comp., *Interpersonal Helping: Emerging Approaches for Social Work Practice.* Springfield, Ill.: C. C. Thomas, 1973, pp. 253–64.

Glasser, W. *Reality Therapy: A New Approach to Psychiatry.* New York: Harper & Row, 1965.

Higdon, H. *The Business Healers.* New York: Random House, 1969. Reprinted by permission.

Robinson, V. P. "A Discussion of Two Case Records Illustrating Personality Change." In J. Taft, ed., *Family Casework and Counseling: A Functional Approach.* Philadelphia: University of Pennsylvania Press, 1948, pp. 133–50.

Salter, A. *Conditioned Reflex Therapy.* New York: Creative Age Press, 1949.

Taylor, F. W. *Scientific Management.* New York: Harper & Brothers Publishers, 1911.

Ziferstein, I. "The Impact of the Socioeconomic Order on the Psychotherapeutic Process in the Soviet Union." In Stanley Lesse, ed., *An Evaluation of the Results of the Psychotherapies.* Springfield, Ill.: Charles C. Thomas, 1968, pp. 262–64. Reprinted by permission.

PRESCRIPTIVE INTERVENTIONS

24

GOALS/OBJECTIVES

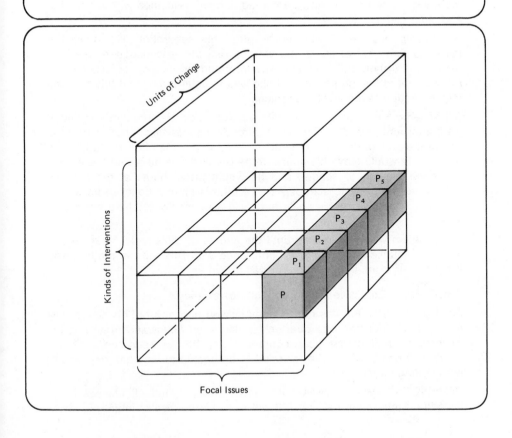

The major focal issues amenable to treatment by prescription appear to involve power/authority, morale/cohesion, and norms/standards. Individual and group problems related to goals and objectives appear to be less susceptible to this consultation approach.

INDIVIDUAL (P_1)

In *contracting,* a cycle-breaking mechanism, the consultant specifies a goal of desired behavior and sets up a series of rewards the client will receive for engaging in this behavior. Since the reward can be had only after the desired behavior has been completed, the approach is termed contingency contracting: if A, the desired behavior, occurs, then B, the specified reward, will follow.

Used to help control a truancy problem, contingency contracting had the following results.

> Bill C., a 16-year-old high school junior, had a relatively clear school record. His cumulative folder indicated no behavior problems. His test scores and grades showed that he was above average academically. Things had started to change, however, during the middle of his sophomore year, when his parents separated and Bill remained with his mother and older sister.
>
> Bill started missing school shortly after this separation. His counselor talked to him several times and warned him of the consequences of his behavior. Further, Bill's mother was informed on several occasions that Bill was not attending school, but she was reluctant to accept this fact and took no action to remedy the problem.
>
> Bill became very adept at concealing his truancy. He frequently attended his homeroom period, during which attendance was taken, but missed the rest of the school day. When he did miss a full day, he often wrote his own excuse. He would leave his house at the precise time he would leave were he actually going to school, and he would arrive home at the time he should had he gone to school. As a result, his mother believed he was in attendance and did not wish to accept the counselor's telling her otherwise.
>
> The problem went unchecked until the middle of Bill's junior year. At this time the counselor arranged a conference with Bill and his mother, and the following contingency contract was drawn up:
>
> PROBLEM: Excessive period and full-day truancy.
>
> BACKGROUND: Bill has consistently missed part or all of his school day for the past year and one quarter. He has been counseled regarding his truancy, his mother has been contacted, and he has been somewhat restricted at home. His mother seemed to be unable to help him because of her working hours.
>
> BEHAVIORAL IMPLEMENTATION: (1) Bill will attend all classes he is scheduled into every day. (2) Bill will have his counselor initial his atten-

dance card at the end of each school day. (3) Bill will exchange the completed attendance card with his mother in accordance with the reward schedule stated below. (4) Bill will chart the cumulative frequency of period attendance on a graph in the counselor's office at the end of each school day. (5) Bill will attend a group rap session once each week.

REWARD SCHEDULE: Successful completion of the above implementation will be rewarded in the following manner:

1. Bill will exchange the signed attendance card with his mother and will receive ten cents (10¢) for each class attended. This money will be saved for a trip to Disneyland on December 31st. (Note: Bill can hold the money himself or have his mother hold it for him.)

2. Bill will be allowed to go to Disneyland on December 31st for the New Year's Eve party.

When school resumes in January, a conference will be held to determine the need for a new contract.

SIGNATURE AND AGREEMENT STATEMENTS:

I agree to follow the provisions of the contract and to dispense the rewards only if the provisions of the contract are met.

_____

Mrs. C.

I agree to follow the provisions of this contract.

_____

Bill C.

I agree to monitor this contract and to make a verbal progress report to Bill and his mother at the end of each week.

_____

Counselor

Bill did not miss one class for three full weeks, and Mrs. C. followed through on her part of the contract. At the end of the three-week period a conference was held, and Bill decided that he thought he could handle full-time attendance. It was mutually decided by Bill and the counselor that for a three-week period the attendance card previously filled out daily need be filled out only on Friday to cover the entire school week. Bill felt that his presenting the completed card to his mother was sufficient reward. After three weeks Bill was maintaining full attendance, so his behavior modification program was discontinued. (Brooks, 1974, pp. 318–19)

It should be noted that this approach involves no effort to deal with underlying causes. The assumption is that attitudes follow rather than precede behavior. Change the behavior, in other words, and the attitude change will follow.

Precision teaching is an approach that ensures the client is treated not as a typical or average student, but as an individual with highly specific learning needs.

Once these have been identified, interventions to fulfill such individualized needs can be introduced. The following consultant-managed procedures are involved.

1. *Pinpointing the behavior* (both in terms of response class and in terms of response class dimension) to be modified in the classroom.
2. *Recording the behavior* to determine its characteristics in the classroom along dimensions relevant to the curriculum.
3. *Changing something in the classroom* to change the behavior in the direction sought and specified when the behavior was pinpointed. This may include changes in teaching method, curriculum materials, motivational procedures, the classroom environment, or anything else that the teacher believes is useful.
4. *Trying again* when the classroom changes in the first plan do not produce the behavior changes sought. (Johnson, 1974, p. 418)

An example of precision teaching in practice is provided by Johnson (1974).

Jerry, a 14-year-old cerebral palsied child, is enrolled in a special education class. Jerry's oral reading performance is well below that expected for his age group, and he also shows poor performance in reading comprehension. In this pinpointed behavior, his recorded rate of making incorrect responses either equaled or exceeded his recorded rate of making correct responses, depending on the reading level of the test.... To change something in the classroom, the teacher decided to introduce a contingency contract in which she agreed to pay Jerry a nickel for every question he answered correctly—a procedure that brought quick results. ... Following this change in classroom procedure, his rate of correctly answering the question exceeded his rate of incorrectly answering questions, suggesting that the procedure worked. This observation eliminated the last step in precision teaching, namely, trying again. (Johnson, 1974, pp. 418–19)

The advantage of such interventions is their specificity. Through Johnson's methodology a client's difficulties in learning are identified and thus become approachable, rather than remaining so vague that intervention is not deemed feasible.

An analysis and summation of some of the implications of the prescriptive approach with individual clients in an industrial context is provided by Steele (1969) in the following. His conclusions are probably applicable to clinical and other situations as well.

I think the role of "expert" is a quite seductive one for the consultant—all the more so in behavioral science since the variables and their relationships are often quite fuzzy and complex. It can be quite personally gratifying to have others see me as someone who really "knows" what is going on or what should be done in a given situation. Besides personal gratification on the part of the consultant, another factor pushes him toward the stance of expert: The client's wish to see himself safely in the hands of an expert who is wise and able so that anxiety over present or future difficulties can be reduced.

Steele has here identified core dynamics underlying the use of the authority-obedience model in prescriptive consulting. He continues,

Both the consultant's and the client's needs, then, may propel the consultant toward exclusive occupancy of the role of expert in their relationship. This may have some benefits such as making it more likely that the consultant will be listened to, but it may also have some costs. One that is usually mentioned is the potential price paid in terms of increased dependency of the client on the consultant—a dependency that may keep the client from developing his own strengths and competencies for diagnosis and problem solving. A second cost—one that is less often considered—is that a focus on the consultant as the exclusive expert may often lead to inadequate decisions. The client often has great wisdom (intuitive if not systematic) about many aspects of his own situation, and an overweighting of the consultant's knowledge-value may indeed cause poorer choices to be made than if there were a more balanced view of that which each can contribute to the situation. (Steele, 1969, pp. 193–94)

Granted these limitations, there appear to be many kinds of client situations that are helped significantly by prescriptive consultation, especially those situations in which the client is unable to act in his or her own behalf. In other instances, structure and reward are introduced into a situation in order to induce purposive behavior—even if the envisaged goal for the moment goes no further than the next nickel. The consultant-envisaged goal, of course, is individual improvement, an objective that in time might be internalized by the client.

GROUP (P₂)

Often prescriptive consultants must deal with personnel problems, and sometimes these difficulties originate at the top of an organization where they crucially affect its capacity for continuity and goal achievement. An example of a breakthrough in a frozen top-management group is provided below.

Telling the truth can prove hazardous. Cole tells the story of one president that retained Cole & Associates to do an organization study. Cole noticed that all of that company's top executives had reached their sixties. No younger men had been trained to replace them. Cole walked into the president's office carrying a set of actuarial tables detailing the mortality rates of men in their sixties. He compared the company to a college with all the members of its football team ready to graduate in the spring. Cole suggested that the company make a concentrated effort to hire and promote younger executives. "The president of that company has not talked to me since that day," says Cole. "We hurt his feelings. He followed our advice, but he didn't like it, and I don't blame him for not liking it." Cole paused. "Still, you've got to tell the truth." (Higdon, 1969, p. 76)

The president's acceptance of the conclusion but rejection of the consultant who offered it seems related to the person-centered resentment so often provoked by prescriptive consultants, even when their prescriptions solve the real problems. By implication, the career risks to an organization member undertaking a comparable role in this situation (Janis, 1973, pp. 148, 216) are apparent in this president's adverse reaction to his "outsider" consultant.

INTERGROUP (P₃)

An intergroup problem exists when two or more groups in an organization are split on the best route to take. In such cases, a prescriptive consultant may be called on to give an outsider's appraisal of the appropriate goals/objectives to pursue.

In the early sixties a major oil company on the West Coast considered adding food-vending machines in their service stations. The top executives divided down the middle on what soon became a major controversy within the organization. "It was like trying to watch a badminton game from under a net," one executive caught in the middle said. "We decided to call in an outsider. He could be impartial, and perhaps most important, he wouldn't have to live with the losers after it was all over." The outsider called in was the management consulting firm Booz, Allen & Hamilton. In keeping with the high status of the corporation (which ranked in the top twenty-five of *Fortune*'s annual list of the 500 largest U.S. industrial corporations), a Booz-Allen vice-president (who ranked high in seniority with the firm) made the initial contacts and interviewed the key executives. Then he left, leaving the assignment in the hands of an "associate," which on Booz-Allen's three-step pyramid is halfway between the bottom and the top. The associate supervised the work of several "consultants" (the title given to the firm's lowest echelon, their so-called bright young men), who interviewed executives of lesser status and began visiting service stations. They also examined what data they could find related to service station operation in the corporate headquarters.

With the research completed the vice-president returned to present the final report. He commented that most service stations have little surplus parking space. "Food will merely encourage customers to remain in the stations longer," he said. "The result will be congestion. In addition, local restaurant owners, who buy gasoline too, may be offended." The Booz-Allen vice-president recommended a trial in several selected stations. This would permit the oil corporation executives to determine how successful food vending would be before fully committing themselves. It was a polite way of saying, "Don't touch food vending with a ten-foot pole."

The chief executive decided to accept the report. Whether food vending in service stations could have proved profitable may never be fully proved, but the members of the organization—including those who had favored the new lost cause—seemed satisfied with the thoroughness and objectivity of the report. It also showed that good consulting is often more art than science. (Higdon, 1969, pp. 41–42)

In this case the recommendation seemed sufficient to close the breach between the two groups over this goals/objectives issue. Equally or even more often, however, the recommendation is supported by the side of the controversy that "wins" and is blocked by those whose position it defeats.

ORGANIZATION (P₄)

Caplan's (1970) description of prescriptive consultation in a government agency provides a clear indication of how a consultant, by imposing his or her own will on a resistant client, may come up with an accurate diagnosis of the problem.

... a consultant was called in by the head of a governmental department to advise on the reorganization of a certain division. On his arrival, after a long airplane flight, he had a short conference with his consultee, who told him that all the technical arrangements for his seven-day stay would be handled by the division chief, who was not available that afternoon but who would meet with him the following day.

The consultation was starting out in the "classical" prescriptive manner; the consultant first met with the head of the government department, the man who had engaged his services. What the consultant had not anticipated, however, was the resistance he was about to encounter from subordinates who were out of sympathy with the entire project. They had engineered a schedule of contacts calculated to insure that his consultation would never probe the real issues.

... the next morning the consultant was surprised when, instead of the division chief, the latter's secretary came around to this hotel to welcome him. She brought a schedule of his appointments over the next five days that the division chief had prepared for him with exemplary efficiency. This program scheduled him in two-hourly blocks to meet with most of the unit heads of the entire department; but the list included very few of the line workers or even the supervisory staff of the division. The secretary hoped that the schedule would meet his approval and had a car outside to convey him to the head office of the department to begin his program. The consultant asked whether he could first meet with the division chief and discuss the schedule, because at first sight it did not seem to be the best way of utilizing his time. The secretary replied that her chief was busy on some urgent business that morning and would not be available till later that day for such a discussion.

Here is how the consultant viewed the situation he faced.

> ... this situation presented the consultant with a dilemma. Apparently,
> the division chief was defensive about his visit and was possibly avoid-
> ing him. There was nothing obviously wrong with the schedule except that
> it filled his time completely and left him little room to maneuver, as well
> as leading him mainly into the general field of forces in the department
> rather than into the internal affairs of the division that he had been called
> in to investigate. And yet it would obviously be rather rude to question
> the arrangements that had been so efficiently made on his behalf and
> that were being so obligingly pressed upon him by the charming girl who
> had been sent to guide him. To accept the arrangements graciously would
> calm the fears of the division chief, and perhaps there would be time
> later that day to discuss the program and negotiate its modification. On
> the other hand, it might be that the absent division chief would persist in
> being otherwise engaged—his own name did not appear on the interview-
> ing schedule until the fourth day! By then it might be too late to collect
> enough information about the division to make a valid assessment of its
> problems. Perhaps the price of being non-threatening was to accept a
> role of impotence.

Because the objective of the consultation seemingly was being thwarted, the consultant decided to take the bull by the horns. He shifted to a forceful confrontation
mode.

> ... the consultant asked the secretary where her chief was at the mo-
> ment. With some reluctance, she divulged that he was chairing a meeting
> of the unit chiefs of his division at one of their divisional office buildings
> on the outskirts of the city, several miles away from the headquarters of
> the department where the consultant's scheduled interviewees were await-
> ing him. The consultant then told her that he was sorry that he could not
> accept the schedule of interviews and asked her to drive him to the di-
> visional office and then to inform his interviewees at headquarters that
> he would see them at a later date. He dealt in a friendly but firm manner
> with her protests, and she took him to the divisional office.
>
> ... once there, he found out where the meeting was being held and, with-
> out more ado, marched into the room. To the consternation of the divi-
> sion chief, he interrupted the meeting; introduced himself to the as-
> sembled group; told them about his mission and about his mandate from
> the head of the department; and said that their meeting provided him
> with an unexpected and marvelous opportunity to meet immediately with
> the principal people whose views on the problems confronting the di-
> vision he was eager to obtain. He then said that if the division chief had
> no objection, he would like to pre-empt the meeting time to discuss these
> matters, since he had traveled several thousand miles to get there and
> had very little time available to reach the core of the situation. The divi-
> sion chief was obviously furious but could do nothing but meekly go

along with this *fait accompli;* and there followed two hours of explosive and illuminating discussion, which laid bare the fundamental problems of the division that underlay the request of the department head for consultation help.

This dramatic action on the part of the consultant initiated a process of rapid fact finding. He was able to overcome the initial authoritarian impression he had made on most of the staff when they became familiar with his style of conducting individual and group interviews. The division chief, however, not unnaturally, never completely warmed up to him, although by the end of the visit even he began to respect the competence and sincerity of the consultant and to realize that his worst fears about him were ill founded.

Such highhanded and defense-attacking coercive behavior should be an infrequent occurrence in this type of consultation, but a consultant should feel free to make use of it whenever the situation so demands. More frequent is the need to influence the staff of an institution to realize that although the latter may perhaps be correctly or incorrectly perceived as authoritarian and coercive, the consultant normally holds his power in reserve and conducts his business on the basis of a free interchange with staff, to whose needs he is sensitive and upon whose personal and professional rights he takes pains not to infringe, within the relatively wide range of latitude that his role usually affords him. Only if there is an obvious attempt to obstruct him or to manipulate him too far off course must he invoke his power. (Caplan, 1970, pp. 229–30)

Given that possibly the consultant did not identify and address the evident cooperation problem between the division chief and the department head, the other interesting aspect of his intervention relates to his zeal in getting these client members back on the track toward the mission's investigative goal. In effect, having been commissioned by the department head to pursue a specific investigation, this consultant, when push came to shove, produced his delegated baton of authority and prescriptively took over the division chief's meeting so as to make the most of his consultation time.

LARGER SOCIAL SYSTEM (P₅)

No published examples of larger-social-system prescriptive interventions are available. If any have been implemented, it is understandable that few clients of this magnitude would publicize the fact that they had required assistance in setting basic goals. In less fundamental yet more technical areas, nonetheless, there are a number of examples of prescriptive interventions into the functioning of larger social systems. Consultants may be brought in, for example, to evaluate telephone rates or to offer solutions to problems of public utilities, transportation networks, hospital services, and so on. In most of these cases the consultant's intervention is premised on expert knowledge and the client has opted for outside consultant services (versus developing autonomous competence) as an economical way of enlisting short- or medium-term technical advice, much of which relates to goals/objectives. These kinds of consultation, while in the prescriptive mode, are more akin to contracting for the delivery of a service and are not further dealt with here.

REFERENCES

Brooks, B. D. "Contingency Contracts with Truants." *Personnel and Guidance Journal* 52, no. 5 (1974): 316–20. Reprinted by permission.

Caplan, G. *The Theory and Practice of Mental Health Consultation.* New York: Basic Books, 1970. Copyright © 1970 by Basic Books, Inc., Publishers, New York. Reprinted by permission of Basic Books and Tavistock Publications Ltd., London.

Higdon, H. *The Business Healers.* New York: Random House, 1969. Reprinted by permission.

Janis, I. *Victims of Groupthink: A Psychological Study of Foreign-Policy Decisions and Fiascoes.* Boston: Houghton Mifflin, 1972.

Johnson, N. J. A. "Precision Teaching: A Key to the Future." In R. Karen, *An Introduction to Behavior Theory and Its Applications.* New York: Harper and Row, 1974, pp. 418–19. Reprinted by permission.

Karen, R. *An Introduction to Behavior Theory and Its Applications.* New York: Harper & Row, 1974.

Steele, F. E. "Consultants and Detectives." Reproduced by special permission from *Journal of Applied Behavioral Science* 5, no. 2 (1969): 187–202.

25

SUMMARY
AND
IMPLICATIONS

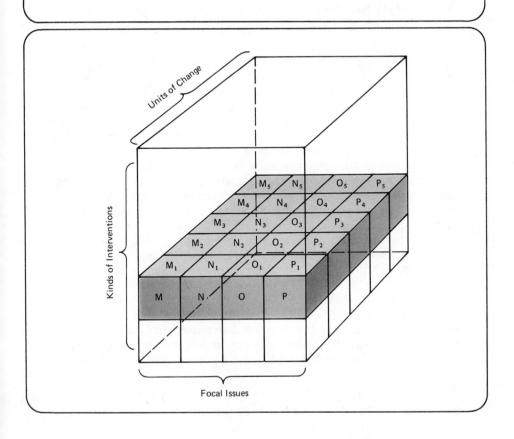

Prescription is an intervention strategy in which the consultant explicitly tells the client what to do to solve his or her problem. Collaboration between consultant and client is based on the assumptions inherent in the authority-obedience model: the consultant exercises authority and the client is expected to comply with the recommendations given. Some prescriptive approaches include built-in arrangements to eliminate or at least reduce the likelihood of client noncompliance. One such arrangement is a strict adherence to confidentiality, more stringent than simply rendering anonymity as in a catalytic approach. Drucker, who has not written about how he works with a client, indicates that he has no "strategies of consultation" but one guideline: he "considers *everything* pertaining to consulting work confidential and not to be discussed or disclosed" (Drucker, personal correspondence dated February 28, 1975).

Prescriptive approaches appear to be most commonly employed in connection with behavior problems involving self-doubt and lost confidence. They are also used to resolve situations that are not presently being addressed by the client (or cannot be, given the technical and other resources available to the client). Other applications include crisis situations, and instances when the client is at "wit's end" or has thrown up his hands in despair.

Jaques (1961) has identified certain weaknesses more or less inherent in the prescriptive approach.

> The very nature of the therapeutic role, however, often makes real collaboration difficult. The situation is often encountered where the social scientist is called in and given a complete mandate to "set things right." Too frequently, such a mandate may represent an unconscious defeatist attitude on the part of the group concerned, with an underlying and understandable desire to evade, if possible, the responsibility for facing up to a complex and unpleasant situation. Because the solution of the problem may seem relatively simple there is a great temptation for the social scientist to jump in and take the responsibility "just for a short time." Having taken full responsibility on his shoulders, however, he will to a greater or lesser degree have precluded the possibility of the group itself developing new roles which would allow them to cope with their own problems by themselves. Thus, although he may clear up the problem, any thanks he receives may be given rather grudgingly, for he will presumably have exposed the inadequacies of the persons concerned without helping them towards new insights and self-reliance. Under these conditions further work is unlikely, and the project may suddenly come to a halt. On the other hand, he may fail with the task, in which case he will likely be left with the blame on his own shoulders for all the previous mistakes and results of mismanagement, and ill effects of which may be displaced and projected in his direction. (Jacques, 1961, pp. 163–64)

For an illustration of the pertinence of Jaques' statement you may refer back to the example in Chapter 24 of a corporate president's "accepting the solution but rejecting the consultant." Such reactions to prescriptive consultation have led many consultants to seek a basis of collaboration with their clients. However, the most common alternative—the catalytic approach—while "solving" the rejection problem may create others, as has already been indicated.

The success of a prescriptive intervention is dependent not only on the degree to which the client is helped to solve the immediate problem, but also on the client's ability to incorporate and self-maintain the pertinent improvements introduced during the period of consultation. Failure to maintain improvements illustrates the disadvantages associated with "behavioral doctoring"—i.e., the client does not necessarily become more effective in his own right simply by having answers handed to him. He is not learning how to solve problems; he is only acting under problem-solving instructions. He may become even less sure of himself than before. A dependency situation is created when a client surrenders his self-will and accepts that of a consultant; he may turn to the consultant whenever stumped or whenever there is disagreement between himself and colleagues as to the soundness of any given course of action. In other words, the "cure" could, over the long term, be more damaging than the symptoms or illness it was intended to correct.

REFERENCES

Jaques, E. "Social Therapy: Technocracy or Collaboration?" In W. G. Bennis, K. D. Benne, and R. Chin, eds., *The Planning of Change*. New York: Holt, Rinehart and Winston, 1961, pp. 163–64. Copyright © 1947 by *The Journal of Social Issues*. Reprinted by permission.

THEORY-PRINCIPLES
INTERVENTIONS

26

THEORY-PRINCIPLES INTERVENTIONS: AN INTRODUCTION

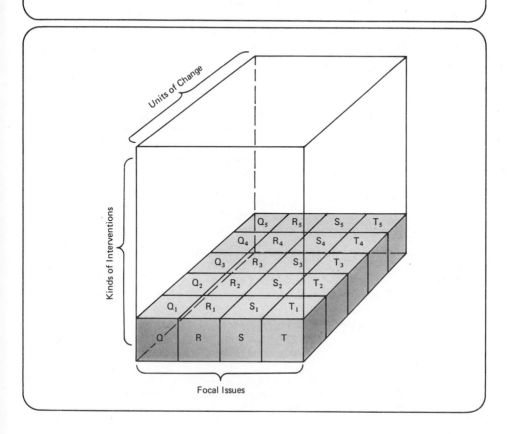

Once consultants realized that theory could be taught to clients, who in turn could use such systematic insights to phase out their own self-defeating cycles, a significant new area of intervention was identified. In other words, a client could be aided through theory-based interventions to comprehend *and* shift the cause-and-effect variables operating in his or her situation. More aware, in terms of theory, of what causes things to be as they are, the client can predict consequences to be expected from whatever specific changes he or she anticipates implementing.

THE THEORY SPECTRUM

Theory-based consultation should not be confused with interventions in which the consultant uses theory solely to guide himself or herself during interaction with the client. A purely prescriptive consultant, for example, neither reveals to the client nor helps the client acquire the systematic insights which he, the consultant, relies upon to guide intervention strategy.

As used in everyday conversation the word "theory" has little to do with theory as used in theory-based consultation. When someone says, "I've got a theory about that . . . ," he may only mean he's got a hunch or that he's playing an angle. Or a person might develop an abstract philosophical doctrine that he describes by saying, "That's my theory. . . ." In both cases the word "theory" is not being used in any sense comparable with its meaning in experimental work or when employed to describe theory-based interventions. Theory, in the behavioral-science sense, is quite different.

The Theory Spectrum shown in Table 26.1 helps in sorting out what theory does and does not mean. On the left side are found nontheoretical bases of action, including trial and error, hunch and intuition. Toward the middle of the Spectrum are commonsense explanations, accounts of what's happening which "make sense in empirical terms." Another degree nearer the theory end are attitudes, beliefs, and convictions. These are often unstated propositions people act upon when deciding

Table 26.1
The theory spectrum

Nontheoretical basis for action	Subjective or empirical explanations				Theoretical basis for action
Trial and error Hunch and intuition	Common-sense expla-nations	Attitudes, beliefs, and con-victions	Cognitive maps and conceptual systems	Plans and planning	Theory expressed in the form of explicit hypotheses that can be tested

Source: R. R. Blake and J. S. Mouton, *Corporate Excellence through Grid Organization Development* (Houston: Gulf Publishing Company, 1968), p. 283.

what to do or not to do to solve given situations. Such attitudes, beliefs, and convictions are based upon accumulated personal experiences and, as practical guides to action, may never have been checked out in an empirical sense.

Another degree nearer the Spectrum's theory end are *cognitive maps* and *conceptual systems*. A cognitive map is a provisional picture that a person creates to explain to himself or to others the character of a problem and approaches to its solution. Such a map is likely to be a complex of commonsense explanations, subjective attitudes, beliefs and convictions, all of which, when put together, are expected to match the real problem in intellectual terms. A cognitive map for a complex problem sometimes has an empirical resemblance to the early New World maps produced after Columbus' voyage. Although these maps bore some correspondence to the shoreline of the east coast of America, their accuracy was insufficient to describe the actual lay of the land and therefore to serve as a sound basis for navigation.

Also close to theory, but still not meeting criteria of a genuine theory-based approach, is a conceptual system, the set of ideas a person uses to account for things. Harrison (1969) has explained the importance of conceptual systems in supporting effective problem solving.

Let us consider how we understand the world we live in, and particularly those parts of it concerning ourselves and our relations with other people. First of all, we organize the world according to *concepts,* or categories. We say that things are warm or cold; good or bad; simple or complex. Each of these concepts may be considered a dimension along which we can place events in the world—some closer to one end of the dimension, some closer to the other.

Actually, we can't really think without using these categories or dimensions to organize our thoughts. Any time we consider the qualities of ourselves, other persons, or events in the inanimate world, we have to use categories to do it. We are dependent for our understanding of the world on the concepts and categories we have for organizing our experiences. If we lack a concept for something which occurs in the world, we either have to invent one or we cannot respond to the event in an organized fashion. How, for example, would a person explain his own and others' behavior without the concept of love and hate? Think how much behavior would simply puzzle or confuse him or, perhaps, just go by without really being perceived at all, for lack of this one dimension.

Concepts do not exist in isolation; they are connected to one another by a network of relationships. Taken all together, the concepts we use to understand a situation, plus the relationships among the concepts, are called a *conceptual system.* For example, we may say, "People who are warm and friendly are usually trusting, and hence, they are often deceived by others." Here we have a conceptual system linking the concepts of *friendly warmth, trust in others,* and *ease of deception.* Because concepts are linked one to another, the location of an event on one concept usually implies something about where the event is located on each of a whole network of concepts. It is thus almost impossible to take in a small bit of information about a characteristic of a person or event without its having a whole host of implications about other characteristics. (Harrison, 1969, p. 65)

Planning and operational blueprints represent still another degree of precision approaching the theory end of the Spectrum. This is particularly so when plans are created from data that forecast the future rather than simply being projections of the past with corrections introduced for rates of change. Such plans represent educated guesses geared to predict specific situations. Although they can be very useful, they are not theory.

Behavioral-science theories are something more than cognitive maps or a conceptual system in the sense Harrison uses that term. A theory is a specific set of explicit statements as to what will or will not occur, predictions that can be tested in action under particular conditions. The degree of accuracy with which such predictions can be made is subject to experimental postevaluation with prior confidence in the prediction expressed in statistical terms. Sometimes referred to as hypotheses, sometimes, less accurately, as axioms or principles, these statements provide the client a basis for evaluating actions in terms of their soundness. Once the client has learned theories and knows how to employ them in concrete situations he or she no longer has to rely solely on intuition or hunch, commonsense, or his or her own subjective conceptual system.

Some consultants reject theory as of little or no use in guiding behavior. Kingsbury (1972) provides an apt description of the "anti" point of view regarding those positions on the Spectrum tending toward the theory end of the continuum.

In the past, I have been more strongly committed than I am now to the idea that it is important for a person to talk through his experiences in a group in order to develop cognitive clarity and a personal theory about the meaning of the experiences he has. Recently, however, I have found myself suspecting that some pretty good things were being talked to death, and that an experience which involved the whole person—mind and body, head and heart, reason and emotion—became so intellectualized that the feeling component of the insight was dulled or lost; the reality, intensity and, I have suspected, the transferability of the insight to other situations was drained away.

Perhaps all I am doing is criticizing the state of the science, but I think something more than that is going on—something that has to do with the denial of the reality of feeling on the irrational ground that is not rational. A lot of "objective" research published in the field of applied behavioral science has the quality of talking valid experience to death. The notion that reason and emotions are mutually exclusive pervades our society. I want reason and emotion unified in my own behavior and experience, and I want to do something better than I know how to do now with these issues in the groups I lead. (Kingsbury, 1972, pp. 111, 112)

In preference to theory-based interventions Kingsbury seems to favor an acceptant orientation, where emotions are felt and expressed as the necessary and sufficient basis for development of new skills or for breaking out of self-defeating cycles.

By comparison, McGregor (1967) points to the contribution that theory can make in fostering development.

> The basic point is that some knowledge of existing theory can guide a group engaged in self-development, not alone by the discussion it provokes but by providing generalizations to be tested by the group both in selecting the strategies it uses for carrying out its primary tasks and in attempting to improve group maintenance. (McGregor, 1967, p. 179)

The theory end of the Spectrum identifies circumstances in which cause-and-effect relationships between action and reaction can be specified. Thus the consequences of any given action can be predicted with a relatively high degree of accuracy. Such theory derives from experiments and field research, mostly in the behavioral sciences. Kingsbury's "complaint" notwithstanding, this kind of theory has reached a degree of sophistication such that predictions can be quite reliable as well as being demonstrative and pertinent.

Theory-based interventions engage a consultant in those activities necessary to assist a client in acquiring a theory basis for governing individual action. The client is freed from blind reliance on common sense and conventional wisdom and is enabled to see situations more objectively by avoiding the distortions that subjective attitudes, beliefs, and untested convictions can produce. Plans and planning can be helpful, but unfortunately they frequently are premised on pragmatic concerns only, with insufficient regard for theory. When tested theory is relied upon, actions can be taken with the expectation that the anticipated consequences will, in fact, occur.

INTELLECTUAL VERSUS EMOTIONAL PROBLEMS

A common reaction to theory interventions as voiced by Kingsbury and others is that, although they might contribute to the solution of intellectual problems, they would not be pertinent for the handling of emotion-based difficulties. However, since ideas and emotions are simultaneous aspects of experience rather than different processes, theory can apply equally to both. For example,

> Sometimes facts are not enough because the problem is not one of fact. It may lie in the emotional attitudes of two persons toward one another which result in stereotypical thinking, persuasive argument, not listening, reacting defensively, closed mind attitudes, and so on. When barriers are present which prevent the use of fact to solve problems the 9,9 approach is to get directly to the cause of the barriers. Then solution of the conflict is to face the emotions that are beneath the surfaces, examine them objectively, and probe for causes beneath them. In order to do this people must be committed to revealing their reactions of frustration, the reasons

they feel misunderstood, and the ways in which their expectations or aspi-rations have been violated. Equally, they must be prepared to identify and to face up to the inherent limitations of competence which may be preventing them from making an effective contribution rather than to cover up or to pass the buck. When this kind of genuine behavior which can only be based upon open and unobstructed communication is achieved, the conditions are right for the surface problems causing dis-agreement to be resolved. When these highly personal attitudes can be forthrightly identified and discussed, presumed injustices and misunder-standings can be cleared up and genuine injustices and misunderstand-ings rectified. This way of confronting the emotions of disagreement and conflict provides a key for the creative resolution of conflict. (Blake and Mouton, 1968, pp. 24–25)

The power of theory to direct technological change is unquestioned. The same is true for biological applications as evidenced in the dramatic strides in medicine that have occurred during the past hundred years. Behavioral theories per se have been clarified for only a hundred or so years, but already they have proved powerful in increasing behavioral efficacy.

HOW CAN THEORY BE MADE USABLE?

The development of theories pertinent for solving everyday kinds of problems blos-somed after World War II as academicians, researchers, and practitioners alike began to learn how to teach theories for problem-solving purposes. What caused this shift towards the actual *use* of theory? There are many explanations, including the following.

1. Techniques for "internalization" of theory. In ordinary classroom learning the teacher may tell a student how things should be while giving little insight as to how the desired conditions can be achieved. The post–World War II differ-ence is a distinction between theory taught in the abstract and theory learned by the client and internalized for personal use and guidance. Internalization permits the client to actually apply the theory to given situations he or she en-counters and thus to test such theories against more characteristic ways of think-ing—trial and error, hunch and intuition, etc. In this way poor mental practices can be replaced with better ones.

2. Strategies for helping a client understand theory sufficiently to be able to apply it in given situations are different from traditional classroom methods. These learning strategies involve several fairly basic steps. The following are quite widely employed by theory-oriented consultants in assisting clients to shift their thinking to a theoretical basis.

Step 1.   The client is presented with some kind of typical situation that he or others for whom he is responsible are likely to meet in daily activities. His reaction, either written or acted out, is called for. Such reactions define his natural bent. This activity is completed *before* any theory is introduced.

Step 2.   The client then studies pertinent theories of behavior, either through a textbook or lecture approach, by the use of audio cassettes, or by viewing a movie that introduces the theoretical orientation. Questions and test examples are provided which enable the client to check out how well he understands the theory.

Step 3.   The client participates in simulated problem situations where "best" solutions can be reached by using theories learned in Step 2.

Step 4.   Postsimulation critiques enable the client to evaluate the degree to which he understood the theories and how well he was able to use them. These critiques also help him to identify any inaccurate assumptions he may have made and any limitations in the theory itself.

Step 5.   Through an additional series of simulations the client is repeatedly provided the opportunity to compare his natural bent for dealing with situations against theoretical specifications. By such self-confrontations the client comes to understand theory in a personally useful way and recognizes the extent to which his second-nature assumptions take over when he is pressured to act. Confidence is built and the client comes to appreciate that he *does* know how to use theory in an effective manner.

Step 6.   When theories have been internalized, further skill practice is provided to enable the client to perfect his capacity to identify and execute the actions and practices the theory requires for breaking self-defeating cycles.

Step 7.   Theory is then employed by the client to reevaluate how he now solves problems in comparison with the natural inclination revealed in Step 1. He again responds to the Step 1 circumstances, this time with theory-based actions.

Step 8.   Generalizations regarding his natural bent are further clarified and differentiated to prevent the client from slipping into habitual ways of responding. This further equips the client for approaching situations that can be handled from a theory-based perspective.

Step 9.   Consultant support and implementation for using a theory-based approach on the job or in social or personal situations is available to assist the changeover from the left side of the Theory Spectrum towards a theory-based approach to problem solving.

Though educational tactics vary from case to case, these steps are as useful with a team, an organization, or a larger social system as with an individual client. A successful theory intervention is likely to include each of these basic steps. Many theory-based approaches, however, bypass significant elements of this internalization process with the result that the theory is rejected by the client because he or she has not experienced its practicality.

WHY THEORY IS A USEFUL INTERVENTION

Science-based theories and principles are fundamental for assisting a changeover from current practices to a more systematic way of doing things. There are a number of reasons why behavioral approaches to management provide such a powerful basis for changing behavior. First, theories are written out and thus are open to public examination. They are objective in the sense of being subject to external proof and are testable for their validity in predicting consequences, not only against research and experimental evidence but in personal terms as well. In other words, they derive authority from a demonstrated utility.

As compared to other interventional approaches, clients engaged in theory-based learning use these theory-based models to observe their own conduct instead of engaging in intuition-oriented or one-to-one exchanges, whether based on acceptant, catalytic, confrontational, or prescriptive approaches. Theory, then, can aid behavior change in a number of ways.

Values.   Theory, with its explicit formulations, brings individuals face to face with their subjective values. What each thinks is right, sound, and valid for relating to subordinates, colleagues, and bosses is subject to common sharing and review.

Defensiveness.   Defensiveness ceases to serve any functional purpose when a person can see and understand that what he or she previously accepted as "right" or "sound" or "valid" is actually untenable. Theory-based understanding of personal modes of managing and their consequences eliminates defensiveness.

Perspective.   Theory provides individuals a social microscope for viewing the present as well as a social telescope for seeing how the past and possible future is affecting here-and-now behavior. Managers are motivated to think through not only short-term consequences but the longer-term implications of various courses of action, an effective curb on impulsive actions and their possibly negative effects.

Communication.   Theory-based language facilitates dialogue between individuals and their subordinates, colleagues, and bosses as to the best approaches for getting results.

Motivation.   Theory specifies the terms of a model of excellence that the individual can aspire to.

Creativity.   Theory helps people to be more curious about what they observe and therefore more imaginative in pursuing creative solutions to managerial problems.

Autonomy.   Theory increases an individual's capacity for self-direction. It is less necessary to consult with others because a person can consult with himself or herself as to the implications of various actions being considered.

The above are general statements as to why theory is an important basis of intervention. But not all theories are of equal significance. Some are overly simple in the sense that so few categories are used that dissimilar behaviors are artificially grouped together and therefore predictive value is severely limited. Others are so overelaborate that people lose their way in attempting to understand them and, as a result, dismiss theory as academic and therefore irrelevant. Still others, although called theories, are little more than philosophical speculation as to the nature of man.

SUMMARY

The key difference between academic theory and theory for use in problem solving is not in the concepts but in the teaching methodology. The methodology used to communicate theories for utilization helps the client internalize the concepts, evaluate them against his or her natural bents, and thereafter do two things: (1) reject natural inclinations when they are inconsistent with sound behavior, and (2) practice theory-indicated sounder behaviors in order to ensure these can be employed with confidence.

The Theory Spectrum is an aid to distinguishing the meaning of theory as employed in a consultation context. Trial and error, and hunch and intuition clearly do not involve the use of theory. Often confused with theory are subjective or empirical explanations that are little more than commonsense explanations; or reported attitudes, beliefs, and convictions intended to account for behavior. Conceptual systems or cognitive maps are more elaborate ideas that clients put together to guide their behavior or as the basis for explaining differences between the actions of people facing essentially the same situation.

Plans and planning are also examples at the empirical level, but here for the first time can be seen an emphasis on anticipating the future consequences of present actions. Thus plans and planning are calculated to anticipate consequences that are wanted and to provide a basis for taking actions that will permit those consequences to be reached.

The theory end of the Spectrum is represented by systematic behavioral-science formulations of the sort that have been experimentally determined to have significant implications for predicting the consequences of behavior. They have emerged from extensive behavioral-science research concerned with power/authority, morale/cohesion, norms/standards, and goals/objectives. Once the client has learned these theories, has tested his or her natural bents against them, and has learned to not only reject natural-bent activities that lead to difficulties but also to strengthen his or her use of theory as the basis for determining action, the theory-based intervention has had its effect. The client is now able to make the shift to a systematic theory-based set of orientations that explain and give predictive value to behavior.

REFERENCES

Blake, R. R., and J. S. Mouton. *Corporate Excellence through Grid Organization Development*. Houston: Gulf Publishing Company, 1968. Copyright © 1968 by Gulf Publishing Company, Houston, Texas. Used with permission.

Harrison, R. "Defenses and the Need to Know." In W. B. Eddy, W. W. Burke, V. A. Dupre, and O. P. South, eds., *Behavioral Science and the Manager's Role*. Washington, D.C.: NTL Institute for Applied Behavioral Science, 1969, pp. 64–70. Reprinted by permission.

Kingsbury, S. "Dilemmas for the Trainer." From W. Dyer, ed., *Modern Theory and Method in Group Training*, pp. 107–115. © 1972 by Litton Educational Publishing, Inc. Reprinted by permission of Van Nostrand Reinhold Company.

McGregor, D. *The Professional Manager*. New York: McGraw-Hill, 1967.

THEORY-PRINCIPLES INTERVENTIONS

27

POWER/AUTHORITY

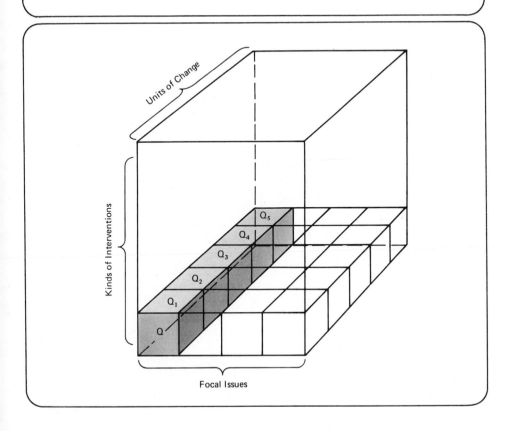

Units of Change

Kinds of Interventions

Q_5

Q_4

Q_3

Q_2

Q_1

Q

Focal Issues

A number of behavioral-science theories deal with power/authority as a central concept. As yet, however, there are only a few published examples of theory interventions where the consultant's objective was to aid the client to internalize a pertinent theory and then apply it to his or her own situation.

INDIVIDUAL (Q₁)

Though power/authority can only be exercised on others, the individual-as-client can be engaged in self-examination as to his or her own assumptions about using power/authority. Many interventions are of this character.

The Managerial Grid® (Blake and Mouton, 1964) contains a set of contrasting theories that enable an individual to gain insight into his or her own power/authority dynamics. The intervention involves the client first in describing his or her managerial behavior in boss-subordinate situations. The individual then studies the Managerial Grid and gains insight into the systematic issues it clarifies. This is first accomplished through reading, but recurs later in an organized seminar situation where participants, through intensive team interactions, have an opportunity to

Figure 27.1
The Grid®

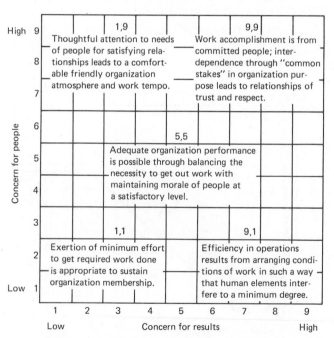

Source: *The Managerial Grid*, R.R. Blake and J.S. Mouton, p. 10.
Copyright © 1964 by Gulf Publishing Company, Houston, Texas.
Reprinted by permission.

see one another's Grid styles. In a final period of activity participants feed back observations on one another's Grid styles by preparing paragraph descriptions, systematically oriented to the Grid, of evidenced behavior. These paragraph descriptions of each individual serve as the basis for aiding participants to carry through their self-examination to meaningful conclusions.

The Managerial Grid, then, provides a framework (Fig. 27.1) for comparative thinking about alternative approaches to management and supervision. It identifies thirteen such theories that are being used in organizations today. Five of these theories—9,1; 1,9; 1,1; 5,5; and 9,9—are "basic." The eight additional possibilities are 9,5 "benevolent autocrat"; 5,9 "consultative"; and combinations such as blended 9,1/1,9 "paternalism," 9,1–1,9 to-and-fro "wide-arc pendulum," intermittent 9,1 line-1,9 staff "counterbalancing," the splitting "two-hat" approach, the 9,1–1,1 "win-leave cycle," and the reactive-around-the-Grid "statistical 5,5."

How a boss deals with a subordinate is very much determined by his or her mode of responding when conflicting ideas are present from a Grid angle. The 9,1 method of conflict resolution is suppression; 1,9 involves smoothing over the differences. 1,1 entails withdrawing into neutrality. 5,5 on the other hand is an effort to encompass the difference through accommodation and compromise on a "half loaf is better than none" basis. The 9,9 approach is to confront the difference by exploring reservations and doubts and by reviewing the facts, data, and logic bases of the difference. The 9,9 mode of confrontation may involve bringing to the surface and working through any underlying emotional tensions that exist between a boss and a subordinate, thereby restoring a functional problem-solving relationship.

One way of evaluating the impact of the Grid intervention is in terms of quantitative studies regarding what participants themselves report to have been the impact of this kind of self-examination.

By the way of summary, the frequency of reactions emphasizing the need for a genuine self-reappraisal is presented in Table 1. These data are based on our judgments of what people said in the post six-month interviews.

It is seen in Table 1 that *all* participants initiated a self-reappraisal in some degree. An indication of what is meant by *Some Self-Reappraisal* in comparison with *Searching Self-Reappraisal* can be seen from the following quotations.

A typical personal reaction placed in the category, *Some Self-Reappraisal,* follows:

"I can't say that I have changed much. At least I haven't modified my approach to people and their ideas too far. I have not shifted away from the direction in which I was already operating. However, I do think I have changed in degree. I am doing a better job now than I was doing previously. I feel more confident that I am on the right track. Therefore, I am working more diligently to increase my skill, but I'm moving in the same direction."

An example of self-reappraisal which is in the *Searching Self-Reappraisal* category is as follows:

"After I got rocked and knocked on my heels a half dozen times at the laboratory and had spent two sleepless nights, I decided that something was basically wrong. A serious, deep review of my own performance was in order: I spent considerable thought afterward in reviewing what I had heard about my own approach and attitudes during the laboratory. I looked into each of the major areas where it seemed to me important suggestions had been made. I set a concrete plan of personal improvement for myself. As a result I have been able to keep constant check on my own progress. While I feel I have not come too far, I remain convinced that it is possible for me to change. I intend to continue my effort."

Another reaction is typical of those categorized as making a *Searching Self-Reappraisal*. This person remarked,

"I continuously use stored-up bits of information gleaned from the laboratory to appraise myself. I do this in terms of trying to understand why I am not so effective in certain situations. I keep in view the question, 'How, through better understanding, might I make a more adequate contribution?' It seems I have been able to make some progress up to this time."

The general conclusion drawn from these reactions is that a widespread self-reappraisal may or may not have contributed to actual increased effectiveness. This question also was explored.

Table 1
The degree of self-reappraisal produced by the laboratory

Initiated no self-reappraisal of my personal behavior	Initiated some self-reappraisal of my personal behavior	Initiated a searching self-reappraisal of my personal behavior
Percent * reporting 0	40	60

Changes in managerial effectiveness after the laboratory as judged by interviewers		
Less effective	No significant change	More effective
Percent reporting 7	20	73

*For ease of reading, in all tables absolute numbers have been converted to percents.
(Blake and Mouton, 1963a, pp. 54–55)

Basic to understanding such changes are altered views of conflict and how best to deal with it. The 9,9 way of dealing with conflict, as already indicated, involves confronting the differences and working them through.

Table 2 reflects our summary of trends observed in interviews with respect to the significance of managing situational conflict.

From Table 2, it is apparent that one of the areas where significant rethinking took place associated directly with the laboratory, is with respect to managing conflict. The two individuals who pointed to *No Change* in thinking about conflict both reported that their characteristic way of dealing with it always was to *confront* it and, in effect, they learned nothing new. For the others, however, the trend of change is in the direction of *confronting* conflict and working it through. Eighty-six percent indicate significant shifts in their attitudes toward situational conflict have taken place.

It is increasingly apparent that conflict is a pivotal area upon which managerial effectiveness hinges. Increased skills in many areas of integrating people into production through making better use of their ideas are readily developed once individuals who work together have learned to understand and to deal effectively with conflict.

Table 2

Significance of understanding situation conflict
and "working it through"

Dealing with situational conflict has become *less* important in my thinking	No change	Dealing with situational conflict has become *more* important in my thinking
Percent reporting 0	14	86

(Blake and Mouton, 1963b, pp. 40–42)

Still another indication of the importance of conflict in solving power/authority issues is provided, in this case through the self-report of an engineer.

The managerial grid seminar taught me that avoiding conflict was one of my most serious management weaknesses, and if I was ever going to be effective as a manager, I'd have to overcome the problem. After the seminar was over, I put what I had learned about myself to work on one of the production men I had to interface with.

My engineering group had designed a semi-conductor, and we had tried to get the production man to agree to be responsible for a particular rate or a particular yield. The second or third day after production started he didn't meet his goals. So he said, "Well the engineer didn't support me." I asked him why he didn't resolve it at the open meeting. He said that he had but that he didn't get the full commitment. So I let it ride for about a week, until I was hearing in the halls that my engineers were dumb. I attended the next meeting and listened to everybody being very polite for about an hour.

The Chairman adjourned the meeting, but I locked the door before anyone could get out and said that I thought there was something we ought
to get out in the open because it was hurting our performance. I said I
wanted the production man to tell my engineer to his face that he was
dumb, so we could see what he had to say about it. The production man
got red in the face and said, "Well I didn't really mean it that way."

"On the other hand," I told the production man, "the maintenance man
here says that you're a dummy. Now why aren't you guys talking to each
other?"

One man said, "Well, everytime I come over to your group, I don't get any
service." And my man got mad and said, "The hell you don't; every time
I give you what you want." This went on for three hours.

Underlying causes were revealed that showed why none of the groups
were functioning as a team. (Frampton, 1973, pp. 76, 78)

Another approach to consultation with individual managers uses two decision-
making models that provide for alternative degrees of subordinate participation in
a manager's decision. As described by Vroom and Yetton (1973) the theory focuses
on power as the central issue; that is, whether the boss uses his or her own power
to make a decision independently or whether and under what conditions others are
involved. Model A is economical in the use of time and minimizes participation;
Model B allows for maximum participation while placing no weight on time con-
sumed. A manager's judgment of a given situation will determine the model used.
If decision quality is all important the boss must decide if he or she has sufficient
information or if the information of others is required before a decision can be
reached. Or if acceptability is all important, those who must implement the decision
may be invited in to help decide. Intermediate degrees of quality/acceptability judgmental weightings by the boss can be matched by intermediate degrees of fusion or
compromise between the "one alone" and "total delegation" alternatives.

In the intervention itself (Vroom and Yetton, 1973, pp. 155–81), part of the
model is introduced and then participants indicate how they would handle thirty
typical managerial dilemmas. An example follows.

"Sharply decreasing profits for the firm have resulted in a directive from
top management that makes it impossible to take on any new personnel
even to replace those who leave. Shortly after this directive is issued, one
of your five subordinates resigns to take a job with another firm. Your
problem is how to rearrange the work assignments among the remaining
four subordinates without reducing the total productivity of the group."
(Vroom and Yetton, 1973, p. 14)

By using a series of eight criteria the client evaluates the best way to go about making a decision regarding standardized situations. Examples of criteria employed are:
Does the boss have sufficient information, or will subordinates accept the boss's
decision and implement it well? Feedback is provided via a computer printout that

contrasts each client's handling of the dilemmas with his colleagues' and with the solutions recommended by the consultants. The model of decision quality/acceptance is close to a theory-based exposition for it provides an ordered framework for thinking. The client is helped to internalize the framework as a basis for predicting the consequences of actions taken, as well as for comparing his natural bent with the requirements of "good management" as conceived by Vroom and Yetton and built into their model.

Transactional analysis, derived from psychoanalytic theory, is a theory-principles intervention at the individual level. Its underlying premise is that each person has three basic yet alternative orientations that may operate upon him as he interrelates with others. One of these orientations is referred to as Parent. The Parent aspect is that of judgmental "should" and "shouldn't" attitudes that typify evaluations of self and others.

A second orientation, the Adult, comprises a problem-solving attitude for dealing with situations encountered in the process of everyday living. The attitude is based on empirical data and proceeds on the assumption that problems individuals encounter are amenable to solution.

The third orientation of transactional analysis is referred to as Child. The Child orientation involves spontaneity, impulsiveness, and, more generally speaking, reactions that are emotionally rooted.

When any two individuals interact both may be operating from the Parent orientation, or both may be responding from the Adult orientation, or from their respective Child's. These are "complementary" transactions, as are situations in which one person is communicating as Parent and the other as Child—in other words, the "lines" between the two persons' orientations do not "cross." Unsymmetrical "crossed" transactions can lead to significant difficulties. Certain consequences follow, depending on which of the three orientations is being employed momentarily by each person.

Transactional analysis as a consultation-based intervention can be approached in a number of different ways. Using it as a basis of self-examination an individual can indicate what his characteristic response would be to certain described situations and then compare these reactions with the theoretical model of transactional analysis. In a third step the individual can be helped to gain insight into the kinds of behavior he "naturally" displays as compared with the kinds of behavior, defined according to transactional analysis, that would be a more effective basis for mature adjustment.

Transactional analysis was originated by Berne (1961) and has been popularized through the work of Harris (1967) and others. Jongeward (1973) provides a series of exercises designed to aid an individual to engage in this kind of self-examination.

Once an individual has learned the basic orientations of transactional analysis and the resulting interactions, he has available a systematic framework through which to view situations as they happen. In this manner he is afforded the opportunity to become a consultant to himself by asking such questions as, "How does the transactional analysis theory apply in this situation and what are my options for converting this interaction into an improved situation?"

Another consultant, Blansfield, describes his use of transactional analysis as a theory intervention with individuals.

> In beginning a program using transactional analysis, I usually explain that I am proposing a more structured beginning methodology than group members may have anticipated. I say that, with their concurrence, I will teach them something about a rather new psychiatric theory and ask them to use this lesson for self-analysis and reporting, and that we will then pursue whatever course the group wishes. At this point I always ask for expressions of feeling about the proposals. It seems very important to uncover feelings of resistance to the intervention and to explore them until the whole group selects another beginning methodology or the resistance is overcome. The possibility that one or more members of the group will withdraw has not occurred in my experience to date. (By the beginning of 1969 I had used this methodology with at least twenty-five groups over a four-year period. Groups of mixed sex and professional background, averaging twelve per group, met usually for a week.) The groups to which I have proposed this approach have generally been enthusiastic about trying something new. Our verbal contract has always contained the clear understanding that during the process group members may ask questions or express resistance. Perhaps four persons of some three hundred have actually done so. Questions arise almost exclusively about Berne's theory, not its use in the group.
>
> I next informally poll the group to confirm that we agree about our immediate methodology. If we do, we proceed to a simplified presentation of the theory, a lecture-dialogue that usually lasts about three hours. I try to cover the information and characteristics of the three ego states, their functioning, and the concepts of age fixation in the Child, executive power, contamination, and decommissioning. Berne's theory of transactions is not referred to at this point; it is dealt with later if appropriate. In this initial phase, I try to convey only enough about transactional analysis to enable each participant to describe himself in terms of his understanding of the theory. Nor do I deal extensively at this point with psychopathology or pathogenesis, for the populations I work with are relatively stable and self-selecting and want increased insight and understanding, not psychotherapy. An early emphasis on neurosis or psychosis might cause them to conceal data they viewed as excessively deviant from group norms. (Blansfield, 1972, pp. 150–51)

Blansfield comments, in conclusion, that his theory-based interventions with individuals are "concerned with organized self-understanding and, where appropriate and possible, with the alleviation of nonfunctional behavior."

The theory approaches described here are among the most widely employed for helping an individual gain insights into how he subjectively perceives his behavior. Though other people may be drawn into the discussions and may offer feedback to help the client clarify his thoughts, the theory intervention focuses on individual examination of personal attitudes toward utilizing power/authority. Other equally pertinent theories are not introduced at this time because examples of their use at the individual level are lacking. Among the most important, however, are McGregor's Theories X and Y, to be introduced in the next section.

GROUP (Q₂)

Theory/principles interventions have also been used in group settings to enable several interacting people to pursue some shared objective. Here the issue of power/authority often is central because in organized groups, such as found in an industrial setting, the real boss and his or her actual subordinates compose the study group.

The general strategy of interventions using a theory/principles approach is to involve participants first in learning the theory/principles (as discussed in Chapter 26) and then in utilizing these theories to diagnose, evaluate, and eventually shift their own bases of interaction. In team building using the Grid as the theory basis of intervention participants first engage in self-examination through Phase 1 Seminar participation. Thereafter, when each of the individual members of the team have acquired this basic understanding, they convene for the purpose of studying their own interactions.

Although this study covers the entire range of variables, including power/authority, morale/cohesion, norms/standards, and goals/objectives, a central part of it is concentrated upon the power/authority issues. A client's self-description of the impact of Grid-based team building is provided by the president of a company.

Work Team Development

The next step was Phase II. These are work team seminars of three days or more as necessary. Our first Phase II involved myself, the executive vice president, vice president for finance, vice president and corporate secretary, vice president for marketing, corporate controller, and director of engineering. This group constitutes the top work team in the company. The tasks undertaken enable each individual in the work team to see how he is viewed as a manager by his immediate associates. This gives him insight into the ways in which he might change to operate more effectively. The group also, as in Phase I, determines what are the barriers to improved effectiveness of the work team. This first Phase II seminar was a most rewarding experience. For a majority of the seven it was even more valuable than the Phase I, and for all of us either confirmed or reconfirmed the validity of the Grid concepts.

Barriers to Team Effectiveness

My work team decided that the greatest barrier to our improved effectiveness was the lack of candor. In our work team and within the company there were certain subjects that were considered too delicate or sensitive to be discussed between us. We defined these as the "sacred cows" of the organization. During our 3-day seminar, the environment was created in which all of these sacred cows were flushed out. As a result, action decisions were made to deal with the sacred cows, whose demise will save the company nearly $1 million in operating costs in the next 12 months.

The second most serious barrier to improved team effectiveness was seen as the lack of creativity. We concluded that, as a team, the lack of candor was also the principal limitation on creativity. If people feel more free to be candid because the right environment for it exists, the flow of managerial innovation, experimentation, and creativity will increase. We are now seeing increasing candor in the work team situation.

When one considers the lack of candor which characterizes many work relationships, it is worth recognizing that we grow up learning never to be totally candid. As children there are things we feel unable to discuss with our parents. As pupils there are things we are not able to discuss with our teacher. In church there are things we cannot discuss with the minister, and in business there are things we cannot discuss with our bosses. Unfortunately, in so many instances it is the things that we feel unable to discuss that are the subjects in most urgent need of discussion and so often of critical nature. It will not be easy to break down the habits of a lifetime which inhibit candor, but if corporations really want to solve their most delicate and sensitive problems, we all need to learn to talk about them. At Simmonds we at least feel we have taken our first steps in the right direction. (Simmonds, 1967, pp. 23–24)

Still another example of Grid team building, involving a top group in a major supermarket chain, is described in the following.

This is the team development seminar. It starts the same way as Phase I, with the boss and his immediate subordinates exploring their managerial styles and operating practices as a work team. They work within the 9,9 management style. Taken together, Phase I & II unblock communication barriers between people, amongst other things. Here's how Grid worked for Gerry Spitzer.

"In the past, when we would set budgets, I would calculate what each department would get. For example, say we had a budget of $300 million. I would say to the fellows: 'You Max Grossner (produce sales manager), you get $30 million'—or however it works out. Then they would yell and complain, 'Why did you give me this?' I would say, 'This is the way it is boys, I'm the boss.' "

"Now, since we went to Grid last year, there's no such happening. I say, 'This is the pie. How are we going to divide it.' Perhaps we've got to reduce our margin in meat. We know we've got to make it up somewhere else. The group comes to a decision. This year it took us an hour-and-a-half to set our budget. Before Grid, we were in there for eight solid hours of table-pounding. But now we were committed. . . ."—Gerry Spitzer, director of Sales, Quebec division. (*Food Topics,* 1967, p. 17)

A comparative investigation within ESB Incorporated (Hart, 1974) shows the impact of Grid team building on manager effectiveness. Basically the comparison is between (a) a control group of "managers innocent of the Grid"; (b) Phase 1 Grid Seminar graduates who have not, as yet, engaged in Phase 2 Grid Team Building; and (c) Phase 1 participants who have also gone on to Phase 2. A detailed statistical analysis of individuals' responses in terms of key questions in areas such as "Decision-Making Analysis" "Analysis of Productivity," and "Most Important Influences" (Hart, 1974, pp. 50–59) demonstrates important positive impact effects of the Phase 2 continuation after Phase 1. The conclusion reached is that, "In short, the Managerial Grid works at ESB, especially where Phase 2 has been adopted as a way of life" (Hart, 1974, p. 59).

Contrasting theories "X" and "Y", which identify two opposing views of human motivation, have been postulated by McGregor (1960). When used as a theory intervention for group study purposes, members can be asked first to indicate characteristic ways of interaction prior to the presentation of Theories X and Y. The theories then can be further employed to test whether or not members see their interaction in the same way *after* the theory is understood. The final step is to plan how to move toward a more desirable interaction mode.

The characteristics of Theories X and Y are summarized in Table 27.1.

Table 27.1
McGregor's theories X and Y

Assumptions	
Theory X	*Theory Y*
1. Work is inherently distasteful to most people.	1. Work is as natural as play if conditions are favorable.
2. Most people have little ambition or desire for responsibility and prefer to be directed.	2. For achieving organizational goals, self-management is often indispensable.
3. Most people have little capacity for creativity involving organization problems.	3. Creativity for solving an organization's problems is widely distributed throughout its membership.
4. Motivation occurs at a bread-and-butter survival level.	4. Rewards which satisfy ego and social needs, as well as bread-and-butter needs, conduce to self-control in line with organizational objectives.
5. Most people must be closely controlled and often coerced to achieve organizational objectives.	5. The capacity for creativity is underutilized in organizations.

Implications for teamwork

Theory X	Theory Y
1. Authority flows unilaterally from superior to subordinate.	1. Authority flows from formal and informal sources, up, down, and across the team.
2. Span of control is narrow and supervision is close.	2. Span of control is wide, with supervision being general rather than detailed.
3. The individual is considered as an isolated unit, and work is organized primarily in terms of his physiological being.	3. The individual is considered as a social-psychological-physiological being and the structuring of his work does not ignore the fullness of man.
4. Work is routinized.	4. The task is a meaningful whole, providing some variety and requiring some skill and judgment.

Using these two models McGregor then developed a set of scales for use in group development. The left side of each scale represents X, the right Y.

Table 27.2

Scale	Theory X					Theory Y
Trust	High suspicion					High trust
	1 2 3 4 5 6 7					
Support	Every man for himself					Genuine concern for each other
	1 2 3 4 5 6 7					
Communication	Guarded, cautious					Open and authentic
	1 2 3 4 5 6 7					
Listening	We don't listen to each other					We understand and are understood
	1 2 3 4 5 6 7					
Team Objectives	Not understood					Clearly understood
	1 2 3 4 5 6 7					
Conflicts	Deny, avoid, or suppress					Accepted and "worked through"
	1 2 3 4 5 6 7					

Members rate their team on these seven-point scales. Then the team as a whole discusses the situation indicated by average scores for any item of less than 5, or for any scales where there is a wide range of individual ratings. Finally team members are asked to consider and identify why the situation is as they have pictured it. In using scales such as these McGregor points out ". . . it is important to agree in advance on a ground rule that there will be no attempt to ferret out the 'author' of any individual rating, although any member may *volunteer* comment about his own rating" (McGregor, 1967, p. 174). If the consultant knows the team by virtue of having worked with it previously, he may complete the scales and his rating may also be used as data, either as a part of the statistical summary or as a basis of comparison in order to give the team the benefit of his "expert" but outsider view. McGregor comments that his experience is that ratings by most groups using these kinds of scales tend to be unrealistically high, particularly when such an attempt is first made. He therefore suggests that after an initial discussion it is often better to wait a week or two and then readminister the scales, this time to a regular meeting dealing with normal operating problems.

One of the advantages of such a set of scales is that the consultant, by the items he or she includes in it, can ask the team to deal with issues it might not recognize as being important prior to the consultant-initiated discussion of them. For example, McGregor's scales include questions concerned with mutual trust and mutual support, communications, listening, team objectives, conflict, use of member resources, how control is exercised, and "organization climate." Most of these are not issues that managers spontaneously raise in day-to-day work meetings in such clearcut terms. These particular questions are not the only ones that might be asked; indeed, a team might be invited to invent the scales to be applied. McGregor points out, however, that to do so can cause managers to become preoccupied with mechanics rather than data. The main purpose is to provide each member with information about how others perceive the team in comparison with his perception and with clues as to how group effectiveness can be improved.

Power/authority problems abound in husband/wife interactions. Unless the conflict involved in working out power/authority differences is resolved, morale/cohesion is likely to be adversely affected with the probable consequence of either further intense combativeness or mutual withdrawal.

A theory-based intervention designed to aid husband-wife pairs to study how they resolve primarily power/authority problems is offered by Bach and Wyden (1968). They have originated a "fight training" approach for improving relations between couples. The idea is this: it is more or less natural for couples to fight; but many, in doing so, do not make their relationships more livable. "Clean" fighting can be part of a healthy basis for living together because, as a means of clearing tensions away, it enables partners to maintain a fresh and vital relationship. The thesis is, "intelligent fighting regulates the intensity of intimate involvement by occasionally creating relief from it. It makes intimacy controllable" (Bach and Wyden, 1970, p. 36).

Fight training utilizes Table 27.3, which shows nine categories of interaction present in ongoing behavior. These categories can be scored by each member of a couple or by the couple together to indicate how "clean" or "dirty" some specific

Table 27.3
The fight elements profile

Category of interaction	1 Reality	2 Injury	3 Involvement	4 Responsibility	5 Humor	6 Expression	7 Communication	8 Directness	9 Specificity
+ or bonding	Authentic, realistic	Fair, above belt	Active, reciprocal	Owning up	Laugh with relief	Open, leveling	High, clear, reciprocal feedback	Direct focus	Specific
0 or neutral									
− or alienating	Imaginary	Dirty, below the belt	Passive, or one-way	Anonymous or group	Ridicule, clowning or laugh-at	Hidden or camouflaged	Static, one-way, no feedback	Displaced focus	General "analysis"

Source: G. R. Bach and P. Wyden, *The Intimate Enemy: How to Fight Fair in Love and Marriage* (New York: Avon Books, 1970), p. 163. Reprinted by permission of William Morrow & Co., Inc., New York.

The "plus" (+) positions on the profile represent good (or "bonding") styles of aggression.
The "minus" (−) positions represent poor (or "alienating") styles of aggression.
The middle (0) positions indicate styles rated as neutral, irrelevant, or unobservable.
The profile is complete when one line is drawn to connect all nine dimensions, intersecting each dimension at the appropriate level. (+ or − or 0). When the line stays predominantly above the "0" level, the fight was fought in a predominantly bonding style. When the line stays predominantly below the "0" level, the fight was fought in predominantly alienating style.

fight they have had has been. The diagram is a comparison model. The higher "positive" end of the column for each category represents *constructive* fighting of the kind that helps the relationship to grow and change; the lower end denotes more and more "negative" fighting, or fighting that leaves bitterness in its wake.

Participants in fight training learn how to use the Fight Elements Profile diagram by attending sessions where several couples, meeting with the consultant, reenact earlier or recent fights, or get into spontaneous fights during the session itself. Through alternately observing and/or participating in these, giving feedback to other couples, and getting feedback from other participants and the consultant over a three-month period, clients learn to describe accurately various kinds of behavior throughout the range of each of the nine element categories. They learn to "pilot" themselves and to study changes in their fight styles as the seminar proceeds.

> Mastering the scoring system (usually after only six fight-group sessions) and then using it to score tape-recorded fights at home and live fights in front of a trainee group (who independently score and later compare) enables trainees to reinforce the all-important belief that they *can* learn to fight fair and informatively with a minimum of injury. (Bach and Wyden, 1970, pp. 350–51)

The scoring system is devised so as to avoid the conclusion that either partner has won or lost. Bach's axiom is that learning how to fight in the context of an intimate relationship is like learning how to dance, not how to box. If *both* don't win, both lose.

Bach and Wyden point out that a man and woman who live together get to know each other's sensitive and weak points ("Achilles' heels"). This enables either person to "hit" the other where it will hurt most. For example, a doctor's wife knew

> that he felt guilty because he treated relatively few nonpaying clinic patients. So she needled him by calling him "money mad." Yet she refused to listen when he tried to level with her. He attempted to find out how she might feel about living on a reduced income, but she would not discuss it. (Bach and Wyden, 1970, p. 84)

Couples may find themselves leveling with each other regarding their motives for "going for the Achilles' heel." The doctor's wife mentioned earlier explained before their fight-training group,

> "Sure I fought dirty! But only when you overwhelmed me and had me in a corner. I got tired of losing practically all the time. Anybody would! So the only way I knew how to slow you down was to get at you with a sort of fifth-column approach." (Bach and Wyden, 1970, p. 84)

Before entering fight training the husband had been unaware of how he had actually prompted her needling tactics. Similarly, she had been misreading his valuation of her as well as his behavior toward her. With these and other mutual misconceptions removed their fighting could more easily move to levels that would have positive, health-promoting effects on their relationship.

Transactional analysis, as already described, has other points of application beyond self-examination. One of them is concerned with aiding husbands and wives to study their interaction in order to move more in the direction of Adult-Adult interaction (Harris, 1967, Chapter 8). In addition, there are examples of how transactional analysis can be employed with parents and children in family group development (Harris, 1967, Chapter 9 and 10).

Parents and children are in a power/authority relationship in the sense that society expects parents to exercise their authority in behalf of their children's growth and development. So as in management or husband/wife relations, the power/authority issue often becomes a win-lose struggle. Gordon (1970) describes a power/authority theory-based intervention designed to help parents use the power/authority available to them in ways that solve rather than create or aggravate parent-child problems. He describes three contrasting ways of resolving conflict: "Parent wins" (Method I); "Child wins" (Method II); and "Both win" (Method III).

In the following example a father and his twelve-year-old daughter resolve conflict by Methods I and II respectively. First, a conflict is generated.

> *Jane:* 'Bye. I'm off to school.
>
> *Parent:* Honey, it's raining and you don't have your raincoat on.
>
> *Jane:* I don't need it.
>
> *Parent:* You don't need it! You'll get wet and ruin your clothes or catch a cold.
>
> *Jane:* It's not raining that hard.
>
> *Parent:* It is too.
>
> *Jane:* Well, I don't want to wear a raincoat. I hate to wear a raincoat.

Then one of the two win-lose outcomes is reached.

> *Parent:* Now, honey, you know you'll be warmer and drier if you wear it. Please go get it.
>
> *Jane:* I hate that raincoat—I won't wear it!
>
> *Parent:* You march right back to your room and get that raincoat! I will not let you go to school without your raincoat on a day like this.
>
> *Jane:* But I don't like it . . .
>
> *Parent:* No "buts"—if you don't wear it your mother and I will have to ground you.
>
> *Jane:* (angrily): All right, you win! I'll wear the stupid raincoat!
>
> *Parent:* I want you to.

Jane: I hate that raincoat—I won't wear it. If you make me wear it, I'll be mad at you.

Parent: Oh, I give up! Go on to school without your raincoat, I don't want to argue with you anymore—you win.

Either or both types of resolution are usually the familiar yet unsatisfying "stuff of life" to those clients who take part in Parent Effectiveness Training. One of the consultant's initial interventions is to trace and compare the different working principles that have operated so as to produce each outcome.

Method I

Parent and child encounter a conflict-of-needs situation. The parent decides what the solution should be. Having selected the solution, the parent announces it and hopes the child will accept it. If the child does not like the solution, the parent may first use persuasion to try to influence the child to accept the solution. If this fails, the parent usually tries to get compliance by employing power and authority.

Method II

Parent and child encounter a conflict-of-needs situation. The parent may or may not have a preconceived solution. If he does, he may try to persuade the child to accept it. It becomes obvious that the child has his own solution and is attempting to persuade the parent to accept it. If the parent resists, the child might then try to use his power to get compliance from the parent. In the end the parent gives in. (Gordon, 1970, pp. 153-63)

In effect, these Method I and Method II summaries serve as simple models that help clarify to parents the dynamics of many such win-lose conflicts. Furthermore, as the assembled parent-clients compare the two win-lose models and discuss with the consultant various longer-term consequences of employing either of them, the "structured ineffectiveness" of both Method I and II probably becomes even more apparent. Such insights are way stations rather than end objectives from the consultant's point of view, for

> The dilemma of almost all parents who come to our P.E.T. classes, seems to be that they are locked in to either Method I or Method II, or oscillate between the two, *because they know of no other alternative to these two ineffective "win-lose" methods.* We find that most parents not only know which method they use most frequently; they also realize both methods are ineffective. It is as if they know they are in trouble, whichever method they use, but do not know where else they can turn. Most of them are grateful to be released from their self-imposed trap. (Gordon, 1970, p. 163)

At this point, then, the consultant introduces Method III as a further contrast to Methods I and II, and as an alternative to them. The summary "model" is as follows:

Parent and child encounter a conflict-of-needs situation. The parent asks the child to participate with him in a joint search for some solution acceptable to both. One or both may offer possible solutions. They critically evaluate them and eventually make a decision on a final solution acceptable to both. No selling of the other is required after the solution has been selected, because both have already accepted it. No power is required to force compliance, because neither is resisting the decision.

For illustration, here is how the raincoat issue was resolved by Method III, as reported by the parent involved.

Jane: 'Bye, I'm off to school.

Parent: Honey, it's raining outside and you don't have your raincoat on.

Jane: I don't need it.

Parent: I think it's raining quite hard and I'm concerned that you'll ruin your clothes or get a cold, and that will affect us.

Jane: Well, I don't want to wear my raincoat.

Parent: You sure sound like you definitely don't want to wear that raincoat.

Jane: That's right, I hate it.

Parent: You really hate your raincoat.

Jane: Yeah, it's plaid.

Parent: Something about plaid raincoats you hate, huh?

Jane: Yes, nobody at school wears plaid raincoats.

Parent: You don't want to be the only one wearing something different.

Jane: I sure don't. Everybody wears plain-colored raincoats—either white or blue or green.

Parent: I see. Well, we really have a conflict here. You don't want to wear your raincoat 'cause it's plaid, but I sure don't want to pay a cleaning bill, and I will not feel comfortable with you getting a cold. Can you think of a solution that we both could accept? How could we solve this so we're both happy?

Jane: (Pause) Maybe I could borrow Mom's car coat today.

Parent: What does that look like? Is it plain-colored?

Jane: Yeah, it's white.

Parent: Think she'll let you wear it today?

Jane: I'll ask her. [Comes back in a few minutes with car coat on; sleeves are too long, but she rolls them back.] It's okay by Mom.

Parent: You're happy with that thing?

Jane: Sure, it's fine.

Parent: Well, I'm convinced it will keep you dry. So if you're happy with that solution, I am too.

Jane: Well, so long.

Parent: So long. Have a good day at school. (Gordon, 1970, pp. 196-97)

It is noteworthy that Jane's actual reason for not wanting to wear her raincoat failed to emerge during either the Method I or Method II disputes. In the heat of polarized conflict she did not find it a useful missile to hurl at her parents. In the joint-search Method III discussion, however, it was identified as *information* that had a bearing on both the problem and a solution.

While parents may quickly *perceive* Method III as a promising new alternative, this by no means implies that they *accept* it or are capable of putting it to work at home. Further stages of training are devoted to strengthening skills. What has been described in these excerpts, however, illustrates the usefulness of contrasting *models* of conflict resolution in bringing to clients' awareness the principal working parts of defective yet established in-home systems of conflict resolution.

The several theories used as the basis of intervention in power/authority problems are both similar and different. The most characteristically shared feature is their common emphasis upon the importance of conflict as a significant issue that can strengthen or weaken relationships, depending on how it is dealt with. The Grid, which identifies five different ways of dealing with conflict, is perhaps the approach most concentrated on conflict resolution. Bach's fight training appears the next most concerned with issues of conflict, with Gordon's approach third. While transactional analysis recognizes the importance of conflict, its treatment is not as straightforward as in these other three approaches. Finally, implications regarding the importance of conflict can be observed in McGregor's Theories X and Y, but the management of conflict is not central in this approach.

The most significant differences among these several theories involve the extent to which they examine and attempt to change correlated aspects of behavior that also determine the quality of relationships. The Grid is the most thoroughly worked out of these various theory-based approaches to intervention, not only in terms of its use for unraveling dilemmas in the area of power/authority but also in regard to problems of interaction that relate to morale/cohesion, norms/standards, and goals/objectives. It is a well worked out theory in terms of its applicability to various kinds of group settings. For example, one application is with regard to management teams, another is its use in unraveling salesman/customer problems, and a third is its use for investigating husband/wife interactions. The Grid has also been utilized in school settings to evaluate teacher/pupil interactions, and so on.

Transactional analysis also has numerous applications. The writings of Berne show its utility in mental-health problem situations. A number of adaptations illustrate its relevance for dealing with managerial and family situations as well.

McGregor's Theories X and Y, Gordon's three methods of problem solving, and Bach's fight training are of a more or less comparable order, albeit within a somewhat narrower scope.

INTERGROUP (Q₃)

Win/lose power struggles between groups are equally susceptible to resolution through theory-based interventions. The strategy already has been described in connection with both group development and self-examination at the individual level.

Beyond all individual members of the contending groups learning theories, instruments are available that enable participants to characterize the situation between them both as it currently exists and as it would be if it were ideal. Once this kind of description has been completed by persons as individuals, the contending groups convene as separate groups to determine on an in-group basis what would constitute the ideal relationship between itself and the other group. The two groups then convene—retaining their character as separate groups, however—to report to each other their ideal-relationship formulations. Once these two images have been presented and shared the two groups, often working through representatives but in the hearing of everyone, reach agreement as to what the future ideal relationship should be.

Returning to work as separate groups, each of them next characterizes what the actual here-and-now intergroup relationship is. Once this is completed the two groups reconvene in a general setting, again as intact groups, and through representatives exchange their images of the present state of intergroup affairs. As a final step the two groups set goals as to the steps necessary for shifting their relationship from what it is to what it should become.

Theory is basic to all of this. Without theory the possibility of achieving 9,9 win-win conditions wherein both groups are able to be more effective by virtue of a good relationship—rather than being separated by a win-lose fight of the 9,1 sort, or having in a 1,9 way to avoid interaction on matters that would produce conflict, or maintaining walls of isolation in a 1,1 sense, or even collaborating but on a 5,5 compromise-accommodation basis—would be difficult to imagine. With the theory for what constitutes a truly sound relationship widely shared among protagonists on both sides of the cleavage, it becomes possible to close that cleavage in terms congruent with theoretical specifications. This means strengthening the integration in order that their interdependence can be productive rather than destructive.

An example of intergroup problem solving premised upon theory intervention and involving a headquarters-field relationship is described below. The headquarters manufacturing vice-president and his group were trying diligently to modernize the entire manufacturing operations of the company. However, the particular plant involved was seen as having a parochial, narrow perspective, paying attention to its own problems but not seeing the larger opportunities for growth and development occasioned by the rapid changes occurring in the company as a whole. Steps as outlined above were introduced. A picture of reactions is provided by a participant in the situation.

"Looking back six months after the headquarters-field team training session, relationships between the headquarters officers, and the biggest plant, are close to being beautiful to observe. Before, they were pretty good, and we bragged about them, but we now see that they were beset by many of the doubts and questions and skepticisms that do so much to undermine real understanding. Furthermore, we uncovered and resolved one whopping issue that was having an adverse effect on profit, but before the training we didn't know how to bring the issue into focus so that we could work on it."

"Both the headquarters and the plant personnel speak frequently about how much better things are as a result of the team training. Really, for the first time, I can say that our headquarters and plant people are collaborating effectively on a basis of mutual assistance. This is something I have been striving for over a period of years and this kind of result is therefore extremely gratifying." (Blake and Mouton, 1962, p. 10)

Another example of intergroup development using theory-based interventions, but now involving lateral rather than vertical groups, is illustrated in the following.

Phase III concerns intergroup relations. It might bring together sales with manufacturing, or warehousing.

At first, the groups meet in separate rooms. Zeke Ferley's group (he's director of distribution) would discuss:

How *does* our department relate to sales?

How *should* our department operate in relationship to sales?

How *do* we see ourselves operating now?

Can we improve?

Then Ferley's people sit down with Spitzer's people and explain their answers. (There's either tacit agreement or heated discussion.) They exchange papers and go off to separate rooms.

"When they return," says Suffrin, "hopefully they'll have reached agreement on key points. If not, they'll set up task force committees to report back to the group on what progress they've made." Phase III lasts three days. (Food Topics, 1967, p. 17)

The two examples above, one of a vertical and one of a horizontal intergroup situation, demonstrate how theory-based interventions can be used to strengthen the integration between groups that must collaborate if they are to contribute to the larger purposes of the organization.

An example of partly theory-based intervention at the intergroup level is by Lorsch and Lawrence (1972), who formulated the contingency theory of intergroup relationships. They base their interventions on a "cognitive map" that is explained to managers prior to intergroup problem analysis. The following are its main points.

1. Any complex social system, such as a company, is composed of differentiated parts.

2. These differentiated parts must be integrated into a unified effort to accomplish corporate purpose.

3. Any part, because of the tasks it performs, develops at least four distinctive attributes, (a) time orientation, (b) interpersonal orientation, (c) internal formal structure, and (d) goal orientation.

The more unlike one another any two interdependent groups are along these four dimensions, the greater the likelihood of difficulties in achieving an effective integration between them.

A case example in which this cognitive map was used is presented in Chapter 11. Evidence that the intervention as a whole was somewhat more catalytic than theory-principle in nature can be adduced from the consultants' practice of first gathering and summarizing interview and questionnaire information, and only then interpreting from this in terms of their theory, as follows.

> We explained that the high differentiation in interpersonal and structural attributes was related to the problems of achieving integration, but that the fact the units were occupying the same task and time space seemed to be intensifying the difficulties in achieving collaboration. In this discussion the managers recognized that two things were needed; first a clearer differentiation of the role of the laboratories and second the development of improved integrative devices. (Lorsch and Lawrence, 1972, pp. 223)

For the participants who are listening this may have the "ring" of theory, but as yet it would not have the "feel" of internalized theory. Consequently, the managers recognized "needs" rather than "what to do."

ORGANIZATION (Q₄)

The idea that the power/authority basis of management and supervision might be changed on an organization-wide basis through the use of theory-based interventions is of very recent date, tracing back to no earlier than the fifties.

The Grid is one approach used to strengthen the effective exercise of power and authority throughout an organization. Participants learn the Grid in the manner described previously except that most organization members gain their Phase 1 self-examination Grid experience in in-company seminars, where study teams are composed of higher- and lower-ranking organization members who are not direct bosses and subordinates of one another. This diagonal slice rather than vertical basis of organizing makes it unnecessary for boss and subordinate to face their power/authority difficulties at a time when they are trying to learn theory-based models of excellence for integrating boss-subordinate relationships.

Team building as a Phase 2 activity utilizes the Grid in functional settings to solve actual power/authority problems; since this step has been described above, it will not be considered further. When all of the intergroup situations where interdependence needs to be strengthened in order for the two groups to work more closely together have been worked through, significant progress has been made in aiding those who manage and supervise an organization to use their power/authority in the most constructive way possible.

Another major approach to organization development via strengthening the use of power/authority makes use of Likert's System 4 theory, combined with survey research and feedback. The Likert model assists the organization-as-client to assess the character of its human organization. Likert has concluded that differences in managerial leadership can be reduced to four different categories: "exploitive author- itative," "benevolent authoritative," "consultative," and "participative group." With scales such as those illustrated in Table 27.4, members of an organization can "pic- ture" the management situation. Summarized, these data can be fed back and eval- uated against the theory so as to identify the character of the human organization currently existing. Furthermore, since the theory and the scales describe what would be required to move to a "participative group" style—demonstrated to be the most facilitating for productivity and satisfaction—it becomes possible to plot the steps essential for change. On the Table 27.4 scales the direction of improvement is toward the right.

The use of data is based on assumptions in the catalytic area and the consultant interventions also are catalytic in character. When additional education-based inter- ventions beyond "data feedback" are required to strengthen managerial effective- ness, Likert (1967, p. 125) points out that training via the sensitivity or Grid ap- proaches can serve to reinforce System 4 values and actions.

Herzberg's motivational concepts (1959, 1966) focus on power/authority rela- tionships from the standpoint of how management and supervision may use power/ authority to create a productive work climate. The approach, which identifies sound and unsound alignments of motivations toward productivity in the industrial situa- tion, is premised on the idea since man's "Animal-Adam" nature is concerned with avoiding "pain from environment," organizations must deal constructively with "hygiene/maintenance" such as work layout and physical job demands, wages and salaries, supervisors' fairness and other aspects of personal security, social climate, matters of job orientation, personal status, and so on. When these are deficient or absent they detract from production motivation. When they are present, however, they do not directly enhance production motivation. The best their fulfillment can be expected to do is to lessen the individual's preoccupation with environment and the accompanying tendencies to find fault with it. A further basic need of man, ac- cording to Herzberg (1966, p. 76), stems from his "Human-Abraham" nature which seeks growth from tasks. Thus the direct "motivators" are task centered and are largely influenced by a person's immediate boss. These positive motivational variables include relevant job information, recognition, responsibility, advancement, and intrinsically interesting work.

Myers has worked as a consultant to increase the alignment between motiva- tional theory and managerial practices in Texas Instruments. His guiding principle is that to become fully effective in supporting productivity, motivational theories

Table 27.4

Profile of organizational characteristics

Instructions:

1. On the lines below each organizational variable (item), please place an *n* at the point which, *in your experience*, describes your organization at the present time (*n* = now). Treat each item as a continuous variable from the extreme at one end to that at the other.

2. In addition, if you have been in your organization one or more years, please also place a *p* on each line at the point which, *in your experience*, describes your organization as it was one to two years ago (*p* – previously).

3. If you were not in your organization one or more years ago, please check here ___ and answer as of the present time, i.e., answer only with an *n*.

Organizational variable					Item No.
1. Leadership processes used					
a. Extent to which superiors have confidence and trust in *subordinates*	Have no confidence and trust in subordinates	Have condescending confidence and trust, such as master has in servant	Substantial but not complete confidence and trust; still wishes to keep control of decisions	Complete confidence and trust in all matters	1
...					
2. Character of motivational forces					
a. Underlying motives tapped	Physical security, economic needs, and some use of the desire for status	Economic needs and moderate use of motives, e.g., desire for status, affiliation, and achievement	Economic needs and considerable use of ego and other major motives, e.g., desire for new experiences	Full use of economic, ego, and other major motives, as, for example, motivational forces arising from group goals	6

Source: R. Likert, *The Human Organization* (New York: McGraw-Hill, 1967), pp. 197–98. Reprinted by permission.

must (1) find expression in the day-to-day behavior and decisions of supervisors, and (2) be used to design the environment within which work takes place. To accomplish the latter the corporation as a system was restructured to fit motivation-maintenance concepts by analyzing functions performed by personnel in terms of their potential for serving maintenance or motivation needs. The theory was then explained to managers through large group meetings where they were informed of the company's plan to implement the theory.

To meet the first-mentioned criterion—that of strengthening the alignment between theory and supervisory practice—consultant/education interventions were introduced. Supervisors, in small seminars of from six to ten participants, were given skill practice in applying the theory within their own supervisory jobs. Supervisors received direct feedback from their subordinates as one way of deepening the impact. An attitude-measurement program was structured around the motivation-maintenance framework and was used to assess progress in satisfying the various maintenance-need and motivation-need areas. The following are conclusions regarding this organization-wide program.

It can be useful as a practical framework for codifying intuitive effectiveness and for guiding the inexperienced, but it will not correct a management failure which, for example, permits the appointment of immature or unscrupulous supervisors. The management philosophy which sparked the growth of TI created a fertile environment for introducing motivation-maintenance theory as a mechanism for achieving company goals by providing opportunities for employees to achieve personal goals. (Myers, 1964, p. 88)

LARGER SOCIAL SYSTEM (Q₅)

Every social system deals in some way or another with the power/authority problem, for it is central to the maintenance of interaction and coordination. Examples have been furnished in earlier sections of interventions at the larger-social-system level which have shifted the power/authority basis of interaction among members of the system. None of these, however, involved change induced by theory intervention. Indeed, there appears to be no well-worked-out example of how theory interventions might be applied to a larger social system to strengthen the effective utilization of authority.

One consideration is whether or not a theory basis of intervention is even theoretically possible at this level. Such an intervention would be possible if members of larger social systems shared common ideas for "best" ways of using power and authority. For example, there is a widespread comprehension of the value of the 9,9 way of managing the power/authority problem, as demonstrated in the following discussion of Grid Seminars. Participants from many different national groupings and cultures have attended these seminars under quite uniform conditions, as described below.

Grid Seminar Subjects

The managers completing the instruments are from the middle and higher levels of business, industry, and government organizations. All are men. All have at least a high school education or its equivalent. The subjects, by geographical breakdown, are from:

- the United States, 1,477 managers from 607 organizations;
- Canada, 166 managers from 144 organizations;
- England, 326 managers from 106 organizations;
- South Africa, 72 managers from 37 organizations;
- Australia, 146 managers from 50 organizations;
- Japan, 178 managers from 52 organizations;
- South America, 59 managers from 32 organizations (Spanish-speaking countries);
- Middle East, 65 managers from 42 organizations in Iran, Lebanon, Saudi Arabia, Iraq, Jordan, and Yemen.

Setting

Managers attended Grid Seminars that were conducted according to the same basic design over a four-year period (Blake and Mouton, 1968b). Translation made it possible for most managers to use their native languages. (Mouton and Blake, 1969, p. 15)

Given these conditions, it was possible to explore a number of the questions embedded in different larger social systems. Three issues of managerial thinking, attitudes, and performance are represented by these questions:

1. What is viewed as effective management across various national groupings? (If there are differences in concepts of effectiveness, a manager working outside of the home country faces values that are in conflict with his or her own.)
2. What similarities or differences are there in managerial attitudes and actions across national groupings?
3. Can educational methods be applied to increase understanding between managers from different countries who work together within the same company?

What Constitutes Soundness?

Organization practices. Managers study Grid theory in their prework and during the Seminar. They are then engaged in an experiment designed to answer the question, "What is the best way for a company to operate?" What managers see as *ideal* is significant, for actions consistent with ideal concepts are bound to be more acceptable than those that are not.

Managers are divided into small study teams and debate twenty questions on particular aspects of business, behavior, and organization performance. Five answers (representing the five Grid theories) are supplied. Managers rank them from "most sound" to "least sound," selecting answers that represent what they think would be sound in an effective organization, *not* what happens in their organizations. If for each of the twenty questions the answer chosen as "most sound" is one representing the same Grid theory or style, the score for that style is 100. If the answer chosen for each of the twenty questions as "least sound" represents the same Grid style, the score for that style is 20.

Data shown in Table 27.5 suggest that regardless of national grouping, managers agree that the 9,9 Grid style represents the soundest way to manage. No between-country differences appear to have statistical significance. The 9,1 and 5,5 ways of managing were chosen as second best with about equal frequency. Next selected was 1,9 while the 1,1 approach was selected as the "least sound" for operating a company.

Table 27.5
Agreement across nations on 9,9 Grid theory
as soundest for operating a corporation

Grid theory for operating a corporation	Seminar participant scores for least to most sound (range 20–100)							
	U.S.	So. Africa	Canada	England	Australia	Middle East	So. America	Japan
9,9	98.2	99.9	99.8	99.9	100.0	97.6	100.0	99.9
9,1	66.7	65.8	62.4	66.3	65.4	67.0	66.0	65.4
5,5	66.0	65.2	66.3	66.5	64.0	60.0	68.0	65.6
1,9	44.1	44.2	46.5	44.5	46.3	47.6	44.5	46.9
1,1	23.4	24.9	25.0	22.8	24.3	27.8	21.5	22.2

Managerial values.   Along with how a company should be operated is the question of how a manager should manage. Each manager in a Grid Seminar identifies what he sees as the best way to solve problems that might crop up with subordinates. Forty forced-choice questions pair each of the five Grid styles with each other style four times. The managerial behavior described involves boss-subordinate interactions in planning, organizing, directing, and controlling work. Managers are instructed to select the answer representing the more effective way to manage. A weight of three points is assigned each pair. The highest score available for any Grid theory is 48, the lowest is 0. Data in Table 27.6 shows that 9,9 again is the theory preferred most. Here 5,5 is second and the others in order are 9,1; 1,9; and 1,1.

Summary.   Results indicate that when complex aspects of management are evaluated, the 9,9 Grid style of managing is endorsed as the theory that makes the most productive use of an organization's members.

Table 27.6
Agreement across nations on 9,9 Grid theory as
soundest basis for individual managerial values

Grid theory for individual managerial values	Seminar participant scores for preference for Grid theories (range 0–48)							
	U.S.	So. Africa	Canada	England	Australia	Middle East	So. America	Japan
9,9	41.3	40.8	40.6	40.9	40.1	39.5	41.0	40.3
9,1	25.6	26.1	24.0	26.4	23.2	28.6	25.9	27.2
5,5	30.7	31.5	31.1	30.7	32.5	29.1	32.2	29.8
1,9	17.5	18.1	18.3	17.4	18.6	18.4	17.5	17.1
1,1	4.9	3.5	6.0	4.6	5.6	4.4	3.4	5.6

Source: J. S. Mouton and R. R. Blake, "Organization Development in the Free World," *Personnel Administration* 32, no. 4 (1969): 16–17.

The above data indicate strongly that a theory-based intervention for strengthening the use of power/authority in larger social systems is a practical possibility. However, that such a theory-based intervention might have practical utility in an actual larger social system remains to be demonstrated.

SUMMARY

The use by consultants of theory-based interventions to deal with focal issues involving power/authority is a post–World War II development. While theories of power/authority were available in the pre–World War II world, they were taught in academic rather than functional ways. This classical teacher-tell manner enabled the student as client to understand what the theories *were,* but did not aid him in testing their *utility* for changing his own situation. One of the first of such theories was developed by Mary Parker Follett in 1924; the initial critical experiment was conducted in the late thirties by Lewin, Lippitt, and White. This experiment identified and demonstrated the consequence of three styles of classroom management, labeled Autocratic, Democratic, and Laissez-faire. Predictions as to consequences were demonstrated in empirical results which permitted the conclusion that democratic classroom practices made a more positive contribution and had fewer innate side effects than either the Autocratic or Laissez-faire leadership models.

But it was only after World War II with the advent of instrumented team learning that consultants learned how to communicate theory to clients so as to help them strengthen personal effectiveness. The steps essential for effective internalization of theory were indicated in Chapter 26 and need not be reconstructed here, beyond saying that theory-based interventions appear to be most effective when an individual is enabled not only to understand the concepts inherent in the theory but also to use the theories to examine his or her own prior assumptions and apply these insights to actual power/authority relationships with others.

Most theory-based consultation in the power/authority area involves either individual self-examination, or group development or team building. The latter takes place in primary groups and most often on an in-organization basis. Such group development, therefore, involves an actual boss and his or her working interactions with subordinates. Theory-based consultation on power/authority issues in such a setting can be a very effective way of bringing into focus issues of interaction that are causing behavior to be unproductive and can encourage more positive team participation.

The use of theory-based interventions for dealing with lateral and vertical intergroup relationships is less common than is the use of a theory basis for strengthening the use of power/authority throughout an organization. The latter, however, is best developed in the Grid approach to organization development and in the survey research use of Likert's System 4.

Basic to the power/authority problem as the focal issue is how protagonists deal with their conflict. All theory-based approaches grapple with this fundamental issue in one way or another, either explicitly or incidentally. The basic approaches for dealing with conflict involve five possibilities: suppression, smoothing, withdrawal, compromise and accommodation, or confrontation. Theories such as transactional analysis make no distinction between confrontation and compromise, and theories such as McGregor's X and Y deal only with suppression as contrasted with confrontation. Gordon's approach to child development deals with suppressing, smoothing, and confrontation. Transactional Analysis and Likert's System 4 are not explicit in identifying alternative ways of approaching conflict situations. Thus, although the theories differ in the degree to which they center upon conflict as the basic power/authority issue, and though they differ in the vividness with which they make alternative possibilities explicit to the client, this feature is basic to each of them.

REFERENCES

Bach, G. R., and P. Wyden. *The Intimate Enemy: How to Fight Fair in Love and Marriage.* New York: Avon Books, 1970. (First published by William Morrow & Company, Inc., 1968.) Reprinted by permission of William Morrow & Co., Inc., New York.

Berne, E. *Transactional Analysis in Psychotherapy.* New York: Random House, 1961.

Blake, R. R., and J. S. Mouton. "Headquarters-Field Team Training for Organizational Improvement. *Training Directors Journal* 16, no. 3 (1962): 3–11.

Blake, R. R., and J. S. Mouton. "Improving Organizational Problem Solving through Increasing the Flow and Utilization of New Ideas." *Training Directors Journal* 17, no. 9 (1963a): 48–57. Reprinted by permission.

Blake, R. R., and J. S. Mouton. "Improving Organizational Problem Solving through Increasing the Flow and Utilization of New Ideas." *Training Directors Journal* 17, no. 10 (1963b): 38–54. Reprinted by permission.

Blake, R. R., and J. S. Mouton. *The Managerial Grid.* Houston: Gulf Publishing Company, 1964. Copyright © 1964 by Gulf Publishing Company, Houston, Texas. Used with permission.

Blake, R. R., J. S. Mouton, and M. G. Blansfield. "How Executive Team Training Can Help You." *Journal of the American Society of Training Directors* 16, no. 1 (1962): 3–11. Reprinted by permission.

Blansfield, M. G. "Transactional Analysis as a Training Intervention." In W. G. Dyer, ed., *Modern Theory and Method in Group Training.* New York: Van Nostrand Reinhold Company, 1972, pp. 149–54. Reprinted by permission.

Frampton, T. J. "Good Managers Are Made." *Electronics Design* 17 (1973): 76–79. Reprinted by permission.

Gordon, T. *Parent Effectiveness Training.* New York: David McKay, 1970. Reprinted by permission.

Harris, T. A. *I'm OK—You're OK.* New York: Harper & Row Publishers, 1967.

Hart, H. A. "The Grid Appraised—Phases 1 and 2." *Personnel* 51, no. 5 (1974): 44–59.

Herzberg, F. *Work and the Nature of Man.* Cleveland: The World Publishing Company, 1966.

Herzberg, F., B. Mausner, and B. B. Snyderman. *The Motivation to Work.* New York: John Wiley, 1959.

Jongeward, D., ed. *Everybody Wins: Transactional Analysis Applied to Organizations.* Reading, Mass.: Addison-Wesley, 1973.

Likert, R. *The Human Organization.* New York: McGraw-Hill, 1967. Reprinted by permission.

Lorsch, J. W., and P. R. Lawrence. "The Diagnosis of Organizational Problems." In N. Margulies and A. P. Raia, eds., *Organizational Development: Values, Process, and Technology.* New York: McGraw-Hill, 1972, pp. 218–28. Reprinted by permission.

McGregor, D. *The Human Side of Enterprise.* New York: McGraw-Hill, 1960.

McGregor, D. *The Professional Manager.* New York: McGraw-Hill, 1967.

Mouton, J. S., and R. R. Blake. "Organization Development in the Free World." *Personnel Administration* 32, no. 4 (1969): 13–23.

Myers, M. S. "Who Are Your Motivated Workers?" *Harvard Business Review,* 42, no. 1 (1964): 73–88.

Simmonds, G. R. "Organization Development: A Key to Future Growth." *Personnel Administration* 30, no. 1 (1967): 19–24. Reprinted by permission.

"Steinberg's: People Are the Pulse." *Food Topics* 22, no. 7 (1967): 9–23.

Vroom, V. H., and P. W. Yetton. *Leadership and Decision-Making.* Pittsburgh: University of Pittsburgh Press, 1973. Reprinted by permission.

THEORY-PRINCIPLES INTERVENTIONS

28

MORALE / COHESION

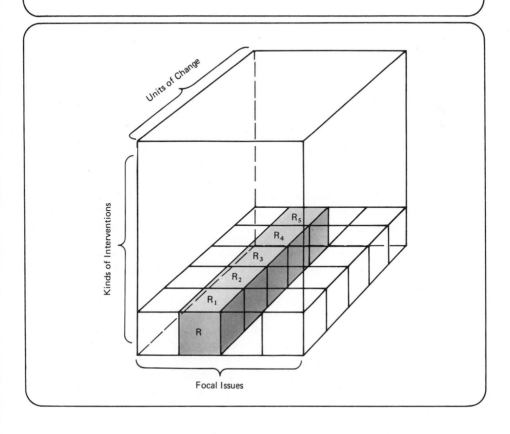

While the importance of high morale/cohesion is widely recognized, it is relatively rare to find theory-based interventions with a morale/cohesion focal issue. The reason may be that morale/cohesion many times is easier to change by changing something else. For example, if power/authority is being misused, it can cause lowered morale/cohesion. The preferred approach to solving the morale/cohesion problem is to deal with the power/authority problem first. Nevertheless, there are approaches that have a theory basis of intervention.

Transactional Analysis as a theory-based intervention was discussed in Chapter 27 and need not be elaborated upon further. An example of its use to help an individual test the possible cohesion of a potential husband/wife relationship is reported by Harris (1969), who provides an example of consultant-assisted evaluation of a prospective husband.

> One of the most helpful ways to examine similarities and dissimilarities is the use of Transactional Analysis in premarital counseling to construct a personality diagram of the couple contemplating marriage. The aim is to expose not just the obvious similarities or dissimilarities but to undertake a more thorough inquiry of what is in the Parent, Adult, and Child of each partner. A couple who enters into such an inquiry might be said to already have a lot in their favor, inasmuch as they take marriage seriously enough to take a long look before they leap. However, one of the partners, having serious doubt about the soundness of the alliance, may undertake such an inquiry on his own. An example is a young lady who was in one of my treatment groups. She asked me to schedule an individual hour for her for the purpose of discussing her dilemma over the fact that a young man she had been dating a short time had proposed to her. Her Child was immensely attracted to him, and yet there was other data coming into her computer which caused her to question whether or not marriage was a good idea. She had learned to use P-A-C accurately and asked that I help her examine this relationship on the basis of examining the P-A-C in each of them.
>
> First we compared the Parent of each. We found she had a strong Parent, which contained countless rules of conduct and many "shoulds" and "oughts." These included the admonition that you don't rush into marriage without thinking. There were certain elements of self-righteousness, like "our kind" are the best people. It contained ideas such as "you are judged by the company you keep" and "don't do anything that is beneath you." It contained the early imprints of a home life that was highly organized, where mother was the head of the house, and where father worked hard and late at the office. There was a great store of "how to" material: How to celebrate a birthday, how to dress the Christmas tree, how to bring up children, and how to handle oneself in social situations. Her Parent came on as an important influence in her life in that the impressions had been more or less consistent. Although its rigidity was sometimes oppressive and produced considerable NOT OK feelings in her Child, her Parent

nonetheless continued to be a constant source of data in all her transactions in the present.

We then turned to an examination of the Parent in the young man. His
parents had been divorced when he was seven years old, and he had been
raised by his mother, who indulged him in material possessions and gave
him sporadic attention. She herself was Child-dominated and emotional
and acted out her feelings in impetuous displays of spending, with intermittent spells of sulking, withdrawal, and vindictiveness. Father did not
come through on the tape at all except as the imprint that he was a "rotten
bastard, like all men." The boy's Parent was so disintegrated and fragmented and inconsistent that it did not come through in present transactions as a controlling or modifying influence over his impulsive, Child-
dominated behavior. Her Parent and his Parent not only had nothing in
common; her Parent also highly disapproved of his. It was readily seen
that little basis existed for a Parent-Parent transaction about any subject,
thus ruling out anything complementary at this level. (Harris, 1969, pp.
128–29)

Her and the boy's "Adult" and "Child" orientations were then diagnosed and contrasted in a similar manner, after which the development of the relationship was
traced in terms of the Parent-Adult-Child orientations model.

As their relationship progressed there became less and less to talk about.
Nothing existed Parent-Parent, little existed Adult-Adult, and what did
exist on the Child-Child level soon produced major disturbances in the
girl's Parent. The relationship then began to settle in a Parent-Child pattern with her assuming the role of the responsible and critical partner
and he assuming the role of the manipulative, testing Child, reproducing
his original situation in childhood. (Harris, 1969, p. 131)

On the basis of what she now saw to be characteristic of the current relationship
pattern and the prospects of its continuation in marriage, she finally decided that she
didn't want him as a husband and broke off the relationship. It should be noted that
this system has an important blind spot since it provides no basis for distinguishing
5,5- from 9,9-oriented behavior. The result is that the "organization man" version
of "Adult" and the mature, independent, self-directed "Adult" are left undifferen-
tiated from each other.

Herzberg's theories of motivation (1959, 1966) have been introduced in Chapter 27, particularly with regard to how power/authority relations can be used either
to stimulate or stifle efforts at productivity and achievement. It can be noted here
also that defective "hygiene/maintenance" provision of environmental factors
(which at most can only prevent downturns from present performance levels), as
well as lack of "motivators"—largely boss-influenced intangibles such as feelings of
achievement, recognition and growth—can have disrupting effects on morale/
cohesion.

IMPLICATIONS

The paucity of examples here may indicate any one of several conclusions. It may be that theory of morale/cohesion is insufficiently developed to make it functionally useful. Alternatively, the theories may be satisfactory, but they have not been converted from academic to utilitarian modes of communication. A third possibility is that theory is of little utility in bringing morale/cohesion to a higher level, though Myers' TI work (Chapter 27) would suggest that this may not be true. A fourth possibility, as mentioned earlier, is that the best way to deal with morale/cohesion is to solve related problems first rather than trying to arouse a high degree of morale/cohesion directly.

REFERENCES

Harris, T. A. *I'm OK—You're OK*. Copyright © 1967, 1968, 1969 by Thomas A. Harris. By permission of Harper & Row, Publishers, Inc.

Herzberg, F., B. Mausner, and B. B. Snyderman. *The Motivation to Work*. New York: Wiley, 1959.

Herzberg, F. *Work and the Nature of Man*. Cleveland: The World Publishing Company, 1966.

29

NORMS/STANDARDS

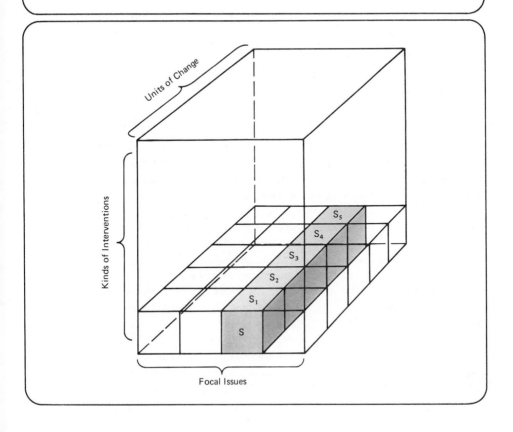

Norms/standards are those either implicit and silent or explicit and publicized bases of shared expectations to which people wish or are supposed to conform. Broadly stated, one's adherence to prevailing norms/standards tends in various ways to be rewarded by other adherents while violations tend to draw "punishment." External regulation, then, can be a powerful perpetuating influence whether or not the particular norms/standards are pertinent to effectiveness.

When norms/standards that relate to a group, an organization, or even larger social systems have been internalized by an individual, they become a basis of self-regulation of behavior; thus any improvement in effectiveness may require that the person's internalized norms/standards be subjected to reexamination. Several different kinds of theory-based interventions have been employed to accomplish this kind of change.

The Grid (Blake and Mouton, 1968) has proved an effective norms/standards intervention, particularly at team, intergroup, and organizational levels. After the Grid has been learned and members are prepared to confront conflict, they use Grid instruments to evaluate "what is," in contrast to "what would be ideal," and then design strategies for shifting from the actual to the ideal. This method of intervention enables members themselves, without further consultation, except on highly technical problems, to engineer their own processes of change.

Another approach that uses a theory-based model of consultation to intervene with individuals makes use of behavior modification. A third, which relates to organization as unit of change, is more problem-focused.

INDIVIDUAL (S₁)

A model for individual development of reasoning skills and their use in the norms/standards area is described by Kepner and Tregoe (1965). The basic idea is that "in management, events proceed as planned unless some force, not provided against by the plan, acts upon events to produce an outcome not contemplated in the plan." (Kepner and Tregoe, 1965, p. 103) Thus any practical problem, being an unwanted effect, can be viewed as a deviation from some standard. The "real cause" of the problem, therefore, is an unplanned and unanticipated or norms change away from "standard" that has been brought about by some specific event or combination of events. Kepner and Tregoe assert that unless and until the actual cause of the problem is precisely determined, any attempts to resolve it—such as by treating one or more of its outward symptoms—represent no more than guesswork and have a high probability of failing. The authors emphasize this point with examples of the ineffectiveness, wasteful expense, and sometimes physical danger involved in taking a managerial decision based on a "false cause."

Rational management, then, consists in valid problem analysis followed by specific related decisions to institute action that will take care of the identified problem. Kepner and Tregoe offer a model of this process, which involves seven initial steps of problem analysis and a further seven steps of formulating the best decision for solving the problem. Briefly stated, these are:

Problem analysis

1. As a prerequisite, the manager has expectations of what the standards of performance in areas of his responsibility should be. He observes what is actually going on, and compares various aspects of the situation against his expectations.

2. Noticing discrepancies between "is" and "should be," the manager selects one out of several problems to work on. He makes this choice according to priorities of (a) the problem's urgency, (b) its seriousness, and (c) its potential for growth if left unattended.

3. He specifies "what the problem *is*"—in terms of its deviation from a standard of performance—by describing accurately its dimensions of "identity," "location," "time," and "extent." To draw a boundary around it, he also specifies what in general the problem does *not* include.

4. Comparing what *has* and what *has not* been affected as deviation from standard, the manager identifies specific *effects* of the real cause.

5. In each "area of distinction" uncovered in the previous step, the manager looks for relevant changes that have taken place and which can be logically connected to the unwanted effect(s).

6. From the array of "relevant changes" the manager deduces possible causes of the deviation. Each such conclusion is put in the form of a testable statement or hypothetical proposition.

7. Each "possible cause" is tested against the facts of the problem specification (established in Step 2). The "most likely" cause of the deviation is described by that tested hypothesis which exactly explains *all* the facts of "what the problem is" (Step 3), not only of what *has* been affected as deviation from standard, but also of what *has not* (see Step 4).

Decision making to solve the problem

1. Now that the problem's cause has been identified and verified, the manager lists the objectives he will try to accomplish in clearing up the problem.

2. He classifies these objectives into (a) "Musts"—requirements that cannot be compromised, and (b) "Wants"—aspects of "best possible performance out of the decision," not all of which can be realized in combination. He ranks and weights the latter.

3. He devises a number of alternative ways of attaining the established objectives.

4. He evaluates each alternative against the objectives, assessing it in terms of how well it satisfies each of the "Musts" and "Wants."

5. He makes a tentative decision, by choosing whichever alternative (or combination of alternatives) appears best able to achieve all the objectives.

6. He explores the tentative decision for any future possible adverse consequences that might be inherent in it.

7. He makes his final decision, which includes (a) specific problem-solving actions to be taken, (b) whatever additional actions he considers necessary for avoiding adverse consequences that might create new problems, and (c) ways of making sure that the actions decided on are carried out.

When this model has been presented an individual can be helped to test against it his presently characteristic modes of problem solving, thereby learning to reject hasty and nonrational "snap judgments." This is particularly crucial when he is under pressure in operational situations where, although time is short, so much is dependent on the quality of his problem-solving analysis that sound information gathering and logical checking procedures are an absolute necessity.

In the overall Kepner-Tregoe intervention sequence with individuals the client begins by studying the model itself and its inherent problem-analysis and decision-making requirements. Next, in a five-day off-the-job training program, he along with others practices using the model to identify and solve, under time pressure, complex problems of a simulated business enterprise as well as selected real-life problems of his back-home situation.

In doing so the individual may indicate his natural bent by slipping into characteristic ways of dealing with problems, regardless of what the logic of the model would suggest. The consultant monitors telephone calls between participants' "offices" as well as the conferences that take place when the daily-assigned general manager, production manager, sales manager, distribution manager, financial manager, and industrial-relations manager of the simulated company meet to discuss problems and make decisions. From his monitoring and the program's designed provision that the cause of each of the company's major problems can be identified if the information available is used accurately and objectively, the consultant is in a position to observe the quality of an individual's contribution.

In the critique sessions scheduled to follow each exercise, each participant is aided by colleagues and consultant to critically evaluate his performance in *using,* for the purpose of arriving at the cause of the problem and making the appropriate decision, the *information* he has been given. This almost-immediate feedback helps each individual to comprehend the extent to which personal norms and standards are revealed in his ways of thinking about problems and the degree to which decisions conform with or deviate from the model. Follow-up interventions are available to aid a given individual to further strengthen his rational problem-solving and decision-making skills in the back-home job situation.

Changing behavior by way of teaching behavior-modification principles to the client who then designs his own application program is an innovative approach to theory intervention (Mencke, 1973). Four basic considerations underlie this approach.

Commitment. This is an absolutely essential precondition for change. No change is possible unless the person is genuinely committed to making a change. Also, such commitments tend to be stronger when made publicly than when made in private . . .

Observable Behavior.   The restatement of the goals to which one is committed in terms of behavior (instead of feelings, thoughts, or other phenomena) has the advantage of making the goal more specific and less ambiguous and will often suggest in and of itself a solution to the problem. Furthermore, when other helping persons are available, the description of the problem, with examples of specific behaviors in specific situations, facilitates communications with the helping person and makes it possible for the helper to provide observations and suggestions and to reinforce desired changes when they occur . . .

A Hierarchical Approach to Goal Attainment.   Frequently individuals fail to execute a desired change in behavior because they attempt to change a total pattern of complex responses all at once rather than beginning with those aspects of the problem that are easy to change and gradually moving in the direction of those that are most resistant to modification. In lay terms, the idea is sometimes expressed in the maxim "Learn to crawl before you attempt to walk." Skinner's concept of "shaping," Wolpe's "desensitization," Gagne's "Learning programs," and task analysis procedures in the human factors area all constitute examples of the value of this approach to applied psychologists. Altogether, there is impressive evidence for the value of this principle of change . . .

Changing Behavior by Reinforcement Rather than Insight.   Much of the success of the behaviorist approach seems to be attributable to the behaviorists' observation that change is relatively unrelated to insight. In order to increase the strength of a desired response, the response must be reinforced rather than understood. Before it can be reinforced, it must occur. Practicing being what you want to be (or some small part of what you want to be) is the best way to become a fully functioning person . . . (Mencke, 1973, p. 98)

The intervention was structured as follows.

Students were required to apply the model to their own behavior to see for themselves if it was a valid tool for producing behavior change. Class activities and grading procedures were based on the behaviorists' translation of the "Know thyself" maxim. That is, some class activities directed students to careful observation and recording of their behavior, while other assignments required analysis and manipulation of the environment.

Two class activities focused on the objective "Know thy behavior." First, the students were required to write a two-page statement describing the problem behavior, its longevity, its frequency, and how difficult they felt it would be to change. At this stage, a very wide range of problems was cited by the students, e.g., study problems, obesity, anxiety about taking exams, shyness, dating problems, depression, lack of motivation, etc. Many of the problems were stated in terms of feelings or emotions and frequently appeared to the student not to involve any overt observable behaviors.

In a second assigned paper students were required to reduce their problem to some overt, observable behavior, to propose a means of measurement, and to collect base rate data. At this point a problem such as "I
can't study" might be expanded to focus on the amount of time engaged
in study, the allocation of time to different subjects by "copying notes,"
"getting organized," or "staring at a book without reading." One ingenious
student in an anatomy course measured the number of definitions she
was able to memorize in a given period of time. In another project a student who complained initially that she was "too flexible," that she did
"very few things spontaneously," measured a wide range of behaviors
related to the problem, including how often she laid her clothes out at
night (an activity that interfered with other, more spontaneous behaviors),
the number of study breaks she took with friends, the number of times
she departed from her rigid study schedule to "have fun with others," and
how often she checked ahead of time with her date to find out what he
had planned to do. In all projects, base rate was compared to similar
data taken at the end of the semester.

A second series of class procedures focused on the objective of knowing
the environment and the relationship between the environment and behavior. Reading and lectures on environmental factors in study and concentration, anxiety, and tensions were accompanied by class exercises
in the identification of environmental reinforcers and relaxation training.
The students were required to write weekly papers describing ways they
applied these ideas to their projects. Many interesting environmental
manipulations resulted from this stage of the project. One student made
seeing or talking to her boyfriend contingent on studying. Another student
asked his wife and a friend to provide regular feedback when he became
abstract and vague in his speech. (His wife loved the job.) For many, the
mere act of recording their own behavior provided enough feedback and
reinforcement to induce change without additional environmental manipulation. (Mencke, 1973, pp. 98–99)

Client reactions twelve months later reveal what aspects of the approach were considered particularly significant.

. . . listing certain behavior patterns which I consider damaging to my
overall personality when I find myself acting them out, and then referring
to the notes later on to compare the feelings involved during both the
deviant and "normal" behavior.

The most important thing to me to realize from Psych. 40 was the idea of
subgoals being so important to achieve before long range goals could
be achieved. I had known this before, but had never really applied it to
a specific problem.

To me, this project was a real catalyst into a total new self-awareness
program for myself. I actually started to be honest with myself—for the
first time. I learned techniques; however, I have transcended into deeper
self-analysis. I've used many techniques in my teaching of children.

... that any behavior can be altered or at least changed to a more acceptable form of behavior by employing the behavior modification steps learned in Psych. 40. (Mencke, 1973, p. 101)

The steps for achieving behavior change through theory intervention as outlined in Chapter 26 seem characteristic of this approach. It is doubtful, however, that this intervention is an example of behavior modification at work. The reason, as the author indicates, is that client commitment to the goal of self-change through cycle breaking is "absolutely essential." "Commitment" is a "mentalistic" concept and is without operational meaning in modification methodologies that focus exclusively on producing specific and externally observable behavior.

GROUP (S₂)

The importance of negative group norms in reducing group effectiveness and the kinds of interventions essential for moving toward more positive norms is described by de la Porte (1974). He maintains that individuals adhere to and, therefore, are controlled by group norms, sometimes without awareness that they are doing so. Thus increased effectiveness is possible only when those susceptible to such norms become aware of and reject them, replacing negative norms with those that promote greater productivity through a series of programmed interventions that include:

- Creating understanding and appreciation of the significance of norms, how they influence organizational effectiveness, and how they contribute to both the creation and the solution of key organizational problems. Group members are taught to think in normative terms and to identify and state norms. The process starts at the top of the company and permeates downward as each organizational level becomes involved in change.
- Establishing positive norm goals through cooperative action. A group can establish acceptable norm goals just as it would establish functional goals.
- Determining the excellence point of norms for the company concerned, and therefore the improvement distance to be covered.
- Establishing normative change priorities. The size of the normative gap is only one factor. More important is the relationship of the norm area to the effectiveness and profitability (or other problems) of the organization. This leads to weighting—and gives more urgent attention to—those norm clusters that have more direct impact than others on the given problem, even though the gap may be narrower than average.
- Developing systematic change strategies by examining and modifying ten specific (and crucial) areas, among which are management commitment to change; information, communication, and feedback on and about results; recognition and reward of consistent employee behavior; and recruitment and selection of new employees. Inclusion of the last recog-

nizes the fact that newcomers can introduce negative norms, just as they can be trained to conform to positive norms.

- Implementing the change strategy. Here, the essential point is to begin at the top of the organization and move downward, with the assurance of top management commitment, support, and modeling behavior.

- Providing follow-through and maintenance on a continuous basis. The emphasis here is on assigning responsibilities for change programs (often best accomplished by setting up a task force or change committee).

- Providing for continuous evaluation of the effectiveness of change strategies, and standing ready to modify plans, by reviewing change strategies if and when they fall short of expectations. (de la Porte, 1974, pp. 65–66)

How participants internalize the concept of norms is not indicated. However, among the advantages claimed for this kind of intervention is that it does not expose individuals to criticism by their peers, for all are equally "guilty" of adhering to the same negative norm(s).

ORGANIZATION (S₄)

An intervention dealing with the entire faculty and supporting staff of one school organization, fifty-four participants in all, is described by Schmuck, Runkel, and Langmeyer (1971). The example is described here because a structured model was taught to participants as the basis for improving their problem-solving procedures. In effect, the attempt was to change the norms/standards for problem solving within the faculty. The intervention began with a six-day interpersonal laboratory in which administrators and faculty members practiced using a group problem-solving approach. The model of the problem-solving sequence involved the following steps: (1) identifying the problem; (2) completing a force-field diagnosis; (3) brainstorming for reducing restraining forces; (4) designing steps to solve the problem; (5) simulating the solution's soundness. The first two days were applied to structured group exercises on simulated problems to demonstrate, through firsthand data gathering, the importance of clear communication and to evaluate the experience in terms of its pertinence for dealing with real-life school situations. This stimulated shared interpersonal feedback.

During the last four days a problem-solving sequence using "real" school problems was introduced to gather data and test the sequence for utility. Identified problems included: (1) insufficient clarity of job responsibility; (2) inadequate use of staff resources; (3) limited involvement and participation of faculty and school decision makers. Subgroupings organized around identified problems provided members with practice in using the sequence. Five training consultants, one working with each of the five groups, provided interventions based primarily on laboratory methods including observation of group process, with feedback of observations, as well as skill development to reinforce new behavior. The consultants sought to enhance task-oriented activity as contrasted with personal growth. "Family" group team building was not involved.

Thereafter participants received day-and-a-half-long "booster shot" training sessions during the school year. The first initiated discussion of the faculty's insufficient use of what they had learned in the first six-day session; the second involved stock-taking in further efforts to revive deteriorating skills. The intervention's operational impact included: (1) classroom application projects; (2) increased influence on school operations from an advisory committee; (3) better interpersonal relations among faculty and administrators; (4) setting up a new internal "facilitator" to serve as a liaison between groups and to help interpersonal relationships, and so on.

SUMMARY

Much is known in behavioral-science research regarding the extent to which behavior is controlled and regulated by norms/standards. Most of this theory, however, remains at the academic level—in other words, it has not been converted to functional use.

The "actual versus ideal" methodology is one illustration of possibilities in this area and the behavior-modification-theory intervention is another example of the potential value of helping clients learn how to replace counterproductive norms and standards with more positive ones, a shift based both upon insight into the process and personal commitment to change. A theory intervention that focuses on practical problem solving may also contribute to the phasing out of inappropriate norms/standards.

The advantage of shifting norms in this manner is that changes in norm-referenced behavior can come about without provoking the intense resistances that are almost inevitable when change is attempted by prescriptive interventions. As was illustrated in the Chapter 23 report by Higdon, not only may the prescriptive consultant be "punished" for rejection of the prevailing norms but, more importantly, after his ouster the client might value and enforce traditional norms even more intensely than before.

REFERENCES

Blake, R. R., and J. S. Mouton. *Corporate Excellence through Grid Organization Development.* Houston: Gulf Publishing Company, 1968.

de la Porte, P. C. A. "Group Norms: Key to Building a Winning Team." *Personnel* 51, no. 5 (1974): 60–67. Reprinted by permission of the publisher.

Kepner, C. H., and B. B. Tregoe. *The Rational Manager.* New York: McGraw-Hill, 1965.

Mencke, R. A. "Teaching Self-Modification in an Adjustment Course." *Personnel and Guidance Journal* 52, no. 2 (1973): 97–101. Copyright 1973 American Personnel and Guidance Association. Reprinted with permission.

Schmuck, R. A., P. Runkel, and D. Langmeyer. "Using Group Problem-Solving Procedures." In R. A. Schmuck and M. B. Miles, eds., *Organization Development in Schools.* Palo Alto, Calif.: National Press Books, 1971, pp. 51–69.

THEORY-PRINCIPLES INTERVENTIONS

30

GOALS/OBJECTIVES

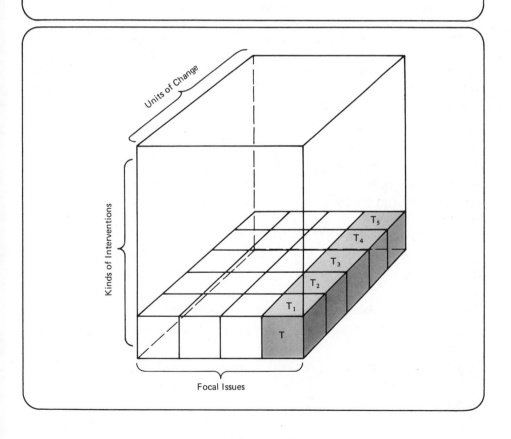

The capacity of goals/objectives to give character and direction to human endeavors is difficult to overestimate. Goals and objectives offer a meaningful orientation to any activity, lend it a purpose. Many activities in modern society are already structured in goals/objectives terms. College education is an example. Graduation represents completion of a planned cycle of activity. Profit is the goal of business. Planned activities are calculated to reach the goal of profit by increasing the return on investment from certain products or by reducing the expense of producing or marketing them. Family life and healthy children constitute the goals of numerous marriages.

Oftentimes, however, goals are expressed in such abstract terms or are so remote from activity that behavior is little influenced. Graduation may be the completion of a college activity cycle, but for the first several years this goal may be too far removed to affect conscious endeavor. The same is true with regard to corporate profit. While certain higher layers in the organization may consider profit crucial, at other levels an individual's contribution to corporate profit is so difficult to evaluate as to be altogether disregarded.

Given the importance of goals and objectives as a foundation for meaningful behavior, the dearth of theory-based interventions with a goals/objective focal issue is surprising. At any rate, in any thoroughgoing theory-based intervention concerning the setting and accomplishment of goals/objectives the consultant aids the client in any one or possibly all four of these ways: (1) goal clarification; (2) goal redefinition; (3) restructuring activities so as to make goals-oriented actions possible; (4) setting of goals in situations where it is possible to designate *what* the goals—especially if unprecedented—should be. The same strategy of intervention has been applied in larger social settings as well.

INDIVIDUAL (T₁)

McClelland and colleagues have identified and researched a motivation that they term "need for Achievement" (*n* Ach). In turn, they have created theory-based intervention designs for the purpose of aiding individuals to increase their capacity for achievement.

Individuals with a high motivation to achieve:

1. calculate carefully what it is they must do to gain a sense of mastery in a situation where the effort they put out can influence whether they are successful or not;

2. set moderately difficult, but potentially achievable goals for themselves;

3. are concerned with the achievement itself rather than the rewards of success per se;

4. show a strong preference for work situations in which they get concrete feedback on how well they are doing.

This research-derived model provides a basis of intervention for teaching people to increase their achievement motivation. The general rationale on which the intervention is based is as follows.

A quest for personal achievement is or can be a continuing stimulus to an individual's financial and economic progress. Comparably, the general or particular population's level of motivation to achieve may be crucial for the financial and social health of a nation. Some individuals, as well as communities and nations, seem naturally to strive toward goals of achievement while others—the vast majority—are far less motivated to do so (McClelland, 1961).

Why one man is perenially motivated to achieve while his neighbor is more or less satisfied to be one of the pack is, of course, a complicated question. To answer it in terms of a particular individual would entail much research into personal history and environmental influences. A more pertinent question, however, is whether or not a presently low level of achievement motivation can be raised through consultant-based interventions. The intervention varies from circumstance to circumstance, but its basic outline includes the following steps.

First, clients are taught how people with a high need to achieve think, talk, and act. This includes demonstrations of how achievement motivation is revealed in imaginative stories as well as how it is reflected in personal goal setting. For example, those highest in need to achieve (a) when given a choice, elect to *work* at a problem-solving task designed to give them about a 1-in-3 chance of succeeding, rather than taking the option of rolling dice in a relatively effortless *game of chance* where the odds of winning are similar (McClelland, 1966); (b) when participating in a *game of skill* (such as throwing darts), set moderately challenging goals for themselves which also tend to have about a 1-in-3 chance of being achieved. Apparently, achievement-motivated people prefer to plan and take *themselves* the actions leading up to success-or-failure outcomes. They enjoy stretching their capabilities; although, at the same time, they take care not to set goals which, in any particular dimensions, are so far out as to be almost impossible to attain.

A related aspect noted by McClelland is that the achievement motivated have a strong preference for work situations in which they get continuing concrete feedback on how well they are doing. Interventions are therefore designed to stimulate participants to set higher, but carefully planned and operational, work goals for themselves—for example, in their work situations covering the next two-year period (Aronoff and Litwin, 1971). As reported elsewhere (McClelland, 1966), interim feedback and critique every six months can be provided during this two-year period.

A third feature of the intervention is that small-group discussions provide opportunities for several participants to evaluate and critique one another's achievement motivations under circumstances where each individual is obligated to explain to the others why the goals he or she set are realistic in terms of his or her present situation, performance, and aptitudes. Other discussants may comment on whether these seem too high or too low. Such discussions can be the stimulus to much broader shared discussion of life goals of achievement as contrasted with making good impressions on others or having many friends (McClelland, 1966). This step is calculated to free participants from old habits and attitudes, i.e., their natural bents; additionally, the small-group atmosphere may produce a cohesiveness among members which sustains mutual encouragement and support for future striving.

Given that participants gain sound systematic comprehension of the dynamics of achievement from the intervention, it has been found in numerous applications that the motive to achieve can be increased over and above its previous level. It has also been demonstrated that such changes in personal motivation translate into improved performance and achievement.

McClelland (1966) points out—but offers no wider basis for solution than the ongoing mutual-support group of clients—that one of the important deterrents to achievement motivation can be the cultural norms and attitudes surrounding an individual. If these are stagnant or negative, the impact of achievement training is likely to be significantly less than if the motivation to achieve within the culture itself is high. Possibly the limited impact of some achievement-motivation projects is due to failure of those responsible for the intervention to address the content and context of economic and financial realities. When setting of goals/objectives occurs in the context of Grid OD projects being carried out by the entire corporation, such barriers to achievement are eliminated in advance.

LARGER SOCIAL SYSTEM (T₅)

Further use of McClelland-innovated training as a precursor to a community development workshop (where participants could begin applying achievement-motivation learnings in an actual social setting) is reported by Berlew and LeClere (1974). While outcomes did not match the objectives set, the project itself provides an interesting case study of a community development attempt.

The activity took place in Curacao, one of a number of islands in the West Indies which since 1954 has been self-governing within the Dutch Commonwealth. Curacao has a population of about 140,000. In the spring of 1969 there occurred a heavy and costly outbreak of community violence. Almost simultaneously the Curacaon Chamber of Commerce intensified its exploration of possible community building opportunities. Berlew was one of the applied behavioral scientists contracted. He traveled to Curacao for discussions with the Chamber and, without going into details, his suggestion that achievement motivation was pertinent to the island's needs initiated the more or less "crash project" that followed.

At 8 p.m. (a few hours after my arrival) I met with the Board of Directors of the Chamber of Commerce and Industry. The President listed four objectives to which the Chamber was committed: (1) to encourage Antilleans to become associated with existing businesses, (2) to increase the amount of commercial activity on Curacao by encouraging Antillean business activity, (3) to create new jobs, and (4) to give Antilleans a sense of participation in their community.

We spent the next two hours reviewing current business and social conditions on Curacao and the prerequisites of an effective small-business development program. I emphasized that while we believe achievement motivation training to be one essential element, the availability of capital and training in business skills are also critical. We ended the Board meeting by planning strategy for a meeting scheduled the next morning with 40 government, community, labor, and business leaders. Our approach, we decided, would be (a) to describe "new behavioral science technologies" such as achievement training; (b) to engage those present in a discussion of how these technologies might relate to the problems of Curacao; and (c) to discuss how we might proceed to apply these technologies, if they were perceived as relevant.

Although the morning meeting was held in the Chamber building (hardly neutral turf), nearly everyone invited showed up. I introduced myself as a "technologist"—someone who did not know much about their specific situation but who was knowledgeable about some new social or change technologies which they should know about and might find useful in solving their problems. During my initial presentation I described achievement motivation training, various types of group training, and "psychological education"; in response to questions, I also discussed community and organization development. Fearing that people might too readily see "cures" to their problems, I tried to be very objective and factual, presenting research findings whenever I could. The meeting lasted over four hours, and each group present appeared to find something relevant to its specific needs, which went well beyond the business development needs of the Chamber. The meeting ended with what seemed to be a general feeling that these new "technologies" were highly relevant and an effort should be made to apply them to the problems on Curacao. (Berlew and LeClere, 1974, pp. 30–31)

A special organization intended to be neutral in terms of the different vested community interests, and that developed its membership from each of them, was set up to spearhead the broad intervention. In due course several hundred of the island residents had participated in either or both the achievement-motivation or community-development activities.

While the achievement-motivation program followed along lines generally comparable to those described earlier in this chapter, the community-development workshop dealt with content issues, such as what the participants would like to see Curacao become, and demonstration projects involving "intergroup competition and cooperation" aspects of community problem solving. Little focus was placed upon team-building skills or the capability of individual members to handle interpersonal or group-based conflict.

The overall impact of the intervention, which had as one of its primary objectives an increase in the number of entrepreneurs and the number of jobs available in Curacao, fell short of the target. Nor did it stimulate continued support by the community and business leadership of Curacao. It is unclear as to why this is so; the character of the interventions themselves may be at fault.

The Curacao intervention may have been unusual in that it was based more on a motivational model derived from psychology or sociology. The motivational model seemed particularly relevant for a number of reasons. First, during initial interview, black Antillean leaders expressed great concern over the lack of an Antillean identity. Specifically, they worried about an almost total lack of initiative by black Antilleans, which they attributed to centuries of dependency, first as slaves, then as Dutch subjects. It was this information that led us to the concept of efficacy and deCharm's distinction between "origins" and "pawns." Second, the lack of an entrepreneurial tradition among black Antilleans suggested that achievement motivation and the development of entrepreneurial spirit should play an important part in the intervention.

It was obvious that the use and distribution of power would have to be a major concern of the intervention. . . .

Unfortunately, we never fully understood the complexities of power on Curacao, although we did come to appreciate its singular importance. (Berlew and LeClere, 1974, p. 50)

The relative lack of success could be partly attributable to the strategies by which the interventions were introduced and carried forward.

This intervention asks people to analyze what they want, when they want to do it, and then to do it, or try to do it. That can create revolutionaries as well as solutions. But unless *some* of the people start thinking in these terms, nothing in the system is going to improve anyway. (Berlew and LeClere, 1974, p. 52)

More fundamentally, though, there appears to have been little in the way of foresighted consultant-client efforts to address the culture-based influences of long-established traditions, precedents, and past practices that run counter to achievement training. Instead, the following serendipitous currents may have helped launch the intervention, move it awhile, and then leave it "dead in the water."

. . . Consultants are accepted because of a funny cross-mixture of the voodoo culture and the Dutch educational system where the people basically believe in voodoo, in magic, in fortune telling, in destiny, and all those things. The motivation training course is seen as something that gives people increased mental powers to control the directions of their lives. And to that extent it's consonant with what I call the voodoo cult. On the other hand, anyone who is a university professor is, by definition, the master. . . . People don't even question the validity of the ideas. So I think the consultant's initial speeches to the community were accepted immediately, whereas they wouldn't be necessarily in other systems. (Berlew and LeClere, 1974, pp. 50–51)

Nonetheless, the Berlew-LeClere experience provides an example of an effort to introduce the members of a large community to behavioral-science–based theories and concepts, several of which aim to shift the cultural basis of interaction in the community to a new and more entrepreneurial orientation.

SUMMARY

Strategies for theory-based interventions designed to aid the client in setting and achieving productive goals and objectives are only beginning to be employed, with the result that relatively little is known about how to take advantage of the academic theory available in this area. The interventions that have been reported are suggestive, but there are significant indications that goals/objectives setting, given the broader norms/standards control over an individual's behavior, is unlikely to be successful.

Evidence to date indicates that when individual members participate in resolving power/authority issues, they begin to feel an increased commitment to finding solutions. Furthermore, when cohesion/morale is high and when norms/standards are consonant with striving, it becomes a practical possibility for members to set goals for their own achievement or for the achievement of the group or organization of which they are members. However, if these other basic dimensions are disregarded, goals/objectives that are set, even as a result of theory-based interventions, are likely to remain unachieved.

REFERENCES

Aronoff, J., and G. H. Litwin. "Achievement Motivation Training and Executive Advancement." *Journal of Applied Behavioral Science* 7, no. 2 (1971): 215–29.

Berlew, D. E., and W. E. LeClere. "Social Interventions in Curacao." Reproduced by special permission from *Journal of Applied Behavioral Science* 10, no. 1 (1974): 29–52.

McClelland, D. C. *The Achieving Society*. Princeton, N.J.: Van Nostrand, 1961.

McClelland, D. C. "That Urge to Achieve." *THINK Magazine* 32, no. 6 (1966): 1923.

31

SUMMARY
AND
IMPLICATIONS

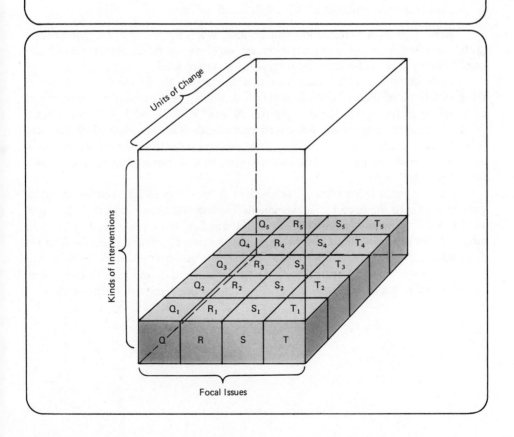

In each intervention described in this section the client has been taught theories pertinent to his or her behavior and has been aided in applying these theories to solving whatever difficulties he or she may be encountering. A significant issue bearing upon the use of theory-based interventions is how to help the client internalize theory so that it becomes a personally useful source of guidance rather than an abstract academic theory.

The dynamics of internalization include the following:

1. Prior to being introduced to theories that may be pertinent, the client is enabled to indicate his or her natural bent in approaching a given problem.

2. Theories are then introduced in any number of different and innovative ways, but the general strategy is that the mode of theory presentation should permit the client to learn through active involvement and participation rather than through passive listening.

3. Opportunities for developing skill in using theory for diagnosis and problem solving are then provided. Along the way the client is afforded the opportunity to test "natural bents" and their implications in the light of the theory, particularly with regard to past behaviors that should be rejected while learning to utilize theory to strengthen new kinds of behavior.

These steps of internalization can be used when the client is an individual, a group, an intergroup, or an organization. As yet there are no good examples of successful theory interventions at the larger-social-system level.

Power/authority is the focal issue that has drawn the greatest attention from those interested in theory-based interventions. There are a number of theory-based approaches, including the Grid, Theories X and Y, Systems 1–4, Transactional Analysis training, and Parent Effectiveness Training. On the other hand, morale/cohesion has barely been approached from the standpoint of theory-based interventions, and the use of theory-based interventions to shift norms/standards is largely unexplored territory.

Goals/objectives have been approached from a theory-intervention point of view in regard to the need for achievement. The interventions reported to date provide a model for what is possible, but are of limited value in demonstrating that this mode of theory intervention can be expected to have significant impact—with the possible exception of its application to individuals in entrepreneurial assignments, i.e., those unencumbered by the norms/standards of group and organization memberships that may prevent them from taking actions involving risk or innovation.

32

THEORY
AND TECHNIQUE
OF CONSULTATION

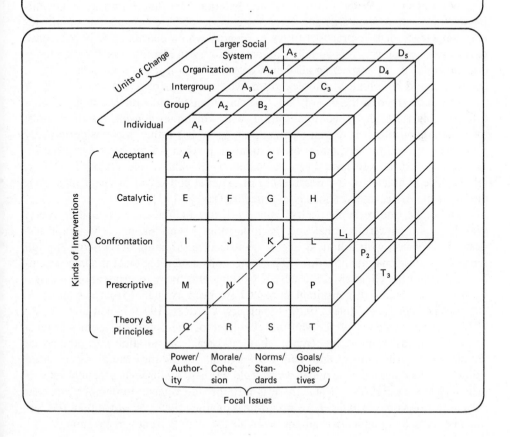

The Consulcube provides a framework within which the various consultant-client interactions can be identified, compared, and evaluated in terms of their richness, variety, and utility. These main features already have been described and discussed in summaries of each of the five major intervention modes. Attention now can be focused on issues that any consultant needs to be aware of: his or her definition of the focal issue, of the consultant's role, of who or what the client is, and of the relationships among them.

WHO IS THE CONSULTANT?

Up to a few years ago the description of a consultant presumed outstanding academic or experience-based qualifications in his or her area of expertise. The consultant had demonstrated, through career and personal success, an unusual knowledge and capacity for assisting clients with specific problems in one or several areas of his or her solution-seeking competency. If not a university professor, the consultant was likely to be employed by a consulting firm.

What was certain yesterday is in a process of flux today, for many now acting effectively in consultation assignments are neither employed by a consulting firm nor by a university. With both internal and external consultants, and with accrediting agencies setting standards and accepting experience-based credentials of individual competence, it is impractical to try to identify who a consultant is by reference to his or her employer. It is equally impractical to try to identify what a consultant's qualifications are by inspecting academic degrees. Even if it were possible to do so, the task would be infinitely complex given two new trends of recent years.

One such trend is the use of "internal consultants," individuals employed on a full-time salaried basis by the organizations with which they consult. In other words, the internal consultant is not an outsider coming in, but rather is an insider already a member of the firm. Dynamics of consultation involving external and internal interventions respectively have been evaluated by Beckhard and Shepard (Porter, 1974). The character of the relationship of external consultant to client most conducive to successful interventions is specified by Davey (1971).

The other, and certainly no less important, trend is the emergence after World War II of the paraprofessional and the indigenous nonprofessional. A paraprofessional is a person with a limited degree of specialized training but without the full range of professional qualifications. The indigenous nonprofessional is someone embedded within the client situation who is working effectively to bring about change. Both of these points of consultant contact have been evaluated from a number of different perspectives (Hines, 1970; Lynch and Gardner, 1970; Nolan and Cooke, 1970). Other evidence of the shifting character of the consultant comes from a number of fields, some quite remote from "classical" consultation and others that are not customarily thought of as consultation at all. Yet all the examples introduced below are documented in clinical work, field studies, or through practical experiments (Riessman, 1965). When there is little or no evidence to demonstrate that the paraprofessional or indigenous nonprofessional are better or worse than the certified or formally qualified consultant, equivalence of effectiveness is presumed.

For example, other things being equal, "dry" alcoholics are often better equipped to help other alcoholics to control their behavior than are psychiatrists, ministers, or other counselors (*Alcoholics Anonymous,* 1955). Working together, ex–drug addicts are equally or more effective in assisting active drug addicts to solve their problems than are medical personnel, psychiatrists, or ministers (Enright, 1971). Ghetto residents who have succeeded in commercial, educational, or upward-mobile social lines of endeavor are equally or more effective in helping other ghetto residents break out of the poverty cycle than are ministers, social workers, and so on (Hallowitz, 1968). Though relevant data are somewhat more difficult to interpret, it appears that people who have themselves been prone to neurotic reactions are sometimes as capable of helping one another to gain insight into and increase their mastery over neurotic symptoms as are psychologists, psychiatrists, etc. (Low, 1960). Criminals in prison, halfway houses, or on probation can be capably assisted in thinking through their pasts and in discovering more constructive modes of behavior by ex-criminals who have successfully gone straight (Buckley, 1972). Programs for adult literacy development have an equal or more impactful result when taught by those who share a common cultural heritage yet who have overcome illiteracy than when taught by experts for whom literacy has never been a problem (Laubach and Laubach, 1960).

When intervening with university students, dormitory counselors who also are students achieve as good or better results than do university counselors who are members of the administration or teaching faculty. Similarly, freshman orientation has been found to be at least as beneficial, or more so, when carried out by upperclassmen as when implemented by the professorial/administrative group (Brown, 1965).

Equally significant are industrial experiments where internal consultants either cooperate on a team basis with external consultants or replace them, and the now-emerging academic experiments in education. Both demonstrate that one student can tutor another student with results that are equal to or better than results obtained by professional educators (Gartner, Kohler, and Riessman, 1971).

Correct generalization from these findings is important in understanding consultation processes. The basic proposition appears to be that the wider the gap between consultant and client, the more numerous and intractable the difficulties encountered in bridging it may prove to be. By the same reasoning, the narrower the gap—particularly when creative ways are found to enable people of equal status to help in bringing about change—the more effective are the changes that result.

The situation is complicated by another factor, however. In many paraprofessional or subprofessional consultant-client contacts, a consultant who does meet professional standards of competence, say a psychiatrist or an OD expert, may be in the picture but *not* visible to the client. This happens because the paraprofessional consultant—a person comparable to the client in socioeconomic, ethnic, and other characteristics—is in the middle, often acting with the client as a member of the corporation or agency. He or she *interprets* the client's situation to the professional consultant and, in turn, gains insight from the professional consultant-expert as to next steps of intervention he or she might consider taking with the client. This middleman role appears to be no less effective and, in fact, more efficient than when an outsider is the consultant, for one professional consultant-expert may advise or supervise ten, twelve, or more paraprofessionals, each of whom may carry a client load of ten, twenty, or thirty clients, depending, of course, on the definition of client and character of the consultation. The multiplier on the professional's competence, in other words, is, in a most conservative circumstance, $1 \times 10 \times 10$: one professional consultant to 100 clients. In direct professional consultant-client contact the load would be ten or so, and without much evidence that outcomes would be superior.

The strengths and limitations inherent in the concept of paraprofessional or internal consultation have yet to be fully worked out. An obvious and significant conclusion is that the capacity for intervening on a consultation basis has little to do with academic credentials, employment by a status consulting firm, accumulated experience, or demonstrated success. As will be seen, in each of these interactions there is a keyed matching in the who-does-what-to-whom relationship between consultant and client. The match often is based on the fact that those involved have experienced common symptoms and so can "understand" one another.

WHAT IS THE FOCAL ISSUE?

In view of the frequency with which it is reported, power/authority seems to be the number one focal-issue problem, outstripping others by about three to one. Power/authority has long been recognized as an endemic source of social disease in modern industrial societies. Freud noted this before the turn of the century when he identified parent-child power/authority relationships as basic to all human adjustment and as causes of much maladjustment. Nowadays these problems seem even more intense and widespread, more "on the table for debate" than in Freud's time.

Power/authority problems are encountered in all walks of life and among people of all ages, although they appear to be more widespread among the young. While most commonly found in the family, such problems repeat themselves in many settings later in life: in marriage, in schools and universities, in industry. They are common in the United States, but possibly no more so than in Europe or Asia where they also abound.

Consultation can be of help in relieving power/authority tensions after the problem has erupted. Much more fundamental solutions are required, however, to get at the root of the problem itself. All intervention modes are employed in seeking to help clients deal with power/authority problems. The acceptant mode is relied upon more commonly when the client is in a subordinate role; for example, a child having problems with adjustment in the home; a student having difficulty in school; a person of lesser industrial rank having difficulties with one of higher rank. However, when the acceptant role is employed the person in the dominant role is unlikely to be brought into the situation, with the result that feedback is unavailable to the source.

The major gain to the client is from the acceptant conditions provided. Once emotional undercurrents are expressed at the surface level and discharged—at least temporarily—then it may be possible for the client to orient his or her thinking about the problem along more objective lines. In turn, these can lead to the client taking actions that will solve the objective problem and remove it as an emotional provocation.

The second most frequently relied upon intervention mode is the catalytic one. Without seeking to change power/authority relationships it facilitates the sharing of information to reduce pluralistic ignorance. In this way it becomes possible to help individuals to anticipate one another's feelings and to provide for an easing of tensions. The likelihood of basic change on either side of power/authority cleavages, however, is remote.

Theory-based interventions are the third most relied upon strategy for approaching power/authority problems. Insights from theory afford the client prospects of rectifying the problem at its source; for example, the client may be helped to reject an ineffective natural bent and to replace it with systematic understanding of human motivations, particularly as they relate to the power/authority problem.

Confrontational and more frequently prescriptive interventions are employed to some extent in the power/authority area. In implementing prescriptions, however, the client is submitting to an external power/authority source, even though under the guise of advice. Thus a prescription tends to reduce the client's degree of capacity for acting according to his or her own power/authority, a condition more likely to provoke antagonisms than to bring about problem solving. Ambivalent feelings germinate under these circumstances. The client brings the consultant into the situation because he or she wants help, but resents the very advice offered when it makes demands that put the individual in conflict with others or in various ways reduces his or her capacity for self-direction. Nonetheless, prescription can be an effective intervention when power/authority is not presently functioning within a system. The classic example is when a client is so down and out that only through the consultant's directions is he likely to ever take steps essential to his own progress.

Confrontation is a useful way of generating insights for clients who have power/authority problems, for the approach "forces" the client to recognize something that previously he or she was unable to see. Since the client was unaware of his or her power/authority problem, he or she is unlikely to have sought out a confrontational consultant for assistance in coping with it. Therefore, confrontational interventions usually are not in clients' frames of expectation and may thus provoke win-lose battles rather than the "Aha" reaction of new insight.

Although by comparison with power/authority other focal issues might seem less important, such a conclusion (while statistically supported) would be misleading. Take, for example, a situation in which norms/standards are lacking with the result that activities are unplanned, disorderly, and unpredictable—even though plans, orderliness, and predictability could lead to the situation's all-around improvement. A conventional solution would be to impose order via power/authority methods. But in due course the consequent reactions would probably lead to the need for consultation to solve problems associated with unacceptable power/authority situations. Had the client recognized that prospect, he or she might have seen in timelier fashion that what actually was needed was structured opportunities for participants to discuss the situation so as to make it possible for constructive norms/standards to emerge. This in turn could provide a coherent basis for establishing order in terms of norms/standards that would regulate behavior and conduct in terms acceptable to all, thus bringing predictability into the situation. Had the client seen the problem in this light he or she would not have approached the situation coercively, but instead would have provided leadership. Power/authority, in other words, is the surface problem under these conditions, whereas norms/standards constitutes the real problem—the focal issue.

Comparable explanations may account for situations in which the real problem is not power/authority but rather the absence of satisfactory goals/objectives. The client's quick power/authority solution is to impose goals, thereby creating the power/authority problem for which consultation is initially sought. The client might, however, have fundamentally solved the problem by creating conditions for getting subordinates initially involved, both in setting and working toward demanding yet mutually accepted goals/objectives. Alternatively, if the client's skill in engendering goals/objectives was insufficient, then the consultation might have dealt with helping this client to increase his or her leadership effectiveness.

Similarly, inadequate morale/cohesion may derive from *anomie*—widespread normlessness and an accompanying lack of shared goals/objectives—which in turn might be an historic consequence of inappropriate or unacceptable exercises of power/authority.

One of the risks of consultation, therefore, is that the consultant will perceive the focal issue as being a power/authority issue when in fact the deeper problem, of which the power/authority problems are but symptoms, continues unrecognized and untreated.

WHO IS THE CLIENT?

"Who is the client?" may appear to be an unimportant question or one for which the answer is obvious. But in reality it is among the most critical, for when a consultant deals with the "wrong" client the consequence is at best unproductive, at worst, destructive. When an individual is reacting out of his or her own history, personal values, and so on, and in the here-and-now context has problems that are uninfluenced by other people, the individual can be considered the client. But the decision as to client becomes somewhat more complex when the following happens. The consultant may be contacted by an individual who complains about problems in his situation that pose barriers to personal effectiveness. In this case the individual may be the initial client, but his situation might on further investigation be found to contain inherent constraints over which this individual has no control, constraints subject to resolution if the others involved in the situation simultaneously participate in solution seeking. The client thus actually may be a group or a team, such as a division, an institute, a counseling office, and so on; the common feature being that several people possess a problem arising from their interactions.

The problem of "Who is the client?" becomes even more complex when the consultant is approached by an individual whose difficulty involves interaction with another person of equal rank who, say, heads another division. The real client may be the person himself, his group, or the intergroup relationship. The following is a way of testing these possibilities. If the individual were to change toward the other person as a result of consultation, would the changes in his behavior, attitudes, and conduct be seen by others within his own immediate membership group as letting them down? Would he be seen as a traitor, or would he be seen as a hero because he was now acting differently toward the other person? If any of these reactions were to occur, the likelihood is that the real client in this situation is the intergroup relationship itself. An example may be helpful.

Consider two segments of a corporation or two departments within a large university—a department of psychology and one of educational psychology. It is likely that the department of psychology, housed in the College of Arts and Sciences, is seen by the educational-psychology department, housed in the College of Education, as "pure," engaging in rigorous research but dealing with trivial problems in a "holier than thou" manner. By comparison, the educational-psychology department may be seen as "loose" in the sense of not being rigorously experimental. To the purists, it seems clinically oriented and even tainted by "mentalism."

Now, if the two chairmen, each representing one of these departments, were to come together and the chairman of the department of "pure" psychology were to agree to a joint professorship for one of the professors of educational psychology, he would likely be seen as "selling out" for some hidden reason or out of personal weakness to the chairman of the department of educational psychology. By the same consideration, if the chairman of the department of educational psychology were to agree to a joint professorship for one of the "purist" psychology-department members, whose life had been devoted to problems of visual discrimination in the monkey, members of his faculty would likely see *his* behavior as "selling out."

It is clear that both decisions might be favorable to the overriding objective of aiding students in learning the fundamentals of psychology. The educational-psychology professor teaching in the College of Arts and Sciences makes a beneficial contribution by helping experimental psychologists to understand "real world" problems that they may approach in an experimental vein. At the same time the pure-psychology professor operating in the educational-psychology department might well be able to communicate an increased understanding and respect for experimental methods.

When decisions about client identity would result in win-lose attitudes between two departments, it is clear that the client is neither chairman, nor is it either department. Rather, the client is the two departments considered jointly. It is they who need the opportunity of studying their relationship and confronting the emotion-based reactions to their differences so that, based on shared understanding, they can reach solutions to their problem of collaboration.

The same line of reasoning applies when the organization is considered as a whole. If the organization has any age, say as much as two or three years, it already has built a climate and a culture of reactions and attitudes based upon tradition, precedents, and past practices, ritual, sacred cows, and so on. These are widely recognized and rarely discussed, but serve as the boundary conditions that define what is okay for people to do and what is beyond the limits of proper responsibility. In such cases the client is the organization as a system rather than the inter-group relationships or the working groups of teams or the separate individuals making up the organization.

Sometimes the problems of the organization are in the larger social system within which the organization is embedded. In the case of a school, for example, these involve issues of community support, taxation, and relationships with parents and interested citizens, law enforcement authorities, and so on. When these interrelationships are among the sources of school problems, then the client is the larger social system, including the school as a subsystem within that larger social system. The interventions necessary must then deal with this broader context.

Thus the question, "Who is the client?" is far more complicated than might appear at first glance. To reiterate, an analytical approach to "Who is the client?" leads to a separation into two categories of individuals who approach a consultant. Sometimes the individual is the real client, i.e., the entire problem that he or she confronts is within the client's capacity to resolve with consultant assistance. Sometimes, however, the client should be seen not as *the* client but as the entry person, that is, an individual through whom access to the *real* client may be possible.

WHEN CONSULTANTS CONTRACT WITH THEIR CLIENTS

Every relationship is based on expectations. Sometimes these are made explicit through formal contracts, either in words or writing, which specify what the relationship is to involve. More often the precise terms are left undefined or at least unstated and informal because expectations are difficult to envisage at the time the contract is inaugurated. Sometimes, in fact, it is unwise or unnecessary to be specific.

But examples of very explicit contracts abound. These are most common in industry where complex, technically worded agreements are reached between two companies, between a company and an individual, or between a management and a union. Such contracts may specify who will do what, to whom, by when, and for how much. Far less specific, marriage vows are nonetheless contractual, too, and indicate in broad terms what each mate expects of the other. Still more general and usually unwritten, except in terms of legal statutes, is the "contract" of responsibility parents automatically assume for rearing their children. What society expects of them is clearer when harm has been done to children than when no flagrant evidence of bad practice arouses community attention.

Other contracts are often implicit or based on intuitive understanding, as is frequently the case between confidants and friends, and in some professional relationships. Each participant is free to end the relationship in a unilateral way when unsatisfied with it; usually there is no basis of redress unless a verbal contract is claimed. It is uncommon, for example, for a medical doctor to enter into a written or verbal contract with a patient (especially with respect to outcomes), although in terms of his or her professional ethic a surgeon attempts to be concrete and specific with patients as to the medical circumstances they face and the treatment likely to be entailed. The relationship between a lawyer and client is usually implicit because, eventualities being what they are, the preparation of a written contract in fixed terms is often difficult if not entirely impractical.

Much the same can be said in the field of consultation. Sometimes a contract is used to specify the character of the relationship (Harris, 1969, p. 231; Kolb and Frohman, 1970, p. 55; Argyris, 1970, pp. 16–17; French and Bell, 1973, pp. 174–75). More often, what the consultation may entail is so difficult to envisage that contract preparation, except possibly for housekeeping and financial aspects, either is not attempted or is deferred until some later time when it would be more practical. A contract may no longer be needed after a consulting relationship has been established and each of the parties has come to appreciate what the situation needs by way of intervention. Thus, in the history of consultation, the preparation of contracts about *process* has been relatively rare, although efforts at mutual understanding of what is to be involved, at what expense, etc., have been characteristic.

This situation is now changing rapidly. The terms of the relationship are being made more explicit and concrete through talking them out, often putting them in writing. There are reasons for this. The most important is that a contract can help both consultant and client crystallize expectations for what the relationship is to be. In this way, unwitting violation of unstated expectations can be reduced and the consultant is freed from untenable demands.

A major limitation in contracting is that the client may never have experienced many of the kinds of consultation approaches possible; in other words, what will occur in the relationship is not understandable to the client at the beginning of the consultation. Under these circumstances, words, whether spoken or written, mean little. By the time a contract is possible it is unnecessary, for client expectations as to what the consultant can do and consultant understanding of client needs have been clarified and crystallized into an acceptable basis of intervention.

There is a partial solution to even this aspect of the problem. It involves stating in contractual terms what the relationship *will be at the beginning* and leaving it open for repeated negotiation as to what it will be as the relationship advances. As experience builds, hastening the rapidity with which consultant and client learn to interact, such expectations are continuously clarified as part and parcel of the consultant's work by process of renegotiation. Some consultants maintain that this process of clarification is inherent in effective consultation in the first place and, therefore, is not some additional aspect brought about by contracting; others see the importance of renegotiation as an additional component that can keep both parties conscious of what is taking place and ready to identify and explore previously unexamined alternatives.

The character of a contract varies with the strategy of consultation, whether cathartic, confrontational, and so on. What follows is a description of contract preparation from each of these major orientations.

Contracting under an Acceptant Orientation

The character of the consultant-client relationship involved in the acceptant mode of intervention is nowhere better described than by Rogers:

> The counseling relationship is one in which warmth of acceptance and absence of any coercion or personal pressure on the part of the counselor permits the maximum expression of feelings, attitudes, and problems by the counselee. The relationship is a well-structured one, with limits of time, of dependence, and of aggressive action which apply particularly to the client, and limits of responsibility and of affection which the counselor imposes on himself. In this unique experience of complete emotional freedom within a well-defined framework, the client is free to recognize and understand his impulses and patterns, positive and negative, as in no other relationship. (Rogers, 1942, pp. 113–14)

Because each such relationship is a unique one acceptant consultation makes contract preparation difficult. Few clients have had prior experience with it or have experienced it in everyday life. They do not know what to expect, and words from the consultant do little to clarify the situation. Only after they have had experience with this approach does it become possible to talk meaningfully about it. Nonetheless some value may come from trying to be explicit. The consultant might say, "In many relationships the 'expert' takes the initiative to assist the one seeking help to resolve the problems for which help is being sought. Other consultants share the initiative with the client in a give-and-take way. It would be my desire that the initiative in our relationship always remain in *your* hands. I will offer whatever help and assistance I can contribute through aiding you to exercise initiative in dealing with your situation. I will do my best to understand what you are experiencing. For me to understand in a manner that will be helpful to you, it is important that I absorb what you are seeking to communicate, and that I do so in a nonevaluative, nonpartisan manner. In this way, it may be that our relationship will offer you the kind of safety that makes it possible for you to explore your own experience so as to gain deeper insight into why you feel as you do; and, further, to see opportunities of change that may not have been as apparent in the past. I may suggest experiments useful to you in entering into an experience, but the initiative for taking part, and for interpreting that experience is yours.

"As we go along you may come to experience your situation in a new light, and in turn this may have a significant bearing on how you relate to others. It might be that by speaking to them I could help them to see your altered situation. But then the initiative would be shifting from you to me. The alternative is that you retain initiative by communicating to them your altered situation as you now or later conceive it. If you wish, I can offer help in providing a safe place to engage in these kinds of interactions with people who are significant to you."

This kind of statement is only the beginning of a contract. Much more is understood than is spoken, in the sense that the client appreciates that he is not about to be told in a directive, advice-giving way what he should start or stop doing in order to deal with his problem.

The Catalytic Contract

Preparation of a contract is somewhat easier for the catalytic consultant than for the consultant who works along acceptant lines, for clients more readily understand the catalytic mode—it is more within the purview of what goes on in their everyday relationships. For example, a person who has a problem expects in everyday contacts with others that they will ask him what the problem is and perhaps help him clarify it. They are likely to do so in ways that leave responsibility for the solution with their "client." The principal effect of a consultant's catalytic intervention impinges on the client's perception of his problem, not through "telling" him what it is, but through aiding the client to test his view of the problem.

A major difference between everyday boss-to-subordinate interactions and the catalytic approach is that the consultant's help often comes through introducing techniques and procedures of data gathering for perception building *that are not in everyday use by the client.* The consultant's expertise, in other words, enables the client to check his perception of the situation in ways he might eventually have been able to grasp, even without catalytic perception-building interventions, at a slower pace. With new insight he may be prompted to act differently, and often more effectively.

The catalytic consultant might go about suggesting contract expectations in the following way. He might say, "The way I see my possible contribution is this: First I want to understand your problem as you define it. Once I am aware of this, I will either gather additional data that will help you to check out your definition of the problem, or I will assist you in designing measuring procedures through which you can test your definition of the problem. I will offer whatever procedural help—such as helping a meeting run smoothly—that may be asked of me in terms of your interpreting the data or your figuring out its implications for your dealing with the situation.

"If the data that are gathered lead to verified or altered perceptions, you may want me to work with others in helping them see the situation differently. I am prepared to do this under the circumstances that you authorize."

A case study of contracting within catalytic assumptions is provided by Weisbord (1973). He goes into some detail about strategies for designing a "fluid" consultant "job description," in this case called a *contract.* This job description covers expectations about consultant-client relations where the consultant operates according to the view that

> ...he hires me to consult to him while he is working on his problem, helping *him* to achieve a better diagnosis of what has happened and what steps he must take to improve things. (Weisbord, 1973, p. 2)

According to Weisbord, the client already is grappling with a situation that makes life difficult and which has three main components:

1. organization crises due to people leaving, excessive absenteeism, cost control problems, budget difficulties, "boss" pressures, interpersonal and intergroup conflict;
2. "significant others" to the client, who number among his sore spots;
3. personal matters, such as uncertainty that "what I have is what I want."

Bypassing categories (1) and (3) above, the client initially nearly always seeks guidance on how to deal with the "significant others" who are paining him. Helping a client cope in a better way with more pertinent organization-related problems —for example, those listed under (1)—is the consultant's "bread and butter" business. How does he go about it? By ". . . gathering information, becoming aware of deeper meanings, making choices . . ." that in the process help the client to:

1. solve the immediate problem;
2. gain insight into his own coping style;
3. acquire greater coping skills.

What kind of a contract do you build with a client in pursuit of these kinds of outcomes? First of all, the client has a right to know what the consultant expects to do in terms of time invested in:

1. interviewing or survey sampling (done anonymously);
2. organizing data;
3. meetings with the client.

The purpose of the job description is to clarify new expectations whenever the situation shifts in any significant way. Thus the contract may be for two hours, a day, or a year, always subject to renegotiation on a moment-by-moment basis and subject to cancellation on twenty-four hours' notice, the proviso being a face-to-face meeting first.

Most significant in understanding the catalytic aspects in this version of consultant-client relationship is the first intervention, described by Weisbord as encompassing the following features.

1. Reacting to his perceived problem, the client sees the intervention as helping him to gain understanding and control over it.
2. Designation of who, when, where, and "why," with the "why" being the client's rather than a "joint" definition or the consultant's task to answer.
3. Diagnosis, based on some kind of collected information; the test of "good"

data being that those who contribute it ". . . will recognize it as critical to their lives together when I collate it and hand it back." (Weisbord, 1973, pp. 1–4)

Most of what has been described in this consultant-client relationship is based on catalytic assumptions, although not completely so, for Weisbord recognizes that under some eventualities either the client or the consultant may compel a "test" of the relationship. These tests, which lead either to deepening the relationship or terminating it, seem more confrontational in character since they promote an "emotion-provoking" exchange. Presumably more basic values and assumptions are being challenged; and when these challenges are successful, the client may come to a new definition of his situation as uncovered values and assumptions put the problem in a radically altered perspective.

A broader example of a catalytic approach is provided by the Tavistock Institute of Human Relations in one of its first projects, at the Glacier Metal Company. Solutions to a number of consultant-client relationship issues were incorporated into the contract in terms of which consultant interventions could be made.

To whom should the consultant team be responsible? This issue was resolved by having the consultant report to the Works Council, a permanent union-management body that for some years had been providing a basis for resolving grievances. As such, it was an elected representative body that was neither management controlled nor worker dominated. The Works Council delegated a project subcommittee as its source of contact with the Tavistock consultants. It was agreed that only public information would be gathered.

Consultants can and do gather information at one level and feed it to another higher level, where it is acted upon. This strategy weakens rather than strengthens management. It reduces boss-subordinate communication and often creates defensiveness, withholding of data, and so on.

The Research Team avoided creating any suspicion of gathering secret information on the premise that the only real value is in information that can be freely discussed. In terms of projects, only those projects were undertaken that had the general approval of the people likely to be affected by the results.

Catalytic aspects of the interventions to preserve the nonsecrecy pledge with individuals or groups were based on the Research Team acting only in an advisory or interpretive role. As they said, "Nothing will be done behind anyone's back. No matter will be discussed unless representatives of the group are present or have agreed to the topic being raised" (Jaques, 1951, pp. 13, 14).

The Tavistock consultants, in other words, were governed by ground rules that put them in a catalytic role relative to helping with the operational problems of the company.

The key strategy in writing a contract is to convey to the client that the consultant's contribution is in assisting in problem definition through approaches to data gathering and data interpretation. This is in contrast with exercising initiative to impose a problem definition on the client or give the client "answers" as to what he should do to rectify the situation.

The Confrontation Contract

The confrontational consultant faces problems in contract writing that are similar to those in acceptant consultation. Since the client usually is inexperienced with this kind of an approach, he or she is not really in a position to exercise judgment as to exactly what the consultant should contribute. After the client has had sufficient experience it is less necessary to prepare a contract: either the relationship is terminated or continued.

Nonetheless, at the beginning of their relationship the consultant can do something to specify what he or she expects to contribute. For example, the consultant might say:

"I see it as my job to aid you to examine and, to whatever degree you find it appropriate, to change the basic assumptions and values that underlie your behavior. I do not see it as my job to judge the soundness or rightness of the values and assumptions you hold. Once having assisted you in recognizing them, my task is to offer whatever additional help can be provided through aiding you to explore the consequences of that conduct on your situation.

"You should not necessarily expect me to accept your definition of problems you face or your interpretation of their causes. At times you may find my interventions personally threatening—not that this would be my intention—and you may experience resentment when I challenge you on what I observe your values and assumptions to be.

"I intend to be as open and responsive to your reactions as I am capable of being. You can expect that I will do my best to provide you concrete and specific evidence as to rationales of the interventions I make, or interpretations of consequences that I report to you from them.

"I do not see it as my job to tell you what to do or to offer advice as to alternative or possibly better courses of action."

The confrontational consultant often explains in advance that until the client reveals the values and assumptions implicit in his or her everyday activities, the consultant cannot point out what kinds of values and assumptions will be challenged. Thus an experiential basis for interpreting this contract is lacking. Once values have been revealed and challenged, though, the client is in a position to appreciate the character of the consultation and to enter into contract writing dependent on his or her readiness to engage further in this approach.

The Prescriptive Contract

The prescriptive approach is the easiest of the interventions to characterize in contract terms. This is because prescription is closely aligned with the everyday experiences people have had as they interact with experts and authorities on various topics. The prescriptive consultant might say to the client:

"I would like to start with your definition of the problem and then to study the situation from my point of view. In due course I will provide you review of my findings and recommendations for action. I will expect to advise you as to solutions for solving the situation that you now face."

By this approach the consultant is in a somewhat better position to indicate the amount of time (and therefore expense) required to study the situation, to prepare a report, to provide advice, and possibly to supervise implementation of the plan.

The key to crystallization of client expectations is in the consultant's readiness to take initiative, to exercise judgment, and to give answers. Since initiative taking, the exercise of judgment, and giving answers is characteristic of relationships in modern society, the client has little difficulty in understanding this contract. What he or she may not understand when agreeing to a contract is the future reluctance he or she is likely to feel towards acting on the recommendations offered.

Contracting under a Theory/Principles Approach

At the outset, a theory/principles consultant finds it difficult to be specific with the client as to what "contributions" can be expected from the intervention. The difficulty arises from the unique characteristics of this mode of intervention. It is the only approach calculated to be educational in character—i.e., the consultant aids the client to gain theory-based understanding of his or her situation based on causal or functional insights that can enable the client to take systematic problem-solving steps. The particular theories and principles the client may need to learn are what make contract writing difficult. While there is widespread understanding of how education can benefit understanding, many present-day adults have been "turned off" school-based learning and have yet to participate in experiential or other relatively new modes of education.

Yet the outlines of contract writing are fairly clear. Points that the theory-and-principles consultant makes in approaching contract preparation are summarized here:

1. Agreement is reached as to the major problem(s) to be approached via the client learning pertinent theories.
2. The method of teaching (whether teacher-tell, case, programmed instruction, instrumented learning) is specific, and one or more modes of intervention for assisting the client to apply these theories and principles in solving designated problems are also discussed. Assistance in evaluating or assessing the extent to which theory-based learning and implementation will have contributed to his or her situation may also be offered.
3. Additional areas that might benefit from a similar approach may be anticipated and noted for study at some future time as the basis for further work.

Even more than in the prescriptive approach, the theory/principles consultant has a basis for anticipating the man hours to be involved in theory and principles learning, expenses such as for learning materials, and the on-site support necessary in assisting the initial educational or implementation phase of the consultation. Support during more extended implementation activities is more difficult to specify in precise terms.

Contracts, whether in words or in writing, can strengthen the process of theory/principles intervention in useful ways. The activity involved in negotiating a contract helps the client to reach realistic expectations as to what the consultant will or will not do. The likelihood of future misunderstandings and disappointment can be reduced this way, and the consultant gains additional insight into the client's present worries, doubts and reservations, unwarranted enthusiasm, excessive dependency, and so on. These observations can be useful in diagnosing how best to proceed in dealing with the client.

A second value of the contract is that the client can place limits on what the consultant does with him or her. By the same token, if what the client is prepared to agree to is viewed by the consultant as inherently unproductive, the consultant need not accept. By pretesting the viability of the situation a sound footing is assured at the outset.

A third advantage of theory/principles contracting is its flexible character. The renegotiation possibilities are completely open; terms can be renegotiated whenever either party wishes to do so. For example, a client who might initially have wanted to go slow may, once he gains experience with benefits, see merit in speeding up. Correspondingly, one who starts by dealing with surface problems may gain the security and convictions essential for grappling with deeper issues.

A major limitation of unprogrammed renegotiation, though, is that it predisposes the consultant toward interacting with the client in terms of felt needs. Since the client does not recognize his or her own *latent* needs and is unable to comprehend undefined needs until the consultant or the newly learned theory or principles bring them into focus, they may never be considered. Also, initiatives by client or consultant to renegotiate might be viewed by the other party as attempts to violate the contract, and so provoke resistance. Even so, without necessarily agreeing to a felt-needs basis for contracting, the theory/principles consultant can define with the client certain areas of freedom to exercise professional judgment and to help the client to become effective by discovering and solving real—though previously unrecognized—problems.

Summary

The contract is one way in which the consultant and client can mutually develop a basis of interaction: the client thus has prestart expectations as to what he or she will gain from the process of consultation and the consultant has a foundation for a period of work with the client.

At the outset of a consultative relationship, acceptant, confrontational, and theory/principles consultants encounter difficulty in "explaining" the character of their intervention, for their modes of intervening usually are not within the client's realm of experience. In the initial contact it is desirable, if at all possible, to demonstrate the character of intervention rather than to rely on explanations of what can be expected. Of these three, the theory/principles consultant has the easiest time in demonstration. He or she can administer instruments on the spot, present theory for using data, and feed back the data, thus giving the client some idea of what to expect and an indication of progress possible in resolving larger problems. The acceptant consultant faces the difficulty of encouraging the client to express feelings freely. If a client is ready to talk, this is no problem; but if he or she resists doing so, the consultant faces the more difficult task of illustrating to the client how they might relate with one another. The confrontational consultant's difficulty is that usually he or she needs to spend some time pinpointing the client's values and assumptions *before* demonstrating to the client how consultant challenges might help him or her to become more objective about the situation at hand.

The prescriptive consultant can explain quite easily, on the basis of an expert approach to the problem, what he or she intends to do and how he or she intends to go about doing it. If the consultant's credentials make sense and his or her presentation demonstrates understanding of the client's problems, then a contract between them is not difficult to prepare.

The consultant who uses a catalytic approach gains acceptance by discussing some aspect of data gathering and then demonstrating its use. In this way, the client can check out whether or not the data make sense in the light of his or her own situation and on this basis decide readiness to take additional steps.

The idea of working out a psychological contract to guide intervention is often advanced as an important aspect of the catalytic approach to consultation. As described by Kolb and Frohman, its characteristics are as follows.

> Once the entry point has been selected, the consultant and the client system, through the entry representative, begin to negotiate a contract. In its use here, the word "contract" implies more than a legal document agreed upon at the outset of the project. The contract will define if and how the succeeding stages of the planned change process will be carried out. The emphasis is on a continuing process of sharing the expectations of the consultant and the client system and agreeing on the contributions to be made by both parties. Mark Frohman has listed 10 areas in which agreement over expectations is important in order to develop an effective working relationship: (1) the consultant's and the client's goals for the project, (2) broad definition of the problem (to be redefined as the relationship progresses), (3) relationship of the problem to the overall system, (4) client resources and abilities applicable to the problem, (5) consultant resources and abilities applicable to the problem, (6) broad mode of approach to the problem, (7) nature of the consultant/client relationship, (8) expected benefits for the client, (9) expected benefits for the consultant, and (10) ability of one party to influence the other. (Kolb and Frohman, 1970, p. 55)

Any approach is likely to establish certain terms of expectations, such as remuneration, but approaches that are based on uncovering as-yet-undiscovered client needs often rely on the tacit understanding that professional judgment will be exercised by the consultant—and honored by the client. Later on, more specific terms can be set, but by that time a contract is hardly necessary.

CONSULTANT PREFERENCES AND/OR "NATURAL BENT"

Many consultants have personal preferences and predispositions that influence their choices or even govern their tendencies to intervene in a certain way. Often these influences are unrelated to a client's real needs. Interventions based on consultant preferences and predilections such as these, rather than on a valid diagnosis of the requirements for helping the client's situation, are of less value than when they are targeted to the client's reality situation. The Grid framework, introduced in the discussion of theory/principles interventions, can be used to illustrate.

Table 32.1

Consultant's intervention preference	Consultant's probable Grid style(s)
Acceptant	1,9
Catalytic	5,5 (and "statistical" 5,5)
Confrontation	9,9 (and 9,1)
Prescriptive	9,1
Theory and principles	9,9 (and 9,1)

Many considerations determine an intervention's effectiveness. But basically a single Grid-style orientation, given that it is sufficiently constructive so as not to rule out consideration of other intervention modes that at some time may become pertinent, can serve to structure the use of an entire range of consultation skills, as illustrated below.

Intervention mode	Grid style	When
Acceptant	9,9	The consultant helps the client to relieve immobilizing tensions and thereby to unblock barriers that have prevented constructive action.
Catalytic	9,9	By aiding the client to build up his perceptions of the situation the consultant assists him in taking fundamental rather than superficial action.

Confrontation	9,9	The client's problem can only be brought into focus and resolved through the client coming to recognize in his behavior the cause of his problems.
Prescriptive	9,9	The client has reached the point of impasse, hopelessness, or despair, and yet action is imperative to avoid further negative consequences.
Theory/principle	9,9	The client can approach and probably solve his problems based on systematic insight, and be in a better position for contending with similar future problems.

But sometimes the intervention mode is more related to 9,1 assumptions on the part of the consultant than to the problem-solving needs of the client.

Intervention mode	Grid style	When
Confrontation	9,1	The consultant derives gratification from shaking the client up.
Prescriptive	9,1	The consultant is determined an action that he sees as valid is taken and is ready to use whatever pressures he can muster to get the client to take the action.
Theory	9,1	The consultant is certain that theory represents the one and only way for the client to solve his problem.

In contrast, the 5,5 consultant assumptions lead to the following:

Intervention mode	Grid style	When
Acceptant	5,5	The consultant reacts in terms of the client's felt needs without being convinced in his own thinking that this is the best thing to do.
Catalytic	5,5	The consultant adapts his response to the client's felt needs, even when it is clear to him, privately, that the realistic solution would entail an alternative definition of the problem.

(Cont.)

Theory	5,5	The consultant presents theory not because he thinks it useful but because he thinks the client wants it.

When the consultant is oriented in the 1,9 direction:

Intervention mode	Grid style	When
Acceptant	1,9	He approaches a client in this manner because high concern on the personal dimension is his sole way of feeling helpful.
Catalytic	1,9	He intervenes because he wants to please the client.

The "burned out," or 1,1 consultant:

Intervention mode	Grid style	When
Acceptant	1,1	The consultant takes a passive, listening posture not out of supportive orientation toward the client but from lack of interest.

A special case of relying on prescriptive intervention can arise out of a consultant's paternalistic orientation.

Intervention mode	Grid style	When
Prescriptive	Paternalistic	He insists, and often correctly, that the client take the recommended action "for his own good," even though the client may not see it that way.

These various intervention modes as evaluated according to Grid-style orientations specify for a particular consultant his or her "legitimate" interventions. When examined as a broad array of alternatives, however, they also make it possible to distinguish between sound interventions and interventions that have inherent weaknesses.

Any consultant whose predilections are other than 9,9 is faced with a dilemma. For example, if his or her orientation is 1,9, would it be better to stay in that mode and concentrate on situations where an acceptant mode would be appropriate, disregarding other modes, or would it be better for the consultant to try to acquire 9,9 flexibility so as to be able to intervene in an effective way regarding whatever specific issue the client has to resolve? A decision to remain within the presently 1,9-delimited mode leads toward specialization, whereas resolution in terms of the 9,9 alternative promotes a generalist orientation.

OVERRELIANCE ON VARIOUS INTERVENTIONS

Any intervention mode, if relied upon exclusively, can sooner or later prove ineffective. A "permanent" acceptant mode, for example, can result in the client becoming so comfortable and accepting of his or her situation, after having been assisted in working through disturbed emotions toward it, that in effect the client becomes satisfied with existing circumstances and loses desire to deal with the source(s) that caused the problem, for which catharsis may have been only the first step toward solution.

The weakness of a perennial catalytic mode is in its shallowness. A catalytic consultant can aid the client to recognize problems, ones that he or she would be likely to overlook without such an intervention, and can then help the client place them in a priority order for action. Such listing may promote the confidence necessary for solution seeking on a step-by-step basis. Yet it is a common observation that this kind of "bridging," even though it aids a client to see aspects of the situation that previously were less visible, rarely helps the client learn to independently diagnose "novel" problems. The consultant becomes a crutch; and as the client gets more help, he or she becomes "weaker."

A risk in a too-long-continued confrontational mode is that of "uncovering" client weaknesses without offering him or her ways to overcome these failings. The dramatic character of even one such exposure—not to mention a series—can be traumatic to the client. He or she can no longer repeat the past and yet is unable to see what alternative actions may be possible. This can be an ultimate kind of defeat.

A weakness of never-ending prescription is that the client is given answers without having learned to think through and to define the problem for which the provided answer is a solution. Thus, as with catalytic interventions, the client may become ever more dependent on continual instruction "from the outside." He or she may completely surrender personal will on a more or less permanent basis, letting the consultant dictate the strategy and actions of daily life.

An unvarying theory-based approach may encourage the client to become too absorbed in intellectual activity, not as a tool for solving problems, but rather as an end in itself. As Kingsbury (1972, pp. 111–12) has mentioned, to the extent that the client can "talk" theory and keep it at a high level of abstraction, it is unnecessary for him to take needed actions. Intellectualizing is, in a certain sense, a way of problem avoidance rather than problem solving.

WHEN TO USE DIFFERENT INTERVENTION MODES

Each intervention mode used in consultation has been pictured as a dominant strategy for given kinds of situations. For a contemporary consultant who is not at the leading edge of his or her field, most frequently one approach or another *is* the customary and dominant approach and shifting from it to another approach is not customary. Yet what was appropriate in an earlier phase of a consultation may be superfluous at a later stage—something else is required if the client is to take another forward step. And, indeed, there is no basic reason why combinations of approaches may not be employed sequentially with the same client as the situation evolves.

Not all modes are equally compatible with one another, even when used on a "well-intended judgment" basis by the same consultant with the same client. Some of the more compatible combinations of approaches are discussed below.

Following Acceptant

Under circumstances where emotional tensions are blocking problem-solving initiative, *only* the acceptant approach stands any likelihood of being able to reduce those tensions sufficiently to permit the problem itself to be examined. The most likely mode to follow, once catharsis has relieved the tensions within the system, is a catalytic approach. The catalytic orientation, which itself is in the nonevaluative and nonjudgmental direction, responds to the felt needs of clients. It is a response to "his" definition of "his" problem, and therefore is emotionally more neutral but consonant with the sympathetic, supportive, warm relationship engendered earlier by acceptant interventions. Furthermore, a catalytic intervention following an acceptant one moves the client forward at the client's own tempo, permitting him to grapple with his problem on his own terms, in his own way, and at his own pace. It is less likely to stir up new anxieties that would make it difficult for the client to build on progress already made.

By comparison, the confrontational approach is likely to jolt the client and to stir resistance by violating his or her expectations of sympathetic support, founded upon experience of the consultant's attitudes in earlier interventions.

The prescriptive solution also is at odds with the support and encouragement characteristic of the acceptant mode, particularly when the prescribed action places the client in a new internal conflict or "forces" him or her to take an action adverse to colleagues or subordinates. A theory-based approach is possible, but less likely, for after tensions have been relieved there often is a need for immediate action and insufficient additional time to shift to a systematic problem-solving approach.

Following Catalytic

This combination is the same as above, but the sequence is in reverse. Should a catalytic intervention stir feelings of anxiety, fear, anger, or even uncertainty, it is natural for the consultant to back off from perception-building activities and to provide the sympathetic support necessary for a client to work through his or her tensions. The interaction is likely thereafter to return to a catalytic basis. In this sense an acceptant intervention within a catalytic sequence is likely to be an interruption of data flow rather than a shift away from the perception-building process.

Following Confrontation

Because a confrontational intervention can have a jolting effect and because it may bring a client face-to-face with problems in ways that prevent him or her from indulging in defensive rationalization, it can cause the client to see disabling personal weaknesses, sometimes for the first time. Once a client is disturbed by self-admission that personally held values and beliefs are unjustified, he or she may "spill" emotions. This overflow of emotions is one way of relieving the discrepancy between the need to maintain a false front and the relief possible through a self-confession kind of reaction. The consultant then may shift from a confrontational to a cathartic basis in order to help the client reestablish emotional equilibrium.

There is the possibility of catalytic intervention when a confrontational mode has not provoked emotional expression but has brought about a major cognitive shift in the definition of the problem. Thereafter the consultant may deal with the client in a catalytic way, aiding him or her in perception building in order to explore action alternatives unavailable under the old definition of the problem.

Prescription also may follow confrontation. Once confrontation has produced a values reassessment, the client may wish to alter conduct yet may have little or no understanding of what new action might constitute a sounder alternative. The consultant may provide direction by telling the client what to do to solve his or her problem and keep the client at it until the new solution becomes sufficiently well established to be maintained without assistance.

Following Prescription

Regardless of how "right," prescription can and often does increase the client's tensions and block effective problem solving. This is so whenever the prescription goes against the grain of the client's history or dramatically shifts interpersonal social or working relationships. After such a prescription a shift of intervention mode may be necessary so that the client can explore, express, and work through the emotions and tensions it aroused. If this shift in intervention mode does not happen at an appropriate time—i.e., when the emotional tensions in the client are at their peak— it is likely to prove ineffective. Once emotions become crystallized or go underground, the client is likely to be more resistant to expressing emotions and therefore would avoid responding to the kind of intervention that would promote this approach. In this case, the only real possibility of further progress is confrontation, sometimes at a quite deep level.

Sometimes the consultant is no longer acceptable to the client after his or her prescriptive interventions have had such disturbing effects. Then catharsis, if introduced at all, comes about through the intervention of a second consultant, most often not connected in any way with the first.

Following Theory/Principle

Although the need for any other kind of intervention may be stimulated by a theory-based approach, prescription is the least probable. Since sound theory provides the client a basis for predicting the source of his or her own actions and for anticipating their consequences, he or she should not need to be "told" by another how to solve problems.

The most probable intervention following theory-based interventions is confrontational in character. Now that the client has an intellectual and emotional basis of insight into the situation, he or she is motivated to take those actions necessary to focus and resolve personal problems. But older values continue to exert a constraining influence. Confrontation can assist the client in rejecting what he or she "knows" to be outmoded values.

Theory-based interventions also may lead to catalytic interventions in the sense that assistance in perception building may be needed to see a complex problem more clearly. Alternatively, an acceptant intervention may aid the client to relieve, focus, express, and work through tensions that were triggered by the theory but were not known about prior to the theory-oriented discovery of them. The resulting catharsis is then of a bridging character, enabling the client to reestablish his or her emotional equilibrium before attempting to move forward.

RECAPITULATION OF A THEORY OF CONSULTATION

A theory of consultation can now be approached based on the many and mixed examples of what takes place in the consultant-client interaction. A basic question is, Which kind of intervention when?

One or another of five basic interventions are used in various approaches to consultation. Although most are "pure," in some situations more than one intervention may be involved, depending on the consultant, the client, and the focal issue being worked on. The client situations that call for one or another of these five basic processes are suggested in Table 32.2.

THE FUTURE OF CONSULTATION

Because of the importance of dealing more effectively with the numerous deep-lying problems that confront modern society, it is probable that consultation is still in its infancy. As greater skill is acquired in helping clients to solve their problems, consultation will become a more and more relied upon means of assistance.

Prescriptive consultation, except in dealing with highly technical problems having little or no human content, is the least likely to expand. The weaknesses inherent

Table 32.2

Intervention	Key words	When indicated
Acceptant	Emotional release	Pent-up feelings are blocking thought and action so that needed initiatives cannot be taken.
Catalytic	Strengthen perception	Poor communication has resulted in pluralistic ignorance that blocks effectiveness.
Confrontation	Value clarification	Values, often hidden, are having negative effects.
Prescription	Giving answers	Client(s) has thrown up his hands or is on the ropes, unable to exercise sufficient initiative to move.
Theory/principles	Insight	Client(s) is ready to shift to a science-oriented basis of problem solving.

in it are obvious. The catalytic approach, except for solving momentary or situational difficulties, is also likely to grow at a slower rate than it has in the past for its contribution is generally of temporary value only.

The three fastest growing approaches are likely to be acceptant, confrontational, and theory-based consulting, in ascending order. Acceptant consultation is of importance in any situation where the client is unable to grapple with personal problems because of a debilitating emotional overload. Only by the emotional release that catharsis can provide does the client stand any real prospect of coping in a problem-solving way with the difficulties being encountered. The confrontational mode is of potentially high significance because the client can thus be assisted to face realities that he or she otherwise might never come to recognize.

Theory-based consultation holds the greatest promise for problem solving in the future. Once the client has learned theory and internalized it, he or she is released from dependence on others for assistance in solving problems and, thereafter, further consultation is unnecessary, at least in the domain of activity defined by the theory. Two current weaknesses of theory-based intervention should be pointed out. First, a client must devote substantial time to the learning of theory in order to permit its internalization. This relatively slow process can turn clients away from the theory-based approach in a world where time is at a premium. The other limitation is that very little work has yet been done in terms of converting the rich store of academic theories for functional use. Years of effort will be required to bring this conversion about, even though the strategies for such conversion and for internalization have been well established.

Once this happens, however, theory-based interventions can be replaced by theory-based teaching in the home, in the classroom, and on the job, such that consultation's instructional role can eventually be taken over by broader strategies of education.

REFERENCES

Alcoholics Anonymous. New and rev. ed. New York: AA Publishing, Inc., 1955.

Argyris, C. *Intervention Theory and Method*. Reading, Mass.: Addison-Wesley, 1970.

Brown, W. F. "Student-to-Student Counseling for Academic Adjustment." *Personnel and Guidance Journal* 43, no. 8 (1965): 811–17.

Buckley, M. "Enter: The Ex-Con." *Federal Probation* 36, no. 4 (1972): 24–30.

Davey, N. G. *The External Consultant's Role in Organizational Change*. East Lansing, Michigan: Michigan State University Studies, 1971.

Enright, J. H. "On the Playing Fields of Synanon." In L. Blank, G. B. Gottsegen, and M. G. Gottsegen, eds., *Confrontation: Encounters in Self and Interpersonal Awareness*. New York: Macmillan, 1971, pp. 147–77.

French, W. L., and C. H. Bell. *Organization Development*. Englewood Cliffs, N.J.: Prentice-Hall, 1973.

Gartner, A., M. Kohler, and F. Riessman. *Children Teach Children*. New York: Harper & Row, 1971.

Hallowitz, E. "The Expanding Role of the Neighborhood Service Center." In F. Riessman and H. R. Popper, eds., *Up from Poverty: New Career Ladders for Nonprofessionals*. New York: Harper & Row, 1968, pp. 92–105.

Harris, T. A. *I'm OK—You're OK*. New York: Avon (by arrangement with Harper & Row, 1967), 1969.

Hines, L. "A Nonprofessional Discusses Her Role in Mental Health." *American Journal of Psychiatry* 126, no. 10 (1970): 111–16.

Jaques, E. *The Changing Culture of a Factory*. London: Tavistock, 1951.

Kingsbury, S. "Dilemmas for the Trainer." In W. G. Dyer, ed., *Modern Theory and Method in Group Training*. New York: Van Nostrand Reinhold Company, 1972, pp. 107–115.

Kolb, D. A., and A. L. Frohman. "An Organization Development Approach to Consulting." *Sloan Management Review* 12, no. 1 (1970): 51–65. © 1970 by the Industrial Management Review Association; all rights reserved.

Laubach, F. C., and R. I. Laubach. *Toward World History*. Syracuse: Syracuse University Press, 1960.

Low, A. A. *Mental Health through Will-Training: A System of Self-Help in Psychotherapy as Practiced by Recovery, Incorporated*. 14th ed. Boston: The Christopher Publishing House, 1966.

Lynch, M., and E. A. Gardner. "Some Issues Raised in the Training of Paraprofessional Personnel as Clinic Therapists." *American Journal of Psychiatry* 126, no. 10 (1970): 117–23.

Nolan, K. J., and E. T. Cooke. "The Training and Utilization of the Mental Health Paraprofessional within the Military: The Social Work/Psychology Specialist." *American Journal of Psychiatry* 127, no. 1 (1970): 114–19.

Porter, L. "An Interview with Beckhard and Shepard—OD: Some Questions, Some Answers." *OD Practitioner* 6, no. 3 (1974): 1–8.

Riessman, F. "The Helper Therapy Principle." *Social Work* 10, no. 2 (1965): 27–32.

Rogers, C. R. *Counseling and Psychotherapy.* Boston: Houghton Mifflin, 1942. Reprinted by permission of the author and publisher.

Weisbord, M. "The Organization Development Contract." *OD Practitioner* 5, (1973): 1–4. Reprinted by permission.

AUTHOR INDEX

SUBJECT INDEX